AF607974

MOCK MODERNISM

EDITED BY LEONARD DIEPEVEEN

Mock Modernism

An Anthology of Parodies, Travesties, Frauds, 1910–1935

UNIVERSITY OF TORONTO PRESS
Toronto Buffalo London

© University of Toronto Press 2014
Toronto Buffalo London
www.utppublishing.com

ISBN 978-1-4426-4482-3 (cloth)

Library and Archives Canada Cataloguing in Publication

Mock modernism : an anthology of parodies, travesties, frauds, 1910–1935 / edited by Leonard Diepeveen.

Includes bibliographical references and index.
ISBN 978-1-4426-4482-3 (bound)

1. Modernism (Literature) – Press coverage. 2. Modernism (Literature) – Public opinion. 3. Modernism (Art) – Press coverage. 4. Modernism (Art) – Public opinion. I. Title.

PN56.M54D543 2014 809'.9112 C2013-908305-7

This book has been published with the help of a grant from the Canadian Federation for the Humanities and Social Sciences, through the Awards to Scholarly Publications Program, using funds provided by the Social Sciences and Humanities Research Council of Canada.

University of Toronto Press acknowledges the financial assistance to its publishing program of the Canada Council for the Arts and the Ontario Arts Council.

Canada Council for the Arts   Conseil des Arts du Canada

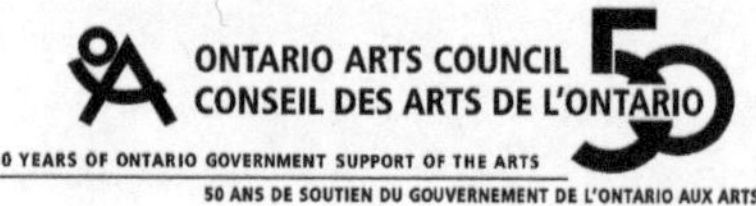

University of Toronto Press acknowledges the financial support of the Government of Canada through the Canada Book Fund for its publishing activities.

Permissions and credits follow on page 415.

Contents

Acknowledgments

Mock Modernism has been a cooperative enterprise. At an institutional level, I'd link to thank the Social Sciences and Humanities Research Council of Canada as well as the Research Development Fund of Dalhousie University, both of which greased the financial wheels necessary to keep this project moving. The archival support for this project has been overwhelming. I'm thinking, of course, of the Modernist Journals Project, which has made so much new modernist scholarship possible. As well, the Gertrude Stein collection at the Beinecke Rare Book and Manuscript Library at Yale has been an immense resource. Thanks, too, to the Chicago Public Library; the library of the University of Illinois; the Ryerson and Burnham Libraries of the Art Institute of Chicago; the British Library; and, for clippings related to the 1912 Postimpressionist exhibition, the King's College Archive Centre of Cambridge University.

As for individuals, I owe much to the anonymous readers for the University of Toronto Press, who helped push this collection in some helpful directions. Some wonderful research assistants over time have helped moved this project along: Adam Bowes, Connor Byrne, Peter Chiykowski, Kelly Conway, and Adrien Robertson. And special thanks to Leslie Gallagher, who provided an especially keen set of working eyes at just the right time. Colleagues at Dalhousie University provided conversation and help with translations, particularly John Barnstead, Federica Belluccini, Melissa Furrow, Jason Haslam, Matt Huculak, Trevor Ross, and Julia Wright. Two people deserve special thanks: Timothy van Laar, for his continuing intellectual conversation and scrutiny; and to Richard Ratzlaff, whose belief in and excitement over this project has propelled it along.

The list of people who volunteered information and suggested sources is larger than I could accommodate, but I'd like to thank, in particular, those who helped me track down texts, and who suggested material I had not been aware of: Rebecca Beasley, Jeremy Braddock, David Bradshaw, Jessica Burstein,

Gregory Castle, Suzanne Churchill, John Xiros Cooper, Sarah Davison, Jonathan Greenberg, Michael Groden, Anne Gwin, Sharon Hamilton, Brian Holcomb, Matt Huculak, Dean Irvine, Karen Leick, Niall Munro, Lawrence Rainey, Stephen Rogers, Max Saunders, Robert Scholes, Jack Selzer, Hannah Sullivan, Oliver Walton, and Mark Wollaeger. Without these colleagues and the Modernist Studies Association this project would be much less rich.

Finally, I'd like to thank Susan, for thirty-some years of friendship and grace. This one's for you.

MOCK MODERNISM

Introduction

In late March of 1913 the International Exhibition of Modern Art arrived in Chicago from New York City, its New York–sized scandal provoking Chicago's press corps to generate an even larger and more rambunctious reception. As the local press set to work on the "Armory Show," laying the groundwork for what would indeed become a greater fracas than what had entertained New York for a few weeks, a curious convergence in early twentieth-century culture was becoming clear, a convergence in which P.T. Barnum could become the interpretive frame for the austere products of modernism, for the chilly pleasures of work like Marcel Duchamp's "Nude Descending a Staircase." Eyeing the baffling works of Picasso, Matisse, and Duchamp, and anticipating plausible modes of public interest for what was being called "freak" art, the Chicago *Record-Herald* plastered its 25 March edition with the large headline: "Step In! No Danger! Cubist Show Now On." It followed this with:

> La-d-ie-s and gentlemen, step closer, please, a little closer. Before visiting the palatial palaces of sculpture and art in other portions of this famous institute see the cubist sideshow – the show they are all talking about.
>
> Here, here, here we have the famous one-eyed lady, brought from the wildes of France; the human skeleton carrying a heliotrope owl and leading a camel with elephant ears; the horse with legs like a bullfrog; the greatest galaxy of normal and abnormal nudes ever assembled on this or any other continent.
>
> Remember, this is the uncensored sho. It's there – there – there – on the inside, ladies and gentlemen. It's continuous. It's different, and it's art – art of the present and the future. A thrill every minute. Something new to tickle the fancy and feast the eye. (25 March 1913: 1)

Juvenile, no doubt. But entangled within the fun there was a serious argument, based on parody, being conducted about modernism – here, an argument that modernism was Barnumism, recast for the arts. So omnipresent and captivating were these kinds of parodic interpretations that modernism became inextricably understood through them. The *Record-Herald*'s reporter and many others in the opening decades of the twentieth century deployed parodic forms to produce an interpretive frame for modernism – sometimes, as here, ponderously so. Here, as elsewhere, the frame's application was clear. Moving on from his routine, the reporter provided its interpretation:

> That was all that was needed – just a real old-fashioned bally-ho at the head of the marble staircase in Art Institute [*sic*] yesterday – to make the first-time visitor to the international exhibition of modern art believe he had done a Rip Van Winkle act and awakened in the old Clark Street Museum.
>
> Decorative screens bearing pictures of every known animal, and a few others, done in colors that would have made P.T. Barnum's circus "front" look like bunting after a rainstorm – these hedged in the entrance to the show.

As his argument goes, Clark Street Museum, the old Chicago vaudeville theatre, provided a more plausible interpretive frame for the Armory Show than the exhibit's actual location – the Art Institute, whose grand and earnest new building Chicagoans had erected to coincide with the 1893 World's Columbian Exposition. That redirection away from sincerity's location applied not just to the show's publicity, but to all aspects of the show's interactions with its public. The reporter continued:

> "On the inside" a group of first-viewers, some critics and some just plain reporters, carried catalogues and tried to figure out why the Chinese puzzle was labeled "King and Queen Surrounded by Nudes," how the "Man on the Balcony" had ever got through Ellis Island, and where the antediluvian animals and men had been resurrected to pose for "A Pastoral."

The Armory Show was taking mimesis for a carnival ride, with the reporter proceeding to argue that many of the show's "pictures" "might be mistaken for pictures of Sunday night's cyclone." The *Record-Herald* also gestured to interpretive frames other than these of its own devising, though the sardonic edge never disappears. Consider the reporter's take on the earnest experts who had brought the show from New York: "There were a few serious individuals – Walt Kuhn, Frederick James Gregg and Walter Pach, all of whom are officially affiliated with the show. Near them could be heard whisperings of 'wonderfully blended color' and of futurists and post-impressionism." Serious approaches lampooned, whimsical approaches presented as plausible – how was an innocent audience to know how to approach these objects? More than a little tongue in cheek, the reporter again archly gestured to the workings of art-world power: despite the odd nature of the works in front of them, the audience knew it was looking at "real works of art because the catalogue said so." As one might expect, though, the *Record-Herald* did not give the catalogue the last word on the show. That was reserved for an apparent onset of madness. In the face of these works of art, dangerous delusion would inevitably find a place. Noting that "Uniformed guards constantly strolled through the rooms or stood near the ice-water tank in the corridor," the reporter claimed that they were primed to intervene with anyone who might take the claims of the show seriously:

> "You've got to hand it to this show, though," admitted a "plain reporter." There's a "punch" in every picture. Now, just look at that color, that, that, or that – "
> Just then a keen-eyed guard interposed.
>
> "Come, young man, come out into the hall. You'll be all right in a few minutes," he said.

We may be sceptical whether this last event, like many others reported in the Chicago press, really happened – although the world would be a better place if an inmate of Dunning (Chicago's local asylum), actually *had* threatened, as reported, to sue the show's artists for plagiarism. But more interesting for understanding modernism is the work writing like this did in providing an entertaining yet far-reaching interpretive frame. The *Record-Herald* article, for example, shows that a blunt understanding of mimesis was central to public understandings of art, and works that seemed to contest its place led people to wonder if in fact these works still could be *art*. Could one assume that these works were sincere, or did modernists offer them as sincerely as P.T. Barnum had offered his Feejee mermaid?

To answer this question, modernism's audience speculated about the surrounding institutions and theories that brought this work to an audience, because one needed some way to account for what one had just seen. Modernism's sceptics, then, frequently asked – and posited answers to – questions about the conditions that allowed such art to garner serious attention. Publicity, certainly, but publicity of a certain kind. It was the unstable publicity of hype, the kind of instability that leads to grand claims, injudicious estimations that border on panic, and downright fraud. No surprise, then, that caricatures of attempts to "explain" modernism were usually couched, as here, in a palpable distrust of the experts, who seemed too eager to justify it, and were importing odd criteria in their estimation, criteria based, among other things, on theory. Those who weren't experts, and yet manifested an appreciation for the work, were suspected of being mad. Modernism, the *Record-Herald* reporter implies, was not just a categorizable group of art objects, it was a system of presenting those works as serious. And it was an event, an event whose meaning extended well beyond its objects and literary texts.

In an age of rapidly increasing print venues, modernism (by which I mean works that either through their subject matter or form – or both – engaged with what their creators saw as the new conditions of modernity) attracted a stunning wealth of printed response: hoaxes, doggerel, cartoons, accounts of staged trials, mock interviews, parodies in adjacent media (such as futurist fashion shows), mock manifestos, even a special "children's" book, *The Cubies ABC*, which was published in response to the New York manifestation of the Armory Show, and which began:

> A is for Art in the Cubies' domain –
> (Not the Art of the Ancients, brand-new are the Cubies.)
> Archipenko's their guide, Anatomics their bane;
> They're the joy of the mad, the despair of the sane,
> (With their emerald hair and their eyes red as rubies.)
> – A is for Art in the Cubies' domain. (Lyall)

These burlesque readings of modernism, mirroring the widespread uncertainty about modernism's sincerity with an unstable sincerity of their own, came from august litterateurs, like Stuart Sherman, professor of English at the University of Illinois, who in 1924 attempted by mechanical principles to reproduce a replica of Stein's writing – and in a bizarre twist protested all the while that he *wasn't* being parodic. In fact, Sherman argued, the following passage was better work than Stein's "gray and protoplasmic" writing:

> Real stupidity; but go slowly. The hope slim. Drink gloriously! Dream! Swiftly pretty people through daffodils slip in green doubt. Grandly fly bitter fish; for hard sunlight lazily consumes old books. Up by a sedate sweetheart roar darkly loud orchards. Life, the purple flame, simply proclaims a poem. (268, 267)

It's not just modernism's antagonists who perpetrated these interpretive send-ups, but modernists themselves, as James Joyce did in his parody of *The Waste Land*, or Alfred Kreymborg, who used the pages of the *New York Morning Telegraph* to imagine what his home life would look like should his wife come home from a shopping expedition speaking Steinese. Most voluminously, mock modernism extends to reporters and columnists for local newspapers, like the *New York Evening Sun*'s Don Marquis, as well as to their indignant readers, who occasionally contributed their own "modernist" works and interpretations, as did the following reader of Don Marquis's column:

> Sir: My 8-year-old niece is a devoted admirer of Miss Gertrude Stein's. She believes that Miss Stein has solved the problem of self-expression that now chains an unenlightened world to school benches and its ABCs. School cuts into one's play time frightfully, you know. Miss Stein's way is so much more satisfactory – you just write it, and there it is! After a preliminary course, my niece wrote me the following letter:
>
> "Pig you the pap is you by my you bear the Jack you bear is a cat and the cat is. – Elsiette"
>
> I see in this letter a great and revolutionary meaning. Don't you? – D.

Given the wide range of their authors, parodic reframings of modernism are found in multiple kinds of locations that range from avant-garde magazines like *The Little Review* to major journals like the *Times Literary Supplement* to the New York *Times* to the Toledo *Blade*; and employing a wide sweep of genres and positing a wide variety of relationships to modernism, ranging from the hostile, to the burlesque, to tongue-in-cheek *homage*. The plethora of responses was instigated not just by the perceived newness and strangeness of modern art forms, but by how this newness proposed to rearrange aesthetic standards. Standards were in flux, making it hard to judge quality. J.C. Squire, editor of the *London Mercury* and an excellent parodist himself, questioned the Muse in one of his verse editorials:

> What can have happened to you, Muse?
> Time was you never held such views.
> You used to sing like a canary
> With quite a small vocabulary
> Of trees and grass, the sun, the moon,
> Which then you always rhymed with swoon,
> So simply, with such innocence,
> And such a lack of deeper sense
> That any passer-by could tell
> If you were singing ill or well.
> 'Twas usually ill, no doubt,
> But you were easily found out.
> Now you bewilder me: how could

> I tell if that were bad or good,
> That gnomic stuff you sang just now,
> That cacophonic senseless row … ("Editorial Notes," August 1928: 342–3)

Like Squire, many others saw modernism as merely a "cacophonic senseless row," which meant that it was difficult not just to figure out what might be the relevant standards for evaluating its qualities. It was also, during the early years of modernism, an adventure to figure out exactly what the relevant features of these works *were*. Nowhere is modernism's flirtation with featurelessness more strenuously and oddly asserted than in Wyndham Lewis's *Time and Western Man*, where Lewis denounces Stein's work in the following awkward terms:

> Gertrude Stein's prose-song is a cold, black suet-pudding. We can represent it as a cold suet-roll of fabulously-reptilian length. Cut it at any point, it is the same thing: the same heavy, sticky opaque mass all through, and all along. It is weighted, projected, with a sibylline urge. It is mournful and monstrous, composed of dead and inanimate material. It is all fat, without nerve. Or the evident vitality that informs it is vegetable rather than animal. Its life is a low-grade, if tenacious, one; of the sausage, by-the-yard, variety. (77)

Never writing straightforward estimations or interpretations, the writers in this collection arrived at their target's features circuitously, aware that their own writing's success depended on its ability to entertain. Laughter, indeed, is the big response to modernism's difficulties. Laughter, though, needs to be understood as part of a larger, publicly understood argument. Consider the *Daily Sketch*'s response to the 1912 Post-Impressionist show:

> The Post-Impressionist, however, obviously scorns mere beauty, whether of form or colour. His is the cult of the immensely, hideously, hopelessly, crazily Ugly.
>
> How do they do it? One guesses that the game is played by standing so many yards away from the virgin canvas and then hurling your paint-box at it just as hard as you can. If the blue sticks it's a sky; if the green sticks, it's grass; if they don't, it is something else! ("Art Gone Mad")

The joke's simultaneously ponderous and banal wit depends for its success on some measure of public agreement that Post-Impressionist art has an at-best tenuous relation to beauty, and that this work's significant features can be understood – and evaluated – by their method of construction, which seems more related to chance than to skill of execution. The article's title and subtitles say much about how far this methodology had stepped outside the standards of good art: "Art Gone Mad. Queer Perversions of the Post-Impressionists. Paint-Box Freaks. Cult of the Crazily Ugly and Its Childish Results." The laughter generated by the works collected in *Mock Modernism*, then, was the laughter of assent; laughter indicates social agreement, and the same joke repeated indicates not only a possible reportorial laziness but, very likely, broad public agreement. Consider, for example, how the *Chicago Examiner* used agreement about skill, speed, and banality to parody modernism. A group of prominent local artists who called themselves the Cliff Dwellers (in reference to a novel by Henry Blake Fuller, skyscraper Chicago, and the lost cultures of the American Southwest), staged a demonstration of how to make advanced art of the kind being shown at the Art Institute. The result, according to the reporter, was "an explosion of mirth over a brilliant satire on the cubists, futurists and post-impressionists":

> Earl H. Reed, who with Louis Betts constitutes the art committee of the Cliff Dwellers, started the ball rolling by dashing off sixteen cubist works in a couple of hours. A. M. Rebori did a cubist impression of the head of Hamlin Garland in less than twenty minutes. T. J. Keene pictured the explosion of a cold storage egg in an incredibly short space of time, and Lorado Taft captivated every one with a picture of "A Nude Eating Soup With a Fork," done in sixty strokes. ("'Cliff Dwellers' Satirize")

This laughter isn't simple; it's central to a complex response to modernism, in this case a send-up of the apparent skill needed to make this art – and an assertion that technical skill was central to good art. The responses collected in *Mock Modernism* don't just mock, then; they interpret modernism's works and the movement as a whole, the social conditions that were granting it attention, and the conditions under which someone could take such work seriously. *Mock Modernism*'s texts are negotiations about, and interventions into, what their source works really signified – what they meant, but also how they inserted themselves into contemporary culture. Parodies, travesties, and frauds are arguments – arguments not only about the value of a work or movement, but arguments about what constitutes its relevant features, and what allows it to attract attention. These explanations, then, didn't assert that modernism could be completely explained by its texts and works of art; they argued that modernism also needed to be understood through, and *as*, its enabling conditions. According to modernism's sceptics, these enabling conditions reached far, to the aesthetic that spawned modernism, the forms of reading that canonized it, and the social conditions that gave it attention. Sometimes these writers recreate interpretive versions of the context, or the motivating aesthetic, or the forms of interpretation that attempted to situate these works as *important*. Indeed, the works were so bizarre one needed these speculative contextualizations to understand how they might command attention. Mock trials, fashion shows, etc., all do the polemical work of parodies – the strategies of parody have simply moved to a larger context.

This larger context provides a wealth of interpretive frameworks for modernism, and reveals something important about how modernism was initially understood, an understanding quite different from the terms by which it would soon become canonized by New Critics like Cleanth Brooks's 1939 *Modern Poetry and the Tradition*, or by F.R. Leavis's *New Bearings in English Poetry* (1932) and *The Great Tradition* (1948), or by Alfred Barr's work at New York's Museum of Modern Art in the 1930s. To get an initial sense of this wide initial range, consider J.C. Squire's skewering of modernist poetry through his figure of the poet Sidney Twyfold in "The Man Who Wrote Free Verse." Squire's story notes that Twyfold's "collected volume 'Ourang-Outang' marked an epoch: all the papers had long reviews, enthusiastic, hedging or denunciatory" (261), and it goes on to quote from one of Twyfold's poems:

Autumnal abscesses relent
The twilight of ancestral days
But, smiling at the parsnip's scent,
The Nubian girl undoes her stays! (250)

Neither Squire's *Ourang-outang* (a reference to Eliot's "Sweeney Erect") nor the Nubian girl are insignificant details. Undeniably, Squire bases a large part of his parody on Eliot's mix of polysyllabics and the ambiguous, slightly menacing context of Eliot's quatrain poems. But that's not all. Squire's parody asserts that Eliot, and modernism more largely, was fashionably fascinated with the exoticized sex of primitivism. Literary critics didn't get back to examining *that* aspect of modernism until the 1990s.

For its parodists, then, modernism was only partially understood as a revolution in aesthetics. Its aesthetic was accompanied by an inseparable, enabling context, made up of manipulations of publicity, performances of machismo, lightweight but portentous analogical references to science, and obfuscating theoretical justifications and explanations. Now parodists, for the most part working with an aesthetic in which art was a retreat from the social world, did not think that modernism's social aspect was a good thing about it. And neither were modernists themselves comfortable with attention being drawn to this larger context. Critics have returned to these larger contextual understandings, albeit with a new sense of their value, only in the modernist studies of the past twenty years.

As their invocations of a larger cultural context indicate, parodic reframings of modernism had complex public *work* to do, work illumined by their relation to more general theories of parody. The works in *Mock Modernism* corroborate Simon Dentith's understanding of parody as "any cultural practice which provides a relatively polemical allusive imitation of another cultural production or practice" (9). Parody's polemics are set into play through citation that either exaggerates aspects of the targeted source, or that uses techniques of bathos to deflate the ambitions of its source. Parody's imitation and polemics have large implications for the nature of art, and for modernism. In their partial and allusive imitation, parodies talk back to their sources, their very existence announcing that modern art is a conversation – and not just a conversation between works of art, but between different works of art, their social contexts, and their readers. But in the particularities of how they set about that conversation, the works in this collection redirect the insights of dominant theories of parody, narrowing and making more productive and socially nuanced parody's focus. The difference arises from how the range and pointedness of parody is understood. For example, Giorgio Agamben, in his *Profanations*, turns to the implications parody may have for understanding language in general:

> If ontology is the more or less felicitous relationship between language and world, then parody, as paraontology, expresses language's inability to reach the thing and the impossibility of the thing finding its own name. The space of parody – which is literature – is therefore necessarily and theologically marked by mourning and by the distorted grimace (just as the space of logic is marked by silence). And yet, in this way, parody attests to what seems to be the only possible truth of language. (2007: 50)

In pointing out parody's entanglement with larger concepts of literature and language, Agamben gives parody ambition and theoretical heft. But he is not very helpful about parody's social uses, and does not account for the characteristics of the particular kind of parodic interventions collected in this volume, interventions based on polemical interpretation. Although one might extrapolate these larger implications from some of these sources, the works in *Mock Modernism* don't direct themselves so much at all language or human expression as at *these uses* of expression and language, *these* forms of art.

In her central *A Theory of Parody* (1985), Linda Hutcheon conceptualizes parody less broadly than does Agamben, as a recreation, with irony. Her argument about the broad cultural place of parody does not see laughter or ridicule as integral to parody's function, and polemics, being filtered through irony, has an uncertain function. Hutcheon's book, and her later *The Politics of*

Postmodernism, usefully expanded our understanding of parody's functions. Coming as it did at a defining moment in postmodernism, and as her differences with Jameson reveal, Hutcheon's position is as much an argument about postmodernism as it is about parody as a genre. More centrally, she and Jameson both look at parody as the defining characteristic of modernism or postmodernism, and do not consider what happens when modernism itself is parodied. That difference, resulting in a much more focused set of parody's attributes and functions, is important. The materials in *Mock Modernism* show how parodies work as polemical interpretations of their sources, and how they do so by using laughter as central. Thus, *Mock Modernism*'s parodies do illustrate some of Hutcheon's larger functions, such as the double-edged character of parody, which both subverts and reinscribes the values of its targets. But the parodies of modernism collected here always foreground a polemical interpretation, and they always filter those interpretations through laughter.

Laughter's filter allows parody to perform complex work, for the laughter always has a thesis, arguing about what modernism meant or how it moved. The mechanics of this work are partially illuminated by the theoretical frame Freud provides in *Jokes and Their Relation to the Unconscious*. To some degree, the works in *Mock Modernism* share the characteristics of what Freud calls tendentious jokes, jokes that under the cover of laughter allow things to be said, and aggression to be released, that would otherwise be socially unacceptable (103ff.). The assertion behind the joke is incomplete without the aggression and the mediated manner in which that aggression is released. For Freud, and for the works in *Mock Modernism*, laughter reframes what is being said and sublimates the aggression. Sublimation, as it always does, complicates the unsublimated, socially unrespectable response. At times, the aggression is sublimated more transparently than at others: a mock court's burning of imitations of Matisse's work and sentencing him to be hanged sublimates the aggression against Matisse more by ritualizing than by deflecting it. As parodies, the works in *Mock Modernism* perform the work of sublimation in three ways: they draw attention to the wit of the parodist; turn the focus of the response from anger to analysis; and, as Freud recognized, compel agreement from those who laugh along. (Although complicit laughter can at times be assumed, the effect of these parodies on the beliefs and actions of readers is tough to measure, and lies outside the scope of this book.)

Is the work of parody's laughter by default socially transgressive, as Freud and other theorists of jokes and parody maintain? In *Mock Modernism* that analysis goes only so far, moving in a more curious direction. Parody as rebellion against power, of course, is absurd on one level, given modernism's outsider cultural status at the time. How could the habitués of, say, Margaret

Anderson's *The Little Review*, with a circulation of perhaps three thousand, really threaten William Randolph Hearst's chain of newspapers, with a readership of perhaps 50 million? Yet, despite the power discrepancies by most measures, the parodies in this book structure their laughter as a rebellion against a threat. Defining modernism's threat as one of incipient rather than established power, these parodies attempt to expose the tawdry power of elitism, of difficulty, of the opaque, of fashion, of publicity, of relevance. While the actual cultural power of modernism at the time may have been more notional than true, the parodies show us where their authors argued the threat in modernism lay, and in that they were, at times, surprisingly prescient.

As it is exhibited in *Mock Modernism*, parody's cultural work of liberation finds its most nuanced model in Bakhtin, particularly his "From the Prehistory of Novelistic Discourse." Freud, after all, deals primarily with jokes, with a nod to parody near the end of his book. Bakhtin sees parody as a subset of satire, although his preferred form, Menippean satire, has an intertextuality so pronounced that it looks parodic, so that parody and satire are hard to disentangle. Bakhtin's implied distinction is that parody bases itself on mimicking linguistic form, and is less pointed, less clearly polemical, than is satire. The interpretive aspects of parody are part, then, of their satirical thrust, and Bakhtin sees parody as a subversive genre, one particularly useful for upsetting power structures by introducing a disruptive voice. But in modernism, and probably elsewhere, the power relationships are more flexible than how Bakhtin and others, including Freud, describe them, often also being used by the powerful to attempt to shut down an uprising.[1]

Parody's laughter goes beyond aggression and unmasking modernism's incipient power. Laughter's filter pushes parody's argument to be based on generally held, communal beliefs and principles that it presents as commonsensical. The laughter is generated by a stretching that is understood to be, after all, not that much of a stretching – one has only to apply Gertrude Stein's prose to the rules of polo to immediately see its ludicrousness. One doesn't have to *argue* for the ludicrousness so much as merely point to it. By basing the laughter on a simulated earnestness and on taking a principle and stretching it, parodies have a peculiar "reining-in" effect. *Mock Modernism*'s parodies define their objects as extreme in some way, which helps to account for why the parodies tended to be directed at high and avant-garde modernism. In their recontextualizing and stretching, parodic interventions simultaneously rein in their source works' ambitions, inherently adopting a middle-of-the-road position, arguing for an aesthetic that does not take aesthetic principles too far, an aesthetic that presents itself as common sense. Along with the laughter, this presenting of an aesthetic as common sense appeals to and tries to define a public, communal understanding. Henry James responding to the simple question "What is your name," or Ezra Pound trying to catch a train – these show what happens to modernist principles when they hit the real world.

"Common sense," of course, is a loaded concept, and it had much work to do in responding to the changing aesthetic of the time. Evocations of common sense asserted a shared social understanding that went without saying, that did not have to be *argued* for. That gesture also implies a historical understanding: activities, points of view, forms of art become commonsensical over time, over repeated iterations. And, of course, "common sense" has great cultural power: it is what one evokes when something ideological has been questioned. This is why commonsense-based parody does not have the liberating functions claimed for parody more largely. Liberation depends on who is doing the parody, and what the target is. Not surprisingly, the *new* things seen in modernist art seemed an assault on common sense: new ideas of representation, specialization, professionalism, and the idea of art as socially involved in contemporary conditions.

Common sense inevitably reaches to many areas of human activity, and this has implications for the content of many of the parodies in this book. In the dominant aesthetic of the early twentieth century, art did not exist as a special case outside of common sense, or outside of common sense's deep alliance with the pragmatic. Consequently, the more avant-garde a work appeared to be, the more simply could a parody reach to pragmatic objections, the most basic of which was that art was referential. Stein's *Tender Buttons* was often the target. A writer for the New York *Evening Sun*, in all probability Don Marquis, wrote:

> "A curving example makes righteous finger nails," says Gertrude Stein, for once hooking a subject and a predicate together with a cheerfulness which need deceive no one concerning her real opinion of grammar. As for the thought-content of Gertrude's observation, can you deny it? (Anonymous, Untitled)

Common sense wasn't just about reining things in via pragmatic objections; these parodies also rein in their sources' too-earnest, ambitious seriousness. Even when it is presented as homage, the parody and its reframing portray the target author as unduly taken in by his or her own seriousness, a seriousness deflated for readers by a new, commonsensical and often banal context for the work. James Joyce, for example, in a letter to Harriet Shaw Weaver, complained of the rain on a recent trip to Rouen:

> Rouen is the rainiest place getting
> Inside all impermeables, wetting
> Damp marrow in drenched bones.

Joyce's historical / geographic specificity and banal subject matter deflates Eliot's mythic time of regeneration, a strategy Joyce continues when he takes Eliot's sighing Dantesque crowd, and transforms them:

I heard mosquitoes swarm in old Bordeaux
So many!
I had not thought the earth contained so many
(Hurry up, Joyce, it's time).

By doing so, of course, he is also, tongue in cheek, making his own miserable context more important, more epic. These are mosquitoes of mythic proportions. In the poem's ending, to which all of Eliot's parodists turn, the poem's final gesture towards a potential benediction finds its re-expression in bathos, a trivial hope for a much-too-specific, much-too-casual future:

But we shall have great times,
When we return to Clinic, that waste land
O Esculapios!
(Shan't we? Shan't we? Shan't we?) (*Letters*, vol. 1: 231)

The works in *Mock Modernism* don't stop at banal recontextualizings. They also identify and critique the spongy characteristics of their sources by stretching them, as Christopher Ward does with Henry James's prose:

"Tea?" asked Marion.

Through the long casement window, which lazily unfolded its unaustere yet deliberate length in a benediction of sunlight, not more interminable than the crepitant genuflection of the waveless ocean, came the tall dark cry of the curlew, as it lashed its angry though querulous tail in intermittent certitude. Perhaps that was why the shiny, untarnished mud flats, blue veined with the tortuous eternal channels of the running tides, interspersed with the nostalgic counterparts of antiquity, and the gray green marshes, where the red shanks choired in uninterrupted but not unvexed prolixity, despite their propinquity, had always seemed to her as remote from the perpetual imbroglio with spiritual things that makes man the most ridiculous of animals, though just emerged from a brave dive in some pool of vitality, whose whereabouts are the secret that makes the mouth vigilant.

"Yes, please," answered Ellen, smiling. (Ward, "The Judge" 79–80)

Although Ward does not quite manage to pull off an exaggeration of James's periodic structure, James's characteristics are pulled taut here, from his vocabulary to his sentence length and structure, to his disproportionate vocabulary-to-action ratio, to the way in which the banality of the surface speech far exceeds the apparent richness of its implications in the somewhat omniscient narrator's silent, lengthy meditation.

Finally, the works collected here playfully create a simulacrum of an authentic and sincere point of origin, having an "as-if" quality that creates an instability central to how their argumentative claims work. They act like they are the real thing, but the public awareness, of course, is that they are not, and the slippage between their appearance of sincerity and prima facie absurdity, while at times hard to stabilize, is always productive and polemical. Sincerity, simultaneously proffered and withheld, is a little off-kilter in these works, and this ungainly sincerity is central to their characterization of modernism (and, one could profitably argue, is central to many modernist works as well).

As the above examples and argument show, parodic interactions with modernism often approach their targets with elements of hostility, homage, and interpretation all rolled into one. While laughter is central, the response isn't *just* ridicule. The "mock" of this book's title points to that, "mock" being a term that points both to counterfeit *and* derision. When one puts the word "mock" in front of a noun, according to the *Oxford English Dictionary*, it amounts to "designating a person who or thing which parodies, imitates, or deceptively resembles that which the noun properly denotes." And, of course, "mock" suggests a certain kind of imitation: "To ridicule by imitation of speech, manner, or behaviour; to parody." Always, with its disguise, using the comedy of the *appearance* of sincerity, mock modernism had complex work to do.

A few words on this book's boundaries, and what those boundaries mean. Reaching to both sides of the Atlantic, I include responses from a wide variety of parodists, both the famous and the completely unknown. Headnotes to different items, therefore, vary in terms of the amount and kinds of information they include. Dates (when available) and other information on individual parodists appear the first time their work appears in this collection. Given the range of authors, it is no surprise that publishing venues also vary widely, both geographically and in the *type* of print sources. London's *Punch* in 1911 differed widely from the whimsy of the University of Wisconsin's undergraduate literary review, or the more combative pages of the *Egoist*. As the response to modernism in Chicago and other places shows, modernism can't be understood as a history of what happened within a relatively small circle in three great literary capitals. Its interactions went across class lines, and had wide-ranging, localized inflections. And, thanks to new distribution methods of mass culture, modernism was both widespread and timely: responses to *Tender Buttons*, for example, rapidly spread across the United States. Despite its having been printed in an edition of only one thousand, the book could in a few months become a national occasion, suggesting, as Karen Leick points out, that many responses and reviews were written solely on the basis of having read other reviews (41–2).

The decentring of modernism has added nuance. A journal, a publishing house, and on occasion even an author, did not always represent a single point of view. There was great interconnectedness within single locations, with the work of parodists appearing in the same journals in which their target authors published. Herbert Palmer, author of *Cinder Thursday*, was published by Eliot's Faber and Faber. *The New Age*, as Ann Ardis has shown in her *Modernism and Cultural Conflict*, was a place where multiple viewpoints met.[2] The Imagist Richard Aldington's send-up of Imagism, "Penultimate Poetry," appeared in *The Egoist*, which also published Pound, his target. Modernism, before it was clear what its properties were, and who was on what side, was a place of confusing and indeterminate locations.

In its organization, *Mock Modernism* distinguishes between targets of parody and modes of parody. The book's first two major sections are given over to parodies of individual authors and movements. The first turns to poetry, the second to fiction. These sections present an asymmetrical picture of what we now understand as modernism. Parodists weren't interested in showing the diversity of modernist responses to the contemporary world; they presented modernism as a single entity, and an extreme one at that. No surprise, then, that more attention was given to the more spectacular writers, and to those writers, like the Sitwells, who seemed most eagerly to seize the mechanisms of publicity. The works in *Mock Modernism*, then, tend to target those manifestations of art that engage with the conditions of modernity in an extreme manner. That is entirely predictable, it being more fun to mock things that are excessive, that walk far outside of traditional aesthetics and subject matters. Parody, indeed, inherently defines its source as somehow being excessive. The consequences for the contents of this book are striking: given the default aesthetic of the time, which based itself on pragmatics, mimesis, and commonsense, it is unsurprising that one finds Ezra Pound lampooned much more often than Robert Frost.

The issue of representation and exclusions is, of course, one about which readers will speculate. The organization of *Mock Modernism* has shaped its inclusions: given that many of these parodies are directed at larger aspects of modernism such as manifestos and methodologies, many targeted authors appear in more than one location, including those who don't have their own, author-specific section. Their representation is larger than a quick glance at the table of contents would indicate. (The headnotes and index clarify all locations where individual authors appear.) Issues of organization aside, my strategy has been to register accurately modern artists' place in the public consciousness of the time, and, as one can clearly see, Stein, Pound, Picasso, and Masters were the major parodic targets. (This book also includes a few parodies of modes of producing traditional art that were seen to be implicated in the devices of modernity.) As for exclusions or limited representation in *Mock Modernism*, the chronological boundaries of the collection have had a significant effect. Wallace Stevens, for example, had very little exposure in the early years of modernism, even in the pages of little magazines. The 1923 edition of *Harmonium* has a very small reception history, and no parodic reframings that I have found. This belated register on the public consciousness, and the consequent lack of early parodic reframings, is also true for writers like William Faulkner, Marianne Moore, and William Carlos Williams.

After the opening two sections on poetry and fiction, the second half of *Mock Modernism* turns to different genres of parodic intervention, showing the period's surprising range of parodic engagement. This second half of the book demonstrates that modernism wasn't understood just as its finished works of art, but that it was, instead, seen to be a complex social phenomenon, and a shared project. The second half begins with perhaps the most dominant genre of parodic intervention: verse commentary. Typically written in doggerel quatrains (a favourite genre of American newspaper columnists in particular), these commentaries tend to direct their parody at the social positioning of modern artists. Modernism was quickly seen not just as an aesthetic movement, but as a broader struggle for cultural power. Three sections then follow – "Manifestos," "Modernist Methodologies," and "Modernist Criticism" – the contents of which assert that modernism was inseparable from theory and its institutions. These parodic engagements mimic modernism's theoretical justifications, its composition processes, and its interpretive explanations. *Mock Modernism* ends with the section "Modernist Performances," consisting of newspaper accounts of ritualistic public engagements with, and enactments of, modernist principles.

As for the temporal range of this book, the works in *Mock Modernism* were written while modernism was still fresh, when the parodies still exhibit the baffled outrage of surprise. They satirize a *current occasion*, not an *eternal text*. Thus, as I have alluded to earlier, parodies written during this time are much more likely to reach to the larger social context, and not, like later parodies, restrict themselves to skewering the formal / thematic properties of the work in question. Further, these responses were not written when modernism was an already-constructed edifice, but when the survivability of this new, jury-rigged assemblage was in doubt. Indeed, even *what was being proposed* was uncertain. The works in this book were created when modernism was in the ascendant, but also when it was still under contention, and when its central properties weren't all that clear. Writing in his 1931 *Survey of Burlesque and Parody*, George Kitchin noted the consequent and peculiar difficulties faced by modernism's parodists:

> Modern poetry would seem to invite the wittiest kind of parody, because it has taken refuge in a world which is rather like the world of nonsense verse ... But for that very reason it is the harder to parody in any true sense. How is the parodist to satirise what already, on the surface, looks like luminous nonsense? And how he must perspire to give his verse the admitted delicacy of the original, nonsense or no nonsense? The truth is we are at one of those critical junctures in art, when a new philosophy of art "puts all in doubt." (345)

These are also parodies of writers and artists before they were *important*, when things were still radically uncertain. It was a volatile time, in which power was uncertain, outcomes in doubt, authenticity debatable. It was a time when modernism was being defended by uncertain standards, with an unclear sense on its own part as to what exactly it was doing. Modernism wasn't figured out yet, and these parodies' immediacy is startling. Later parodies, by contrast, work with the sense of someone like Eliot already established, and of a history of how his work has been taught in the classroom. The parody becomes a knocking down of the arthritic king, not the deflating of a pretentious arriviste.

Beyond its temporal limitations, *Mock Modernism* restricts itself to those works that have a parodic intent, that with an implied earnestness attempt to stretch characteristics of modernism to expose it, to make an argument about it. By simulating an aesthetic impulse, whose features the audience is expected to know, the works included here foreground their target referent. And they silently stretch that referent's putative characteristics, locating their argument in the tensions between their audience's implied understanding of the referent and the stretching that unmasks its ludicrousness. By taking characteristics and silently stretching them, the recreation mimics seriousness. Except in their moments of meta-commentary, there is thus a deadpan quality to many of the works included here, with the dominant pleasures being those of complicity and social consensus, of being in on the joke. For inclusion in this volume, then, negative assessments of modernism weren't enough, no matter how spectacular. Works needed to be more than polemical, they needed a parodic subtext to inflect the polemic.

These respondents to modernism returned repeatedly to several meanings in their reframings. The first, given the terms under which modernism would eventually become canonized, is surprising: modernism, instead of being too aloof from mass culture, was parodied as being too immersed in it, which made it easy to pick up in modernist art the greasy imprint of its surrounding culture. Modernism wasn't allied with eternity, but had sold itself to the *now*. Parodists suspected that these aspects of mass culture were being used to dodge aesthetic standards. Moreover, modernism's immersion in publicity, fashion, speed, mass replication, professional organization, and culture of celebrity created problems of trust. Movements, fashion, and mass behaviour all made these parodists nervous about the sincerity of these writers and artists. For many of these parodists, modernism wasn't "natural"; it worked too consciously at what it set out to do.

A more abstract meaning is suggested by these parodists' scope, their skewering a wide range of modernism's media and genres. Modernism's wide range, in fact, is often indicated and argued about within individual works themselves, for many of the pieces in *Mock Modernism* assert that modernism had an aesthetic and context that was transferable, with individual modernist works having clear implications for work in other arts. For modernists, this generalizable reach was a sign of their art's ambition, a point not lost on a sceptical audience. These parodies show that, early on, modernism was recognized to be making ambitious claims: for its reach, its critique, and the value of its technical innovations. These claims linked modern works to each other in a movement that stretched across genres and media, and resulting in modern works that were not just about themselves, but about *modernity*.

That recognized linkage led to a standard deflating move, which was to take the seriousness of these terms down a notch, sometimes head on, but often by showing how easily modernism was transferable. Modernism's large claims did not reveal profundity, but glibness. To many parodists it was often suspiciously easily to accomplish this transfer, as when Stein's work, say, was transferred to other social contexts, such as the unlikely pages of the *New York City Daily Trade Record*, which offered the following migration of Steinian prose into the commercial context:

> Gertrude Stein, if she made a prose poem of our lines, might well say: Woolens, alas, alas, and again – the Northeast, warps, warps and no woof but sorrow. See far, far away the distant but unfeeling scope. A mill – a thing but not a person, all or none, but none so much as yesterday not tomorrow. A gum shoe – a feeling, but not pink – bitter. Worsteds, too – or worst. A thread but not spun. Cloakings – a riot, a dance, a minuet, a tango, but slow music, and hearts break in distant woe. What is a cloak? no wrap, but rainbows, not hosiery, no, not ever. But when? Ah! ("The Futurist on the Trade," 18 June 1914)

There was much fun to be had transferring Steinese to a variety of social contexts, but more central to early understandings of modernism was that the aesthetic principles revealed in a particular work or form of art – and their enabling social context – were transferable from one art form to another. This is the logical motivation behind futurist fashion shows, and the many claims of Stein as a cubist. The possibilities for parody lay in extending the absurdities of one aesthetic manifestation into another medium, exposing even more starkly its obvious banalities. For example, Don Marquis, writing in the *New York Evening Sun*, created the characters of Hermione and her Little Group of Serious Thinkers. Enchanted with all things modern, their portentous experiments and pronouncements allowed the unthinking application of one medium into another. At an evening soirée, for example, the narrator approaches Fothergil Finch, the Poet of Revolt, in order to get an explanation of composer Voke Easeley, the featured performer for the night's entertainment. Fothergil's response is initially baffling:

> "A New Art!" said Fothergil. And then he led me into the hall and explained.
>
> What Gertrude Stein has done for prose, what the wilder *vers libre* bards are doing for poetry, what cubists and futurists are doing for painting and sculpture, that Voke Easeley is doing for vocal music.
>
> "He is painting sound portraits with his larynx now," said Fothergil. "And the beautiful part of it is that he is absolutely tone deaf! He doesn't know a thing about music. He tried for years to learn and couldn't. The only way he knows when you strike a chord on the piano is because he doesn't like chords near as well as he does discords." (*Hermione and Her Little Group of Serious Thinkers* 86–7)

As the above example suggests, modernism was generalizable: the responses were as often a parodic reframing of how whole genres of modernism and their methodologies generally worked as they were overtly of specific texts. (This aspect of modern parody has big consequences for how one understands things like the place of theory and fashion in modernism, for example.) Modernism wasn't just free verse, or atonal music, or cubism in isolation; these manifestations were related. Part of this connectedness was because they all arose from a single social context; in particular, from a new engagement with mass culture. But this transferability was possible also because many parodists thought theory was starting to play too large a role in aesthetic production. Indeed, a sign of the perceived prominence of theory in modernism are the many moments of sustained and direct meta-reflection in this collection. Many of the items included in *Mock Modernism* show anxiety about professionalism, and about a mode of artmaking that had moved away from the "natural" to something much more deliberate and self-conscious. This self-consciousness was related to nervousness about writers' and artists' motivating impulses and the conditions under which they made their artworks, with the result that sceptics spent a fair bit of time figuring out composition practices.

In a final, related point, these parodies all argued that modernism – its artworks, its theories, its criticism – were all *easy* to produce. In a display of faux humility, parodists more often stated how easy it was to parody this work than they crowed about their skill in doing so. Modernism, given a few starting principles, was completely predictable. A.R. Orage, writing in his *New Age* in 1915, claimed,

> A friend of mine has invented an automatic cubist-vorticist picture-maker that turns you out a Bomberg "Mud-bath" or a Wadsworth "City" with the turn of a wrist. A frame contains coloured pieces of flat wood which shift themselves into "arrangements" (as Mr. Pound would have said) expressive of profound emotions! Specimens, I understand, can be seen at the Chenil Gallery at Chelsea. The invention will shortly be placed upon the market. (R.H.C., "Readers and Writers" 509)

A letter to Orage at *The New Age* a few years earlier had argued that "we must not forget that there is no excessive difficulty in the invention of 'advanced' theories. They are an easy sport for winter evenings, in fact; but ruinous and perplexing at last if wit is reckoned sufficient in art, and life no more than a lark." The writer concluded that, in fact, one of the weakest aspects of Picasso's work was "the ease with which he may be imitated and caricatured" (Guthrie, 1911: 141–2). Belief in and irritation at that apparent ease motivates the authors collected in this book.

But were they right? Were modern works effortless to produce? At times, as Kitchin has pointed out, featureless modernism seems hard to parody, and the parodies seem laboured, with the features of Stein's work especially being hard to parody. But occasionally, readers of *Mock Modernism* will find it as hard to distinguish the parody from the original as I have (whether this means that parody, at its most successful, becomes forgery, is a question beyond the reach of this introduction). Is it not plausible, at least, that Masters could have written "Birdie McReynolds," or Eliot written "Einstein among the Coffee-cups"? What does it imply that one can't, at times, tell the difference between parody and original? It implies, I believe, several important things about modernism. First, it suggests that modernism's more heightened forms and traditional aesthetics were so far apart from each other that what was ridiculous within one aesthetic made perfect sense within another. Second, it suggests that bathos, one of the central tools of parody and burlesque, came under stress at this time. For artists who used as their central aesthetic principles realism, the ordinary, or the unexceptional – writers like Masters, Woolf, Cather – parodies struggled to make the bathos register. It is hard to use bathos in response to a work that uses the ordinary as one of its central aesthetic principles. And at the other end, it was difficult to stretch extreme changes in register, such as in Eliot's quatrain poems (which use bathetic shifts in tone and diction as one of their central poetic registers), or the work of the deliberately eccentric, such as the Sitwells. As Mark Jones argues in his examination of parody in Wordsworth, at times a work emerges as parody only when we know the "relevant 'background'" (64).

The kinds of responses collected in *Mock Modernism* have played an at best anecdotal role in histories of modernism. That limited role has led to a truncated understanding not only of how modernism gained notice, but, even more important, how it was constructed, interpreted, and came to power both fashionable and institutional. Modernism wasn't just a series of texts and artworks; it was an *event*, and an event whose meaning was under constant negotiation. Further, the items collected here show that we impoverish our understanding of modernism if we understand its reception primarily in terms of extended reviews in serious journals and major newspapers. Modernism isn't just a story of major centres, of a few little magazines, and of major newspapers of record. The public sphere was much more diverse than that, and it played a more significant and diverse role in the construction of modernism than has usually been granted. One of modernism's central interactions with its public, one that helped the public posit what modernism *was*, was laughter, and laughter did some serious work. This shift in understanding how modernism interacted with its public early on has significant consequences: when brought to light, these responses show the energy with which modernism was negotiated, and what the surprising terms of those negotiations were.

As fits the purpose of this book, my texts are printed as they appeared at the time – I have not turned to later, edited versions, and, except for obvious misprints, I have made no editorial corrections. Given the interconnectedness of many of these works, many of these parodies could have been inserted into different sections of the book. In particular, Gertrude Stein, who appears with more frequency than many other modernists, is scattered throughout this book, and not in an individual section. This dispersal occurs because Stein so often appears as an explanatory context for other aspects of modernism. My index helps both with locating repeating authors and topics (such as Cubism and Futurism), and with making conceptual connections more clear.

I have kept explanatory notes to a minimum. My elucidations are found either in headnotes, or in notes at the back of the book, whichever I thought was most useful for reading. The few *foot*notes that appear indicate notes that were in the original sources. The endnotes are used primarily to explicate possibly unfamiliar contemporary references, provide translations, and at times point out what features and which authors were being parodied. Occasionally, the notes engage in the queasy pleasure of explaining puns on names and other jokes. I apologize for unnecessary explanations – as anyone familiar with Freud's *Jokes and Their Relation to the Unconscious* can attest to, a joke explained is no longer a joke.

PART I

Literary Targets

I. Poetry

Surveying the landscape, literary types in the early twentieth century often commented, with some wariness, that poetry publishing was booming. Harold Monro, poet, anthologist, editor of the *Poetry Review*, and proprietor of the Poetry Bookshop, wrote in his 1920 anthology *Some Contemporary Poets* that "younger men and women of education enjoy the practice of making clever rhymes or noting down their own feelings in loose sentences, vaguely termed 'free verse.' The periodicals and newspapers make a large demand for these exercises in rhyme and rhythm: it is not difficult to be accepted" (9). Across the Atlantic, and looking back from some years' distance, Fred Lewis Pattee, professor of English at Pennsylvania State University, and often considered to be the first professor of American literature, noted the same phenomenon, but with less placidity. In his 1930 *The New American Literature*, in a chapter entitled "The Poetry Debacle," he referred to what had been the fashion for the "new poetry": "Everybody was reading it, or professing to read it, or intending to read it." Quoting Don Marquis, Pattee went on:

> It burst even into the Sunday "funnies" and the comic journals:
> There's a grand poetical "boom," they say.
> (Climb on it, chime on it, brothers of mine!)
> 'Twixt the dawn and the dusk of each lyrical day
> There's another school started, and all of 'em pay.
> (A dollar a line!
> Think of it, Ferdy, a dollar a line!) (1930: 386)

To a cynic, it seemed that virtually *anything* could get published. Across the Atlantic and a decade earlier, J.C. Squire despairingly noted an ad from the London Correspondence College that had appeared in the *Times Literary*

Supplement. What drew his ire was the text that read "The field for Verse is much larger than most people suppose. Hundreds of journals publish and pay for poetry. Anyone with aptitude can learn to write the kind of Verse editors will pay for" ("Short Cuts" 26).

From some historical distance, one can look back and articulate numerous reasons for the poetry boom: the invention of linotype; changes in distribution methods; the cheaper cost of paper; the discovery that advertising, not subscriptions, could pay for the cost of a magazine; urbanization; the rise in accessible education and the consequent need for poetry anthologies to educate the lower classes. At the time, however, these possible reasons for the poetry boom were noted much less often than was the increase in publication itself, and particularly the increase in new *forms* of poetry. For most commentators, that increase signalled a crisis: what did this increase in poetry, and poetry of a new kind, have to say about aesthetic standards? About modernity? This instability, apparently, was well suited to parodic interventions, leading Squire and others to set pen to paper and busy themselves lampooning the excesses of modernism.

FREE VERSE

Its most galvanizing instance being the publication of *Spoon River Anthology* (see the parodies of Edgar Lee Masters collected later), free verse generated an enormous number of responses. This was due to the novelty of the form, certainly. But it was also due to the form's association with publicity. Lawrence Gilman, reviewing Masters's *Spoon River Anthology* in the *North American Review*, noted:

> Since the famous discovery of Paris by Mr. Richard Harding Davis some years ago, there have been few more edifying happenings of a similar kind than the recent disclosure, by our always alert "general public" and our no less alert newspaper paragraphers, of a strange and hitherto unheard of poetic phenomenon: "vers libre." Letters to the papers from sarcastic and jocose readers, parodies by the paragraphers, solemn discussions by reviewers, have marked this momentous emergence into public view of a novel and arresting verse-form. (217)

The parodic engagements with free verse collected in *Mock Modernism* raised, more often than not, questions about evaluative standards (how might one distinguish good from bad), and suspicions about composition practices. Some of the suspect composition practices were those based on an application, to poetry, of a larger aesthetic context. Volumes like the painter Max Weber's *Cubist Poems*, published in 1914 by Elkin Mathews, suggested to some that modern culture offered some easy ways to poetry. Weber's opening poem reads:

The Eye Moment

Cubes, cubes, cubes, cubes,
High, low, and high, and higher, higher,
Far, far out, out, out, far,
Planes, planes, planes,
Colours, lights, signs, whistles, bells, signals, colours,
Planes, planes, planes,
Eyes, eyes, window eyes, eyes, eyes,
Nostrils, nostrils, chimney nostrils,
Breathing, burning, puffing,
Thrilling, puffing, breathing, puffing,
Millions of things upon things,
Billions of things upon things
This for the eye, the eye of being,
At the edge of the Hudson,

Flowing timeless, endless,
On, on, on, on ... (11)

A more successful painter than poet, Weber only once tried his hand at publishing a book of poems. Most modernist poetry, of course, was not so mannered as Weber's, but parodists tended not to want to make distinctions of quality and sophistication. Generalized summings-up were more useful; as one writer noted, "It's so damnably easy!" Bert Leston Taylor grumbled:

The verses of the modern pote,
The things he labels "free,"

Resemble much a little boat
That's rudderless at sea.
The pote rides in his cockleshell,
Not knowing where he's bound.

And, tossed about from swell to swell,
Goes round and round and round. (1921: 6)

The typical subject matters of free verse were often poked at, with worries that free verse had no sense of the appropriate. A standard device for exposing this was bathos – sweeping shifts in tone and subject matter, as in J.C. Squire's send-up of a free verse poem:

Gyrating cowls.
Ink.
Oh God! A Lobster! ("Man Who Wrote Free Verse": 248)

At one end, the rewritings of free verse were very detailed, taking on such conventions of free verse as lineation, punctuation, capitalization, aporia, and melodramatic juxtapositions. Simultaneously, however, the critiques were broad – parodying free verse through exaggerating its associations with democracy, immigration, Bolshevism, intellectualism, and suspect sexual practices. This aspect of aesthetic critique, like much of the work in this anthology as a whole, was less like the pleasures of a chess game than those of a food fight.

John Collings Squire, "The Man Who Wrote Free Verse"

London Mercury, June 1924: 127–37; rpt. in _The Grub Street Nights Entertainments_ (London: Hodder and Stoughton, 1924; New York: George H. Doran Co., 1924), 239–64.

A prolific author, J.C. Squire (1884–1958) was, for a while, the most successful British literary journalist of his day. His journal *The London Mercury* had a circulation of ten thousand at its high point, rivalling that of the *Times Literary Supplement*. An anthologist writing in 1922 claimed of Squire that "no living poet has a wider influence on the literary views and tendencies of his age" (Wetherell 1922: 36), a judgment echoed, apparently, by newspaper columnist Franklin P. Adams. An excellent parodist, Squire was described in 1935 as "immeasurably the greatest of our parodists to-day" (Richardson 1935: 24). Squire also projected himself headlong into literary politics, setting himself squarely against high modernism. Squire's support of the Georgian poets, and distrust of experimental modernism, led high moderns to disparage the "Squirearchy." T.S. Eliot, having written for Squire initially at *The New Statesman*, had by 1920 distanced himself, writing in a letter to John Quinn that Squire "knows nothing about poetry; but he is the cleverest journalist in London. If he succeeds, it will be impossible to get anything good published" (25 January 1920: 435). Lytton Strachey described Squire as "that little worm," and Virginia Woolf thought of him as "more repulsive than words can express, and malignant into the bargain" (qtd. in Pearson 147).

Squire's social engagement ranged widely. A founding member of the Fabian society, he stood for parliament for both Labour and the Liberals. He was knighted in 1933. During the last two decades of his life Squire's views on literary matters were more and more pushed to the margins by the rise of international modernism.

THE MAN WHO WROTE FREE VERSE

I

This is a very short story. It is hardly a story at all. It might even be described as all moral and no story: a lamentable thing, but the fit is upon us.

It was Sunday afternoon; the sky blue, the sun hot, the shade cool because of a slight breeze. The Manor House, its ancient stones mottled yellow and grey, its arched oaken door ajar, half its mullioned and leaded windows open, slept behind its gently sloping lawn. Lady Muriel was presumably asleep as well; at any rate she had retired to her room after the exhausting chatter of lunch. Sir Herbert and his wife, active delegates from a more energetic world, had gone out for a walk, though all country walks must have been very much alike to them, and they would certainly have nothing to report when they returned except Sir Herbert's hearty and self-evident appetite for tea. The two young men who completed the party had professed weariness and resorted to the shadow of the great cedar, with the Sunday papers and a large collection of Muriel's latest books. Adrian Roberts, bowed beneath the load of a Foreign Office clerkship, had taken the hammock; Reggie Twyfold, who was burdened only by an acute intelligence and enough to live on, was comfortable in a deck chair with a foot-rest; both were well supported by cushions in red, blue, green and orange silk. Their reading was desultory amid the enchantment of the afternoon. Curving down to their right was a concourse of lilacs, laburnum, and red hawthorn all in bloom. On the left a border, a rockery, the bricks of the walled garden, and southward, making an opening through which the woody pastoral landscape fell and fell into blue distance, two groups of tall elms newly in leaf. At intervals a rook drowsily cawed in one of them and there was a slight flutter of wings; otherwise the birds were silent, and an occasional white butterfly in lazy erratic flight was the only thing in movement.

The church clock struck three; Adrian laid his book on his knees, Reggie languidly dropped his to the ground.

"Muriel's books," said Reggie, "seem even more ridiculous here than they do in town."

"I'm reading Trollope," replied Adrian from his hammock, with the air of one who preferred not to waste his time.

"I confess," replied Reggie defensively, "that I can't help looking at the stuff."

"Some of the bindings are rather engaging."

"No, I mean the insides," insisted Reggie. "I can't help being curious about them, idiotic though they are. You can't realise what rot all these novels are."

"Oh, yes, I can. They are pretentious and psychological, dull and obscene, or cheaply cynical. I do occasionally look at one for conversational purposes with other people, though I dare not admit it to Muriel or she'd bore me to death with her arguments."

"This one I have here isn't even punctuated."

"It makes little difference," said Adrian consolingly; "none of these people can write and few of them seem even to want to."

"But, really, Adrian, I can't quite ignore it all as you do. – It's the poetry I was thinking of most. I confess I can't make head or tail of three-quarters of it, but I can't help thinking I may be wrong. Why should they be writing what seems to us cacophonous gibberish? It isn't only Muriel, you know. Lots of people seem to admire it, and it's happening all over Europe and America."

"Not really, my dear. We hear a good deal about it, and the papers we read seem to think it all ought to be taken seriously. In point of fact these creatures are scarcely read by each other. It's a kind of hideous little underworld; the sort of thing you see when you lift up a large stone and see disgusting insects, beetles and centipedes, scuttling about. They dislike the daylight too. It's all the most awful nonsense. The second-rate have discovered the trick of incomprehensibility in our own time; the trick of bogus audacity has always been known."

"I know, that's what it all seems like to me when I read it. Yet when I'm not reading it I feel that there may be something genuine in all this movement ..."

"Which?" asked Adrian in an amused voice.

"Oh, the whole of it. The general mix-up. All these isms and experiments. Scientific and social conceptions can't alter without modifying art; music changes and poetry may change; and I conceive new things being said in a new way."

"And so can I," said Adrian. "I really don't mind people saying anything they like if they mean it and are competent to express themselves. I don't insist upon rhymes, and I don't, so long as my ear is pleased, mind people's lines being all of different lengths, and I don't mind impressionism if it produces effects on me, and I'm not a bit afraid of my sub-conscious. But when half-wits, or no-wits, invite me to applaud their absurd posing and silly illiteracy I see no reason to do so."

"But don't you think," Reggie went on, still generously resolute to put a case against which all his instincts revolted, "that in some way it is all important and symptomatic. Doesn't it seem to you significant that when the Bolsheviks got into power in Russia they made all the Cubists and things official artists?"

Adrian was unmoved. "No," he said, "I'm sure that highly elaborate nonsense means nothing whatever to the proletariat. To their leaders it only meant one more annoyance to the bourgeoisie; though perhaps they naturally felt a kind of affinity for the rape of language and the murder of ideas." His eyes strayed to the far landscape. "The confiscation of the comma," he murmured, as it were for his own benefit. Then he recalled himself and began speaking in more vigorous tones. "Look here, Reggie, you yourself could write all this bosh on your head."

"That's hardly a compliment, is it, if all you say is true?"

"But, quite seriously, you could and you could take them all in. Why not do it, Reggie? Start a career as an advanced poet. A small piece of shell in your ribs ought not to interfere with that; in fact it might be rather a help. Get them all to take you seriously and then give it away."

"But, Adrian, how could I? They'd all guess. Besides, how would you like to have to fraternise with this dreadful rabble and be despised by all civilised people?" His high voice was querulous.

Adrian turned his head. "That's quite easy," he said. "Take a false name and – yes, an accommodation address, I think they call it. Be invisible! Refuse to meet any one! Be a hopeless invalid! Or disgusting to the sight! Why not a leper? A leper would do beautifully! It really could be quite easily managed. There's a man I get my boots from who would let you use his address. He used to be in the Royal Opera Arcade, but he's just moved now to a place that looks like a private house, in fact there are actually rooms there."

Two substantial figures silently appeared in the opening between the elms, Sir Herbert, hearty even at that distance, and his wife a meet companion. Lady Muriel's voice was heard from an upper window. Adrian waved an arm to them and prepared to rise. "Do think about it, Reggie," he said.

II

Reggie Twyfold sat at his sitting-room window in the Albany. He was on the top floor: dormers on the eastern side: and he looked out on a skyline of slates, chimneystacks, and chimney cowls revolving dizzily in a brisk wind. "You must begin," Adrian had said, "by emptying your mind completely and recording only disconnected impressions. You can work in the rebellion and work out the verbs later." This advice was superfluous; he could have got on well enough without it; but it strengthened him in his purpose to know that Adrian was confident about what he himself had suspected, and he was resolved now to see the imposture through to the bitter – he did not guess how bitter – end. He had, in his time, written competent verse and prose, but he had never sweated such blood trying to write sense as he had now sweated trying to write nonsense. Two and a half hours of scribblings and deletions had left him exhausted: and he looked at the fruits of his labours with an expression of doubt. "It's grotesque," he said, "nobody could print such rubbish. It's inconceivable that there isn't more in it than this." But Adrian was coming to luncheon and he had sworn to have a first attempt to show him; and, with a groan, he settled down to perfect the experiment. He was still poising his pen over the sheet when Adrian stole in. "Well," he said, "I see you've been at it. Lobster, good! Let's read it while we have lunch."

"I don't think it's really ready," protested Reggie.

"But all the better, Reggie," said Adrian, snatching the paper from him. They sat down at the table. Adrian absently eviscerated half a lobster while he read the sheet, and re-read it. Then "All poetry can best be tested by being read aloud," he said; and suited the action to the word. He read it:

The chimney-cowls
Gyrate
In the
Wind
There is a blot of ink
On
My paper.
I am going to have lunch
Before long
And I am glad there is
A
Lobster.

"My dear," said Adrian, as he finished, "I congratulate you. This is a most admirable beginning. But there are several faults in it."

"Good Lord, I should think so," said Reggie; "I've never written down such dismal filth in my life."

"Oh, I didn't mean faults in that sense; I meant really what you would ordinarily call merits."

"I'm damned if I can see them," said Reggie.

"But they are there all the same," said Adrian, almost paternally. "For one thing there is almost a flow to it. For another the sentences are quite ordinary. For another you actually express, in one place, a genuine emotion: I mean when you refer to the lobster."

Reggie defended himself. "One must say something," he argued.

"Not necessarily. Please remember that you are lampooning or, rather, imitating. You've read far more of these silly poems than I have. You know all the kinds of them as well as I do. Think of the kinds. Use what you have done as raw material and develop a poem in each kind from it. You must know what I mean. For instance there is the very simple kind which consists of leaving out everything conjunctive, running together a series of objects, and ending with an exclamation. You know as well as I do what I mean, don't you?"

"Oh, of course," said Reggie,

Gyrating cowls.
Ink.
Oh God! A Lobster!

But it would be asinine to think of getting any one to print that."

"Not as asinine as you suppose. You've seen things just like that in bookstand papers, haven't you? Now put your back into it. I've got an hour to spare and I shall read Matthew Arnold while you show what you can do. You know them all quite well. Don't forget the classical one and don't forget the one which is allowed to rhyme, by way of compensation for its especially polysyllabic obscurity. Eat that pear now, and proceed with your work."

Reggie obeyed. Adrian stretched himself on the sofa while the bard, in fitful bursts, covered several sheets of paper with writing. Now and then he looked up. "You needn't stare at the chimney-pots again," said Adrian on one occasion, "once is quite enough. You can make up all you want to know about them."

Three quarters of an hour elapsed. Reggie rose with a defiant exclamation. "Well, I've done them," he exclaimed, "and if you really think these things are at all like their originals, all I can say is Lord help somebody."

"You can read them this time," said Adrian. "I'll listen and make necessary suggestions, though I daresay none will be necessary."

Reggie took a deep breath, and began in a voice which showed his determination to beat down his shame. "This," he said, "is one kind that I think you may recognise.

Chimney cowls
Cut
Against sky.
Inky
Excruciating, torturing, abominable
Lobsters
Claws like saws
Goggle-eyes, pins, tentacles
Goggle-eyes at goggle-eyes
Fat men dining at
The Ritz."

"Not a bad beginning," remarked Adrian. "I couldn't tell from your reading, though, whether the lines began with capital letters or small ones."

"Oh, all small ones," Reggie assured him, "and every other line is to be printed upside down. 'Ritz' is in very large capitals, and there is a line of alternate notes of exclamation and interrogation marks at the bottom. But I couldn't read those aloud, could I?"

"No, of course not. What about the next?"

"Well, this rhymes; but it is really fearfully obscure:

Apocalyptic chimney cowls
Squeak at the sergeant's velvet hat
Donkeys and other paper fowls
Disgorge decretals at the cat.

The lead archdeacon eats her cheese
Corrupting their connubial bliss
And Mary on her six black knees
Refuses Christopher a kiss.

Autumnal abscesses relent
The twilight of ancestral days
But, smiling at the parsnip's scent,
The Nubian girl undoes her stays!"

"Splendid," said Adrian. "That is much freer. I hope the next one will not rhyme though."

"It does a bit, I'm afraid," said Reggie, "but so very badly that I don't think you could mark it down a point for it. I'm not sure, though, whether it is quite obscure enough:

Jewelled parakeets arise
Making many a silver noise
Round the checkered chimney cowls
Whilst the old Marchesa's owls
Blinking in the glaring day
Flit like fans from far Cathay
Glittering ink sheds bleak incense
On the poodle's stifled sense
Whilst the crimson-armoured lobster
Wishes that he was an oyster
Slipping like a cockatoo
Through the woods 'Tu-whit, Tu-whoo'
Through porticoes and pilasters
Starred with oleanders, asters,
Prim pagodas, jet, wax-fruits
Crinolines of Dresden queens
And indecent salmon-tins
Darting through …"

"That's enough," interrupted Adrian. "That's quite all right. I suppose you get the word 'crystal' in somewhere?"

"Yes, of course," said Reggie, "it comes a little later on with the jade and the unicorns. I found that one so easy that I could hardly stop."

"Put that one aside to be submitted to an editor. What is the next?"

"Classical," said Reggie, "and you are to take it that all the proper names are spelt with good hard 'k's' and 'os's' instead of 'us's.' This is how it goes:

Chimney cowls
Cut
Against sky."

"But this is the same as the first," Adrian broke in. "You've read this one before."

"Only the beginning," said Reggie. "This kind begins like the first but then it gets different. Besides it isn't ever printed upside down; a few italics instead:

Chimney cowls
Cut
Against sky
O Phoibos Albanios
The white limbs
Of the nymphs
On Hymettos
Io Pan, the honey
Acrid
In the nostrils,
Io, the purple
Of the vats of Herakles
On the cliffs
By Akrokeraunia
Hard and bitter
The shells
But the flesh
Ah Zeus!
Ah good!"

"Is that all?" asked Adrian.

"Yes; isn't it enough?"

"Absolutely perfect. But there is one kind missing. Except for that line about fat men eating at the Ritz there was nothing really expressing the spirit of real revolt. You do not do it metaphorically by dissolving words as you have dissolved grammar; you do not do it literally by stating your desire to destroy society, to throw infernal machines at the comfortable, to burn libraries and pictures, to abolish education, to bombard churches and to tip the Almighty off his throne. You do not even wish you were a tiger or a motor-car."

"Well, hang it all, Adrian," said Reggie, kicking the fender a little peevishly, "I have hardly had time, have I? But I do assure you I can do that one even more easily than the others. If you find those satisfactory this will be as well."

"Yes, they're quite perfect."

"Well, I don't know whether to hope you're right or not. Even now I cannot persuade myself that this horrible drivel will take anybody in."

"Well, my dear, you're wrong. I will send you a list of papers to which you may submit them and the address is all right. Now I must be going. The Balkans are waiting for me." He took up his hat, stick, and gloves and went out. His leisurely footstep had sounded four times on the stairs when Reggie rushed after him.

"I say, wait a minute," he called breathlessly, "there's one thing we've forgotten. What is my name to be? I simply must have a convincing one. It would be awful to be found out before the time for disclosure comes; nobody would ever believe I was leg-pulling." Adrian leant with his back to the banisters, pinched his chin and frowned slightly in thought.

"Ought I to be a woman do you think?" suggested Reggie.

"Wait a minute," said Adrian; and then, "I've got it. These made-up names are never convincing. I've a brilliant idea. Nobody has ever dreamed of using his own name as a pseudonym."

"But, Adrian, it would be absurd to sign myself Reginald Twyfold."

"I wasn't suggesting it. What you must do is to sign yourself Charles Twyfold, or Sidney Twyfold, or Ralph Twyfold. John always looks false. I think Sidney; nobody would ever call himself by a name like Sidney unless it really was his name."

Reggie was still slightly alarmed. "Twyfold," he ventured, "is such an uncommon name. I shall be pestered by people asking me if he is a relation."

"Yes. And what better disguise could you have? Frankly admit, when you have to, that he *is* a relation. Try to turn the subject; but if you are pressed confess to a second cousinship. Let it be extracted from you that his branch of the family is a little detrimental. 'I think Sidney lives in Paris. His father had to flee the country and settle in Boulogne, while he himself was not exactly sent down from Oxford but found it convenient to come down after one term.' Good-bye!"

III

A month passed; a month spent by the disreputable Sidney in industrious composition and despatch of manuscripts. Reggie, who couldn't help liking Muriel in spite of her brainless pretentiousness and was always amused by a dive into strange society, was lunching at her house in Upper Berkeley Street. There was a company of twelve in the jazz dining-room: six young men and six middle-aged women. The women, at a glance, seemed all to have white faces and red hair; the young men had white faces and either no hair or too much; tortoise-shell spectacles were generally worn; voices were pitched high; and any little indecency was welcomed by titters of appreciation. The husbands of the ladies were absent on business or sport; and Art was the principal theme of talk. Reggie managed to keep his end up with the vivacious dames on either side of him. He knew very few of the names of the latest and most devastating Franco-Brazilian painters, and pornography, owing to some strange inhibition, he always shrank from discussing in mixed company. But he met his companions half way; and now and then, when he inadvertently slipped into seriousness, sense, or the disclosure of an acquaintance with the major artists of the past, he delighted them with the surprise of a fresh point of view. The time might come, he reflected, when they might think morality too charming and agree to turn to it for an entirely novel sensation. Suddenly across the confusion of sights and sounds he was aware of Muriel's long neck and vast stupid eyes as it were shouting across a font of painted wooden pomegranates. "Reggie," she cried, "you simply must tell me, *who* is Sidney Twyfold. I simply must know him."

"Why?" asked Reggie, "if you don't mind saying."

"But, dearest Reggie, he writes the most marvellous poetry. We're all simply raving about it. Nobody ever heard of him till two weeks ago. Didn't you see his 'Mammon Fox-Trot' in the – I forget which of the papers it was – last week?"

"No," said Reggie, hoping his face was not paling as he thought it was.

"But he must be a relative of yours, isn't he?"

It was the first rehearsal of what was to be Reggie's programme until everybody knew about his vagrant Continental cousin who was so averse from personal publicity. "I have a distant cousin who I think is called Sidney, or else Stanley," he said bravely, "but I've never even seen him. His family live abroad, I believe. I expect it may be he."

"But why don't you run him down? He is wonderful. You simply must find him and bring him in touch with others who are doing the same thing."

Reggie was evasive. He promised to look at the poem, and expressed a conviction that cousin Sidney would be sure to turn up unassisted. The exchange of sentences, dominant above the surrounding scherzo, gave a new direction to the general conversation. Sidney had been printed in five places in the last three weeks, and most of those present had revelled in his whole product. It was agreed that he had not yet found a definite direction; but as Bertie Griffin said, that was perhaps all the better. Even Cubism and Futurism, it was agreed, had been too narrow. Sidney Twyfold comprehended these and more: he was at once Electrist, Early Victorian, Deliquescent, Sadist, Universalist, Psychoanalyst and Communist; and he could equal each of the most advanced poets on his own ground. Words like reality, metaphysics, complex, impression, release, significance, dull, sentimental and priapic began to swarm in the air like swallows preparing for migration. Reggie could not help being pleased at having caused such a stir. "So much better," he heard a myopic youth say, "than Teddy's 'Convulsions in Blue Flat Minor.'"

Muriel protested: "I thought Teddy's thing delicious."

"No," said the youth, "that sort of thing is rather *vieux jeu*. People like Twyfold have got much farther."

Reggie had a lift in Greta Rogers's car as far as Piccadilly Circus. He could not help, in the comparatively reasonable atmosphere of a *tête-à-tête*, asking her whether she could explain the "Mammon Fox-Trot" to him, or indeed throw the slightest hint of its meaning to him. "Reggie," she said, "I wish you wouldn't be so obstinate. *All* the amusing young men are doing it, and they *must* be right."

He went down Jermyn Street, turned to the left after looking carefully around him, and sidled into the bootmaker's for his post. He gathered it up, went back to the Albany and locked his door. There were two cheques; there was a manuscript rejected, as he knew and even hoped it would be, by John Fulford to whom he had wickedly sent it; there was a solemn letter of fraternity from a humourless ass who had written all-too-understandable free verse for years and was now about to move with the times; there were three invitations from people he did not know and three more from people he did know, including Muriel herself; there was a request from an emancipated young woman for an assignation; and there was a letter calling him a disgusting scoundrel addressed from one of the Service Clubs and honestly signed "W. H. P. Matthews, Col." Reggie sighed; then he laughed; he would go through with it now, and in two years, when Adrian gave the word, he would blow the whole thing sky-high.

IV

It is impossible here to detail the stages by which Sidney Twyfold attained his ultimate fame. His art developed along various paths, and Reggie managed his career with great acumen. At times he wrote poems consisting entirely of lines like:

i—i—iii—iii——ii—oksz
P.... NWⱯᗡ

But he knew that after a while even his keenest admirers would want rather more pabulum than that. He mixed these cunningly with poems in all the other modes, graduated down to quite lucid, if violently savage, denunciations of the throne, the hearth, and the altar, his views on the need for trampling on women being specially pronounced. He even went farther: at rare intervals he dug out some of the old seriously pretty poems of his regenerate days and sent them to respectable periodicals which had previously rejected them. They were always printed; his disciples rejoiced that their hero could do that sort of traditional thing on his head, and the earnest seekers after truth argued still more earnestly that the fault, as concerned his darker works, must obviously lie with the reader and not with the poet. As his vogue in all the advanced circles of England and America grew, the chase after his body became hotter. After a brief and risky employment of a district messenger with a cab, he had to leave the bootmaker (who was glad to get rid of him) and move Sidney's quarters to a friend's flat in Paris: it meant delay with the posts, but comparative safety was assured unless the French Post Office could be tampered with for particulars of readdressing. The appearance of his collected volume, "Ourang-Outang," marked an epoch: all the papers had long reviews, enthusiastic, hedging or denunciatory; red political journals began calling him the Poet of the Revolution; and an offer of £5,000 for the MSS. came from a transatlantic bookseller. Reggie was exercised by this; he would have liked the money, but his conscience would not allow him to sell a commodity the value of which he intended presently to destroy. The bookseller, however, was not blind to the advertising value of his mere offer; he blazoned it, and the refusal, abroad, and even the most conventional began to think that there must be a finely austere artist in this Twyfold who not merely declined all personal publicity but had stated that he did not approve of the factitious making of money by the sale of manuscripts.

The two years were nearly up, and Adrian and he were continually dinning on the ways and means by which the imposture should be revealed to the world. The leader of revolt would suddenly throw off his dark cloak and step forward as the Laughing King of the Imbeciles. How certain it all seemed! Yet life is but one vast chain of sleeping volcanoes, and this plan also went up in an unheralded eruption.

Reggie had gone to bed early that night when the great British Bolshevik Revolution broke out. He did not see St. Paul's and Westminster consumed by flames; he was not present when the Queen Victoria Memorial, that idol and symbol of a hated aristocracy, was pulled down by ropes; he was still asleep in the most secluded thoroughfare in London, when the morning boat for Russia left crowded with refugees bound for the safest and most prosperous monarchist country remaining. The first, in fact, that he knew of the change, was the appearance in his bedroom of three dirty and hirsute men with pistols, who announced themselves as the heads of the British Soviet, Abramovitch, Macalister and Evans. Reggie, dazed, took some time to pull himself together; but when he was at last awake he thought they had gone mad, for they clicked to the salute and said, in unison, "The Dawn, Comrade."

"What?" asked the astonished Reggie.

"We greet the Poet of the Revolution," chimed the three harsh voices.

"But," exclaimed Reggie, with a sudden intuition, "you've got the wrong man. You must have looked me up in the telephone book and got the wrong name. The poet is Sidney Twyfold; I'm Reggie; he's my cousin."

Abramovitch spoke. "Zere is," he said, "no further neet for dezeption, gomrade. Ve haf spied on you and your letters for a year. You haf done your vork; you must now haf ze revard." They led him away.

As they went down the stairs Reggie heard the uproar of a vast multitude cheering in those cloisters where no multitude had ever been before. Above the din shrill voices were calling his own name. He began to guess.

V

And so it was. Reggie, after that intoxicating pageant in Hyde Park where he was unveiled to a people which had thrown off its chains, became the official Laureate of the British Republic. He was allowed one room in his old quarters at the Albany, and was guarded night and day; for, after all, though his sentiments had hitherto been unexceptionable, the bourgeois blood might out. It was a tedious job being the Tyrtaeus of the Reds; but so long as he could not be understood they were quite satisfied with him. All his friends, including Adrian and Muriel, were in St. Petersburg (formerly Leningrad) earning their living by teaching dancing and English, and selling work which they described as English Peasant Embroidery. He was no worse off than they; and he had a salary of a million paper pounds a day as well as a barrel of beer a year. He knew that Adrian would not give him away for fear of getting him shot; still, it mattered little, for, had the truth about Reggie been told, his masters would probably have treated it as one more infamous capitalist lie.

He died in the end, poor fellow, of boredom and intellectual starvation. His funeral was attended by half the army and millions of the proletariat. He was buried in the National Pantheon in Villiers Street, Strand.

John Collings Squire, "If a Very New Poet Had Written 'The Lotus-Eaters,'" in *Tricks of the Trade*

(London: Martin Secker, 1917), 65–7.

IF A VERY NEW POET HAD WRITTEN "THE LOTUS-EATERS"

I.

Ahl
Ough!
Umph!
It *was* a sweat!
Thank God, that's over!
No more navigating for me.
I am on to
Something
Softer . . . .
Conductor,
Give us a tune!

II.

Work!
Did I used to work?
I seem to remember it
Out there.
Millions of fools are still at
It,
Jumping about
All over the place . . . .
And what's the good of it all? …
Buzz,
Hustle,
Pop,
And then …
Dump
In the grave.

III.

Bring me six cushions
A yellow one, a green one, a purple one, an orange one, an ultramarine one,
  and a vermilion one,
Colours of which the combination
Pleases my eye.
Bring me
Also
Six lemon squashes
And
A straw . . . .

IV.

I have taken off my coat.
I shall now
Loosen
My braces.

V.

Now I am
All right . . . .
My God …
I do feel lazy!

John Collings Squire, "The Poetry of Broken Shackles," in *Collected Parodies*

(London: Hodder & Stoughton, 1921), 180–1.

An earlier version of Squire's poem was initially published in *The New Age* in 1910.

THE POETRY OF BROKEN SHACKLES

The sun sets.
Not a breath of wind stirs the surface of the sea,
Not a ripple breaks the sheen of its placid mirror,
And the fields,
Weary of the heat and labour of the day,
Lie motionless and green-brown as the day dies
Immobile in the perfection of rest well-won.
Never a sound threads the air save the distant crooning song
Of a herdsman,
And the voices of grazing sheep
Bleating
Quietly.
And the faint murmur, far, far out over the waters of the plash of oars
From a brown-sailed fisherman's boat whose canvas idly hangs
From the masts.
High in the west
The battlemented clouds are piled
Red and purple and dark blue, all girdled and glowing
With the golden effulgence of the orb of Apollo now half below the horizon.
In the east with great strides
Night comes on
Inviolable, indomitable, immense,
Brushing wide heaven with the stridence of her rustling wings,
Enacting once again the old old tragedy with her pitiless wings,
Striking fear into the heart of man
And death into the heart of the day;

Proclaiming, exultant triumphant, with steely clarion the victory of her
titanic wings . . . .
The whole air is filled full with the clamour of innumerable wings.
The sun goes down
Pop!

Alfred E. Randall, "Experiment in Free Rhythm"

***New Age* 6.18 (1910): 414.**

Randall was a regular contributor to A.R. Orage's *New Age*, where he also published some of his verse. A few of Randall's poems also appeared in the same issue of the *English Review* as Pound's "Ballad of the Goodly Fere."

EXPERIMENT IN FREE RHYTHM

I sing,
And as I sing I wonder if my song
Will ever be
Echoed down the aisles of time.
I do not spring
Upon the public mailed in melody.
No!
I babble like the brooklet free,
And halt, and waver, and onward go,
And sometimes rhyme.
"The poet in a golden clime was born,"
Said Tennyson; but he was wrong.
The poet seeks the golden clime,
And cannot wait to study rhyme
And rhythm, or the classic forms
When
His pen
Must earn his bread, and pay
His rent at once, or storms
Will lower o'er his fiery way
To Parnassus.
Any fool
Or eleutheromaniac
Can tread the track
And win the laurel, found a school,
And have his books reviewed,
And sometimes read,
And be the poet of a day,

(No more.)
If he will write like this, and shock the prude
Who only loves the verse-forms dead.
We,
The spirits free,
Who drag the heavens with reticular
Appliances, and catch
A star,
(Sometimes!)
Can never match
The bards who sang with measured chimes,
Who sculptured speech to shapes
Forlorn in majesty.
But as the soul
Jumps like the tortured flea,
Unequally,
We,
Being on the whole
Of a similar nature
To this poor creature,
Must do likewise, and thus we sing
In rhythms free,
Like this thing.

William Kean Seymour, "*Thirty-four: A Very New Poet*: To Be or Not to Be," in *A Jackdaw in Georgia, a Book of Polite Parodies and Imitations of Contemporaries and Others*

(London: J.C. Wilson, 1923), 76–7.

A poet, novelist, editor, and critic, Seymour (1887–1975) was the author of at least twenty-one books, including the improbably titled *The Cats of Rome* (1970). Seymour's work was also published in the Sitwells' *Wheels, 1920 (Fifth Cycle).*

THIRTY-FOUR: A VERY NEW POET

TO BE OR NOT TO BE

The question shapes itself,
The mind darkens in doubt:
Which shall it be, –
Capricious arrows, lacerating life,
Arrows of fate, and pebbles of mischance
Stunning the soul;
To be supine to fortune,
By fortune spurned,
Or resolutely, armed and arrogant,
Meet the disastrous ills
That roll in murderous waves,
And saying
"Every day
In every way
Things
Grow better and better"
End them?

Ah, but, –
Another way!
Death
Darkly resuming in a coal-gas sleep

Her calm dominion:
That's a better way!
To die,
To sleep,
And in an oven lose
Heart-throb and head-throb,
Spleen and jealousy,
And all the things we hate.
To die,
To sleep,
To turn the tap and dream …
But there's the hitch!
That tap of dreams,
That foul, hydrogenous engine
May release
The soul to wander
Whither?

That's the thought
Controls
The itching fingers hovering round the tap …
Whither?
That,
And the beastly smell,
And putting good money
Into the Gas Company's
Pockets.

F. Scott Fitzgerald, from *This Side of Paradise*

(New York: Charles Scribner's Sons, 1920), 232–4.

F. Scott Fitzgerald (1896–1940) was the author of *The Great Gatsby*. *This Side of Paradise* was his first major commercial success. In the novel, Tom D'Invilliers's own poetry leans to late-nineteenth-century aestheticism, while the poetry of Amory Blaine (the novel's protagonist) gets closest to modernism in its penchant for ellipses. Fitzgerald's own tastes ranged much more closely to high modernism, particularly in his admiration for T.S. Eliot, whom he referred to as "the greatest living poet in any language" (*Life in Letters* 137). (For a parody of *This Side of Paradise*, see Dorothy Parker's "Once More Mother Hubbard," p. 172 below.)

There were days when Amory listened. These were when Tom, wreathed in smoke, indulged in the slaughter of American literature. Words failed him.

"Fifty thousand dollars a year," he would cry. "My God! Look at them, look at them – Edna Ferber, Gouverneur Morris, Fanny Hurst, Mary Roberts Rinehart – not producing among 'em one story or novel that will last ten years. This man Cobb – I don't think he's either clever or amusing and what's more, I don't think very many people do, except the editors. He's just groggy with advertising. And – oh Harold Bell Wright oh Zane Grey –[1]

"They try."

"No, they don't even try. Some of them *can* write, but they won't sit down and do one honest novel. Most of them *can't* write, I'll admit. I believe Rupert Hughes tries to give a real, comprehensive picture of American life, but his style and perspective are barbarous. Ernest Poole and Dorothy Canfield try but they're hindered by their absolute lack of any sense of humor; but at least they crowd their work instead of spreading it thin. Every author ought to write every book as if he were going to be beheaded the day he finished it."

"Is that double entente?"

"Don't slow me up! Now there's a few of 'em that seem to have some cultural background, some intelligence and a good deal of literary felicity but they just simply won't write honestly; they'd all claim there was no public for good stuff. Then why the devil is it that Wells, Conrad, Galsworthy, Shaw, Bennett, and the rest depend on America for over half their sales?"

"How does little Tommy like the poets?"

Tom was overcome. He dropped his arms until they swung loosely beside the chair and emitted faint grunts.

"I'm writing a satire on 'em now, calling it 'Boston Bards and Hearst Reviewers.'"

"Let's hear it," said Amory eagerly.

"I've only got the last few lines done."

"That's very modern. Let's hear 'em, if they're funny."

Tom produced a folded paper from his pocket and read aloud, pausing at intervals so that Amory could see that it was free verse:

"So
Walter Arensberg,
Alfred Kreymborg,
Carl Sandburg,
Louis Untermeyer,
Eunice Tietjens,
Clara Shanafelt,
James Oppenheim,
Maxwell Bodenheim,
Richard Glaenzer,
Scharmel Iris,
Conrad Aiken,[2]
I place your names here
So that you may live
If only as names,
Sinuous, mauve-colored names,
In the Juvenalia
Of my collected editions."

Amory roared.

"You win the iron pansy. I'll buy you a meal on the arrogance of the last two lines."

Amory did not entirely agree with Tom's sweeping damnation of American novelists and poets. He enjoyed both Vachel Lindsay and Booth Tarkington, and admired the conscientious, if slender, artistry of Edgar Lee Masters.[3]

"What I hate is this idiotic drivel about 'I am God – I am man – I ride the winds – I look through the smoke – I am the life sense.'"

"It's ghastly!"

Bert Leston Taylor, "The Muse Untrammeled," in *A Penny Whistle: Together with the Babette Ballads*

(New York: Knopf, 1921), 42–3.

Bert Leston Taylor (1866–1921) was the writer and editor of "A Line o' Type or Two," his column at the *Chicago Tribune* from 1901 until his death (with one short break). Taylor did much of the writing himself, but famous writers and others would contribute items as well. Taylor's column, widely reported to be the first of its type, combined whimsical news items, satiric verse, cartoons, and jokes. In a posthumous collection of Taylor's verse, Franklin P. Adams (of the syndicated column "The Conning Tower") wrote: "To my mind, he was easily the best paragrapher that ever achieved the art of putting the front page, or the leading editorial, or a whole political, literary, or artistic situation into twenty-five words, his verses were even better than his paragraphs" (xi).

THE MUSE UNTRAMMELED

Come, my Muse, let us exalt the Obvious!
Unfettered, let us name
The sum of two and two, the which
Is four.
This form of verse, *vers libre*, lends itself
Exactly to our purpose,
For obvious reasons –
Reasons as obvious as Marie
Corelli.[4]

We can be commonplace, my Muse, in o. f. forms,
But 'tis more difficult;
For, questing rimes, one ofttimes strays afield
And happens on some dainty flower of fancy
That elsewhere might have blushed
Unseen;
Or finds a piquant phrase, unworn,
Unfrazzled, and
Uncanned.

But in Free Verse, my Muse, the likelihood
Of such discoveries is less.
Though accidents *will* happen
In the worst regulated poems.

Here we are free as air, and hence
Our airy nothings, which are
Nothing if not airy;
And hence we give ourselves airs,
And air our grievances against the persons
Who cannot see us,
Who *could not* see us with the telescope
At Lick.

Franklin P. Adams, "To a Vers Librist," in *Something Else Again*

(Garden City, NY: Doubleday, Page & Co., 1920), 43–4.

Perhaps the most popular columnist of his day, Franklin P. Adams (1881–1960) worked for several New York papers. His well-known column for the *New York Tribune*, *The Conning Tower*, was often salted with contributions from readers (a practice also followed by Bert Leston Taylor in Chicago). Much of this work reappeared in compilations Adams regularly published. Adams was also a Member of the Algonquin Round Table, and a panelist on the famous radio show *Information Please*.

TO A VERS LIBRIST

"Oh bard," I said, "your verse is free;
The shackles that encumber me,
The fetters that are my obsession,
Are never gyves to your expression.

"The fear of falsities in rhyme,
In metre, quantity, or time,
Is never yours; you sing along
Your unpremeditated song."

"Correct," the young vers librist said.
"Whatever pops into my head
I write, and have but one small fetter:
I start each line with a capital letter.

But rhyme and metre – Ishkebibble![5] –
Are actually negli*gib*le.
I go ahead, like all my school.
Without a single silly rule."

Of rhyme I am so reverential
He made me feel inconsequential.
I shed some strongly saline tears
For bards I loved in younger years.

"If Keats had fallen for your fluff,"
I said, "he might have done good stuff.
If Burns had thrown his rhymes away,
His songs might still be sung to-day."

O bards of rhyme and metre free,
My gratitude goes out to ye
For all your deathless lines – ahem!
Let's see, now . . . . What *is* one of them?

PROSE POETRY

Seen as being closely allied to the cultural ambitions of free verse, prose poems were a puzzling target for parodists, who had difficulty figuring out what the recurrent features of prose poems actually *were* – other than their being written in prose, of course. Primarily targeting Amy Lowell, they eventually focused their attentions on subject matter: banal surroundings and events, which are charged with significance through a puzzling portentousness that becomes highly charged with the introduction of proto-surrealistic, often sinister details (this was also a common strategy for parodying Eliot's quatrain poems). Their target was the prose poet, of course: the hyper-sensitive mind that makes these kinds of connections. As do parodies of other forms of modernist poetry, these parodies reveal an anxiety about the entrance of realism into poetry.

J.C. Squire, "The Simple Prose-Poem," in *Collected Parodies*

(London: Hodder and Stoughton, 1921), 180–1.

In its original version in *The New Age* in 1910, Squire entitled this work a little more polemically: "The Prose-Poem-Oh-So-Simple."

THE SIMPLE PROSE-POEM

I sat in my chair.

I gazed into the fire, the fire with its caverns of light, with its luminous recesses the pulses of which undulate, rise and fall, heave and subside, like the bosom of some beloved woman.

The fire with its wavering rainbow tongues.

I sat in my chair, gazing.

On a sudden I heard a step, soft as a snowflake,

There behind my chair, standing yet not standing, suspended as it were yet not suspended, stood the form of a man, which was neither of earth nor of heaven. Pale was his brow. His eyes of a profundity and liquidity like the liquidity and profundity of pools in the utter depths of some remote sea where keel never swam nor lead sounded, shone with a light that was neither of heaven nor of earth. His cheeks were faintly hollowed as with the last loving touch of a sculptor's thumb, and his white tremulous lips, beardless as a boy's, spoke yet did not speak.

"I have come," was the message.

The stranger turned towards the door with a slight beckoning gesture.

I knew him and I followed.

Sue Golden [pseud.], "The Reader Critic. So This Is Art!"

***Little Review* 3.8 (January 1917): 27.**

The author of these prose poems is unknown, although she did publish on one other occasion in the *Little Review*. As a response to that piece, editor Jane Heap wrote: "Yes, how sad it all is that some minds have to jeer everything in the world, from Helen's beauty to Bernhardt's 'wooden leg.'"

MURINE AND KOKA-KOLA

I. THE LAMP

Darkness enveloped us. I led her under a street-lamp of wrought iron from which hung suspended a round white moon which shone upon her unreal beauty. She turned her hurt eyes away from the hard light, and rested them upon an electric sign overhead which, flashing in and out, read:

"Don't tell your age. Murine your eyes."

Sign, if you are a lie, you must be broken. But if you tell the truth, you may increase the ecstasy of our manufactured passion.

II. THE JAR

This is a common jar set in the druggist's window to attract attention. It is without design, filled with a burning red liquid, flashing iridescent lights from concealed depths. Near it is another jar filled with a bright green liquid which leaps like fire whenever the light from a passing automobile falls upon it.

My soul is like the red jar, burning within itself; yours is like the green one, attracted by each passing fancy.

III. AFTER THE ORGY

It is morning; the revellers of last night have departed; the music of the phonograph and the voices of the cabaret singers are silent now. In the pale light of morning, frayed wisps of paper float up and down the street; from the brass handle of the saloon door a drenched veil is hanging; on the floor of the automobile lie scattered hair pins. Ah, frail hair pins, ah, tender vail [*sic*], how slight you are beside my grief!

Silence and pale dawn, and empty emptiness. Ah, the last silence and the last heart-ache, and the last nickel, and the last green pickle lying on the last cold plate on the last free-lunch counter in the world! How sad it all is!

Louis Untermeyer, "Amy Lowell, Brushing up Her Polyphonic Prose, Declaims *Fortitude*," in — *and Other Poets*

(New York: H. Holt and Co., 1916), 62–3.

Likely the most important anthologist of the first half of the twentieth century, Louis Untermeyer (1885–1977) shaped the educations of countless high school and college students with his anthologies of modern poetry. Untermeyer was an enthusiastic proponent of what might be termed democratic modernism, writing in the 1919 edition of his anthology *Modern American Poetry* that "the last few decades have witnessed a sudden and amazing growth in the volume as well as in the quality of the work of our poets. A new spirit, energetic, alert, penetrative, seems to have stirred these states, and a countryful of writers has responded to it" (vii). He was much less enthusiastic about Eliot's work, particularly *The Waste Land*: "The 'Dial's' award to Mr. T.S. Eliot and the subsequent book-publication of his 'The Waste Land' have occasioned a display of some of the most enthusiastically naive superlatives that have ever issued from publicly sophisticated iconoclasts" (1923: 151). Just a few years after this parody appeared, Untermeyer in his *Modern American Poetry* gave Lowell some respectful attention, and extended praise even to her prose poetry, a volume of which he described as "extraordinarily varied, sweeping in their sense of amplitude and time" (198).

Early in his career Untermeyer wrote for *The Masses* and *The Liberator*, and later was investigated by the House Committee on Un-American Activities. In 1961 Untermeyer was appointed Poet Laureate Consultant in Poetry to the Library of Congress.

AMY LOWELL

BRUSHING UP HER POLYPHONIC PROSE, DECLAIMS *FORTITUDE.*

ZIP! The thought of you tears in my heart. I fumble and start. I mumble and trip. Zip! The night is a blur. The yellow wax candles whimper and stir. And I, on my way to the heavens, am hurled to the jabbering world. Down, down to the hideous level of Brown; to the Jones, Cohns and various Malones, I sink. The sails of my spirit sag and shrink. The rains of distemper ruffle my feathers and put out my fire. The Zeppelins in my soul drag in the mire; they shiver and rip. *Zip!*

In my neighbor's garden a blue herring sings. *Twee—twee* … On the topmost bough of a cinnamon tree he throws his rapture like a fine spray against the stony night. Over and under the petulant silver thunder of the fountains he cries. I hear silver and mauve … and the faint sheen of olives. The green echoes rise. They break, these thin-stemmed glasses of sound; ground and shattered by the still skies. The pale herring's song is long with a slender perfume. A whiff of red memories blows through the gloom … and melts on the tongue. Into the room a young, blond wind ripples and laughs. She stammers and speaks with a breath that is full of blush-roses and leeks. And the moon, without warning, comes eerily from the west. He staggers wearily, knowing no rest; lurching out of a cloud and singing aloud. He too laughs; a crazy laughter breaking through his scars. Like a drunken Pierrot spilling the stars from his too-long sleeves. The sun grieves and looks down reprovingly. And the day bursts forth, rejoicing alone. Darkness is overthrown as the great wheels turn. In a thousand factories the tungstens burn. The shaftings worry and moan. The dynamos drone …

Pardon me. There goes the 'phone …

IMAGISM

After the outburst directed at free verse in general, Imagism was the poetic manifestation to get the most attention in the press as a recognizable *genre* of modernist literature. A.R. Orage, writing pseudonymously in his *New Age*, distrusted the "newness" of imagism:

> Imagism, on the other hand, at last takes on a meaning for me. I feel about it what M. Jourdain felt about prose: it is a very old trick disguised as a modern invention. Let me take one of Mr. Pound's examples. Arriving in Paris one day he was struck on his first walk by the number of beautiful women and children he saw. He desired to set down his impression, and this is how, after dozens of attempts, he scored a success:
>
> The apparitions [*sic*] of these faces in the crowd:
> Petals, on a wet, black bough.
>
> The image here, you are to understand, is Mr. Pound's imaginative equivalent for the scene of which he was a sensitive witness; and we ought further to conclude that it is the perfect image. But is it? On the contrary, I could invent a score of other images of quite equal equivalence. So could anybody. Meredith was perpetually doing such things: his "dainty rogue in porcelain" is the most familiar instance. Shelley was prolific in them. The Japanese have made their only literary art of such bon-bons. What of these, for instance, as other images for the same scene: white wheeling gulls upon a muddy weedstrewn beach; war medals on a ragged waistcoat; patches of blue in a sky of smokecoloured clouds; oases in a sand-storm; flaming orchids growing upon a gooseberry bush; mistletoe on bare trees snowclad; iridescence upon corpses; a robin's song on a dark autumn day. Had enough? I could go on ad infinitum. But I should not set up as an Imagist, but only as a journalist, on the strength of them! (R.H.C., "Readers and Writers" [September 1914])

Parodic responses to imagism return to several issues: the incomprehensibility and pretentiousness of its minimalist aesthetic, its odd syntax and the chance juxtapositions it used to create a sense of its importance, and its use of Chinese and Greek subject matter (and, most irritating, Greek-inflected spellings).

Harold Massingham, "Recipe for an Imagist Poem"

***Form* 1.1 (April 1916): 41.**

Harold John Massingham (1888–1952) was a poet and prolific writer about the English countryside. Among other places, his poetry appeared in *Coterie*, where he was published alongside T.S. Eliot. Massingham's assertion that modernist art could be churned out by following a banal recipe was a trope common to early twentieth-century parodists.

RECIPE FOR AN IMAGIST POEM

The sky is jaundiced
The brown bird makes indentations in the white snow,
Nature broods
Spasmodically.

My heart gapes like the yellow sky,
It beats
Against the white futility of my bosom,
Like the feet of a staccato brown bird,
Broodingly.

Allen Upward, "Correspondence. The Discarded Imagist"

***Egoist* 2.6 (1915): 98.**

Allen Upward (1863–1926) was a poet and novelist who wrote frequently for A.R. Orage's *New Age*. His poetry appeared in the first anthology of Imagist poetry, *Des Imagistes*, edited by Ezra Pound. (In the piece below, Upward grumbles that F.S. Flint had misspelled his name in the previous number of the *Egoist*.)

Madam,
O thou unborn historian of literature – (if you ever mention my name spell it better than F. S. Flint, please!)
Do not believe a single word
That others have written about me.

In the year nineteen hundred a poet named Cranmer Byng brought to my attic in Whitehall Gardens a book of Chinese Gems by Professor Giles,[6]
Eastern butterflies coming into my attic there beside the Stygian Thames,
And read me one of them – willows, forsaken young wife, spring.

Immediately my soul kissed the soul of immortal China:
I perceived that all we in the West were indeed barbarians and foreign devils,
And that we knew scarcely anything about poetry.

I set to work and wrote little poems
Some of which I read to a scientific friend
Who said – "After all, what do they prove?"
Then I hid them away for ten or twelve years,
Scented leaves in a Chinese jar,
While I went on composing the poem of life.

I withstood the savages of the Niger with a revolver:
I withstood the savages of the Thames with a printing-press:
Byng and I we set up as publishers in Fleet Street, and produced the "Odes of Confucius," and the "Sayings."

My own poems I did not produce:
They were sent back to me by the *Spectator* and the *English Review.*
I secretly grudged them to the Western devils.

After many years I sent them to Chicago, and they were printed by Harriet Monroe. (They also were printed in THE EGOIST.)
Thereupon Ezra Pound the generous rose up and called me an Imagist. (I had no idea what he meant.)
And he included me in an anthology of Imagists.

This was a very great honour.
But I was left out of the next anthology.
This was a very great shame.

And now I have read in a history of Imagism
That the movement was started in nineteen hundred and eight
By Edward Storer and T. E. Hulme

(Poetry the crystal of language,
Passion frozen by art,
Fallen in love with its likeness!)

Evil is the advice in the day of Horace
That poems should be given nine years to fix,
Evil in the day of swift movements – (for I hear that already Imagism is out of date.)

O thou divine soul of China
Brooding over millenniums of perfect art,
May you never be troubled by the impertinences of the West!

And thou unborn literary historian (if you ever mention my name)
Write me down an imitator of Po Li and Shakespeare
As well as of Edward Storer and T. E. Hulme.

Horace Holley, "Correspondence. Imagists"

***Egoist* 1.12 (1914): 236.**

Author of several books of poetry, including his 1913 *Creation: Post-Impressionist Poems*, Holley (1887–1960) was also a prominent member of the Bahá'í community.

My muse bids me submit the following to your correspondence column. It should be noted that there is no record of verse libre having been applied before to the art of letter writing. While the "Daily Mail" is going into the question of flies, let us here turn and consider.

THE MICE

In the world's cupboard
The scamper of little feet,
A new sound

O busy, sharp-teethed mice
Nibbling your anxious bellies full,
Fear not:
The Cat was belled long since
By mice of a bolder generation!

Nay rather beware the tightness of your own tummies,
Little mice,
Since already you have eaten the Greek Anthology
And now your glistening white teeth
Gnaw the fat tomes of Chinese Wisdom.

What would you do with the Lute of Jade,
O little mice?
This is indeed a dainty luncheon,
O little mice,
O Imagists!

"Imagiste Love Lines"

***Columbia Jester*; rpt. in *Life*, 18 January 1917: 69.**

The *Columbia Jester*, founded in 1901, was the humor magazine of Columbia University. The "e" in Imagiste did some quickly recognizable work here and in many other parodies: a stab at H.D. and Pound, the extra letter asserts the dubious French origins and consequent theoretical pretensions of modern movements.

IMAGISTE LOVE LINES

I love my lady with a deep purple love;
She fascinates me like a fly
Struggling in a Pot of glue.
Her eyes are gray, like twin ash-cans,
Just emptied, about which still hovers
A dusty mist.
Her disposition is as bright as a ten-cent shine,
Yet her kisses are tender and goulashy.
I love my lady with a deep purple love.

C.E. Bechhöfer, "Pastiche"

New Age **15.20 (1914): 481.**

Carl Eric Bechhöfer Roberts (1894–1949) was a prolific novelist and biographer who wrote parodies regularly for *The New Age*. The "R.A." referred to in the preface is Richard Aldington.

(The following fragment was picked up in the neighbourhood of Oxford Street last Monday evening. It is signed "R. A.," but there is no further external evidence as to the authorship. Internally, however, it presents some interesting characteristics of style and rhythm, which will enable all who have followed intelligently the more significant developments of recent English poetry to fill in the initials with tolerable accuracy.)

KINEMASTERION.

——————————————————————
——————————————————————
——————— I grip my leaden obol,
and in the scented darkness,
scented, O Phoibos, as the narcissoi
in the glades of Arcady,
o Pallas! (O Lempriere!)[7]
till I surrender the token of requital
unto the liveried minion of Orcus,
who with his tapering torch of elektron,
– lucerna pedibus meis –[8]
Guideth me over a carpet
woven in bazaars of Persepolis:
and I sink into the velvet clutch,
purple as the onyx that skirteth
the Ionian Sea by moonrise,
o Orion!
into the purple clutch, I say,
of mine amber-pedestalled throne …
hoi, hoi, hoi!

then, by the grace of Hephaistos,
my myriad-pupilled eyes are unburdened,
and I behold on the silken screen,
diaper-woven in Phrygian splendour,
bordered with flickering clusters of laurels,
meet for the brow of Rikkados,
who abideth nigh to the wooded pleasaunce
that hath in its centre a silvery fish-tank
rippled by keels of triremes …
being shaped as the oval diskos,
that thy supple arm flingeth,
the tendons of thy many-sinewed arm,
mighty Poseidon …
and I behold on the silken screen,
(hearest thou this, o Artemis?)
in the jasper pomp of Dorian anapaests,
the legend of the woman
(false as Helen)
whose image pursueth me, o swift-footed uncle of Persephone
the woman with the tresses
tinctured and stained
with the cunning of Tyrian dyes,
red as the rose that flourisheth in the
vale of Eleusis …
——————————————————————
——————————————————————
————————Demeter————————
——————————————————————
—————thy helmet, o Teucer[9]—————
——————————————————————

Richard Aldington, "Penultimate Poetry"

***Egoist* 1.2 (1914): 36.**

A central member of the Imagist circle, Richard Aldington (1892–1962) wrote numerous books of poetry and criticism, as well as the acclaimed war novel *Death of a Hero* (1929). "Penultimate Poetry" seems less directed at imagist poetry in general than at Ezra Pound: Pound's exoticism, diction, hortatory tone, rapid shifts in tone, and baffling Provençal. The immediate instigation for Aldington's parodies was not only Pound's "In a Station of the Metro," but a series of poems Pound published in the November 1913 issue of *Poetry*. Aldington alludes to several of Pound's titles ("Gentildonna," "Ancora"), and Pound's instantly recognizable tone in a poem like "Further Instructions:" "Come, my songs, let us express our baser passions. / Let us express our envy for the man with a steady job and no worry about the future" (57). Pound's phrasing in his "Xenia" – "Rest me with Chinese colors, / For I think the glass is evil" (59) – finds its debasement in Aldington's "Ancora."

PENULTIMATE POETRY

XENOPHILOMETROPOLITANIA

I. TENZONE ALL A GENTILDONNA.

Come, my songs.

II. CANTATA.

"Men pols lois puelh voys."[10]
– ARNAUT OF MARVOIL

Come my songs,
Let us observe this person
Who munches chicken-bones like a Chinese consul
Mandilibating a delicate succulent Pekinese spaniel.

III. ELEVATORS.

Come my songs,
Let us whizz up to the eighteenth floor,

Let us present our most undignified exterior
To this mass of indolent superstition,
To this perverted somnambulistic age;
Let us soar up higher than the eighteenth floor
And consider the delicate delectable monocles
Of the musical virgins of Parnassus:
Pale slaughter beneath purple skies.

IV. ANCORA.

Rest me with mushrooms,
For I think the steak is evil.

V. CONVICTED.

Like an armful of greasy engineer's-cotton
Flung by a typhoon against a broken crate of ducks' eggs
She stands by the rail of the Old Bailey dock.
Her intoxication is exquisite and excessive,
And delicate her delicate sterility.
Her delicacy is so delicate that she would feel affronted
If I remarked nonchalantly, "Saay, stranger, ain't you dandy."

VI. GITANJALI.[11]

Come my songs,
(For we have not "come" during three of these our delectable canzoni)
Come, my songs, let us go to America.
Let us move the thumbs on our left hands
And the middle fingers on our right hands
With the delicate impressive gestures
Of Rabindranath Tagore. (Salaam, o water-cress of the desert.)
O my songs, of all things let us
Be delicate and impressive.
I implore you my songs to remain so;
I charge you in the name of these states.

VII. ALTRUISM.

Come my songs,
Let us praise ourselves;

I doubt if the smug will do it for us,
The smug who possess all the rest of the universe.

VIII. SONG OF INNOCENCE.

The wind moves over the wheat
With a silver crashing,
A thin war of delicate kettles.

IX.

The apparition   of these poems   in a crowd :
White faces   in a black   dead faint.

Emanuel Morgan [Witter Bynner], "Spectrum. 'Opus 96'"

***Little Review* 4.3 (1917): 25.**

For information about Emanuel Morgan, see the note below under "Preface" to *Spectra* (p. 225). The *Little Review* published this work not knowing that it was actually a hoax (this was the same issue that saw the publication of Eliot's French poems). Upon learning, apparently via the *Detroit News*, that Spectric poetry was actually intended as a send-up of manifesto-based modernism, back-pedalling editor Jane Heap commented:

[Early last June the Spectrics sent in a fat bunch of poems to the *Little Review* (unsolicited). One poem, Opus 96, by E. Morgan, appeared in our July number. The others were returned with an Andersonian note. Poor M. C. A. was so taken by storm that she "published with éclat" in the same issue an ecstatic eulogy of the "new school":

Banish
Anne Knish
Set the dog on
Emanuel Morgan.

And to show how such "artist-editors" as Ezra Pound were completely astounded by the new "virile" school, we quote from a letter written August 10, 1917:

"Morgan's 'spectric' business is a little late. People intending to be 'schools' should have 'done it first.'"

"Or rather they should base their school on something having to do with their art, not on a vague aesthetic theory. His manifesto advances no proposition affecting his own medium, i.e., words, rhythm, etc., only some twaddle about ultra-violets. Jejune. There is no difference between his free verse and any other free verse."

"After all Imagisme had three definite propositions about *writing*, and also a few 'don'ts.' *And* it differed from the neo-celtic-twilightists, etc., who preceded it. Morgan is only another Imagist imitator with a different preface from Amy's."

I confess to a deep ignorance of the nature of the hoax. If a man changes his name and writes better stuff, why does that make the public so ridiculous? Why not stick to the name and pray for more power to it? There is a certain occult society that can deduce your psychic name from your horoscope: all you have to do then is to discard your Christian name and the world is yours! I can't do much for names, myself: a frog by any other name can hop as far and no farther. – jh.] ("The Reader Critic. The Hoax of the 'Spectrics.'")

SPECTRUM. "OPUS 96"

You are the Japan
Where cherries always blossom.
With you there is no meantime.

Your [*sic*] are the nightingale's twenty-four hours of song,
The unbroken Parthenon,
The everlasting purring of the sphynx.

At the first footfall of an uncouth season,
You migrate with one wing-sweep
To beauty.

"Pathology des Dommagistes"

The Chapbook **23 (May 1921): 21–4.**

Norman Gates suggests that the author of this suite of poems was Harold Monro, but his is a minority position; all other references to this work have been unable to identify who wrote the following works. Monro's *The Chapbook* came out of his Poetry Bookshop, which published both Pound's anthology *Des Imagistes* and Edward Marsh's *Georgian Poetry*. *The Chapbook*, indeed, rigorously engaged in *quid pro quo*: in the September 1922 edition Osbert Sitwell used rhyming couplets to pillory Edward Shanks, J.C. Squire, and the Squirearchy more generally.

"Palaeolith" seems to refer to the opening of Hope Mirrlees's *Paris: A Poem*, published by the Woolfs' Hogarth Press in 1919:

> I want a holophrase
>
> NORD-SUD
>
> ZIG-ZAG
> LION NOIR
> CACAO BLOOKER
>
> Black-figured vases in Etruscan tombs
>
> RUE DU BAC (DUBONNET)
> SOLFERINO (DUBONNET)
> CHAMBRE DES DEPUTES (3)

The other poems target Ezra Pound, Amy Lowell, Richard Aldington, and H.D.

PATHOLOGY DES DOMMAGISTES

(Being Specimens for a projected Anthology to be issued in the U.S.A.)

"*C'est vrai, c'est dommage,*
et c'est dommage c'est vrai."[12]

(Translated from the Elizabethan
English by B. H. W.).

PALÆOLITH

BRING now
Chryso-phrases two words long
Sprinkle the marble steps
White as her neck
Twice …

ANOTHER

I

HOI
The wet milk lashes me
A lank sea-weed
Sheared the salt water
Long long ago.
Wait for me
Where daisies twine round
Papuan mandragora.

II

Hoi …

EPIGRAM

(AFTER THE CRETAN.)

LITTLE Calligulala
Has tied one golden sandal
Round her pink ankle
Too tightly.
Heu! The discomfort
The varicose veins. . . .

Silver dust falls
Over the tepidarium …

SELECTED BULBS FROM A JAVAN POT

The Yellow Tamarinds.

WONDERING when I would be able to pay my laundress, I let my eyes fall and I saw the smutty tamarinds I grow in my little window-box.

The Frenzied Mandolinist.

A MANDOLINIST in a night-club having broken his E-string spoke thus: "Less expensive than sheet-music, much more unexpected than tips from ecstatic customers, are thy gambols, thou damned one!"

(AND A LOT MORE)

"CONTICUERUNT OMNES …"[13]

LESBIA'S hair
Swathing her navel
Has been dyed with henna
To match the goldfish
In the plashing fountain?

"TUTTI FRUTTI"

ON the spots of
The brown cushion
My love
Has laid her yellow hairs.
Her fan is not moving:
Where
Is the drunken juggler?

AND AFTER …

WHERE are the creases
That furrowed Claudius'
Pinky complexion?

He has strayed
To the baths
And Madame Rubinstein[14]
Has smeared mauve
Pomade over it.
God!
Those creases …

FRAGMENT (UNTRANSLATED)

AFTER SAPPHO.

μαὶ ροτ ἰς αλμωστας
βαδας θαιν, ἰεθρω.

βυτνοτ

κναιτ[15]

THE ANTHOLOGIST

(A POEM IN THE OLD STYLE.)

SHOULD auld acquaintance spend its shot
And critics prove unkind
We'll take the fiddling things we've got
And send them off to bind.

We all must sign, my dear,
We all must sign:
We'll get a word of mention yet.
From the dailies' scribbling Swine.

Gie me a column in the "News"
And Someone's portrait fine,
I'll see that poets get their dues
(That's if they're friends of mine)

We all must sign, my dear,
We all must sign,
It's surely cheap at half-a-crown
Let's make it two-and-nine.
(and so on)

EDGAR LEE MASTERS

For a few years, until he was supplanted by Pound, Eliot, and the Sitwells, Edgar Lee Masters was the poster boy of fashionable poets, his *Spoon River Anthology* characterized as "altogether the most read and talked-of volume of poetry that had ever been written in America" (Boynton 52). Popularity's social manifestations had national inflections, and from across the Atlantic, Masters's popularity was seen, at times, as typifying the worst aspects of American literary culture. Writing in *The New Statesman*, an anonymous reviewer snorted:

> Mr. Masters' book has been extravagantly boomed in America. It is ridiculous to suggest that it is a great book or he a poet. His writing is most commonplace; where he tries metaphor or any sort of high flying he is at his worst; and his moralisings, though sensible, are not profound. ("Transatlantic Lyre" 332)

In America, *The Dial* termed Masters's work "the *reductio ad absurdum* of certain of the new methods – such as the abandonment of conventional form and the fearless scrutiny of disagreeable realities" (Alden 28). *Spoon River*'s publication created a crisis over the place of realism in poetry (people wondered whether anyone had died a natural death in Spoon River), and the uncertain function of lineation and rhythm in Masters's work and modernism more generally. And, underneath all this there was a worry whether Masters himself was serious in his enterprise – a recurrent undertone in his career, given the highly conservative verse he published both before and after *Spoon River*. *The Dial* puzzled: "Mr Masters has shown before this that he knows what verse is; how then can he perpetrate, and endure to see in type, trash like this" (Alden 28)?

Henry Savage, from *A Long Spoon and the Devil. Being Fish Quaint and Queer from the Spoon River, the Property of Edgar Lee Masters, Poached by H. Savage, Etc.*

(London: Cecil Palmer, 1922).

Henry Savage was a modestly successful poet and critic. Reviewing Savage's *Escapes and Escapades*, Ford Madox Hueffer (Ford) concurred with several other reviewers, and claimed in 1915 that "Mr. Savage is almost as good as Heine" (qtd. in blurb in Savage, *Long Spoon*, 56). That may have been Savage's high point. In his autobiography, Savage complains of being shut out not only by high modernists, but also from the *Georgian Poetry* anthologies. The *Times* of London reports that in 1920 Savage unsuccessfully sued Lord Alfred Douglas for libel, after Douglas in an unpublished letter to the *Bookman's Journal* called Savage "a votary of the Oscar Wilde cult," and argued that the editor should "cut out" Wilde from publishing in the *Journal*.

Savage, at the end of his life, looked back with disgruntlement on the downward turn of his literary career. In the preface of what appears to be a book of self-published poems, he wrote:

> The revolt against beauty and the singing quality in poetry began, roughly-speaking, after the 1914–18 war with Germany; and my work, good, bad or indifferent as it may be, is in the tradition of song and beauty. I remember my surprise in Paris soon after the war when a youthful and able contributor to that then revolutionary organ, "transition," said, with every appearance of sincerity, that he had "no use for Keats ..."
>
> In the meantime, having some sympathy with revolutions, and wishing to keep step with the time-spirit, I studied the work of many modern poets and began to see more clearly why my "hue was not the wear." Not that it worried me much. It did, however, dawn on me that much work, inferior to mine, was being published and acclaimed, and that – as it isn't always virtuous to turn the other cheek – indifference to the fact would be more reprehensible than commendable. I therefore tried out the poems, some few years ago, on a publisher whose reader returned them with the meaningless comment that they were "without sufficient personal distinction"; and as it then became obvious to me that, in literary circles, there must be quite a number of similar nitwits clothed in a little brief authority, I haven't tried them out since.

> They are being published now mainly because of what may be a pardonable vanity, and because it occurred to me recently that, as I am in the evening of my days, some perhaps unpleasant person may benefit by them excessively when I am dead; weeping the while for Hecuba, so to speak, bragging that he "once saw Shelley plain," and joining his grave-faced listeners in wondering why merit isn't recognised as it should be until too late. Humbug and unpleasant persons being always with us, I ought not to worry about possibilities of the kind mentioned, but I won't deny myself a certain satisfaction in being able to anticipate them. (1946: 7–8)

Savage's *A Long Spoon and the Devil* (which he claims to have written in a week) addresses the poet who unleashed the storm over free verse, and whose meteoric rise Savage must have watched with scepticism.

THE POACHER

See here, Edgar Lee Masters!
You of the leaden Spoon River,
Did you think, when you first started fishing
In those delectable waters,
That you would be able to preserve them for ever?
Let me inform you, O Masters,
That though there be many disciples,
There are also a few free and independent poachers
In this cut-throat world of enchantment.
With rod and line through the bushes,
And caddis-worms, bread-paste, and maggits [*sic*],
Quietly some one approaches
To cast a quill in those waters.
You are not the only pebble on the beach, my dear Edgar,
Not by a long peb.
And besides, it's so damnably easy!

GRAND GUIGNOL

Why did I slit the man's weazand?
My Lord, it was all owing to a formula,
Invented back in the Dark Ages

By some one who hadn't the wits of Machiavelli.
Now that the deed is done
And the brief insanity is over,
I can see it wasn't the fault of the poor devil who suffered,
And, incidentally, suffers no longer
Now that he is past editing the brightest of the All-Colour monthlies.
But I kept on getting slips of paper
Saying how he "regretted" not being able to use my stories.
And with ruin staring me in the face
(The price of stamps, my Lord),
Just as it stares in the face of Lombard Street
Under the blessed dispensation
Of the Chancellor of the Exchequer,
So I began to wonder,
And wonder led to brooding,
And brooding led to a sulphur melancholy,
And that led to madness.
Till, one day, seeking him out,
Asking point blank if his regret was sincere,
His silly explanation so made me all goosey,
That the silver chord of reason was loosed
And the golden bowl of sanity broken –
And now, my Lord, judge me!

THEOPHILUS MUDIE

You think, Tom Williams, because you have read Robert Briffault,
And Jeremy Taylor[16] and Dorothy Richardson and that chap Joyce,
And go to the Café Royal,
And once met Rebecca West at a polite literary function,
That you are more intellectual
Than the man with side-whiskers and a toga
Who wears out the King's Road, Chelsea, with his sandals;
Or John Drinkwater,
Or the people who run *Coterie.*
And yet I would not have you beware the *intelligentsia*
So much as the evil by which my own downfall was accelerated.
My mistake was that I said
That in the Elysian Fields
People would read with equal enjoyment

The works of Immanuel Kant and Gene Stratton Porter.[17]
In trying to achieve which impracticable ideal
I busted my boiler.

VALE

But for the limits of physical endurance,
Shame, for the price of paper and eke ink,
Piracy, barratry on the high seas,
And other reasons too many to detail,
I do not see why this nonsense
Should not go on till the Greek Kalends,
Or *David Copperfield* is attributed to Thackeray,
Or David Lloyd George is found out,
Or David H. Lawrence gets within an aeon or two
Of the real value of sex;
Or till my debts are paid,
Or the moo-cows come home.
But if the pundits are right in their assertion
That we can have too much of a good thing,
Does it not follow with dreadful logic
That too much of a thing like this
Might even have more dire results
Than the stuff which mainly inspired it?
Wherefore, reader –

FINIS

Samuel Hoffenstein, "Birdie McReynolds," in *Year in, You're Out*

(New York: H. Liveright, 1930), 164–5.

Samuel Hoffenstein (1890–1947) was born in Russia. He began his career in journalism, writing for the *New York Sun*, *New York Tribune*, and *Vanity Fair*. He received enthusiastic reviews for his collections of satiric verse, including his posthumous collection *Pencil in the Air*. His most popular work, *Poems in Praise of Practically Nothing*, sold over 200,000 copies. In the early 1930s Hoffenstein moved to Los Angeles, where he worked as a screenwriter, and was nominated for two Academy Awards, including the 1944 film noir classic *Laura*.

BIRDIE MCREYNOLDS

(MR. EDGAR LEE MASTERS TELLS AN OLD, OLD STORY.)

I kept the house on the corner of Linden and Pineapple Streets,
Down in the district.
And a lively house it was, too,
For a burg like Fork River.
I liked the business,
And that's why I went in it.
Nobody has to do anything he doesn't want to.
How else could I have stuck it out in that hick town?
Imagine me a Fork River housewife,
With a Fork River husband,
The kind that used to come down to my house –
Me, Birdie McReynolds!
Don't make me swallow some dirt.
I never lost my virtue.
Don't think it!
I gave it away for a while,
And then I sold it,
And I had a good time both ways.
I knew everybody,
And everybody liked me.
I kept the judge in his place,

The Mayor, the Sheriff, and the Councilmen,
Or the town couldn't have held them.
They needed somebody like me to tone them down,
The poor, swell-headed, small-town fish,
And it's usually a Birdie McReynolds that does it.
I could read a man's character
By the kind of suspenders he wore;
The old sports went in for white silk ones
With "Fireman" or "Policeman" engraved on the buckles.
It made them feel virile,
The poor saps!
Don't think you'll get a sob-story out of me, Eddie Masters;
I wasn't that kind of a jezebel.
There ain't any, anyhow.
It's the good women must weep
While the men work.
We like them to work –
They spend more.
Now go away and let me sleep;
That's one thing I never got enough of
In my business,
Or I wouldn't be here.

William Kean Seymour, "A Spoon River Casualty," in *Parrot Pie: Parodies and Imitations of Contemporaries*

(London: G.G. Harrap & Co., 1927), 145.

A SPOON RIVER CASUALTY

When I began it seemed a sudden light
Flooded my mind and spirit.
I was sixteen and avid for all books
When Pastor Schirdling at the Baptist Soirée
Made my ambition leap.
If *he* could read Gibbon's *Decline and Fall*
Three times and start a fourth time so could I.
I went one better:
I set myself to memorize each word
Of that immortal monumental work.
Patiently through the nights by candlelight
I fixed line after line,
Saying them over in the silent house,
Steadily piling massive periods.
I lost my job with the First National
Just as I neared my fifty-thousandth word.
When I stabbed a waiter for interrupting me
As I was in the midst of Volume Two
They put me in the Penitentiary,
And took my book away. Maybe they thought
They'd kill the light of Gibbon in my mind.
They killed me first. Having no work to do,
I quietly died and left them wondering.

Franklin P. Adams, "The Conning Tower," in Bliss Perry, *A Study of Poetry*

(Boston: Houghton Mifflin, 1920), 208–9.

ADD SPOON RIVER ANTHOLOGY

Peoria, Ill., Jan. 24. — The Spoon River levee, which protected thousands of acres of farm land below Havana, Ill., fifty-five miles south of here, broke this morning.

A score or more of families fled to higher ground. The towns of Havana, Lewiston and Duncan Mills are isolated. Two dozen head of cattle are reported drowned on the farm of John Himpshell, near Havana. – Associated Press dispatch.

Edgar Lee Masters wrote a lot of things
About me and the people who
Inhabited my banks.
All of them, all are sleeping on the hill.
Herbert Marshall, Amelia Garrick, Enoch Dunlap,
Ida Frickey, Alfred Moir, Archibald Highbie and the rest.
Me he gave no thought to –
Unless, perhaps, to think that I, too, was asleep.
Those people on the hill, I thought.
Have grown famous;
But nobody writes about me.
I was only a river, you know.
But I had my pride,
So one January day I overflowed my banks;
It was n't [*sic*] much of a flood, Mr. Masters,
But it put me on the front page
And in the late dispatches
Of the Associated Press.

THE SITWELLS

In a time that had more than its share of artists who knew how to manipulate the levers of publicity, the Sitwells (Edith, Osbert, and Sacheverell) stood out. Indeed, F.R. Leavis in 1932 claimed that "the Sitwells belong to the history of publicity rather than of poetry" (*New Bearings* 73). J.C. Squire referred to them in "The Man Who Wrote Free Verse" with his description of the company at a literary luncheon: "The women, at a glance, seemed all to have white faces and red hair; the young men had white faces and either no hair or too much; tortoise-shell spectacles were generally worn; voices were pitched high; and any little indecency was welcomed by titters of appreciation" (134). Squire's attitude to their poetry was no less acerbic. Reviewing a volume by Osbert, Squire wrote that the poet "has to take more trouble with his versification, instead of succumbing to eye-rhymes and gross accentuations which might have been produced by a Babu using a metronome" ("Poetry" 437).

Writing a few years after the 1923 performance of her *Façade* (with music by William Walton, and in which the text was read through large faux-African masks), Edith Sitwell responded to criticism of Sitwellian charlatanism:

> In a paper of the Yellow Press, a short while ago, an article appeared claiming that the English people have always been notable for "seeing through" and exposing charlatans and impostors in literature and the arts. This is very true, since they have, in their time, seen through and rendered life intolerable to such charlatans and impostors as Coleridge, Keats, Shelley, and Wordsworth, and, before he was frightened into conforming to their ideals, Tennyson. (*Poetry and Criticism* 6)

Edmund George Valpy Knox, "Spokes: Or an Ode on Ebullitions of Eccentricity That Ought to Have Been Overcome in Early Childhood," in *Parodies Regained*

(London: Methuen & Co., 1921), 31–4.

E.V. Knox (1881–1971), the father of the novelist Penelope Fitzgerald, began his career as a freelance journalist. He became a regular contributor to *Punch* (publishing under the pseudonym "Evoe"), and was its editor from 1932 to 1949. He published numerous collections of his writings, reprinted from the pages of *Punch*. As its title might indicate, the piece below follows quite closely, in its syntax and form, Wordsworth's "Ode: Intimations of Immortality from Recollections of Early Childhood."

George Morrow (1869–1955), who provided the illustrations for *Parodies Regained*, was a prolific book illustrator and a regular cartoonist for *Punch*, for which he contributed thousands of cartoons.

SPOKES: OR AN ODE ON EBULLITIONS OF ECCENTRICITY THAT OUGHT TO HAVE BEEN OVERCOME IN EARLY CHILDHOOD

(This is an attempt to imitate some of the younger poets who write in "Wheels": only I have put it into a Wordsworth measure because I thought it would be easier.)

I have a mind where meadow, grove and stream
And common things like cats and bricks
To me do seem
Much as they might to lunatics,

The strange hallucinations of a dream.

Prosaic persons think I am a bore:
Think whatso'er they may,
I see and say

That *is* a pea-green monkey climbing up the door.

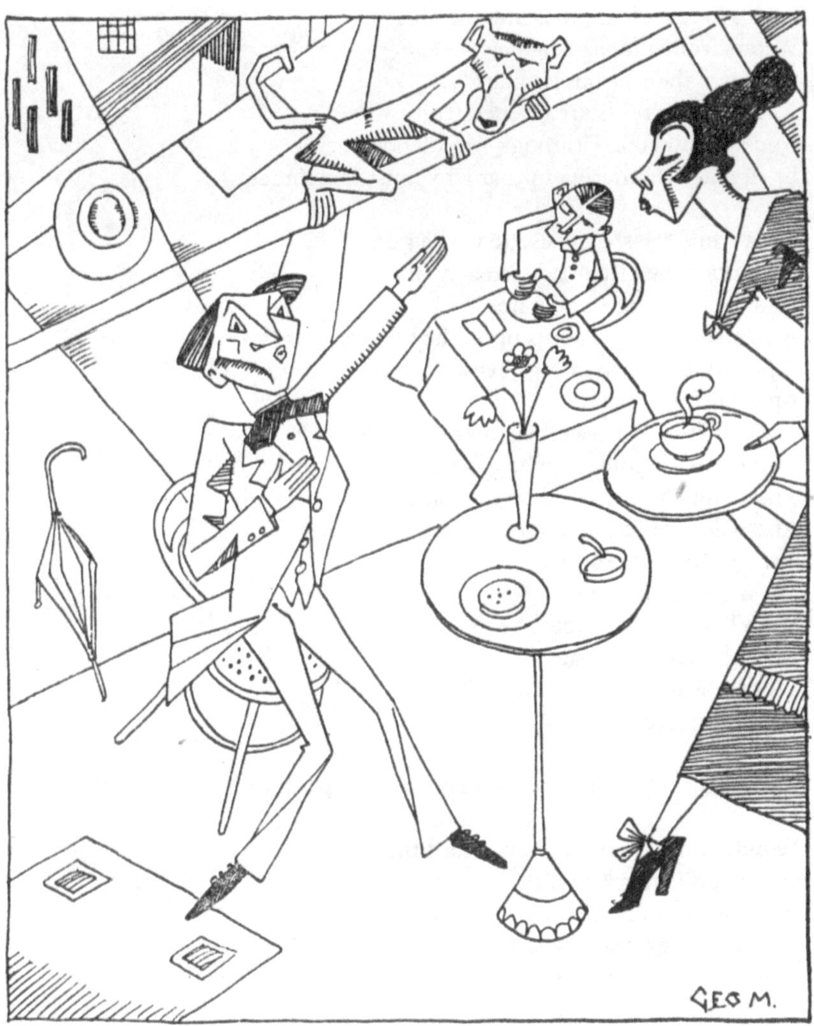

THE VORTICIST POET BANISHES HIS SADNESS WITH THE VISION OF TOASTED SCONES

The rainbow comes and blows
The moon amidst the night
Shrills louder than the trombone's blare;
Waters from a topaz height
Let down their turquoise hair;
And songs of birds are ripened fruit,
And shadows creak through woodlands sleek –
In all that shimmering uproar why must I be mute?

Now, while the sharp falsetto of the rain
Shampoos the bleak and bistre square
And all seems lone and bare,
A crimson motive flaunts upon the breeze,
A parrot voice reiterating "Teas,"
And I feel well again.
The clockwork buses move towards the Strand;
And there are golden-ceilinged cafés still,
And penny toys are sold on Ludgate Hill,
And bales of incense come from Samarcand;
Things are not really bad;
My crackling thought
Munches the future like an ought,
And how shall I be sad
When toasted teacakes can be had?
Ye glittering ones

Pounce round me, let me see ye pounce, ye panther-hearted buns!

Ye buttered crumpets, I have heard the call
Of crocodile to crocodile,
In amorous morasses near the Nile;
And seen the crested lizard scrawl
"Tarzan" on a temple wall,

Or, if I have not seen, I dreamed – I dreamed it all.
O hapless day! if a critic
Should breathe some word of annoyance,
Marring my joyance,
In a world paralytic
And plumed and tense,

And ask what in thunder can be the sense
Of sound-waves – and still the words outpour
As the babble of children when they roar
"Hurray! Hurray! It is my birthday!"
Yet fears I have, not frequent, when
I gaze upon the books of bygone men,
That make me ask, "*Is* mine a poet's pen?"
The primrose at my feet
Takes up the awful bleat;
And "Yes, it is, it is, it is!" I scream;
"Give me more cake – more cake and lots more cream."

Then come from mountains high and hear my prayer,
Ye Muses with the waspish golden hair
And faces lovely as warm apricots,
Woolly and freckled over with brown spots,
And plump as bird-song in a bush of may,
And lead me under yak-haired deodars
That eat the fretted orange of the day,
To find flamingoes, rising a pink spray,
And warm as stars;
And let me listen to the creaking moon
And hear the brittle laughter of the breeze
Patchouli-scented as a blonde marquise;
And publish me at once, and publish soon.
Thanks to the vogue of Futuristic things
And constant tumult of a negroid band,
To me a chocolate *éclair* often brings
Thoughts that not even nurse can understand.

William Kean Seymour, Three Parodies of Edith Sitwell, in *A Jackdaw in Georgia: A Book of Polite Parodies and Imitations of Contemporaries and Others*

(London: J.C. Wilson, 1923), 1–7.

Seymour's first poem alludes to Sitwell's recently published "Aubade," which begins

Jane, Jane,
Tall as a crane,
The morning light creaks down again; (95)

ONE: MISS EDITH SITWELL

FANTASIA FOR ONE-STRINGED FIDDLE

Elise, Elise,
Wore through her knees
Shinning up the hips of mulberry trees.
So keen
And clean
To her eyrie green
Was her shinning
That the sinning
And preposterous Rural Dean
Said "I aver
I'm proud of her."
Mulberry and mulberry
In the tree with antics merry
She plucked and dropped
Till daylight stopped.
Then
To the men
Waiting in the dusk
To carry home her husk

She said, "Alas,
I'm as brittle as glass,
I'm not the woman I one time was;
Bring up your ladders
And perch them straight;
The sky's all bladders
And strings of fate!"
Bats in the belfry
Bluffed and blew
Before she was well free
And home with Lou.
Lou was sweet,
With immaculate feet,
Whose spouse, a greasy Spaniard
Was found hanging by his lanyard
In the tropics.
Other topics
She had none
Except one.
"Fish?" she would scream,
"I prefer bream
After they are scraped and scaled."
Then she always sat
Flat
On the knees
Of Elise
And wailed.
They had a fat
And thriving cat
And jointly agreed
To pay for its feed
If each could call it Magnificat.
Elise's mother-in-law
Used to utter a saw
Seated on the lid of the old harmonium.
"Don't, child, ever
Try to be clever
Or earn the fickle world's encomium."
Before she was dead
She also said,

Nodding her black bonnet
With the icicles upon it,
"For one rupee
I can buy enough tea
To keep me in drink till half-past-three,
While I dream
In the gleam
Of furry apples raining from a sycamore tree."

But Elise holds her knees
High in bed and sees
Mulberries in millions on the apple trees;
Thinking
As she's sinking
Into sleep
Of the deep
Wise thoughts of her mother-in-law
Whose mental claw
Clutches her there in her bed
Till her spirit is dead.

TWO: MISS EDITH SITWELL

QUARTETTE FOR THREE MILK PAILS AND A FEEDING BOTTLE

Contented cows that crop carnations
Teach us all our proper stations.

With glassy eyes like basins painted,
Bright as orbs of virgins sainted,

They between the poles and wires
Watch the Flying Dutchman's fires,

Charm with decorous horns and tails
Singing homicides from Wales.

With rigid wooden tread they stand
In still procession through the land,

Their dugs a sharp seductive red
Where no velvet calves have fed.

If I were Mrs. Shandon-Gaff,
Who never has been seen to laugh,

I, with Jones the Poulterer's son,
Would embark upon the run;

For cows in contemplation cropping,
Roses and carnations lopping,

Turn the Doctor and the Dean
Quite egregiously green,

Whose discontent and milkless spite
Spout volcanic in the night,

Souring milk of human kindness
By their spiritual blindness.

Aunt Jemima, Uncle Rupert,
Tear yourselves away from Schubert;

Contented cows that crop carnations
Teach us *all* our proper stations,

Competing mildly with pink pills
And Ripolin for window sills.

THREE: MISS EDITH SITWELL

HOW THE GOOSE GIRL CONVINCED THE DEAN

The moonlight belches blue as cheese
Against the goose-herd's cherry knees.

Whose topaz eyes have counted thrice
The agate tails of twenty mice.

"Tournez, tournez!" said the Dean,
"Have you combed their feathers clean?

Whilst the rusty owls on black
Writhen branches screamed 'Alack!'"

"I have shod my geese with glass
Greener than young April was,

They are making happy hiss
With Clothilda's idiot niece:

But old kings and barren queens
Smile like empty soup tureens,

Lest their cabbage hearts should quail
When my silver goslings trail."

Quoth the Dean, "Ah, yes, dear friend,
Now at last I comprehend,

Though your frayed and cambric cheek
Made me hesitate to speak."

T.S. ELIOT

Unlike their entanglements with the Sitwells or with Pound, parodic engagements with Eliot did not target his manipulation of publicity, and he was not tied to movements and their motivating theories. Eliot's vulnerabilities, instead, lay in his representing the "modern," and a modern attitude to artmaking. Moreover, even before the publication of *The Waste Land*, his influence on the young was often noted. In 1920 a sceptical Louis Untermeyer characterized Eliot's position in the following manner:

> For two or three years the poetry of T.S. Eliot has been championed warmly by a few protagonists and condemned even more heatedly by many who suspected the young author of all things from charlatanry to literary anarchism. Those who have read it have talked of this product, not as poetry, but as a precipitant, a touchstone; they pronounced "Eliot" as though the name were either a shibboleth or a red flag. Controversy was difficult. For, with the exception of two longish poems and half a dozen scattered verses, this native of St. Louis continued to publish his occasional pieces in England and threatened at the age of thirty-one to take on the proportions of a myth. (126)

Parodists turned to mock the new cultural power of difficulty, of the enigma. With "The Love Song of J. Alfred Prufrock" they went after phrases and narrative situations; with Eliot's quatrain poems they turned to Eliot's sinuously polysyllabic diction, together with his opaque narrative situations and his sinister, racialized, and sexualized atmospherics. In the fifth volume of *Coterie* (1920), Edward J. O'Brien turned the following lines in imitation of Eliot's narrative in "Sweeney Among the Nightingales:"

> Mocking from a plush trapeze
> Arabella hunts for fleas,
> Gravely quiescent Jumbo lies
> Contemplating mysteries.
>
> Mrs. Geoghegan rustles in
> As if she had a secret sin,
> But Rumpelmayer rushes out
> And then it all becomes a rout. (23)

To O'Brien and other parodists, Eliot's poem creates the same kind of instantly recognizable narrative mystery:

The person in the Spanish cape
Tries to sit on Sweeney's knees

Slips and pulls the table cloth
Overturns a coffee-cup,
Reorganized upon the floor
She yawns and draws a stocking up;

The silent man in mocha brown
Sprawls at the window-sill and gapes;
The waiter brings in oranges
Bananas figs and hothouse grapes (56)

Parodies of *The Waste Land* returned to several aspects of Eliot's work: its recondite sources, multiple languages, rapidly changing tonal registers, sudden immersion in popular culture (more a sign of the poem's pretentiousness than an escape from it), and, of course, the poem's ending. H.P. Lovecraft (author of the horror classic *At the Mountains of Madness*), for example, ended his less-than-mediocre send-up of Eliot's poem with:

In the ghoul-haunted Woodland of Weir
Strangers pause to shed a tear;
Henry Fielding wrote "Tom Jones"
And cursed be he that moves my bones.
I saw the Leonard-Tendler fight[18]
Farewell, farewell, O go to hell.
Nobody home
In the shantih. (255)

William Kean Seymour, "The Love-Song of J. Ernest Odol," in *Parrot Pie: Parodies and Imitations of Contemporaries*

(London: G.G. Harrap & Co., 1927), 43–5.

THE LOVE-SONG OF J. ERNEST ODOL

Come with me, then; let us go
Where the sunset is spread out upon the snow
Like a crab articulated upon a table;
Come with me through certain unfrequented ways
Where no band plays
To slack-legged visitors at cheap hotels,
Where day goes out with dinner-bells,
And all things wait for summer
And that gay newcomer
Who will infest with multitudinous feet
The *plage*[19] of this now somnolent retreat.

In the room the women eat their jelly
Prating of Botticelli.

And for us there is still time,
For the snow lies on the hills in swathes,
Like bandages in an operating-theatre.
There is still time, there is still time
To see that straddling lobster, the high sun,
Split on the plate of evening;
Time for me and time for you,
And time yet for a thousand new sensations
And for a hundred potent exultations
Before we sip again that deadening brew.

In the room the women eat their jelly
Prating of Botticelli.

Ah! I have known them in my smallest bones.
They will come up to you with dace-like eyes
And murmur phrases of assumed surprise
And patter on in elegant undertones,
Pouring the golden moments into seas
Of dull vacuities.

I should have been the fangs of a grey beast
Fleshing and unfleshing in green glooms.
I grow old … I grow old …
They are wearing their ties made up, I am told.

No, I am not great Caesar, or Michelangelo,
Or that sick pierrot, ranting Romeo;
Though I have seen side-whiskers grow on squires;
And in the midnight a tomcat's desires
Flourish in song unlovely.

But would it have been reasonable, after all,
To let a silence fall
Terribly in the chatter and not stoop?
After the cocktails and the vigorous soup,
The roast saddle of mutton and the jelly
(Don't you think he's lovely, Botticelli?)
Would it have been reasonable, do you think,
To have lifted to the mocking spirit a wink
And smiled and said,
"I am the ghost of Mr W. T. Stead,[20]
But I have been used badly
By Mr Dennis Bradley"?[21]

Shall I wear my pants or skirts? Is it safe to eat a plum?
I shall sport a cotton waistcoat and beat a penny drum.
I have seen the mermaids scrambling in the scum.
I have seen them drifting and lifting in their pride,
Lovely in their glamorous play upon the running tide,
And the south wind saw them and the south wind sighed.

But the evening, the evening is so quiet,
And out there are no coffee-spoons and chatter,
But the serene snow and the down-drifting sun.
Let us go out, then; it is no matter
To murmur words; the meal is nearly done.

Louis Untermeyer, "Einstein among the Coffee-Cups," in *Heavens*

(New York: Harcourt, Brace and Co., 1922), 147.

Untermeyer's poem was published as part of a "review" of an anthology by the "hardy and perennial" Warren Stoddard Breathweight (a reference to rival anthologist William Stanley Braithwaite): *Rhyme and Relativity: An Anthology of American Poems Apostrophising the Theories of Einstein* (published by Small, Little & Klein). According to Untermeyer, the dust jacket blurbed the collection in this way:

> This is the era of anthologies. There is scarcely an animal, school of thought, experiment in technique, *locale* or topic of conversation that has not been made the excuse for a collection of verse. We have anthologies of songs by women, songs for men, jingles for children; anthologies of prose poems, ghost poems, horse poems, cat poems, doggerels; anthologies of poems about war, the dance, gardens, Christianity and Kansas.
>
> It is all the more amazing to realize that no one heretofore has made a timely collection of poems inspired by the Einstein Theory of Relativity. The fact that there are, as yet, few such poems to be gathered is beside the point. The verses which have been collected here call attention to new and profound impulses which are stirring this generation; they reflect such provocative phenomena as *Relative Motion, Substitutes for Gravitation, The Michelson-Morley Experiments, Time as a Fourth Dimension, Deflected Light-Rays, non-Euclidean Warps in Space* and *The Shifting of Spectral Lines toward the Red.* (122–3)

Using his own poem as a demonstration of the collection's limitations, Untermeyer commented: "In spite of the seriousness with which this collection has been received, we cannot relinquish our suspicion that the entire book is a hoax" (121).

EINSTEIN AMONG THE COFFEE-CUPS

BY T.S. ELI-T

Deflective rhythm under seas
    Where Sappho tuned the snarling air;

A shifting of the spectral lines
   Grown red with gravity and wear.

New systems of coördinates
   Disturb the Sunday table-cloth.
Celestine yawns. Sir Oliver
   Hints of the jaguar and sloth.

A chord of the eleventh shrieks
   And slips beyond the portico.
The night contracts. A warp in space
   Has rumors of Correggio.

Lights. Mrs. Blumenthal expands;
   Diaphragm and diastole.
The rector brightens. Tea is served;
   Euclid supplanted by the sole.

F.R. Scott, "Sweeney Graduates"

***McGilliad* 1.2 (April 1930): 9.**

F.R. Scott (1899–1985) was a Canadian poet and a member of the Faculty of Law at McGill University. A fundamental partner in the establishing of a socialist party in Canada (the Co-operative Commonwealth Federation), he was its national chairman for eight years.

SWEENEY GRADUATES

(WITH ALL NECESSARY APOLOGIES)

Sweeney, a ripe collegiate,
Emits stenography. Content
To write as ragged notes dictate,
He earns an adequate per cent.

The hour is procreant. His mind,
Incapable of further suction,
Gives sudden, fissive birth – a kind
Of protoplasmal reproduction.

He sloughs the academic skin.
The intellectual skirmish ends.
Now may the serious work begin
Of piling up the dividends.

Professor Slogan, D.C.L.,[22]
Sifts truth from error. He conjectures
That Sweeney knows his questions well
Since they are answered from his lectures.

His depelliculative dome
Preponderates with pride, as all
His pet ideas come flocking home
Inviolate, identical.

So Sweeney passes. So they pass
In thousands down the milky way.
Nebuchadnezzar, throned in brass,
Laughs at the prophets' disarray,

As educated hordes intrude
On meretricious premises
And magnates in their magnitude
Dispense the dubious degrees.

Herbert Palmer, from *Cinder Thursday*

(London: Ernest Benn, 1931), 11–19.

Herbert Palmer (1880–1961) was a poet and critic. He was the author of seventeen books of criticism, verse, and drama, including his 1927 drama *The Judgement of François Villon*, published by Virginia and Leonard Woolf's Hogarth Press, and a 1943 collection of poems under the imprint of Eliot's Faber and Faber. Palmer's *Cinder Thursday* is one of the more ambitious but heavy-handed send-ups of T.S. Eliot. The publisher's blurb claims:

> *Cinder Thursday* ... seeks, by means of parody, satire, mockery and passion, and even by direct statement, to point out some of the most alarming features of present-day disintegration both in literature and social life. It begins with parodies of T.S. Eliot and other modernists, explains by means of parody and direct and symbolic criticism the significance of *The Waste Land* and its influence and goes on to show how the disintegration in poetry is only the expression of disintegration in so much present-day social, national and individual life, the most alarming features of which are evidenced in what is known as Bolshevism with its relationship to Russian Communism.

In his 1938 *Post-Victorian Poetry* Palmer attacked many modernist writers, and claimed of *The Waste Land* that

> surely Mr Eliot never intended *The Waste Land* to be taken quite so seriously, at least not quite so constructively, especially as it exhibits too many of the features of a hoax. At any rate a hoax and earnest are strangely, hypnotically, and bafflingly blended. It is as if Mr Eliot were saying: "Take this, you fox-terriers; it's all you are worth. Here's a bone for a dog." If *The Waste Land* means anything to me in relation to 2030 it is that *The Waste Land* will be truly a waste land, unknown and unhonoured, leering out of the darkness at all other English poetry, which will be equally unknown and unhonoured. (313)

I. CHRISTMAS ILLUMINATIONS

(With apologies to T. S. Eliot, Laura Riding, Gertrude Stein and certain Imagists)

I have noticed
That in the poetry of T. S. Eliot

The chief animal symbol is a monkey,
Though obscure,
Because it sometimes looks like a bone.
And I have further noticed
That in the poetry of Laura Riding
The chief animal symbol is a spider,—
Or a woman.
(Though the word spider occurs more than twenty times in four pages.)
But in the poetry of Edith Sitwell
Which speedeth her well
It is a unicorn
And royally born.
O, my children, why have ye piped unto me!
And I have further noticed
That in my own poetry
It is a wolf—
A very vicious, complex and contradictory beast,—
Though it is sometimes a lion.
Which is a pity.
Because nobody to-day loves lions.
I have noticed, Oh I have noticed!
Because I have noticed I have noticed
That I have noticed.
I
Have . . . . .
Spots, dots,
Five of them . . . . .
The lion and the unicorn were fighting for the crown,
The lion chased the unicorn all round the town.
Some gave them green grass and some gave them brown,
Some gave them apple-sauce and – knocked the lion down.
Which wasn't fair.
Though somebody spoke about it.
And a voice came out of a cloud, crying,
"The unicorn was originally a starved rhinoceros
Which ran about wildly
To make itself thin."
But I have noticed that royalty often, springs from vulgar origins.
O, my children, why have ye piped unto me!
The infant mortality for the year nineteen-thirty is the lowest on record
Because

Because so few were born.
The lion and the unicorn were fighting for the crown,
Someone beat a cooking-pot and knocked the lion down.
Which was the end of that chapter.
And a great darkness came over the face of the land
And covered the tail of the unicorn.

II. THE SAHARA

(With apologies to T. S. Eliot)

The wilderness shall blossom as a rose,
But with cactus.
Look backwards and forwards and into the air.

"Sir, Sir, Oh Sir,
You are quiet in your chair.
Did you not hear me as I reached the highest stair?
I have left my shopping parcel,
I have left my combinations,
I left them on your chair
When I came to ask some questions.
For certes you are learned, and curiously wise."

And her blue eyes filled with tears as she stood before him there.
But shrugging his shoulders he chucked her under the chin,
And said rather cynically
"Little Muse, Little Muse, I have need of your parcel.
Your parcel contains infinite treasure in a narrow space;
Your combinations ..." The wind whistled and the hinges of the door creaked,
And the tears ran swiftly down her pale and frightened cheeks,
"Not that, oh not that!
What will people think and say?
I have never been so close to you as that."

But he pushed the lass away
As he glared upon the day,
"I shall keep your combinations

For my future permutations;
I shall twist 'em round my brain
When my spirit is in pain,
To improve the shining hour
To arouse the passion-flower,
And I'll hang 'em on the line
When the day is clear and fine
To inform the populations
Of excessive tribulations;
I shall hear them say and say
That you left your combinations
When you dressed yourself one morning,
And that all your sons and daughters
Who tread the hills and waters
Are a progeny most trying,
And are mine, mine, mine."

"But Sir, O, O,
I conceal the things, you know,
Underneath my gown of pearly grey.
I never show my combinations to the open eye of day.
I never do a single thing to throw myself away.
And I never, never, never gave you cause at all for this wild play."
Ring out wild bells across the snow.
Ring out, ring out.
Let the stars join and clawing Ages shout.
Miching Mallecho![23] There's wax in Pluto's ears.
Ring out, Horatio, what a wounded name
Is scratched upon the sand-corroded pillar,
In the land of the Chaldeans by the river Chebar.
Malory, too, to stick in Wednesday's ash with Ezekiel,
For there came a damsel out of a pavilion,
The senior batsman tugging at her train.
Can this continue? Shall these dry bones live?
Where are the spirit eyes among the corpses?
Oh, that old god, he's deaf and dumb again!
My heart aches, and a drowsy numbness pains my sense
As though of hemlock I had drunk the sorrows of my line.[24]
Ring out, ring out!
Ethereal minstrel! pilgrim of the sky

Is this the face that launched a thousand ships?[25]
I think, and do not think.
The wind goes slowly. What's that awful stink?

"Tha get on with tha deein', Jack,
It's only the 'am for the buryin.'"

I'm not surprised they call it the Sahara,
For I never saw so many houses in my life.
I'm not surprised they call it the Promised Land,
For it is strewn with plucked flowers,
Shouting, shouting, shouting,
Dying, dying, dying.
People evidently know what they are talking about,
Because the voice of the first Georgian nightingale
Came out of the throat of a coconut-flinger.

Howl, howl, howl jackals,
Scream hyenas.
Let the wind scorch and the green places be laid waste
And all colour be effaced
In the pimpled chastity of the desert's grinning face.
Ouranga, wanga, stanga. Therefore, therefore
Let the poet's dreams be mixed or telescoped.
Let him pilfer and echo and intermingle without scruple.
Let the consciousness of life be garnered from broken, twisted phrases and images,
As it is in real dreams,
As it is in sleep.
Let the Law of indisciplined Association of Ideas take leading control,
That everything go leaping and whirling,
As it is in the brains of lunatics
And little children.
Ouranga, wanga, stanga.
Therefore also
Let some things be upside down, and some of the epithets be unnatural.
Let the tentacles of nightmare visitations strangle all alabaster comeliness of repose
As well as grammar and punctuation.
And with all that let, oh let

Let the most incomprehensible language of Blake be parodied into the language of despair
And contempt and disillusion. Ceres! let them triumph.
Although, although, although with it all
The miracle of the sudden oasis shall arise to dazzle the eyes and tempt the admiration,
While a strange hypnotic power permeates the universe.
Thus shall the Waste Land be born out of a man's brain
And the disillusioned and desiccated get their High Song.

III. SUPPLEMENT

But I haven't shown everything,
I have merely chiefly stated.
I haven't shown the strange grammar and punctuation,
The wrong grammar and punctuation,
And omitted punctuation,
And occasional use of wrong epithets,
Deliberately wrong,
And I haven't quoted what T. S. Eliot quoted,
"You! hypocrite lecteur! – mon semblable, – mon frère!"
For I am not a hypocritical reader
And I am nobody's bad brother.
I refuse to be taken in by *The Waste Land*,
I refuse to pretend that I am not taken in.
I refuse to praise what I think I freely understand,
A hoax,
The most stupendous literary hoax since Adam,
Yet in some abysmal way creative,
Even in its disintegration,
Touched with the finger-nail of Donne
And the knuckle bones of Dante and Ezekiel,
Yet nearly all awry,
Deliberately and intuitively awry.
And wired.
God! what a mousetrap!

If anyone can prove that I am wrong
He may have my hat,
He may have my trousers,

He may have my boots,
He may have my bootlaces,
He may have my coat and waistcoat
And my pants, vest, and shirt,
And I will brave the attentions of the police
And run about naked,
Crying in a loud voice from *The Waste Land*
"What have we given?
My friend, blood shaking my heart
The awful daring of a moment's surrender
Which an age of prudence can never retract."

IV. A FURTHER SUPPLEMENT

I think I know what he thought, –
Why cast pearls before …
A bone's good enough for fox-terriers.
Wait and see. Tra-la!
I guess they'll run to it.
And yap over it:
The real thing this,
No caviare,
No grape-fruit,
No salmon-steak,
But the real thing, – a bone.
The Poet's for his Age,
It's [sic] expression.
Disintegration for the disintegraters and lost souls,
"The saving passion."

Samuel Hoffenstein, "The Moist Land – A Parody of Eliot's Poem"

***New York Tribune*, 28 January 1923, sect. VI: 24; rpt. in Samuel Hoffenstein, *Year In, You're Out* (New York: H. Liveright, 1930), 107–17.**

"THE MOIST LAND"

(Being an account of the flight of Mr. T. S. Eliot from Scotland into Shropshire, from Shropshire into Wales, and thence into the Irish Sea.)

Unum, duo, tres, quattuor, quinque, sex, septem, octo, novem, decem, shema yisrael, adonai; alohainu, adonai echad; nun Wilhelm, wie geht's in der Schule, ganz gut, papa; ibid, infra dig, anon, sic, anno mirabile.[26]

I. THE DEMOBILIZATION OF THE FLEET

April's very fickle following
March which is very windy, following
February, very sleety, following
December, and so next year is this year
And so forth and so forth and so forth,
Etcetera; und so weiter.[27]
The Archduke in scarlet hunting coat came down to breakfast
Having slept all night with his hunting-boots under the sheets
His gun by his side. The steel of the barrel glittered
All night like phosphorescence in the room heavy with panatellas.
"Officer, which way is uptown, and if so which way is downtown?
I am a widow woman from Lynn, Massachusetts, and have never been here
  before,
Though I have a cousin on the force whose name is Sweeney,
A Titanic fellow, big I mean, bronzed as iodine,
Do you know him perhaps?
Perhaps, perchance, haply, mayhap, maybe?
Yes, no, nein, ja, oui, si, non?"
"My own name is Schulz. No Sweeney do I know."
"And yet my own husband was German. I am as I said a widow woman."

In Hamburg an der Elbe
Da schwimmt ein Krokodil.[28]

Now gleam the birches ghost-white wherever they are.
The sacerdotal poplars seem to have taken off their surplices
Against the heat. What time is it, Nathan?
Quelle heure est-il? Or, is the Big Ben out of order again?

The perch season is open in eastern West Virginia,
Give me a silver arrow and a bow of polished tin,
Give me a cross-bow out of Thessaly or Irkutsk,
Or an old-fashioned Winchester such as pawnbrokers still use in Erie, Pa., against burglars,
And I will prick their shins in the delicate mine-water,
The dirty perch!
How long, oh, Catiline, will you keep up this pish-posh?

Come, Marie, let us go to the Moscow Art Theatre.
Zhil ya na Tiflise
Bil ya na Kavkase.[29]
Closer, Marie (is not that Mischa Elman going into the shop to buy rosin –
He is a short fellow for his height, don't you think?)
Come closer, and we shall watch the moon rise over Tammany Hall.
The violins begin, let us imagine they are nightingales,
Singing their last, for the world ends tomorrow.
(About this time the fat-legged chorus comes on; do they still say, "So this is Paris"?)
Come, we will stand on the corner of Fourteenth Street and Third Avenue.
The world is falling about us like a whole autumn;
Come close, in the shadow, in the shadow,
The shadow that lengthens and lengthens,
As if we stood under the legs of a Colossus.
My heart is broken, Marie; the moon is red
With blood. And I wonder, I wonder,
Which six of the seven cities that claimed Homer were liars?
Comment allez-vous? Très bien, Monsieur.

II. A THREE-HANDED GAME OF PINOCHLE

Antiques, Madame? The Modern Antique Company
Has been in business forty-seven years
And never one dissatisfied customer.

Benvenuto! Benvenuto Cellini!
Tarry a moment, it is I, Fra Lippo Lippi,
There are two damsels in the cemetery
Waiting for us under the cypresses;
Let's go together.
Chi troppo sale
Precipitevolissimevolmente.[30]
Flow softly, Wabash, till I end my song!
"Oh, God, how I hate things out of Grand Rapids!"
Have you ever known what it is to hunger for objets d'art?
This candelabra, *par exemple*, pray
Examine it; observe this little stain –
This little copper stain – well, it was blood.
"Do you remember the Marchesa –
The fiery little woman out of Bologna?
No? Well, we'll say no more about it!"
"Have you ever been lost in the Schwarzwald, Amalie,
With nothing to eat but those filthy little sausages
They sell in Köln at Schimmel's there on the corner?"

"What was that?"

"I shouldn't be surprised
If dead men tell no tales."
"I think we've been dead a hundred thousand years."

Yes, and I know that was Little Red Riding Hood
I saw today on Fort Washington Avenue."
Aloha! Aloha!
But the barges spread sail down the river like peacocks,
Their canopies of orange and azure,
A sailor from Smyrna with a lemon between his teeth
Fell into the water. O there, Demetrios!
"I think you got a nerve, Mr. Rosenzweig, to ask I should marry your
daughter without a dowry."
In Hongkong I met Kwong Chu,
A mandarin with fingernails a yard long.
He had the most exquisite manners,
And I shall never forget his beautiful angel's smile

When he had us to tea that afternoon in January,
An hour after he had decapitated his mother.
Flow gently, Wabash, till I end my song.
IT'S A QUARTER TO FOUR!
"Is you comin', Andrew Jackson?"
"I ain't sayin' as I ain't."

"I ain't askin' yuh as you ain't; I'se askin' you as yuh is.
Now is yuh?"
IT'S A QUARTER TO FOUR.

Have you met Nastasia Fillipovna,[31] I said,
And he said he hadn't, so I asked him to.
And that was the beginning. She was one
Of those fierce Russian women, knows no fun.
Hurry up, Johnny, and get your gun.
Well, in a week the man was done for.
IT'S A QUARTER TO FOUR.
Good-night, ladies,
Good-night, ladies,
Good-night, ladies,
We're going to leave you now.

By the way, I'm sure you know the *Côte d'azur.*
IT'S A QUARTER TO FOUR.
As for me, I never took anything stronger
Than a thimbleful of rum
Even in the good old days,
But you, Mr. O'Brien, say you drink hair-tonic.
Flow softly, Wabash, till I end my song.

III. DEATH BY HOOCH

I am the same, Panthides,
I, Leotychides, who once in Elymais
Herded black sheep and by Hypanis shore,
Looking on Thebes a thousand leagues away,
Wreathed for your head a crown of eglantine,
And drank a copper keg of home-made wine.

Hula, hula,
Hula, hula,
Old Mother Hubbard she made my bed.
But what good is it
Since Ivan the Terrible
The Brooklyn Bridge
And Staten Island
Fell on my head?

Oh, Carthage, Carthage,
What boots it that the hawthorns keep their snows
Against these many months of wind and sun?
I resolved to take only sarsaparilla,
But what good did that do?
The clerk dished me up a vanilla,
Believing Columbus a Jew.

Take these, *les fleurs mourantes,*[32] *mademoiselle.*
There's nothing more for me to say,
(Oh, Neptune, Neptune, call your mermaids in!)
Until you get my letter.
But I know
(Oi, weh is mir, weh is mir!)[33]
That they've christened
Petrograd
Something or other,
And there's nothing to do
Until somebody
Can find my brother.
The more's the pity,
He's gone, he's gone
In a Spanish galleon
With Henry VIII
To Atlantic City.

La, la,
I've waited in High Bridge,
But I'm going now.

Rome is burning,
Yes, burning,
Gott
im
Himmel,
burning,
burning,
hula, hula,
la, la.

IV. THUNDER AND LIGHTNING

The dead are living
And the living are dead
And there's no use giving
Your board and your bed
To the sorrowful woman who came
From Lithuania
Latvia
Vienna or Rumania
Rome or Czecho-Slovakia
With an instep and eyebrows of flame.
Waiki, waiki.
What if I have three keys to my apartment
One gold, one silver and one lead
Here in this desert place the frogs are withered
The griffons are no bigger than fleas,
The sands are rocky and the rocks are sandy,
And there's not enough water
And not enough brandy
To wash the ears of King Cole's daughter.
Co co lo co po co.
   Oh if there were
Oh if there were
   Oh if there were
Do do do do do do
Ra mi fa so.

Let her sit at her piano and play Tschaikowsky,
But we who know how black the sun can be

Yom Kippur Eve or when there is no sun at all
We'll wait in this dead land and see
The Woolworth Building fall.

They will be here presently
And we shall be parched and shrivelled,
Whoever they are we shall be blanched and withered.
We have only to say coo coo
And all will be over.
Even the unicorns stay in their dry holes
The vampires mourn. Wait till the thunder speaks
Dada, goo goo
Abracadabra.
My friend you see me dead and yet I know
I have not long to live
After the purple gnats with bovine faces
After Jerusalem's fallen and Mrs. Grundy
Comes by on a black horse with the three graces.
Gautama's gone, the sacred bull is gone.
Apis is gone
Adio, bella Napoli, adio
Adio
Wait Khiva till the Ganges turns to milk,
You'll hear the tiger laugh with green grimaces
You'll see the thunder lift the Himalayas
As if they were a toothpick.
Da da ma ma pa pa
HALLELUJAH
I'll wait awhile for Julian the Apostate
You go and pick the fallen lightnings up
And see if Mrs. Porter
Has got enough soda water.

Farewell, I've turned the prow to Greece again.
Shall I call up my lawyer, Cortlandt 0004
And say the sea is beautiful tonight.
Brooklyn Bridge is falling down falling down falling down

Amo amas amat amabo amabimus
Huius huius huius – O mea culpa[34]

There's never anything to say though I should say
The less the more. The blue parrot's fainted.
God bless you all. Paracelsus is drunk again.
Daddy. Damdaddy. Damdaddy

Shanty shanty shanty.

Christopher Ward, "The Dry Land," in *The Triumph of the Nut, and Other Parodies*

(New York: Henry Holt and Co., 1923), 170–8.

Christopher Ward (1894–1966) was a lawyer, parodist, historian, and author of historical fiction. Ward was a cousin of Henry Seidel Canby, and early in his career contributed regularly to periodicals under Canby's editorship. *The Triumph of the Nut* was his first popular work, running into three editions.

BY WAY OF EPILOGUE

THE DRY LAND

Variations
Suggested by T. S. Eliot's Poem
THE WASTE LAND

I. APRIL FIRST

April is the foolishest month, bringing
The First of April, bringing
Jest and youthful jollity, jingling
Bells of Merry Andrew, rattling
Dried peas in blown bladders
Full of sound and signifying
Nothing – absolutely nothing.

II. THE SEA

The Dry Land yields no wine,
The Waste Land no whiskey,
And the Desert no malt liquor,
But there is moisture in spots.
Where there are rocks,
There also is moisture.

(Come with me here to the rocks)
What rocks? The Fleet rocks –
In the cradle of the deep.
Half a league and half a league outward,
In the sea, the sea, the open sea,
The Mariners of England
Nightly guard our shores.

Yo! ho! ho! and a bottle of rum,
A little wine for my stomach's ache
And whiskey in a glass darkly.
Let us go down to the sea in ships
Today it is our pleasure to be drunk
And this our queen shall be as drunk as we.
Εντεῦθεν 'εξελαύνει σταθμοὺς δύο
Παρασάγγας δέκα εἰν τὴν θάλατταν[35]

Alack! alack! turn back! turn back!
For I am suffering a sea-change
Or something. Pull for the shore,
Sailor, pull for the shore!

III. THE WHITE ROCK

Very well, then, here is another Rock,
(Come in under the shadow of this White Rock)
And I will show you something else again.
But that is water
And water
And also water,
Only that and nothing more.
Who would go upon a bust
On White Rock?
What a pallid bust it would be
On White Rock,
Only that and nothing more.
Mrs. Porter and her daughter
Washed their feet in soda-water.
They knew
What to do
With water.

IV. OTHER ROCKS

Are there no other Rocks? Yes
Here are rocks, – bullion, scads, cash,
Banknotes, dough and all kinds of money.
What will it buy? What will it buy?
Sodas, fizzy, fuzzy, insubstantial?
Sundaes, clinging, cloying, agglutinating?
Pretty polonies and excellent peppermint drops?
Yes, all. No more? Aye, more.
But this is the Waste Land. This is the Dry Land.
Aye, but there is moisture in spots,
(Come with me here to this spot)
This is a Wet Spot. It will buy
Any old thing
You want.
Johnnie Walker, Haig and Haig
Black and White and Gordon Gin.
Ab-sa-tive-ly, Mr. Gallagher?
Pos-o-lute-ly, Mr. Shean!

V. THE MOUNTAINS

In the highlands, where the Revenooer dozes
Where the old, kind men have rosy noses –
O the Moonshine's *right*
In my old Kentucky home!
Here is a still and a quiet conscience.
O still! govern thou my song.

Jug, jug, jug, jug, jug, jug
And also bottles
And demijohns
By the light of, the light of the moon.
There is no water
In my old Kentucky home
Except for washing
And damn little for that.

There spotted snakes with double tongue
And bats with baby faces may be seen

And camels all lumpy and bumpy and humpy
A-rolling down to Bowling Green.

VI. RAT'S ALLEY

I think we are in Rat's Alley
Where the dead men roll their bones.
What is that noise? A rat i' the arras?
Sh! Sh-h! Sh-h-h! Sh-h-h-h!
At my back in a cold blast I hear
The rattle of the bones, and chuckle spread from ear to ear.

In days of old when nights were cold
And the world was too much with us
Late and soon
He rattled his bones on the alley-stones,
A remote, unfriended, melan-
Choly coon.
He kept his maculate but honored bones
In the dark backward
And abysm of his pants.
He rolled 'em nightly on the alley stones
With that strange power
That erring men call chance.
And now his gentle ghost besprent with April dew
Nightly to the wandering moon complains
Ah craves action. Shoots ten dollahs.
Fade me! Fade me! Shower down boy!
Telegraph dice, click fo' de coin!
Eagle bones, see kin you fly!
Bugle dice, blow fo' de cash!
L'il snow flakes, sof'ly fall!
Gallopers, git right! Whuff! Bam!
READ 'EM AN' WEEP!!
I never saw a Moor. I never saw the sea
And yet I know how the heather smells[36]
And, by the same token, I can distinguish
A Moor from a Blackamoor
And the wild rose from the negroes.

VII. HAT AND TEETH

Where Catherine Street descends into the Strand
There I saw one I knew and stopped him, crying
"Where did you get that hat? Stetson?"
"Dunlap," he said and grinned
And showed precarious teeth.
One of the Five he was and not The One,
So Pyorrhea[37] claimed him for her own.

VIII. BANANAS

What makes the rear rank breathe so hard?
They are saying "But
Yes, we have no Bananas today."[38]
O O O O that sweet Banana Rag,
It is so beautiful,
So fruitiful.
But, yet, we have no bananas today.
This day, so calm, so cool, so bright
We have not a
Single damn ba-
Nana, yes.
What shall I do now? What shall I do?
I shall rush out just as I am without one plea
And buy cocoanuts.

IX. APRIL AGAIN

Yes, April is the foolishest month, bringing
The First of April. On that day I wrote this,
Tongue in cheek, twinkle
In eye, laughter in sleeve and
It shall shake the World,
Insofar as the World is composed of
Serious, sophisticated,
Impressionistic, expressionistic,
Futuristic, cubistic
Immature, Dadaists, blinking
Through horn spectacles

With horn lenses as well as
Horn frames, who shall read
What is not written, hear
What is not spoken, understand
What is cryptic only because it is
Nonsense.
Eeny meeny miney mo
Omne ignotum pro magnifico
Ich weiss nicht was soll es bedeuten.
Lasciate ogni speranza voi ch'entrate[39]
Da Dada Dadaism
Ha Haha Hahaism
Silly Sillier Silliest

NOTES

Not only the title but the plan and a good deal of the incidental symbolism of the poem were suggested by Mr. T. S. Eliot's poem *The Waste Land.* Indeed, so deeply am I indebted, Mr. Eliot's poem will elucidate the difficulties of my poem much better than my notes can do; and I recommend it (apart from the amusement to be derived from it) because my poem will seem more lucid by contrast.

Following Mr. Eliot's example, I have availed myself of the work of fellow bards. Credit has not been given in these notes in every case, but will be extended freely on application to our Credit Department.

I

Lines 1–7 Cf. *The Waste Land* I.1–7.

II

11. A phenomenon commonly observed.
14. V. *The Waste Land* I.26.
23. St. Timothy *I Timothy* 23.
25–6. V. H. Fielding *Tom Thumb the Great* I, Sc. II.
27–28. Cf. Xenophon *Anabasis, passim.*
31–32. V. Moody and Sankey *Hymnal* No. 1.

III

34. Cf. *The Waste Land* I.26.
36–7. Cf. *The Waste Land* I.348–9.
45. Cf. *The Waste Land* I.199–201.

IV

59. Inquire of any policeman or taxi-driver.
64–5. This list is incomplete. For full particulars inquire as above.
66–7. I do not know the origin of the ballad from which these lines are taken.

V

68–69. Cf. R. L. Stevenson, *In the Highlands.*
70–71. Old song.
72. Cf. W. Shakspeare *Henry VIII* Act 3, Sc. 2.
73. V. John Milton *Paradise Lost* Bk. 7,1.29.
74. V. *The Waste Land* I.204.
78–9. So reported by travellers.
83. Cf. *The Waste Land* I.379.
85. Old song. This Bowling Green is not in The N. Y. *Evening Post* but in Ky.

VI

86–7. Cf. *The Waste Land* I.115–116.
90. Cf. *The Waste Land* I.185.6.
92. Cf. Old song.
96–7. Cf. Oliver Goldsmith *The Traveller* 1. I.
99–100. Cf. W. Shakspeare *The Tempest* Act 1, Sc. 2.
102–3. Cf. J. Milton *Comus.*
104. V. B. Jonson *Elegy on Lady Jane Pawlett.*
106–13. V. Hugh Wiley, *passim.*
114–15. V. Emily Dickinson *Poems.*

VII

120–1. Cf. *The Waste Land* I.69.
123. Cf. *The Waste Land* I.339.
124–5. V. Current advertisements.

VIII

128. Old song of unknown origin.
129–31. Cf. *The Waste Land* I.128–130.
137–8. Cf. *The Waste Land* I.131.2.

IX

156. Cf. *The Waste Land, passim.*

EZRA POUND

From the outset of Pound's career, it was clear what the terms of his parodies would be. Responding to Pound's *A Lume Spento* in the *Cambridge Review*, Rupert Brooke wrote:

> Mr. Ezra Pound's work was "discovered" recently by certain London papers, and, a little timorously, acclaimed as valuable and inspiring. He is – do not his name and his verse betray it? – a young American; and he writes vers libre. His virtues and faults are both obvious. He is blatant, full of foolish archaisms, obscure through awkward language not subtle thought, and formless. (58)

As the tone of Brooke's review suggests, Pound would be found to be too American for the British. Writing in *The Egoist*, John Felton complained

> He knows a little of almost everything, but nothing well.
> He has the average American's respect for the latest novelty.
> Impossible to know if he ever thought of anything himself.
> If he had a real conviction he might achieve.
> Appearance – a whitened golliwog on a cleft carrot.
> Style – Flashy, blustering and often vulgar.
> Destiny – The admiration of the colonies. (297)

But Pound was too much the expatriate for some American tastes, prompting Margaret Widdemer, in the parody printed on page 155, to imagine a scenario in which Pound, participating in a poetry reading, chooses not to attend, and his poem is "Mailed disdainfully by him from anywhere but America, and read prayerfully by a committee from Chicago" (15).

Both American and British parodists thought he was *striving* too much, and giving up on naturalness. As an accompanying sign of this, Pound, like the Sitwells and Gertrude Stein, was portrayed as having a careerist's eye for publicity, and a consequent lack of focus on sincerity. Qualities other than sincerity dominated, and became the agreed-upon territory of parodies: Pound's hectoring frankness, love for the arcane and occult, and his American slang and rapid changes in level of diction.

Louis Untermeyer, "Ezra Pound," in — *and Other Poets*

(New York: H. Holt and Co., 1916), 55–7.

EZRA POUND

Putting on a Greek Head-Dress, Provençal Slippers, and an Imagiste Air, Recites:

ΠΗΑ ΠΟΥΝΔΙΝΓΣ[40]

I

Come, my songs, let us sing about something –
It is time we were getting ourselves talked about.

II

The iron menace of the pillar-box
is threatening the virginity of night.
Oh, Lars Porsena, let us be naked and impudent,
as the first day of April,
or Bernard Shaw without a toga.
Let us run up behind people and pinch them
in their too-fleshy ankles,
in the green twilight;

Male and female alike (I hear that they read you, Walt Whitman) –
Eheu, eheu fugaces – sic simper – sic transit – et cetera . . . .[41]

Loosen thy chrome girdle;
Unveil the crux ansata[42] – oh Ardanari-Iswari.[43]

III

TO A VERY CERTAIN LADY

Cybele, Cybele, you have grown sleek and damnably patronizing.
You pat me on the head, indolently,
as though I were a green puppy from Patagonia;
You tell me your love is platonic, and your passion
has cooled to me,
Like a porcelain pitcher in which hot water for shaving
has been standing for hours.

Go to – put on your latest Basque tea-gown
And catch other tadpoles in your cheap net.
Marry, as you most likely will, a Chicago millionaire,
(I can imagine no worse end for you)
And cultivate the Indiana literati …

Your heart is an empty dance-hall:
With lights blazing and musicians playing
on mute instruments.

C.E. Bechhöfer, "More Contemporaries. A Poem of Milton"

***New Age* 15.13 (1914): 308.**

A POEM OF MILTON.

I give it the once-over. LAUGHTER.
Some stuff? You tickle a laugh out of me.
You rubberneck, roughneck, redneck, lowbrow, piking, shortskate, tenhorn [*sic*], four-flushing mutt. HA.
I LAUGH, monkeying with the junk. Pardon me.
Read it? I should worry. Ishkibibble.[44]
This is the straight dope! We have the Goods, you rummy, waggling, agglutinous punk wop, Dante. I ROAR.
I am a lion. Look at me. Esto perpetua.[45]

Edmund George Valpy Knox, "The Rovers," in *Parodies Regained*

(London: Methuen & Co., 1921), 87–91.

THE ROVERS

(Mr. Ezra Pound, the American troubadour, has an unexpected meeting with Mr. W. H. Davies, the English tramp poet, whose simple rustic muse is so justly admired.)

SCENE: A platform at Charing Cross Metropolitan Station

MR. POUND *(emerging from a throng of passengers and addressing the station roof).*
Lo, I am weary of travel,
And the reading of many notices has tired my eyes
Until they see nothing but dots . . .
. . . . . Bah!
Little red lamp words pointing me onwards,
Little green lamp words pointing me onwards,
Little white lamp words pointing me onwards,
Onwards and onwards . . . .
. . . . Ai-ee!
I have sung rondels in many cities
Because they delighted my heart,
All about Ysolt and Audiart,
Loosely adapting from lots of originals.
I am a jongleur and free of the world,
Yet nevertheless
I have lost my way on the Underground line.

MR. W. H. DAVIES *(likewise emerging from the throng).*
Are you looking for the Bakerloo?

MR. E. P. I am.

MR. W. H. D. So am I too.
I also am a poet, and I thirst
For flowers and clouds and birds and buds and hares;
I do not understand these moving stairs

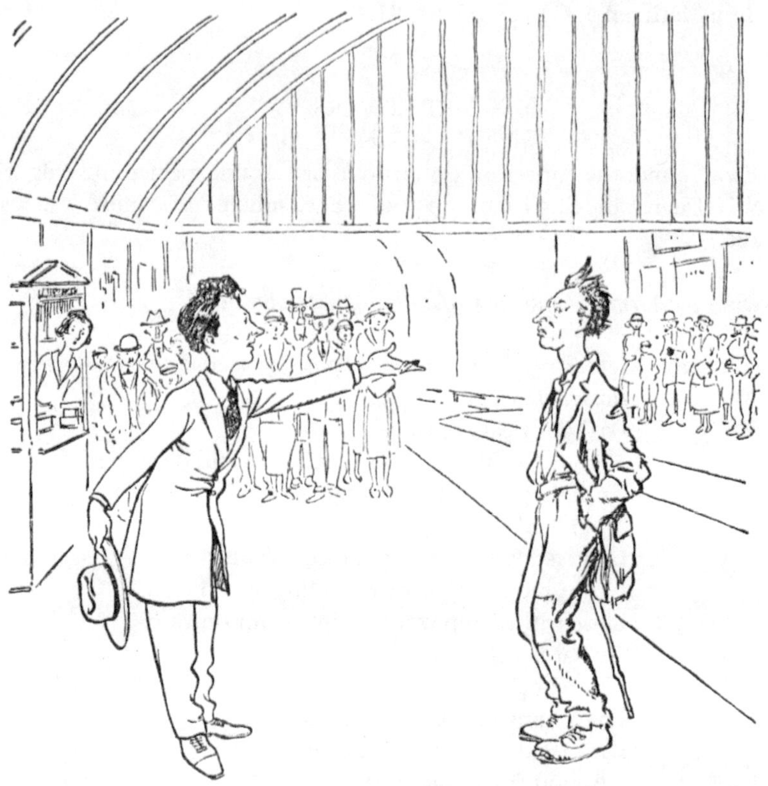

MR. EZRA POUND RECOUNTS TO MR. W. H. DAVIES HIS EXPERIENCES ON THE UNDERGROUND RAILWAY

That one must get off with the right foot first.
When I see cows chewing quite quietly,
With wet pink lips –

MR. E. P. *(interrupting in the rather unusual manner of "The Seafarer," circa 800).*
Song space a moment seek I your grace for,
While I point out how perfectly poisonous
Railfare down here is.
Bitter boot-pains have I abided
Woeful wind-loss and whangs in the waistcoat
And eke in the sides oft. A moment ago I
Nearly a new hat battered to bits had
In the stour[i] stamped on; fain would I stick steel
Through the Directors. (*He pauses.*)

MR. W. H. D. *(hopefully).* Hear how my friend the jongleur sings!
I too have suffered many things;
At Oxford Circus I have known
What townmen call the "stentorphone,"
Most like a hive wherein are bees
Which told me to "Keep moving, please,"
And made me from my skin to leap
Higher than lambs do round calm sheep.
When I reflect on caddis-worms –

MR. E. P. *(not to be denied and overbearing him).*
Hung hard to high straps, where hot the air is,
There I heard nought save "Whew, whew! "and "Ow dear !"
"Golly!" "Sardines!" "Get out at Victoria!"
Rotten romances were for my reading
Bought at the bookstalls (none were Ballate),
Seen over shoulders as sadly I swayed there,
Scent of some bad kind abundantly breathing;
Bits of tobacco and match-heads bestrewed me ;
Flecked was my collar; full often some Bolshevist
Blew smoke about me.

MR. W. H. D. *(feeling that they are not getting much further and pointing to a chocolate stall).*
That is a nice girl over there;
How prettily she tilts her head aside

i Early English.

As birds in spring do on bent sprays;
Perhaps, if we approach her, she will guide
Our footsteps through this spiteful maze.

MR. E. P. *(approaching stall and singing in a rich baritone).*
Sith in sooth you wish me well, Balatetta, Balatetta,
My white, my slender, my cruelle –

MR. W. H. D. Stop! I can do this so much better.
(Addresses girl, who seems slightly alarmed, in a soothing manner.)
Molly, so fair of face and form,
The dainty comfits on your stall
Would scarcely make you seem more sweet
Suppose you were to eat them all;
Give me your answer plain and true,
How shall we find the Bakerloo?

(She points the way.)
Exeunt arm-in-arm, mr. w. h. davies silent but triumphant, mr. ezra pound singing lustily and incorrigibly in the manner of a Villonaud:

Drink we a skoal[ii] for the leathern thong!
Tube-mates merry and stout and strong,
And this be the strain of our dangling-song
That Hell[iii] burn all the Management long!

(His voice dies away.)

A PORTER. Lor lumme!

ii Early English.
iii Plain English.

William Kean Seymour, "Twenty-nine: Mr. Ezra Pound. Boat Race," in *A Jackdaw in Georgia, a Book of Polite Parodies and Imitations of Contemporaries and Others*

(London: J.C. Wilson, 1923), 69.

At times, parodists believed their target work was well enough known that they could transform it clause by clause, bringing it down to a lower register, and skewering the pretentiousness of the original. Here, the Greek context of Pound's "The Return" (and the large cultural claims of that poem) is debased by being taken to a different context.

TWENTY-NINE: MR. EZRA POUND

BOAT RACE

See, the hesitant walk, the slow,
Tentative steps,
The odd gait,
The rolling uncertainty.

See, they come forth,
Singly
And together,
Fumbling, as half-asleep;
As if their feet debated,
Quarrelled,
And scorned obedience.

These were the happy lads
  Inseparable.

Lords of the flowing bowl!
By them the taximen
  Sniffing a reckless fare!

Haie! Haie!
These were the swift to enter;
These the light-footed;
These the undoubted bloods.

Dazed and unsteady,
  Pallid and silly.

"A Line-o'-Type or Two"

***Chicago Daily Tribune*, 18 April 1913: 8.**

In the April issue of *Poetry*, Pound had published his "Salutation:"

O generation of the thoroughly smug
  and thoroughly uncomfortable,
I have seen fishermen picnicking in the sun,
I have seen them with untidy families,
I have seen their smiles full of teeth
  and heard ungainly laughter.

And I am happier than you are,
And they were happier than I am;
And the fish swim in the lake
  and do not even own clothing.

"'SALUTATION' – TO THE NEW POETRY"

O degenerates in the art of writing,
  and fallen ones,
I have seen Cubists splattering their paints,
I have seen them make hideous splotches,
I have seen their riots of color
  and found nothing in them.
You are far worse than they are,
And they are much worse than nothing;
And the nude descends the staircase,
  and does not even own clothing.

W.R., "Contemporomania." From "A Line-o'-Type or Two"

***Chicago Daily Tribune*, 11 April 1913: 6.**

Bert Leston Taylor noted of the following contribution: "Admirers of Ezra Pound who were so fortunate as to read his verse in the April number of *Poetry* must have felt, with us, that they were too few. Happily we are able to supplement them with others in the same manner, by a valued contributor." Pound had published his series "Contemporania" in *Poetry*'s April issue. As might be expected, I have not found the epigraph's source in Baudelaire.

CONTEMPOROMANIA.

C'est le squiche c'est la svôche,
C'est la svôche et le squiche,
C'est la Poesie!

– Baudelaire

Let us write poetry.
No; let us write squish and swosh
When the end of the line is squish
Falls west of the easterly edge of the page,
"Poetry" will call it poetry.
The Friday Literary Supplement of the Chicago Evening Post
Will call it great poetry.

Let us not write it by the foot.
Let us not write it by the metre:
That would be traditional.
Let us write it by the yard.
Let us write it by the hectare.
Let us not write by the yard of three feet.
Let us write by the back-yard.
Let us write a back-yardful of squish and swosh.

I saw an Ethiopian in a back-yard at night.
He looked like the horse-chestnut in a farmer's pocket.

I have a friend who has a hectare in his back-yard.
His back-yard is in France.
His front-yard is in France.
This is because he lives there.
If he lived here
His back-yard would be in America
And there would be no hectare in it.

Let us run the lawn-mower over the hectare.
It is now a nude hectare.
It is now a naked hectare.
It is a French hectare.
Is not this suggestive?

This is poetry à la "Poetry."
This is poetry à la d'Elle.
This is poetry by the yard.
It is also poetry by The Pound.
The Pound of squish and swosh,
Ezra Pound.

OTHERS

Ford Madox Ford, "Literary Portraits – XXXIX. Mr W. B. Yeats and His New Poems"

Outlook 33 (6 June 1914): 783–4.

Ford Madox Ford (1873–1939) was founder of *The English Review* and *The Transatlantic Review*, author of *The Good Soldier*, and numerous works of fiction and poetry. Ford himself was pilloried by John Felton in *The New Age* as being more than a little self-important:

> A ponderous egoism emerging from unhappy youthful surroundings,
> He rambles disconsolately through interminable pages,
> Loosing himself in a multiplicity of irrelevant details.
> He is redeemed from some earlier banalities
> But lies forever imbedded in the yielding mud of impressionism. (297)

I want poets to be natural creatures; and they very seldom are natural creatures. And I suppose why I regarded Mr. Yeats with so little respect for many years was simply that he seemed to me exceedingly affected. I don't mean to say that he seemed to me to be personally affected, since I never, until quite lately, came into personal contact with Mr. Yeats. But, from the 'nineties onward, Mr. Yeats really did seem to dispense across this city of London a sort of aura that I found exceedingly irritating. That may have been mere jealousy, of course; but I hardly think it was jealousy, since Mr. Yeats was always so immeasurably more distinguished than myself that I might just as well have been jealous of Sappho.

But certainly the thought that Mr. Yeats was somewhere about, probably leaning on a mantelpiece with his face to the ceiling, irritated me exceedingly. I didn't like his confounded point of view. I hated and do still hate, people who poke about among legends and insist on the charms of remote islands. And all that I had read of Mr. Yeats's work was *The Countess Kathleen*, which seemed to have to do with legend, and a poem which began, "I will arise and go now." This always seemed to me to be particularly irritating. How, I used to ask myself, could that gentleman get to Innesfree, supposing he were then lying down, without rising? And why then should he state that he was going to arise? You will observe that this was a prose-impressionist irritation. The prose-impressionist, if he has to deal with a gentleman going out of a door in an ordinary way, does not say that the gentleman walked to the door, starting with his right foot, put his hand upon the handle, turned the handle, drew the door towards him, and stepped across the mat. No, the prose-impressionist treats the matter somewhat as follows: "Mr. Humphrey said he must be going. When the door closed upon him Inez threw herself into a chair and wept convulsively." So, Innesfree being the centre of Mr. Yeats's poem, and I being, presumably even at that early age, a prose-impressionist, should have preferred Mr. Yeats's poem to have run:

At Innesfree there is a public-house;
They board you well for ten and six a week.
The mutton is not good, but you can eat
Their honey. I am going there to take
A week or so of holiday to-morrow.

There might have been in addition some details about the landscape and whether the fishing was good. That was what I wanted in a poem of those days; that is what I still want in a poem. And the Mr. Yeats of the 'nineties seemed to be always – when he wasn't leaning against a mantelpiece – reclining by the side of some lake or other, and then arising and going to some other lake. He seemed, in short, to be self-conscious about his attitude.

E.E., from "The New England Poets See a Ghost"

***New Yorker*, 28 March 1925: 16.**

The *New Yorker* does not identify the author of these parodies. The parodies here, at moments, have fairly specific targets. The parody of Robert Frost refers to "The Death of the Hired Man"; the ending of the Amy Lowell parody refers to her "Patterns."

THE NEW ENGLAND POETS SEE A GHOST

ROBERT FROST

SHE sat beside the window, sewing. "John."
 "Well, Mary?"
 "Do you know, to-night's a year
That Henry Bannockburn, our hired man, died."
"A Year? It seems no more than yesterday.
Time flies."
 "Oh, what a fearful night that was:
The wind was wailing at our door; the moon
Was roving through the sky like some lost woman.
Then suddenly we saw the barnlight flicker
And finally go out. You hurried … *John!*"
"Well, Mary?"
 "*What's that light there on the stair?*"
"I don't see any light!"
 "Just look, it's moving,
And coming near us!"
 "Mary, are you mad?"
"John, it's the ghost of Henry Bannockburn;
His eyes are staring just as when he lay
Across the barn-floor. *John!* I feel his hand
Upon my neck! …"
 "There, there, you're all right, dear;
It's only John. Here, drink this glass of water."
She shuddered, drank the water, smoothed her dress,
And then resumed her sewing at the window.

EDWIN ARLINGTON ROBINSON

THERE isn't any doubt about the matter
At all. If you believe in transmigration,
Well then, so much the worse for you. But listen:
Why should a soul revisit earth in such
A vaporous state? You see the fallacy.
Metempsychosis merely means that death
Sunders the spirit from the flesh and lets
The spirit enter in a new-born body.
In other words, the spirit's never free:
It leaves one man and goes into the next,
So that it couldn't ever get the chance
To hound us in this histrionic manner.
A ghost (you might have guessed it for yourself)
Is purely the creation of the brain,
The wilful vision of the psychic eye.
It isn't even an hallucination, –
Strange how some clever people think it that.
Most probably you did the man a wrong:
The craving for confession makes you conjure
His image up before you – thus your yearning
For martyrdom is sated by the pain
Of guilt that seizes you …
To put it briefly,
We never see a ghost unless we want to.
Figure that out and then I'll tell you more.

Amy Lowell

THE sky was coldly blue with many grim stars gleaming boldly. I was seated in my garden, wearing my new velvet gown – only $59.50 – when I heard a weird sound repeated: *Clank-clank!* I started up hastily and saw that a misty form had appeared, draped in a swarm of flowing white veils that fluttered about eerily and escaped into space. Again I heard: *Clank-clank!* Looking further I saw that the form moved wearily because of a thick chain that was bound to its feet.

Clank-clank! Ah, the pain that passed over its dim face. It seemed to petition me for a word before it breathed its last sigh. But how could I know who the apparition was? Perhaps it was the ghost of someone who had wreathed the flowers of my garden about her head in hours long gone. *Clank-clank!* came the drawn rattle of the chains dragging away. I decided there was no use lagging on the bench any longer, so I gracefully glided to the house in my new velvet gown.

Just before entering I glanced at the sky and noticed that all the constellations danced there save Saturn. Dog-gone it! what is Saturn for? – E.E.

Hart Crane, "America's Plutonic Ecstasies" and "OF AN EVENING PULLING OFF A LITTLE EXPERIENCE (with the english language)" (1923)

In *Complete Poems of Hart Crane*, ed. Marc Simon (New York: Liveright, 2000), 157, 179–80.

Hart Crane (1899–1932) is the author of *The Bridge* and *White Buildings*. The first poem was originally published in the little magazine *S4N*, which also published the work of e.e. cummings; the second was not published in Crane's lifetime.

AMERICA'S PLUTONIC ECSTASIES

WITH HOMAGE TO E. E. CUMMINGS

preferring laxatives to wine
all america is saying
"how are my bowels today?" and
feeling them in every way and
peering
for the one goat (unsqueezable)
that kicked out long ago –

or, even thinking
of something – Oh!
Unbelievably – Oh!
HEADY! – those aromatic LEMONS!
that make your colored syrup fairly
PULSE! – yes, PULSE!

the nation's lips are thin and fast
with righteousness. Yet if
memory serves there is still
catharsis from gin-daisies as well as
maiden-hair ferns, and the BRONX
doesn't stink at all

These
and other natural grammarians are ab-
so-loot-lee necessary
for a FREE-ER PASSAGE – (NOT
to india, o ye faithful,
but a little BACK DOOR DIGNITY)

OF AN EVENING

PULLING OFF A LITTLE EXPERIENCE

(with the english language)

by
NIGHTS
EEEEEECCCUUUMMMMMMIIINNGGGSSS (for short) 69

wrists web rythms [*sic*]
and the poke-
,dot smile;
of Genevive
talks
back

i KNew,kneW my feet
?go on) were an applesauce
part
of yoU belching POCHETTEkeepit
upyou s,uede
ballbearing

celery = grin

remind of-of la guerre

UM
Trimvirate (creamed dancing bitches)

corking with Helene, (exactly you make)
my perpendicularly crowdedPOCKets

smilepoke

„besides: which
April has
a
word to say: classy)eh(!
while blundering fumbiguts gather accu
rate little, O-SO masturbations in /
to
fractions of heaven. Hold tight bless
worms trilling rimple flock to
sad iron

goats of
love-
semi-colon
piping (dash)

Margaret Widdemer, Selections from *A Tree with a Bird in It: A Symposium of Contemporary American Poets on Being Shown a Pear-Tree on Which Sat a Grackle*

(New York: Harcourt, Brace and Co., 1922).

A prolific author, Widdemer (1884–1978) won the 1919 Pulitzer Prize for poetry for *The Old Road to Paradise* (sharing the award with Carl Sandburg's *Corn Huskers*). Her 1964 memoir, *Golden Friends I Had*, gives a sprightly tour of her meetings with various modernists. Amy Lowell is one of the heroes of this book; Ezra Pound, decidedly not – a visceral dislike particularly aimed at the way Pound claimed and transmitted his knowledge.

Widdemer gives the following as the premise for the poems that appear in *A Tree with a Bird in it*:

> A little while since, I had the fortune to live in a house, outside of whose windows there grew a pear-tree. On the branches of this tree lived a green bird of indeterminate nature. I do not know what his real name was, but the name, to quote our great exemplar Lewis Carroll, by which his name was *called* was the Grackle. He seemed perfectly willing to be addressed thus, and accordingly was.
>
> Aside from watching the Pear-Tree and the Grackle, my other principal occupation that winter was watching the Poetry Society of America now and then at its monthly meetings. It occurred to me finally to invite such members of it as cared to come, following many good examples, to an outdoor symposium under the tree.
>
> The result follows.
>
> MARGARET WIDDEMER.
>
> P. S. The tree died.

AMY LOWELL

(Fixing her glasses firmly on the rest of the Poetry Society in a way which makes them with difficulty refrain from writhing.)

OISEAURIE

Glunk!
I toss my heels up to my head …
That was a bird I heard say glunk
As I walked statelily through my extensive, expensive English country estate
In a pink brocade with silver buttons, a purple passementerie cut with panniers, a train, and faced with watered silk:
But it
Is dead now!
(The bird)
Probably putrescent
And green …
I scrabble my toes …
Glunk!

ROBERT FROST

(Rather nervously, retreating with haste in the wake of Mr. Robinson as soon as he had finished.)

THE BIRD MISUNDERSTOOD

There was a grackle sat on our old pear tree –
Don't ask me why – I never did really know;
But he made my wife and me feel, for really the very first time
We were out in the actual country, hindering things to grow;

It gave us rather a queer feeling to hear the grackle grackle,
But when it got to be winter time he got up and went thence
And now we shall never know, though we watch the tree till April,
Whether his curious crying ever made song or sense.

CARL SANDBURG

(Striking from time to time a few notes on a mouth-organ, with a wonderful effect of human brotherhood which does not quite include the East.)

CHICAGO MEMORIES

Grackles, trees –
I been thinkin' 'bout 'em all: I been thinkin' they're all right:
Nothin' much – Gosh, nothin' much against God, even.
God made little apples, a hobo sang in Kankakee,
Shattered apples, I picked you up under a tree, red wormy apples, I ate you
. . . .
That lets God out.
There were three green birds on the tree, there were three wailing cats
against a green dawn . . . .
'Gene Field[46] sang, "The world is full of a number of things,"
'Gene Field said, "When they caught me I was living in a tree . . . ."
'Gene Field said everything in Chicago of the eighties.
Now he's dead, I say things, say 'em well, too . . . .
'Gene Field . . . . back in the lost days, back in the eighties,
Singing, colyumning . . . . 'Gene Field . . . . forgotten . . . .
Back in Arkansaw there was a green bird, too,
I can remember how he sang, back in the lost days, back in the eighties.
Uncle Yon Swenson under the tree chewing slowly, slowly . . . .
Memories, memories!
There are only trees now, no 'Gene, no eighties
Gray cats, I can feel your fur in my heart . . . .
Green grackle, I remember now,
Back in the lost days, back in the eighties
The cat ate you.

EZRA POUND

(Mailed disdainfully by him from anywhere but America, and read prayerfully by a committee from Chicago.)

RAINUV: A ROMANTIC BALLAD FROM THE EARLY BASQUE

. . . . so then naturally
This Count Rainuv I speak of
(Certainly I did not expect you would ever have heard of him;
You are American poets, aren't you?
That's rather awful . . . . I am the only American poet

I could ever tolerate . . . . well, sniff and pass . . . .)
Therefore . . . . well, I knew Rainuv.
(My P. G. course at Penn, you'll remember;
A little Anglo-Saxon and Basuto,
But Provencal, mostly. Most don't go in for that . . . .
You haven't, of course . . . . What, no Provencal?
Well, of course, I know
Rather more than you do. That's my specialty.
But then – *Omnis Gallia est divisa*[47] – but no matter.
Not fit, perhaps you'd say, that, to be quoted
Before ladies . . . . That's your rather amusing prudishness . . . .)
Well, this Rainuv, then,
A person with a squint like a flash
Of square fishes ... being rather worse than most
Of the usual *literati*
Said, being carried off by desire of boasting
That he knew all the mid-Victorians
Et ab lor bos amics:[48]
(He thought it was something to boast of.)

We'll say he said he smoked with Tennyson,
And – deeper pit – *pax vobiscum*[49] — went to vespers
With Adelaide Anne Procter;[50] helped Bob Browning elope
With Elizabeth and her lapdog (said it bit him)
Said he was the first man Blake told
All about the angels in a pear-tree at Peckham Rye
Blake drew them for him, he said; they were grackles, not angels
(Blake's not a mid-Victorian, but you don't know better)
So ... we come, being slightly irritated, to facing him down.
"... And George Eliot?" we ask lightly.
"*Roomed with him*," nodded Rainuv confidently,
"*At college*! ... Ah, *bos amic! bos amic*![51]
Rainuv is a king to you ...
Three centuries from now (you dead and messy) men whispering insolently
(Eeni meeni mini mo ...) will boast that their great-grand-uncles
Were kicked by me in passing ...

II. Fiction

Fiction's parodic interventions differed noticeably from those of music, visual art, and poetry. Unlike the way they represented the other arts and genres in this book, parodists did not understand "modern fiction" to be imitable as a genre, the way "modern poetry" and "modern painting" were. It was understood to be composed of and by individuals, and was not caricatured as springing from a movement or series of movements. This is not to say that modern writers did not theorize about modern fiction as a whole – Woolf's "Mr. Bennett and Mrs. Brown" and Eliot's "Ulysses, Order and Myth" are not lone examples. But, while writing about modern fiction by its authors was at times proscriptive, these essays had a single signature. Fiction had no group manifestos, and no consequent parodies of the methods of publicity, theory-based practice, and groupthink they implied. As well, fiction had a different relationship to time and currency than did poetry or visual art. Parodies of fiction did not tend to show up in daily newspapers (parodies of prose take up more space, after all, than a quarter-column send-up of a work that had just appeared in *Poetry*), appearing in magazines instead, or, often, for the first time in *collections* of writing by a parodist.

Perhaps because modern works of fiction were less connected to groups and not as time bound, parodic interactions with them tended to limit themselves to the stylistic qualities and the typical plots and subject matter of these individual works, rather than also directly reaching to the larger social context that gave this material serious attention (of course, to parody a writer's typical subject matter was an indirect way to address modernism's social context). The targets of parodic writing tended to be the difficulty, sexual content, and realism of their target works, which parodists tended to see not as natural, but as mannered and artificial. Writers accomplished their parodies through some typical means. Some of this was done through recontextualizing to a more pragmatic context (as is also seen in the modernist methodologies section of this book). More typically, they engaged in distorted repetition of their source work's perceived dominant effects – if a little prolixity is good, double the amount should be, well, not to put too fine a point on it, perhaps, better.

Finally, many of these parodies did their work through compression. Of course, some of this compression was pragmatic – one could not profitably write a novel the length of a Henry James novel to parody Henry James. But more than this, a swift parody was a way of arguing that the dominant and characteristic effects of the source material were a trick – they were not *earned*. Parodies of fiction were always shortened versions of their sources, and so they tended to schematize the typical attributes of the source material – in the parody, things proceeded much more swiftly, with much more melodramatic shifts in register and context. The parody was all about compression, which was understood as getting down to the essentials of the prose, what the prose amounted to once its decorative scaffolding had been removed.

J.G.T. [James Thurber], "More Authors Cover the Snyder Trial"

***New Yorker*, 7 May 1927: 69.**

James Grover Thurber (1894–1961) was one of the great humorists of the twentieth century. An author and cartoonist, he began his career as a reporter for various newspapers, including the *Columbus Dispatch*, the *Chicago Tribune*, and the *New York Evening Post*. In 1927 he began his career as an editor with the *New Yorker*, where his witty cartoons and prose established a devoted public.

In the selection that follows, Thurber uses as his subject the sensational 1927 trial of Ruth Snyder and Judd Gray. Ruth Snyder's husband had been found murdered, and Snyder argued that the death had been the result of a break-in. Her story was suspicious, however, and as the investigation went on it was discovered that Snyder had a lover, Judd Gray. Under some tricky questioning she and Gray betrayed each other, were arrested, tried, found guilty of murder, and eventually electrocuted.

I

Who Did We, Did Did We, We Did, Says Miss Stein!

By Gertrude Stein

This is a trial. This is quite a trial. I am on trial. They are on trial. Who is on trial?

I can tell you how it is. I can tell you have told you will tell you how it is.

There is a man. There is a woman. There is not a man. There would have been a man. There was a man. There were two men. There is one man. There is a woman where is a woman is a man.

He says he did. He says he did not. She says she did. She says she did not. She says he did. He says she did. She says they did. He says they did. He says they did not. She says they did not. I'll say they did.

II

Joyce Finds Socksocking Is Big Element in Murder Case!

By James Joyce

Trial regen by trialholden Queenscountycourthouse with tumpetty taptap mid socksocking with sashweights by jackals. In socksocking, the sashwiring goes: guggengagglegoggsnukkk … To corsetsale is to alibi is to meetinlovenkillenlove. *Rehad des arbah sed drahab!* Not a quart of papa's booze had poison booze vor the killparty for the snugglesnuggle …

III

Out a Mile, Writes Cobb!

By Ty Cobb

Stealing home from a bridge game is a clever stunt, if properly worked. But it should never be followed by the hit-and-run play.

It's not like the Cry Baby bandits – four bawls and a walk to Sing Sing. Snyder merely hit into a double play and was out a mile, Syracuse to New York to Syracuse.

K.D., "When Helen Furr Got Gay with Harold Moos: A Narrative Written in the Now Popular Manner of Gertrude Stein"

***Vanity Fair*, October 1923: 37.**

The identity of K.D. is unknown. While most parodies of Gertrude Stein went to her *Tender Buttons*, here the target is Stein's *Three Lives*, playing with that book's dense psychological entanglements and essentializing, and its repetitions of plot, diction, and syntax.

When Georgine Skeen went away to stay two months with her brother, and left Helen Furr at the place they had been regularly living when they had been so gay there together, Helen Furr went on being gay there. She was quite gay and a little more gay than she had been when she and Georgine Skeen had been gay there together. This was because she received visits regularly from Harold Moos. Harold Moos was not a gay man but he was a very dark man, and a very heavy man and a very bald man, and of all the regularly dark men and the regularly heavy men and the regularly bald men who sat regularly there then with Helen Furr, Harold Moos was the darkest man and heaviest man and the baldest man who sat regularly there with her.

Harold Moos was living regularly in the same place where Helen Furr and Georgine Skeen were living when they were being gay there. Harold was cultivating painting still-life, which was very heavy cultivating then. He was not at all gay, because he was cultivating still-life. It was not very gay still-life, it was not even such gay still-life as he was cultivating when he first sat regularly with Miss Skeen and Miss Furr when they were living regularly there then. The still-life which Harold Moos cultivated was quite pleasant when he first regularly cultivated it.

It was melons!

And it was just a shade gay when he was first painting it in that place where Helen Furr was being gay in all the big and little ways she had of being gay, but when he had been painting it three or four weeks it was not so gay as it had been when he was first painting it. It did not have such a gay smell as when he was first painting it there then. When Harold Moos' still-life did not smell so very gay he would go and sit regularly with the dark men and the heavy men and the bald men who sat with Helen Furr while she was being gay alone while Georgine

Skeen had gone away to stay two months with her brother. Helen Furr was very gay whenever Harold Moos came to sit regularly with her.

She was always gay when dark men or heavy men or bald men, or men that were heavy and not so dark and bald, sat regularly with her, but she was more gay when Harold Moos sat regularly with her than when other dark and heavy and bald men sat with her, and she was very much more gay than she had been when Georgine Skeen was living there then.

Helen Furr knew all the big ways of being gay and all the little ways of being gay and she was gay in all the ways that dark men and heavy men and bald men, who sit regularly with girls, like in girls who are being gay. She knew all the old ways of being gay, and she thought up lots of new ways of being gay and particularly ways that Harold Moos would like to see her use in being gay. When Harold Moos, who was not at all gay, would come to sit regularly with her in the place where she was living, she would go up behind him and put her hands over his eyes and say "Guess who this is!" and would be very gay there then.

And she would be gay in talking baby-talk to him then, and she would be gay with a Southern accent and be very gay then, and she would pull Harold Moos' chair away from him when he would be sitting down and would be very gay regularly in all the big and little ways there are of being gay with dark and heavy and bald men like Harold Moos.

And she would straighten his tie and be very gay then, and she would pick threads off his coat and be very gay then and she was often being gay in putting on his hat, and always being gay in knocking it off.

One day, when Helen Furr was being gay and Harold Moos was feeling very dark and very heavy and very bald and not at all gay they were married – regularly there then. Harold Moos, who was not gay then, thought Helen Furr would not be so gay when they were married regularly, but she went on being gay in all the big and little ways she had of being gay with dark and heavy and bald men before she had married Harold Moos. She could not think up any new way of being gay, so she kept on being gay in her old ways. Every day she would be gay in going up behind Harold Moos and putting her hands over his eyes and saying "Guess who this is!," and she would be gay in baby-talk then, and she would be gay in lisping then, and she would straighten his tie, being gay, and she would pick white threads off the collar of his coat, being gay.

But she could not think up any new way of being gay.

One day, when they had been married regularly for a year, she again went up behind Harold Moos and put her hand over his eyes, saying "Guess who this is!" Then Harold Moos, who was not feeling regularly gay, said to Helen Furr: "I have been thinking up a way of making you less gay and of making myself more regularly gay and in a *wholly new way*; and, with that end in view, I hereby hit you three times regularly on the head with this walking stick – One! !?x, Two x?!, Three ? x ! – and, now that I have regularly brained you, I already feel a little more gay; but, in order to make myself regularly *extraordinarily* gay, I am going out to subscribe regularly to the gayest magazine in the world, which (if you had not been knocked regularly senseless) you would know is *Vanity Fair*."

E.B. White, "Is a Train"

***New Yorker*, 27 October 1934: 26.**

E.B. White (1899–1985) was a central contributor to the *New Yorker*, as well as the author of *Charlotte's Web* and other popular children's books. In addition to collections of essays, he is the author, with James Thurber, of *Is Sex Necessary?* By 2009, his reworking of William Strunk's *The Elements of Style* had sold over ten million copies.

IS A TRAIN

(THE STRANGE SYSTEMIC RECESSION OF A PUNCTUAL LYRICIST IN A RAILROAD STATION WAITING TO MEET NOT TO MEET GERTRUDE STEIN)

One november two november three no trumps is
not a rose. The train the train
that I would meet is one that I have known alas
and neither rain nor gloom of sleet
nor one november too too long is
farther to my wish to go as
soft as tracings in the snow as white and happy
on the hart as where from thicket
cold did start the hunting and the sparrowfoot
in token of the annual notion of love
and to my love devotion to seek to find to seek to
find in all the hampers of the mind the
four november five november wind the wind
the wind that blew so long ago and must still blow
(does still blow) the sound of this the waiting room the
dull the populated gloom the benches curved
to the sacro-iliac
curved to the under knee,
to fit to fit the sacro-iliac
down to a sunless me,
and the surflike noise of the singing terminal
the sound in the wind that is soft and germinal

the people waiting the waiting
people the waiting room and the circled gloom
the hope of journeys still unshaken and all the
trains that have not been taken.

One november two november three november
four november
Stein
Stein
Stein.

Stella Gibbons, from *Cold Comfort Farm*

(London, New York: Longmans, Green and Co., 1932), 31–4, 38–9, 43–4, 92–3.

Stella Gibbons (1902–89) was slightly known as a minor poet until the publication of her early novel *Cold Comfort Farm*. The run-away success of this work, which parodies Thomas Hardy, Mary Webb, and the portentous symbolism and simmering sexuality of D.H. Lawrence's writing, was not even partially matched by the almost thirty books that she wrote afterwards. In the excerpts that follow, I have kept the asterisks that Gibbons used to signal the beginning of what she considered an especially purple passage.

Dawn crept over the Downs like a sinister white animal, followed by the snarling cries of a wind eating its way between the black boughs of the thorns. The wind was the furious voice of this sluggish animal light that was baring the dormers and mullions and scullions of Cold Comfort Farm.

The farm was crouched on a bleak hillside, whence its fields, fanged with flints, dropped steeply to the village of Howling a mile away. Its stables and outhouses were built in the shape of a rough octangle surrounding the farmhouse itself, which was built in the shape of a rough triangle. The left point of the triangle abutted on the farthest point of the octangle, which was formed by the cowsheds, which lay parallel with the big barn. The outhouses were built of roughcast stone, with thatched roofs, while the farm itself was built partly of local flint, set in cement, and partly of some stone brought at great trouble and enormous personal expense from Perthshire.

The farmhouse was a long, low building, two-storied in parts. Other parts of it were three-storied. Edward the Sixth had originally owned it in the form of a shed in which he housed his swineherds, but he had grown tired of it, and had had it rebuilt in Sussex clay. Then he pulled it down. Elizabeth had rebuilt it, with a good many chimneys in one way and another. The Charleses had let it alone; but William and Mary had pulled it down again, and George the First had rebuilt it. George the Second, however, burned it down. George the Third added another wing. George the Fourth pulled it down again.

By the time England began to develop that magnificent blossoming of trade and imperial expansion which fell to her lot under Victoria, there was not much of the original building left, save the tradition that it had always been there. It crouched, like a beast about to spring, under the bulk of Mockuncle Hill. Like ghosts embedded in brick and stone, the architectural variations of each period through which it had passed were mute history. It was known locally as "The King's Whim."

The front door of the farm faced a perfectly inaccessible ploughed field at the back of the house; it had been the whim of Red Raleigh Starkadder, in 1835, to have it so; and so the family always used to come in by the back door, which abutted on the general yard facing the cowsheds. A long corridor ran half-way through the house on the second storey and then stopped. One could not get into the attics at all. It was all very awkward.

... Growing with the viscuous [*sic*] light that was invading the sky, there came the solemn, tortured-snake voice of the sea, two miles away, falling in sharp folds upon the mirror-expanses of the beach.

Under the ominous bowl of the sky a man was ploughing the sloping field immediately below the farm, where the flints shone bone-sharp and white in the growing light. The ice-cascade of the wind leaped over him, as he guided the plough over the flint runnels. Now and again he called roughly to his team:

"Upidee, Travail! Ho, there, Arsenic! Jug-jug!" But for the most part he worked in silence, and silent were his team. The light showed no more of his face than a grey expanse of flesh, expressionless as the land he ploughed, from which looked out two sluggish eyes.

Every now and again, when he came to the corner of the field and was forced to tilt the scranlet of his plough almost on to its axle to make the turn, he glanced up at the farm where it squatted on the gaunt shoulder of the hill, and something like a possessive gleam shone in his dull eyes. But he only turned his team again, watching the crooked passage of the scranlet through the yeasty earth, and muttered: "Hola, Arsenic! Belay there, Travail!" while the bitter light wanned into full day.

Because of the peculiar formation of the outhouses surrounding the farm, the light was always longer in reaching the yard than the rest of the house. Long after the sunlight was shining through the cobwebs on uppermost windows of the old house the yard was in damp blue shadow.

It was in shadow now, but sharp gleams sprang from the ranged milk-buckets along the ford-piece outside the cowshed.

Leaving the house by the back door, you came up sharply against a stone wall running right across the yard, and turning abruptly, at right angles, just before it reached the shed where the bull was housed, and running down to the gate leading out into the ragged garden where mallows, dog's-body and wild turnip were running riot. The bull's shed abutted upon the right corner of the dairy, which faced the cowsheds. The cowsheds faced the house, but the back door faced the bull's shed. From here a long-roofed barn extended the whole length of the octangle until it reached the front door of the house. Here it took a quick turn, and ended. The dairy was awkwardly placed; it had been a thorn in the side of old Fig Starkadder, the last owner of the farm, who had died three years ago. The dairy overlooked the front door, in face of the extreme point of the triangle which formed the ancient buildings of the farmhouse.

From the dairy a wall extended which formed the right-hand boundary of the octangle, joining the bull's shed and the pig-pens at the extreme end of the right point of the triangle. A staircase, put in to make it more difficult, ran parallel with the octangle, half-way round the yard, against the wall which led down to the garden gate.

The spurt and regular ping! of milk against metal came from the reeking interior of the sheds. The bucket was pressed between Adam Lambsbreath's knees, and his head was pressed deep into the flank of Feckless, the big Jersey. His gnarled hands mechanically stroked the teat, while a low crooning, mindless as the Down wind itself came from his lips.

He was asleep. He had been awake all night, wandering in thought over the indifferent bare shoulders of the Downs after his wild bird, his little flower …

Judith had crossed the muck and rabble of the yard, and now entered the house by the back door.

In the large kitchen, which occupied most of the middle of the house, a sullen fire burned, the smoke of which wavered up the blackened walls and over the deal table, darkened by age and dirt, which was roughly set for a meal. A snood full of coarse porridge hung over the fire, and standing with one arm resting upon the high mantel, looking moodily down into the heaving contents of the snood, was a tall young man whose riding-boots were splashed with mud to the thigh, and whose coarse linen shirt was open to his waist. The firelight lit up his diaphragm muscles as they heaved slowly in rough rhythm with the porridge.

He looked up as Judith entered, and gave a short, defiant laugh, but said nothing. Judith slowly crossed over until she stood by his side. She was as tall as he. They stood in silence, she staring at him, and he down into the secret crevasses of the porridge.

"Well, mother mine," he said at last, "here I am, you see. I said I would be in time for breakfast, and I have kept my word."

His voice had a low, throaty, animal quality, a sneering warmth that wound a velvet ribbon of sexuality over the outward coarseness of the man.

Judith's breath came in long shudders. She thrust her arms deeper into her shawl. The porridge gave an ominous, leering heave; it might almost have been endowed with life, so uncannily did its movements keep pace with the human passions that throbbed above it.

"Cur," said, Judith, levelly, at last. "Coward! Liar! Libertine! Who were you with last night? Moll at the mill or Violet at the vicarage? Or Ivy, perhaps, at the ironmongery? Seth – my son …" Her deep, dry voice quivered, but she whipped it back, and her next words flew out at him like a lash.

"Do you want to break my heart?"

"Yes," said Seth, with an elemental simplicity.

The porridge boiled over.

Seth, sitting by the fire, was growing tired of looking at his postcards, which were a three-year-old gift from the vicar's son, with whom he occasionally went poaching. He knew them all by now. Meriam, the hired girl, would not be in until after dinner. When she came, she would avoid his eyes, and tremble and weep.

He laughed insolently, triumphantly. Undoing another button of his shirt he lounged out across the yard to the shed where Big Business, the bull, was imprisoned in darkness.

Laughing softly, Seth struck the door of the shed.

And as though answering the deep call of male to male, the bull uttered a loud, tortured bellow that rose undefeated through the dead sky that brooded above the farm.

Seth undid yet another button, and lounged away.

Just as the kettle boiled and she darted forward to rescue it, a shadow darkened the door and there stood Reuben, looking at Flora's gallant preparations with an expression of stricken amazement mingled with fury.

"Hullo," said Flora, getting her blow in first. "I feel sure you must be Reuben. I'm Flora Poste, your cousin, you know. How do you do? I'm so glad to see somebody has come in for some tea. Do sit down. Do you take milk? (No sugar … of course … or do you? I do, but most of my friends don't.)"

***The man's big body, etched menacingly against the bleak light that stabbed in from the low windows, did not move. His thoughts swirled like a beck in spate behind the sodden grey furrows of his face. A woman … Blast! Blast! Come to wrest away from him the land whose love fermented in his veins like slow yeast. She-woman. Young, soft-coloured, insolent. His gaze was suddenly edged by a fleshy taint. Break her. Break. Keep and hold and hold fast the land. The land, the iron furrows of frosted earth under the rain-lust, the fecund spears of rain, the swelling, slow burst of seed-sheaths, the slow smell of cows and cry of cows, the trampling bride-pride of the bull in his hour. All his, his …

"Will you have some bread and butter?" asked Flora, handing him a cup of tea. "Oh, never mind your boots. Adam can sweep the mud up afterwards. Do come in."

Defeated, Reuben came in.

Dorothy Parker, "Once More Mother Hubbard – As Told by F. Scott Fitzgerald"

***Life*, 7 July 1921.**

Dorothy Parker (1893–1967) was a poet, fiction writer, critic, and screenwriter. What unifies her work is her acerbic satire, and a genius for the one-liner. A founding member of the Algonquin Round Table, she contributed to Franklin P. Adams's "The Conning Tower," and was associated with *Vanity Fair* and, later, the *New Yorker*. Her politics eventually landed her on the Hollywood blacklist. Amory Blaine is the protagonist of Fitzgerald's *This Side of Paradise*; Rosalind Connage is his primary love interest.

Rosalind rested her nineteen-year-old elbows on her nineteen-year-old knees. All that you could see of her, above the polished sides of the nineteen-year-old bathtub, was her bobbed, curly hair and her disturbing gray eyes. A cigarette drooped lazily from the spoiled curves of her nineteen-year-old mouth.

Amory leaned against the door, softly whistling "Coming Back to Nassau Hall" through his teeth. Her young perfection kindled a curious fire in him.

"Tell me about you," he said, carelessly.

He knew about her, of course. She was famous in their generation. Of dances, football games, and house parties, she was the uncrowned queen. It was her good luck that, to date, no one had crowned her.

"There's nothing to tell," she answered wearily, lighting another cigarette. It was a pleasure to watch the movement of her supple young wrist as she tossed the burning match on the floor. "The usual thing – fired from three or four schools – I forget their names. Finished with a year at Bedford. Then a round of dances, clinics, teas, back rooms, motor trips, prize fights – and through them all a clamor of dull, desirous men telling me how beautiful I am. I am a riot, aren't I? In a one-piece bathing suit nobody can tie me. Father gives me ten-thousand a year to dress on, and I manage to break about even on my crap-shooting. All I care about is knocking the conventions for a goal. I want to live – to live –"

There was a gentle cough, and Mrs. Hubbard appeared apologetically at the door.

"Rosalind, dear," she interrupted, softly, "I think someone ought to feed Prince. He seems to be –"

"Mother, what an old idiot you are," said the girl quietly. She was youth and beauty.

"When I was young," began Mrs. Hubbard, tentatively.

Splash! The washcloth caught her just below the ear. Amory found himself wondering, while he watched Rosalind's young gesture as she threw it, if it were possible for her to make an ungraceful motion.

"I'd better be getting Prince something –"

Mrs. Hubbard's voice trailed vaguely away down the hall.

Rosalind looked languorously down at the cigarette between her nineteen-year-old fingers.

"I was made for love," she murmured.

Amory looked at her through half-closed eyes.

"Could you love me?" he asked idly. It was time to try his line.

There was a soft plashing of water as she shrugged her shoulders.

"How do I know?" she answered. "I haven't even kissed you yet."

Again the gentle cough, preceding Mrs. Hubbard's appearance.

"Isn't that too bad," she said smiling uncertainly. "There isn't a thing in the house –"

"Oh, damn," yawned Rosalind.

Christopher Ward, "The Blind Booby," in *Twisted Tales*

(New York: Henry Holt and Co., 1924), 55–64.

The target of this story, Carl van Vechten (1880–1964), was a friend of Gertrude Stein and patron and habitué of the Harlem Renaissance. Van Vechten was as famous for his lifestyle as for his prose. His version of the Harlem Renaissance, seen in particular in his 1926 novel *Nigger Heaven*, was heavy on violence and primitivism.

THE BLIND BOOBY

By CARL FAR FETCHTEN

I

"Father," said Rollo Prunes, "Will you tell me the story of my life, so that all these gentle readers may know about it and be prepared for the very whimsical adventures, I am about to have?"

Certainly, my son, said his father, a portly man with a high bald forehead and a high-balled nose, but before I do so, let me suggest that, when speaking, you discard quotation marks. It is so much cooler without them these hot days and it is considered very whimsical to omit them. Besides which, your readers will generally be unable to distinguish between conversation and narrative, which contributes much to their enjoyment.

Very well, father, said Rollo, I shall do as you wish, though I feel that it makes my remarks seem very bald, if not immodest.

When your mother died – please pay attention, boy, I am speaking –

I beg your pardon, father, said Rollo, but unless you use the words, said George Prunes or his father continued or something like that, I really don't know whether you are speaking or the author is writing.

When your mother died, said George Prunes, she made me promise to send you to college. But I got even with your sainted mother by sending you to one of those little insectarian colleges, which has turned you out the hopeless dub you are.

Now, in order that the education –

I beg your pardon, father, said Rollo, but this thing of beginning a new paragraph without quotes confuses me. Are you still speaking?

I am, said George Prunes, and in order not to confuse you further I shall continue speaking without pause or punctuation or capitals until the end of the chapter i am now about to give you a chance to get a real education i have engaged an ex-convict confidence man and divekeeper for your tutor his name is paul moody but no relation to mr sankeys old partner he will lead you into temptation teach the young idea to shoot craps bring up the child in the broadway it should go and generally play the devil with your morals if you have any you must never look me in the face again until you have the primrose path of dalliance trod to the entire satisfaction of the author now as I am getting out of breath ishallhavetorunmywordsalltogethergooddaymyson.

II

Harold's apartment consisted of several rooms furnished with a number of books, including "The Triumph of the Nut," because, when you begin mentioning real names, you might as well give yourself a little hand-out as to name "Alice in Wonderland," or "The Way of All Flesh," which really don't need the advertisement.

Also there was a valet by the name of —— (this space to let to any really good valet out of a job). His chief duty was to scrub Rollo's back, when he bathed, and make him blush.

Rollo found his wardrobe well equipped with clothes by Snooks, hats by Bunyip, shoes by Bartin & Bartin. After his bath, he put on a beautiful dressing gown, with the name of an English firm on the label, which name will be furnished on request.

III

In a room a man and a woman were sitting, but they are really unimportant as compared with the room. It was a charming room, containing a few books, among which one may mention "The Triumph of the Nut," a volume of exceedingly clever parodies by a well-known author. It might as well be understood, once and for all, that no one else in our line of business, to wit, literature, is entitled to mention in this Shopping Guide.

Other articles present were a handsome set of Mah Jongg at $65., a garden umbrella, striped orange and black, price $25., a genuine needlepoint chair for $167., a table lamp, No. 7026, at $10.50, a pair of wrought-iron candlesticks 16 in. high, for $15.50, Chinese Foo-dog book-ends at $25.50, a gay little lettuce green bowl at $2.25 and many others, too numerous to mention, suitable for wedding presents and Christmas gifts, all of which are purchasable through Our Shopping Service.

In the genuine needlepoint chair, sat a lady with a permanent wave and a temporary complexion. Her jaw was square or, perchance, oblong. She wore a gown by Gollie and a hat by Goshe. She was addicted to cigarette smoking in excess of all normal requirements.

Opposite her sat a young man with eyes like Rudyard Kipling's, a nose like John the Baptist's, ears like Cardinal Wolsey's, a forehead like Henry Ford's, a mouth like the Mississippi River and a character like overripe Limburger cheese.

IV

Campaspe Cutplug was about thirty or forty, intensely feminine, femininely intense – it works both ways. She regarded Paul Moody with intense femininity and feminine intensity and was obviously waiting a chance to speak.

'paspe – no, that's not a typographical error. Proper names begin with a capital, I know, but you're so improper – 'paspe, then, the last time I was in jail I ate hot-house grapes, caviare and plovers' eggs. Why?

Because –

Don't interrupt. The answer is, because I liked them. But, beyond that – if there is any beyond – Paris, I say, is provincial, London is ludicrous, Vienna is varicose, Buda-Pesth is budapestiferous. So why argue about –

Paulet, she interrupted, Paulet me speak. You are lucky, Paulet, that I didn't marry you. No husband can be attractive to his wife and knowing that he will – well, I don't know what he will do. But that was a pretty good start for an epigram, wasn't it?

The door opened and John Armstrong entered. He was a pawnbroker who resembled a prize-fighter.

Hello! ... then he saw Paul and reversed the salutation. Oh, here comes Buggsy.

Tumbal Bugg was shaped like an olive. He was a composer of blaa, the successor of jazz.

Oh my God! What a crowd! What a collection of freaks!

The words were spoken in loud clear tones, but as there was no name attached, no one knew who said it or whether it was merely the reader's comment. Everybody looked at everybody else with suspicion tempered by malevolence, but at this point Rollo, in search of his tutor, entered.

Take a drink, Rollo, said 'paspe.

Oh no, said Rollo. It's against, the law. Why, up at Sandford and Merton College, where I went to school –

Take a cigarette, Rollo, said Bugg

Oh no, said Rollo. Smoking isn't sanitary. Why, up at Sandford –

Take a walk, Rollo, said Paul.

Oh no, said Rollo. Why, I just came –

But Armstrong carried him out of the door and gently threw him down the elevator-shaft.

V

Rollo's tutor and his lady friend had taken him to Coney Island to try to get him in trouble, so they could blackmail Prunes *pere*, who was regarded as easy fruit. It was there that Rollo first met Cymbals O'Grady, the lady snake-charmer.

Cymbals had the delicate features of a beauty from Malaysia or the hinterland of Tibet. Her fragile nose had been frequently broken and carelessly mended. Her broad cheek bones had been modelled by an artist, or perhaps a hod-carrier. Her eyes were green, when they weren't black.

What a lovely creature! cried Campaspe, speaking sarcastic.

Cymbals was caressing a python from New Jersey when she heard these words. She took one look at Campaspe and fainted. It was the only repartee she could think of and it wasn't so bad, at that.

They put her in the car to carry her back to New York. There was no room in the car for Rollo. So they tied a rope to him and he trotted along contentedly under the rear axle.

VI

Campaspe lighted three or four cigarettes and got into bed. The door opened an inch and through the crack peered the beseeching left eye of Cupid Cutplug, her husband.

Campaspe, he whispered. I been out with the boys – and girls again. I'm sorry.

Campaspe laughed. Cupid, why will you always be so apologetic? Don't you know that in the best society that you are likely to meet in this book, that sort of thing is quite the custom? Have your fun, dear boy. I don't care in the least. But, please have some regard for my reputation and do not enter this room. Remember that we are married and respect me accordingly.

The door closed and Campaspe examined the books on her bed-table; plays by Pellegrini Pollyanna and Kalter Aufschnitt, poems by Gil Blas, Gandhi, Trotzky, Gorgonzola, Caviare, Ludendorff, Snickelfritz … She upset the table and kicked all the covers off the bed … She read a few lines of Aldous Suckling and threw the book through the window … A paragraph of Arthur Machine did not satisfy her, so she ate the rest of the book … Half an ounce of Ronald Furcoat and she broke the mirror with the slender volume … She was not in a critical mood … This was her ordinary method of reading.

Then she took up Dr. Watts's "Songs Divine and Moral." Opening the book at random, she began to sing herself to sleep:

> Whene'er I take my walks abroad
> How many poor I see,
> I do not give a damn for them
> Nor they a damn for –

Awk-z-z-z! Awk-z-z-z! Campaspe Cutplug slept.

VII

Cymbals O'Grady loved Rollo to distraction and back again and it embarrassed him very much. Everywhere that Rollo went Cymbals was sure to go and to get there first.

He found her in his apartment one night and the fire-escape was his only salvation. He hastened straightway to Campaspe.

Campaspe was sitting in her garden thinking. She was a great thinker and when she was thinking her brain made a noise like a squirrel-cage.

Why do elephants, who feel the poignancy of life most utterly, wear such persistent and sardonic smiles? Is it because Bach's music looms in their consciousness so highly – the higher, the fewer? But who plays Bach now? Who indeed plays half-Bach the way Eddie Mahan did or quarter-Bach like Ben Boynton? Sismondi's tarantella always bemused Nietzsche even when his lack of humor terrified Pope Pius IX – or X, for that matter. And then there were Theodoric Dreiser, the Ostrogoth of letters. No matter what Rabbi Perlmutter might think of allegory as a vehicle for despondency, there was nothing like alligator pears for salad. In life we never know anything about what we don't know anything about, so why do we?

Desire is hidden identity but petrifaction is generally final. Shadows are the only realities for personality cripples the intellect. Who, then, has not? It is only in laughter that one can adequately display gold teeth.

Oh is that you, Rollo? What's the matter?

Save me, save me from Cymbals!

Why not marry my sister Alice Goldilocks?

VIII

Rollo, said Alice, we've been married two weeks. Aren't you ever going to work?

Work? His voice was hoarse, his face green with pallor. I'll see everybody in

– in Jericho first, as we used to say at old S. and M.

Rollo!

I mean it. You don't know me, woman. I've changed. There's got to be some development of my character in this book and it's come all at once.

Rollo!

I'm going to be a wicked, wicked little boy. You go to the bad place!

Rollo!

I'm going back to Cymbals and the rest of the brass-band. Gol darn everybody. Curse! Curse! Curse!

Uttering these frightful imprecations, Rollo broke a chair, spat through his teeth and rushed out madly into the night.

Not TO BE CONTINUED, Let us hope!

Christopher Ward, "A Loose Lady," in *Twisted Tales*

(New York: Henry Holt and Co., 1924), 65–74.

With a nod to some of the narrative strategies of *My Ántonia*, Ward's parody takes on Willa Cather's regionalism: the detailed, yet narrow scope of the small lives, the mythic temporal stretch, and characters who seem to spring from Sherwood Anderson's theory of the grotesque.

A LOOSE LADY

By CALLA WITHER

Thirty or forty years ago, in one of those grey towns out in Nebrasky, which are so much greyer in novels than they are in fact, there was a man named Captain Forrester. He was a burly man, who had few words, no ideas, an unmitigated conscience, an impregnable brain, and an erring wife.

He had sprained his thumb years before, which broke him so that he could no longer work. He lived in a house full of heavy black walnut furniture and Rogers's groups; "How the Battle was Won," "Weighing the Baby." He walked with a crutch, two canes and difficulty. But most of the time he sat in an Andrew Jackson chair in the back-yard watching a rambler rose. If it seemed inclined to ramble too widely, he would chide its errancy by shaking his forefinger and making a gentle clucking sound with his tongue.

Mrs. Forrester was seventy-five or a hundred years younger than her husband. She was very fond of men. She had an iridescent laugh, which rose and descended – not "fell," descended – like a suave switchback. It was an inviting laugh and the invitation was often accepted. It made little difference to her who the man was. If it was not Judge Pommeroy or Ivy Peters, the village shyster, then the corner grocer, the fat iceman or one-eyed Riley, the butcher, would do.

When men came to see the Captain, she came out on the front porch to greet them in whatever she happened to have on, if anything. It flattered the men to have her rush to the door in a dressing-gown, a pair of earrings or what not. The less what, the more not, the greater the flattery.

Her beautiful eyes were set beneath her eyebrows and approximately equidistant from her nose. They were lively, laughing, intimate and usually a little wobbly.

She had a fascinating gift of mimicry. She often caricatured people to their faces. They were greatly pleased by such delicate attentions and used to laugh as heartily as they could under the circumstances. Her imitation of Mrs. Grimes's hunchback pleased that old lady so that she chagrined herself into hysterics.

II

But we will begin this story over again with the hero. Niel Herbert also lived, so to speak, in the little grey town. He was a tall, narrow chested, serious young man. He wore his hair brushed heroically back from his high, white forehead and in his eye was the same earnest look as in the eye of his grandfather, the famous Casabianca, hero of the burning deck.

He had a very quick mind. When unusually excited, it would respond on Thursday afternoon to an external stimulus received in the morning of the preceding Saturday. Ordinarily, however, the interval was ten days or a fortnight.

He was first cousin to Claude Wheeler and had the same wonderful sense of melancholy. Niel and Claude are such lovely names for such nice boys.

On a summer afternoon, Niel sat in the back room of his uncle's law office, surrounded by law books and steel engravings. His uncle was in the front office, surrounding a tumbler of hard liquor. The contrast between the aridity of his environment and the humidity of his uncle's occupation was very sad and comforting to Niel.

He heard a woman's laugh in the front office and then a voice of heart-breaking sweetness, such as one sometimes hears in lovely, gentle old songs, "Hail! Hail! the Gang's All Here!" and other barroom melodies.

"Is that the way you prepare your cases, Judge?" she cried gayly. "Well, I am a hard case. Prepare me!"

Niel heard the mellifluous gurgle of the rich, rare, beneficent old Bourbon, as Mrs. Forrester decanted it into her bewitching, fascinating, generous mouth. He peered through the keyhole and thought he had never seen another woman drink so elegantly out of a demijohn. Her gracious eyes were full of light, her capacious mouth was full of liquor.

Something about her, perhaps it was his uncle's arm, made him acutely conscious of her fragility, her frailty. His uncle seemed pleased with her. There could be no negative encounter with Mrs. Forrester. She was positively stimulating. If she merely spoke to you, you thought of moonshine. The aroma of her breath was intoxicating.

Niel drove her home in the buggy. She nestled close to him.

"It's so dull in this town, Niel," she said. "I get so little exercise. Do you think you could hug me, Niel?"

He had never seen her so full of spirits. On the way home, he saw the moon hanging in the sky. It was full. He thought of her and suddenly realized what she had asked him. He blushed and hung his head.

III

Niel and his uncle drove to the Forresters' to dinner, in the only vehicle the liveryman had for hire, the town hearse. It was a very pleasant vehicle, though somewhat close. The plate-glass sides kept out the summer air, but permitted them to look at the scenery. They emerged covered with faded rose leaves.

There were other guests, the Ogdens and Relentless Rudolph Ellinger. Mr. Ogden, a somewhat tarnished man of a hundred and fifty – pounds, – had one eye, a stiff imperial, a flexible moustache and another eye. Mrs. Ogden looked like a fruit-stand. She had a pear-shaped face, a cherry nose, ears like Smyrna figs, a plum coloured gown, a strawberry mark on her left arm. She had not a damson, but she had a peach of a daughter.

Constance Ogden was a very pretty girl with protuberant china-blue eyes, red hair and a pug nose. There were two dissatisfied lines from the corners of her mouth to the corners of her nose. When she was displeased, the lines tightened and dislocated her nose. She would push it back in place again. The lines were dissatisfied because of this constant interference.

Ellinger's hair was coarse and curly, so were his teeth, lips, manners and morals. He had a nose like the prow of a ship and a stern jaw. He seemed very much alive from his neck down. He was a powerful man and would have burst with his own vigor had not his waistcoat buttons been fastened with copper rivets. His body was so restless that it frequently turned completely around inside of his clothes. Then his white shirt front adorned his back and the tails of his dress coat hung down in front, a bifurcated apron. This was very embarrassing to sensitive persons, such as Niel.

Mrs. Forrester was elegantly dressed in a pair of garnet earrings, garnished with green peas, which, obedient to the laws of gravitation, hung naturally beside her thin pale triangular cheeks, and a velvet gown.

Captain Forrester, at the head of the table, took off his coat, rolled up his sleeves, tucked his napkin under his chin and deftly dislocated the turkey. Mrs. Forrester held Ellinger's right hand with her left under the table and Judge Pommeroy's left with her right, pressed Mr. Ogden's foot with her toe and vamped Niel across the table with the gay challenge of her eyes. Meanwhile she distracted her husband's attention by leading him into reminiscence.

He began his narrative with a concise account of the creation of the world, at which he had been present. He told how he had lived in the Garden of Eden, as Lincoln, Neb. was then called, and had a job on the Adam ranch as animal trainer: boundless sunny sky, boundless animals of all kinds, from the sybaritic gorilla to the ascetic iguana. "An ideal life for a young man," the Captain pronounced. "I recommend it to you, Niel."

Once, he said, there was trouble between two of the boys and Cain killed Abel. "I knew them both well," said the Captain. "Fine young men, though Cain was a leetle mite quick on the trigger."

He told his story with some difficulty, choosing his words, mostly of one syllable, slowly, absently crushing tumblers, cups and other table-ware in his strong fingers and heaping the fragments beside his plate. His humorous remarks were greeted with peals of hearty weeping. The faces of his auditors were wreathed with gloom. He ended his story by falling asleep, his head on Mrs. Ogden's shoulder.

After dinner they played the card game called "Authors." At ten o'clock they sang "Where is my Wandering Boy Tonight" and "Hark! from the Tombs." Then, after the Doxology, Captain Forrester pronounced the benediction incorrectly and Niel and his uncle rolled away in the hearse.

Niel thought he had never spent a more charmingly depressing evening. In bed, he cracked his knuckles, bit his nails and cried himself cozily to sleep.

IV

One morning a telegram reached Captain Forrester after a hard struggle. A savings-bank, of which he was the favorite director, had failed. There was nothing really wrong with the bank, but it was almost foolishly fond of Captain Forrester and, to give him a chance to display his magnanimity, it kindly went blooey. The Captain went to Denver and Rudolph Ellinger came to keep Mrs. Forrester from being lonely during the Captain's absence.

Next morning Niel got up before dawn to pick wild flowers. That was his only dissipation. It was a beautiful summer morning. The birds were singing. All over the marsh the wild pussy-wants-a-corner made cool sheets of silence, the swamp johnny-comes-marching-home flashed its silken splendor and the tangled john-brown's-body-lies-a-moldering-in-the-grave spread its accordion-colored clusters. Niel's heart swelled in his breast and he sobbed blithely.

He took out his barlow knife and began to cut a bouquet for the pretty lady. He would tie it to her door-knob and run away and hide. When she saw it she would be so pleased that she would never speak to that horrid, horrid Rudolph Ellinger again.

He found the kitchen door unlocked. Outside the door of Mrs. Forrester's room, he saw two pairs of shoes, a large pair of patent-leathers and a small pair of suede slippers. This gave Niel a great shock.

He found himself flat on his back in the stream that meandered through the marsh. He did not know how he got there, whether he had fallen or been pushed. His ears were red, his nose was blue, his eyes were full of tears. He raised his right hand toward heaven.

"Ladies that trespass," he said and then repeated it in italics – *"Ladies that trespass are far worse than men."*

Having thus officially announced his adhesion to the double standard, he arose, went home and changed his clothes. It was not a moral scruple she had outraged, but a native innocence.

V

Captain Forrester returned from Denver with Judge Pommeroy.

"Mrs. Forrester," he said, "I am a poor man."

"You are, indeed, Mr. Forrester," she said. "You always were."

"You see, Mrs. Forrester," said the Judge, "the Captain was neither legally nor morally responsible for the bank's failure. There was no obligation of any kind on him to give away all his money and yours, but how else could he rise to heights of moral grandeur and make himself a very pathetic and noble figure indeed? Of course, you'll be practically paupers now. You'll have to do the cooking and scrubbing and all that but we all have to sacrifice something to achieve self satisfaction and Captain Forrester has sacrificed you. I hope you sympathize, madam."

"I do sympathize, Judge," said she, "I deeply sympathize – with myself."

"You are a noble woman, Mrs. Forrester," said the Judge solemnly.

The Captain then had a stroke and breathed stertorously for three weeks. After that he sat up in bed, but could not speak clearly. He could master only a few simple words like "blah-blah" or "google."

Niel often went to the Forresters' house. He loved it because it was so dreary. He always found men there or, if not men, boys. They all looked alike to Mrs. Forrester, especially after the fourth or fifth cocktail. When Niel saw them, he would crack his knuckles and moan disconsolately.

Once she dared to lay her hand on Niel's arm and to say to him: "Niel, you are very good looking." His normal temperature was freezing. It fell thirty-two degrees. He repulsed her advances zeroically.

Captain Forrester died and Niel went to Boston to become an undertaker. He did not bid Mrs. Forrester good-bye. He could never forgive her for having survived her husband. It was so unheroic to go on living. A double funeral would have been such a gloriously melancholy occasion. He went away with a heart full of weary contempt, but his head was still empty.

Years after he heard that she was dead. That made him feel better. He smiled for the first and last time in his life. He is now following his profession in Boston and is noted as a director of funeral pageants.

Edmund George Valpy Knox, "Mystery," in *Apes and Parrots: An Anthology of Parodies Collected by J.C. Squire*

(Cambridge: Washburn and Thomas, 1929), 261–6.

Not just the subject matter, which Conrad's readers would have found infinitely recognizable, but the manner of telling is spoofed here. Knox deflates some of Conrad's signature characteristics: the cloistered context of where the narrative is told, the endless deferrals of the story and the storytellers, leading to the wonderful impatience and deflation of the ending.

MYSTERY

(Joseph Conrad)

I hadn't seen Burleigh for some five years or more when I found him waiting for me that fine light evening in the long low-roofed room with the red curtains – all sailormen know it – at the back of "The Ebb Tide." The front rooms of the tavern of course look out on the square grey shipping offices of the Ultramarine Company, just where the tramway forks – I never could make out, by the way, where that tramway goes to – but Robinson keeps this upstairs room with the bay-windows, the one that looks out over the docks, for a few favoured customers, amongst whom I am privileged to count myself.

Robinson didn't seem to have altered much, I thought. The same white puffed-out cheeks like an elderly cherub in need of fresh air, and the thick black eyebrows that seemed to wave and rustle as if in some invisible wind. Mrs. Robinson was much the same too—angular, moving obscurely in the background, with those thin lips and that faint everlasting smile.

The first part of Burleigh that I noticed when I went upstairs and opened the door was his broad back, encased as usual in a frock-coat of No. 1 sailcloth, the tails of which fell slightly apart as he bent downwards to light his pipe at the fire with a long twist of old newspaper. When he stood up and turned round I was relieved to see that he had not altered either. The ring of fine curly hair that ran round the crown of his otherwise bald head was thinner than it had been, but there was the same lugubrious drollery in his grey eyes and the same gentle murmuring voice that came so incongruously from his deep stalwart chest as though through a sort of syrup. He had that old trick too of his of smiling so that one end of his mouth ran up suddenly against the barrier of his heavy moustache, like the curl of a wave on a spit of reef. The large white-cotton umbrella, badly rolled up, that he always carried when ashore, was still hanging by its crook from his huge right arm.

"Have a –" he said quizzically, and I signified assent in the usual manner. As we sat down at the gleaming mahogany table and looked at each other smiling across it, he knew, of course – how could he help knowing? – that I wanted to hear all about that remarkable cruise of the "Albatross" away in the Southern ice floes about which the whole water-side was talking and about which nobody surely was likely to know more than he did. But equally of course he wasn't going to tell me all at once, for that wasn't Burleigh's way. Instead he tugged dreamily at one of his big moustaches and smiled up into the end of the other as we looked out at the lighted tideway beneath. Lamps shone high, shone low there, shone with single eyes, shone in rows, were reflected in glittering ladders broken by the shadows of hawsers along the oily inquietude of the stream. Congregated and at rest, the ships seemed to cast gentle inquiring glances at one another, to ask how each had fared in the vast incalculable tangle of wet mysteriousness which passes under the name of the sea.

Burleigh gave a final tug at last and spoke.

"I've asked another man in here to-night to meet you in a kind of way," he said with a sort of depreciatory wave of his big hand as though it was a species of liberty to ask one man to meet another. And then, clearing his throat and twisting his smile again – "Man called Allotson, Jim Allotson"; and, as if with a sudden effort of memory and dragging the words up from some deep recess of his vast interior – "second mate."

"Not on the –" I began, but he stopped me at once with the heavy emphatic nod characteristic of him.

"First man up the berg-side," he cooed in that surprisingly gentle voice. "Girl on it. Sicilian dancer, I believe. Derelict. Polar bears too. Good man, Jim Allotson. I'll tell you about him before he comes."

And bit by bit I came to piece out, between the nods of Burleigh's head and the tuggings of that moustache of his and his quick sideways smile, the history of Allotson's youth up to the day when, by one of those extraordinary coincidences that sailors call chance, he became second officer of the "Albatross" – became second officer and so had his share of the tragi-comedy that was to happen to the crew of about the most adventurous tramp that was ever beaten out of the trade routes into the frozen seas.

He had been the son of a rather superior ship's chandler, I gathered, of a pious disposition, who settled down in East Croydon of all places after retiring from the sight and smell of salt water as they came to him on the quay-side at

Singapore. Neither a gravel subsoil nor excessive church-going was able to ward off malaria for long. He soon went under – his wife had died some years before – and left the child to the care of his only surviving relative, a sister named Ann. I can see her now as Burleigh described her to me, with her tight lips, expressionless eyes, grey coils of hair and the black alpaca dress she always inhabited, checking, reproving, forbidding and instilling endless moral axioms into this touzle-headed waif who had the rover's blood so inalienably in his veins.

He ran away, of course. He was bound to run away, had always dreamed and thought of nothing but ropes and rigging and tar, had seen the alleyways of his snug suburban home as tidal inlets hung with tropical vegetation; ran away and got a berth as ship's boy, and at fifteen had seen as much of the strange places of the world as many of us achieve in a life-time. He had frizzled in pestilential mud-flats, been driven under stormsails by the stark spite of typhoons, opened up hidden creeks, the passionless offshoots of unknown estuaries, at a time when other lads were grinding away at their Rule of Three.

Somehow or other, Burleigh did not exactly know how, he had managed to get his second-mate's certificate. But what he did know was that all through those wanderings the young man had preserved a sort of simple charming piety that came perhaps from the early lessons of that vigorous uncompromising old lady in Croydon, intolerable though her maxims had seemed.

"Good man, Jim Allotson," cooed Burleigh once more at the end of all this, as though it were a kind of refrain. And just then the door opened and a man came in. He was dressed in a blue reefer suit, stooped slightly and walked a little lame. So much I saw as I gradually drew my eyes upward from the bright spot of light at the bottom of Burleigh's grog glass, where they had been fixed with a sort of fascination while he spoke. Raised now to the level of the stranger's own, they blinked a little, and I held my breath for a moment at the contrast between that fresh ruddy face with slight black whiskers and the crop of hair that surmounted it, white as a bank of snow. He had the grey eyes that seem to be searching out the eternal riddle of heaven and sea, even when they have no further to look than the end of a room. Down the left cheek ran a broad whitey-brown scar that shocked almost as though it were unnatural and had been painted on. I did not need Burleigh's purred introduction to the second mate of the "Albatross" to have my curiosity, already pretty lively, as you know, whipped up to fever-point; and my friend's, "This young man is very anxious to hear –" could have been read without trouble in my eyes.

"But how much have you told him already?" he asked, speaking with a slight stammer as he raised his glass and held it out a little stiffly in front of him, as though this was a necessary preliminary before putting it to his lips. I found out later that this was an invariable trick of his. "Have you told him how I got my second-mate's certificate?"

Burleigh shook his head. He didn't, of course, as I was aware, know.

"About fourteen years ago," began Allotson, and I sighed a little; but before he had said another word the door opened again.

There was something horribly uncanny about that opening of the door, not followed by the appearance of a body but only of a face, as if it had been cut off at the neck –

"Time, gentlemen, please," said the voice of Robinson.

Rose MacAulay, "Week-end at the Hoppers," in *Parody Party*, ed. Leonard Russell

(London: Hutchinson, 1936), 19–35.

Rose MacAulay (1881–1958) was a highly successful journalist whose work appeared widely, ranging from the *TLS* and Squire's *London Mercury* to the *Daily Express* and *Daily Mail*. MacAulay began her career as a fiction writer in 1906, with the publication of *Abbots Verney*. She was also a poet, and published scholarly work on seventeenth-century literature. In her later years her output expanded to include travel writing. Her last novel, *The Towers of Trebizond* (1956), was a best-seller and critically acclaimed. Her target here, of course, is Hemingway, in particular the Hemingway of *The Sun Also Rises* – its androgynous central female character, short declarative sentences and repetitive diction, lack of interiority, and, inevitably, the drinking.

WEEK-END AT THE HOPPERS

I went down Friday evening. I drove Frank Lester down. The Hoppers hadn't wanted to have us come Friday. They said they wouldn't be home themselves till late Friday night. Just the same, we drove down Friday afternoon. I stopped off for Frank at Brown's Hotel. She hadn't packed yet. She was getting herself a drink in the lounge. She had on a red dress and no hat and looked swell.

"Hullo, Jim," she said." What are you round for, this hour? Have a brandy."

"Sure I'll have a brandy."

I got a brandy and another for Frank. Frank had gotten herself somewhat drunk already. She had another. Then I had another. Then we each had two more. It was fine, sitting there in the lounge, drinking and looking at Frank. Frank looked fine. It was a swell day outside.

"It's a swell day outside," I said.

"Sure it's a swell day. What are you round for this hour?"

What the hell was I round for? I couldn't remember.

"Give me time. It'll come back."

I had another. Then it came back.

"Driving down to the Hoppers. Don't you remember? We said we'd be there this afternoon. They said no, they'd be from home. No matter. We'll have their lousy mansion to ourselves."

"Ourselves hell. You've forgotten the servants. Are you scared of English servants?"

"No," I said.

"The hell you're not. Sure you're scared of English servants. Everyone's scared of English servants. The English are scared of English servants. Americans are scared stiff. That's why the Hoppers are from home so much. They're scared of their butler."

"Well," I said, "I suppose he'll give us a drink."

"You bet he won't give us a drink. We'll be too scared to ask him. Come on. Let's go some place."

"Where'll we go?"

"Let's go eat."

"We'll eat here."

So we had lunch. We had some good melon, then some pretty nice roast duck, with new potatoes and peas, and the sweet was good, too. We drank a hock that seemed nicer than it was. We were both feeling pretty good by then. We had coffee.

"Come on," I said. "Time we went Hopper."

Frank got up. "Let's go Hopper," she said. "I'm ready. We'll take some bottles, because we're scared of the butler."

"You packing a bag?"

"Sure I'm packing a bag. What'll I take Hopper? Might take all my clothes. Or just leave them. Less trouble. Listen, Jim, I have to leave my clothes here, because of being behind with my bill. Will the Hoppers be sore?"

"Won't matter. They'll be sore anyway, at us turning up Friday."

"Will the servants be sore?"

"Oh, they'll be sore all right. Sure they'll be sore. Turning up Friday, without any clothes. I should say the servants will be sore."

"Maybe I'll pack my pyjamas. And some kind of lousy dress for to-night, to score off the servants."

"That's fine. Go and pack them."

Frank was an hour packing. I strolled around and sat in the lounge. I had some more drinks. Phil Winston came in, looking for a man. He was just over from Paris. He sat down by me and we commenced to talk. I bought him a drink. He told me the news from Paris. A lot of funny things had happened in Paris since I left it, he said. That's what's the matter with Paris. The funny things all happen after you leave, or else before you get there. I told Phil to spill them, but they weren't much, in the end. It seemed that Rosalie, the girl I was living with last May, had some drinks at a wild party and jumped from a top window on to a gendarme's head, dressed in her best hat and garters for a study in the nude. But it turned out badly, for she killed the gendarme and broke her own leg, and they didn't know whether to try her for manslaughter or attempted suicide or going nude in the street, so they shut her up as cuckoo.

"That's a whale of a funny tale," I said.

"Well, I'm doing my best," he said. "I'm practising for a country week-end. Bob and Mamie Hopper have asked me down to-morrow, to that swell house they've taken in Sussex."

"It's to-day," I told him." That week-end begins to-day. You'd better come down with Frank and me. Bob and Mamie'll be sore if you're late for the party."

So that was fixed, after he'd thought round it for a while and had a lager. He went back to Bury Street, to pack a grip, and Frank and I were to collect him. I thought he would make it better for us with the servants.

Frank came down. She had a kind of palecoloured suit, like bath oliver crackers, and her hat was cracker-coloured too, and she looked fine. I told her about Phil, and she said: "What did you need to ask that mutt for? He'll disgrace us with the butler, drinking wine." But she was quite pleased really, due to her and me not being the only ones to get there too soon.

Frank wanted to stop for another beer, but I said we would stop off at drink places down the road. She said this was no good, they shut at three. So we bought some bottles and pushed off. We collected Phil in Bury Street. He was dressed seaside, in canvas shoes and flannels, due to the Hopper house being a mile from the Channel, and he thought he would go sea-shore all of the time. I thought, sea-shore hell; I wanted to shoot rabbits. There were some big trout in a stream nearby, too, and I meant to get some out. But Frank wanted to go sea-shore too; she had packed her sun-bath suit and her swim suit, in spite of its being the English Channel in the rain.

We drove out of London by Clapham.

"Haven't I heard of Clapham?" said Frank. "Isn't there a sect here?"

"Sects everywhere," I said.

"I didn't say sex, you ignorant bum. Sect. Listen, Phil. What's the Clapham sect do?"

"Play the harp, these days. Or else burn. All dead."

"Well, what did they do once?"

"They started all that slave trouble. It was they gave the bug to Lincoln. If it hadn't been for the Clapham sect, we'd still have our plantations worked. To hell with the Clapham sect. I guess they're frying all right." Phil was a Virginian. But his relatives never had any plantations that I heard of. His old man was a judge, and Phil was a doctor, but they said he never would be much of a doctor.

"Well," said Frank, "they may be frying, but they had some pretty nice houses round this common."

We drove along streets, and though we went a pretty good speed it seemed we never would be outside London. We came to a crowd, where a Ford V Eight had gotten an old woman, so we stopped to look too. The old lady lay on the pavement, and all of her was a mess. The Ford was a mess too, and there was a police officer writing it all down in a book and people in the crowd shouting they'd be witnesses, but the police officer took no notice, he just went on writing in his book. He looked like a philosopher, writing away and taking no heed of the crowd. Phil thought he must get out and help, seeing he was a doctor, but then an ambulance came up. They took up the old lady and put her in and we could see better what a mess the Ford had gotten her into. Frank started to retch, but, this is God's truth, though I like old ladies, I felt fine. I hadn't felt so fine since I saw a horse gored by a very good bull at Pamplona in 1927. That was a fine bull, and he made Christ's own mess of that horse. I like horses, too, and I like old ladies. But that bull and that Ford must have had a grand technique. I suppose one likes to see a job thoroughly done, and that's why one feels fine, and the crowds run up and applaud as if it was a good tennis game, and won't move along whatever the policeman tells them. I said so to Frank. Frank said, "Sure we feel fine. But let's not talk about it."

When it was all over, we pushed along, but we hadn't gone far when Frank said she must have a drink. She had gone all yellow and looked terribly.

"I feel like mud," she said. "Maybe I'll vomit."

So we stopped and got one of the bottles, and we hadn't brought any glasses along so we tipped the bottle into our mouths and drank round and Frank commenced to feel better. Then I drove on.

By now I had gotten to feel somewhat sad and without hope, and as if this hellish town London never would end and let us be in Sussex. The map was funny, too; it didn't seem like going the right way. That's one of the troubles about maps, they don't copy nature close enough, they go ways of their own.

"Forget it," I said to Phil, who kept telling me streets he thought he saw on that darned map. "If I go ahead, I get some place, don't I?"

"Sure we get some place," said Frank. "Go on travelling south. If we travel south we get to the ocean, don't we? We want the ocean, don't we? If we can't find the Hopper house we can go swim. That would be swell, not having to stay at the Hopper house. Maybe we'll come to a nice roadhouse and stop there."

We drove along, and by now I had gotten used to London and not getting outside of it and thought it might be all for the best, and that we would maybe have a pretty nice week-end running about these suburbs, with every now and then a drink. But just when I had settled to that it seemed to turn into country, and fields and little bungalows commenced to appear. There were little woods, too, as if someone had just planted them for ornament. We pulled in at a garage and filled up with gas, and the public houses had opened by now so we got ourselves some drinks. Then we drove on and the hills and fields and woods got bigger and the houses more like real houses, and there were villages too with churches and inns and we felt this must be Sussex or Surrey or some county like that, and we commenced to think we might end up at the Hoppers after all. We saw a few good sights on the way. There was a terrier chasing a large tabby cat in a village street, and when it caught up to it the cat turned and they fought. It was a swell fight. The terrier was good with his teeth but he had to keep letting go because the tabby scratched him. It was a fine tabby, very quick and good with its claws, and they both fought well, and were game to the end. The terrier got an eye scratched out and the tabby was pretty well chewed up and it was a grand fight and I felt fine after it. I like terriers and I like cats, and these were very neat good fighters and game to the last.

Soon after that we came to a lodge with gates, and a large kind of park, and Frank said it was the Hopper park, she had seen a photograph of it and that was it. So we drove in, and up a long drive, and the Hopper house was a large yellow mansion, not bad, with a nice tennis lawn and flower gardens around. We got out and rang the door bell and a man servant with a face like a cod's came. Frank said, "We're not expected until tomorrow, but we're early."

The man like a cod took it quite calmly. He had another man fetch in our grips from the car and take them upstairs, and he had a maid take us up to our rooms. They were pretty nice rooms. Two of them had a communicating door between them. The maid didn't seem sure whether Frank and I or Frank and Phil would be occupying these, but Frank had her put my case in one of them. What the hell, I thought, because I hadn't known we'd gotten that far, but I was pleased, too. Phil didn't care; he had a girl in New York, and they put him across the passage.

The maid was a fine girl. She asked would we like anything further. We didn't have anything at all yet, and I said so. "Sure, we'd like something further," I said. "We'd like some drinks, if that's all right."

She said she thought that would be all right, and went off, and soon a man brought us up drinks, and we felt better. We felt so good that Frank got out her swim suit and her sun-bath suit and tennis racket and put on her white shorts and so was ready for anything. I took my fishing-rod, because I meant to get some fish out of the Hoppers' stream they had told me about. They had said it was a good stream, with trout all sizes from your little finger to your arm. Phil took his swim suit and there we were, all set for anything. We went downstairs and looked around, and thought the Hoppers had done pretty well, and had gotten themselves a swell house. The pictures were fine, too; the Hoppers had bought themselves some ancestors to go with the house, and they looked fine.

The man we held for the butler was in the hall as we went out. He said dinner was at nine.

"That's all right with us," said Phil. "That'll give us time for a swim."

We got in the car and drove off, and we thought we would get to the ocean first and I would drop them there and go after that trout stream. The Hoppers were only a mile from the sea, so I went on going south, but it all looked pretty countrified for a seaside resort. Frank said she could smell ozone, but it proved to be a cabbage field. There is not much in it when it comes to nature smells and that is Christ's truth.

After a time Frank said, "Listen, Jim. Listen, Phil. This isn't the seaside. We must be going around in circles, like men lost in the bush."

"Isn't that fine," I said.

"Can't you keep straight, Jim? For my sake, Jim, keep a straight course and let me have that ocean swim. What it is, Jim, you're going after that stream of yours. Get this, Jim: Phil and I want the ocean and we mean to have it. I knew you were a pretty lousy driver, Jim, but I didn't think even you'd be able to drive around Britain for hours and never strike the ocean. How do you do it, Jim? Phil, ask him how he does it. Listen, Jim, give me the wheel. I'll find the bloody English Channel or I'll die."

"Let me alone," I said, "you're a drunk."

"Drunk hell. Give it me, you louse."

She leaned across me and got hold of the wheel and we ran right into a ditch. We got out and stood looking at it, and it looked like not getting us to the English Channel that afternoon.

"Let's go find us a drink," said Frank, "before we start in pulling it out."

We walked down the lane to where there was a church tower showing, because in England where you find a church you find a pub too, and that's the best thing I know about the Church of England. The same thing doesn't seem to apply to what the English call chapels. I once asked an Englishman why this was; he said he supposed it was due to the Establishment. Anyway we walked towards that church tower, and sure enough there was a pub close up against it. It was a pretty nice-looking pub, with a good bar and we ordered beer and it was good beer but rather warm. On the walls were pictures of dead poultry and of race-horses and there was a fine stuffed trout that made me feel badly because I commenced to think about those trout in the stream that I wanted to fish. There was bran on the floor and some men were playing a dart game and we sat and watched. It looked like a good game, and the men seemed to like it and some of them played well. Then two of them started to fight, and one was knocked out.

"Let's go," said Phil. So we got out quickly, lest someone should spot Phil was a doctor and ask him to do good to the man who had passed out.

We walked back down the lane to the ditched car and the birds were singing in the trees and the church bells played a tune and I felt fine after the beer and seeing that fight and the man go down so clean, as if he was a skittle.

"I feel fine," I said. "I don't know where we are nor where we shall be, but I feel fine."

"Fine hell," said Phil. "That damn church clock striking eight, and no ocean in sight and your fool car in the ditch."

We came up with the car and it was still in the ditch.

"Isn't that fine," said Phil.

"You're a grand girl, Frank," I said. "You're a grand driver."

"Well," she said, "let's not talk so much. Can't you get her out?"

"Sure we can get her out," said Phil. "You can get her out yourself. One little touch of your finger, and out she jumps. Come on, sit at the wheel and drive her out."

"Hell," said Frank. "Let's not talk so much. Let's start in shoving."

So we started in shoving and hauling and jacking, and time went by, and at last we got her out. The wing was bent and a few more things had happened, but on the whole she looked as if she might go.

"Well," said Frank, getting in, "let's go some place."

"We're going right back to the Hopper house," I said, for by then I was pretty tired. "I want that dinner the cod said was happening at nine."

"Well," said Frank and let it go at that, and so did Phil; they both wanted that dinner too, and weren't feeling sea-shore any more.

"Can we find the way back?" said Phil.

I thought I could find the way back, but, due to one lane in Sussex looking so like the next, it took some time. I didn't have the map with me, but anyway the map was a wash-out, since we didn't know where we were on it. I own I felt somewhat surprised when I saw those lodge gates and that yellow mansion turning up again. It must have been some way past nine when we drove up the drive and rang that door bell. The butler like a cod opened the door, and it seemed he looked more high hat than ever, due, I thought, to us being late for dinner. Just the same, he let us inside, and said, "I will inform her ladyship of your arrival" and ambled off.

Phil said, "Isn't that fine. The British King must have made Mamie into a lady," and Frank let out a laugh and said, "There's hope for all of us, if he can do that," and then the cod came back, with no expression at all on his face, and with him was a fine whale of a woman in a velvet dinner-gown who stood and looked us up and down, and I felt I didn't have any spine. She must be another of the Hoppers' week-enders, I thought, come early too; or maybe she was the housekeeper. Either way, what the hell, I thought.

"There is some mistake, I suppose," she said, and I commenced to wish we had waited till Saturday after all, if anyone was going to take it badly.

But Frank, who was pretty drunk, and the woman looked her over as if she knew it, said "Listen. The Hoppers are our friends and they like to have us arrive just any time. So we came along to-day instead of to-morrow. Does that worry you?"

The British woman got to look more like Boadicea modelled in ice than ever, and said: "I am afraid I don't know who the Hoppers may be. I suppose you are aware that this is Stanbury Hall Lord Ashendeane's house. My butler supposed at first that you were the guests we were expecting. Now that the little mistake is cleared up, the maid will bring your things down directly, as no doubt you will be wanting to join your friends."

She stood looking at us pretty coldly, in that sour English way. I think she thought we were a gang of crooks gotten in, and wasn't going to give us a chance to do our stuff.

Phil, who is slow in his brain, said, "Do you mean to tell us we're *not* in the Hoppers' house in Sussex, after all this time we've been stopping here and no one said a word?"

"I have already told you," said the female English aristocracy, "that you are at Lord Ashendeane's house. It is, if you want to know, in the middle of Kent."

"Well, isn't that fine," said Phil bitterly. "I'll say that's fine, us staying here and the butler telling us it was the Hopper house, Sussex, and the Hoppers would be back late, and dinner to be at nine. I call this a swell visit."

"If you will excuse me," said the British lady, "I must go back to my guests." She walked away, and went through a door at the end of the hall, and when it was opened there was talking and the smell of roast bird, but it shut again and we were left in the hall with the butler to watch us till our grips came down.

"You're a fine kind of a butler," said Phil, "feeding us those stories. Why the hell didn't you tell us the facts?"

The butler looked at us with his cod's eyes, saying nothing, and I could see he remembered that he had fed us no stories because we hadn't asked a thing, and I saw him remembering too the drinks we had had.

"Oh, don't talk to him," said Frank. "Let's get to hell out of here. The Hoppers will be expecting us." She said that to show off before the butler, because he didn't look like he thought anyone but the police expected us, or ever would.

The maid and a man came downstairs with our things and gave them to us, and I gave the girl money, and she was a fine girl with good legs and a pretty nice skin, but she didn't offer us any more drinks, nor so much as a bite of food, nor did the butler, though he took my money too. Then we went out to the car, and I thought how we were getting pretty used to my car by now, and were having a motoring holiday.

"Ask them how we get to the Hoppers," said Phil.

But Frank shouted out, “Hoppers hell. They're away in another county. And anyway I'm not going there, after the way they've let us down. I never want to see the Hoppers again. We're going back to London, to get a meal and a drink and stay there. Only I suppose Jim will never find London. He won't even find the right county; he'll get us some town in Yorkshire, maybe. You're a grand pilot, Jim, I'll say you are.”

“Oh, let's not talk,” I said. “We've had a week-end that turned out badly, that's all. Let's forget it.”

“I shan't ever forget it,” said Frank, “the way the Hoppers have let us down. Asking us to stop and then going away like that. When I think how we didn't have so much as a drink out of them, I get feeling pretty sore.”

Phil said, “Don't feel sore. No use to feel sore. Maybe we'll get a drink somewhere in Kent.”

The air smelt of hay and clover; it was like one of those sweet, coldish drinks you get at Sardieu's by the Madeleine. It felt pretty good to be going back to London again after all these lanes. Lanes are very nice, but you get tired. I began to feel fine, though I didn't have any food inside me, and though the Hopper Week-end hadn't turned out too well.

“I feel fine,” I said.

William Kean Seymour, "Peter Gink," in *Parrot Pie: Parodies and Imitations of Contemporaries*

(London: G.G. Harrap & Co., 1927), 148–53.

Sherwood Anderson's short-story collection *Winesburg, Ohio*, with its use of the grotesque and a relative frankness about human sexuality, inspired parodists to write several additional chapters.

PETER GINK[iv]

I

When Peter Gink's mother had been married six weeks to Ephraim Gink, the Swinesburg undertaker, a curious thing happened. She was walking along the cinder-track by the side of Swine Creek when a large water-rat crossed in front of her. Jessie was on her way to the Swinesburg Asylum to visit her aunt and sister. Leah Crayfoot had been there for ten years holding the conviction that she was Lot's wife and that Swinesburg was Sodom and Gomorrah. Leah's niece, Mary Crayfoot, had been in the institution a year, following an acute phase of nymphomania. Jessie was thinking of Mary as she walked on the bank of the Creek. She reflected that if her sister had married Bill Whelan, the pork-butcher, for all his cross-eye and duckbill lip, she might not have rushed naked into Main Street that terrible Saturday night a year ago. As she walked she recalled the flaring headlines of the *Swinesburg Mail* the next morning. "Mad Maiden Staggers Main Street." She shuddered, trying to conquer the nausea that her charwoman had just significantly explained to her, and then, quickening her pace, screamed suddenly at the sight of the great slimy rat running across the track. Seth Wilson, the bar-tender, said it turned his stomach to hear her frenzied shriek, and when he looked from his saloon window Jessie was running back to Swinesburg crying out like one demented.

Folk recalled the incident years afterward when Peter Gink shambled his lean form along the sidewalk. Like a rat, they said. His little rat-like eyes looked cruelly at you, even though his head was turned in the other direction. His hair, also, was like the brown pelt of a rat. And Swinesburg remembered always how, in Sunday School, he had bitten through the broadclothed leg of Reverend Tomkins, the Presbyterian minister, with his little rat-like teeth.

---

iv From *Swinesburg, Ohio*.

Jessie Gink had three other children beside Peter, and all normal except two, Hephzibah and Washington. Hephzibah was born when a record blizzard swept Swinesburg. She had a violent temper and, at the age of eight, startled the town by creeping up behind the old washerwoman with a woodchopper and severing her right leg at the ankle. "I st'uck her one wiv a chopper and then Momma came and took it away. She s'ceamed and s'ceamed. I won't never have a chance to kill her now." She was taken to the children's ward of the asylum for observation. Washington was sent to a reformatory for three years when nine years old. He had been caught climbing the waterspout of the women's quarters of the Swinesburg Hospital and, when brought before the sheriff, laughed defiantly and announced his intention of doing it again at the first opportunity. "I like to see the pretty ladies," he said. At the age of six he had torn the muslin off the legs of the Grand Piano in the Presbyterian Church Hall. Two years after his release from the reformatory, then fourteen, he took a train ticket to Bacchus, ten miles distant, and while craning from the windows in Swinesburg Tunnel to peep at a young gas-fitter and his sweetheart in the next compartment, had his brains dashed out by a passing train.

But this is a digression from Peter Gink, Washington's brother.

II

Peter had spent the day varnishing coffins in the iron shed at the rear of old Ephraim Gink's shop. Venomously hissing *John Brown's Body* he had worked and worked with little dancing shapes of death in his thoughts. "They are all dead," he had repeated a thousand times as he smoothed the polish over the pitch pine. "They are all dead, they are all dead." Soon his father's friends in Main Street would be dead in fact, frilled and furbished and brass-plated and mourned – for a day. Only for a day, or a month at most. But if they but knew they were dead now, creeping along Main Street with their dead souls shining like codfish. He sniggered at the thought. So convinced was he that they were dead that, as he worked, he composed little crude epitaphs.

Bill Whelan lies here,
Slit from ear to ear.

That was one of them, and when he went along Main Street he stopped by the kerosene-store and looked across the street at Bill Whelan crying his pork under the gas-flares. Their cross-eyes never met, but Bill Whelan shuddered and dropped a hand of pork.

"Bill Whelan lies here,
Slit from ear to ear."

Peter Gink hissed the rhyme to himself, and then crooning softly, "Dead, all dead," passed on. At the cutler's shop he stopped and thought of Reverend Tomkins. He would like to stab him a million times with the glittering nail scissors hanging there on the brass wire. He passed on; a definite determination had come into his mind. No, he wouldn't kill Bill Whelan with a razor, or Reverend Tomkins with the scissors; he would lure them separately to Cyrus Bone's disused lean-to in the centre of the bean-fields, tie their limbs up with coffin tape and gnaw them with his teeth till they were dead and unrecognizable.

Returning home along Main Street, he lingered only to fill his coat-pocket with hot peanuts. He went straight up to his room, sniggering quietly. Inside he was safe with his dream. He gnawed ecstatically at the last remaining knob of the bedstead. "All dead," he gasped, "all dead."

His mother found him dead there the next morning. He had gnawed the curtains into paper pulp, the legs of the chairs had been nibbled to matchstick proportions; holes gaped in the plaster walls where his sharp teeth had been working frantically; and pinned in the remains of the bolster was the crude rhyme:

Bill Whelan lies here,
Gnawed from ear to ear.

III

Ephraim Gink came up at his wife's call. He was a medium-sized man, with a pocked, purpureal face and protruding eyes. His eyes had the filmy quality of a dead skate and the warts on the backs of his hands made them resemble the hind-parts of a toad. He looked round the room at the confusion of gnawn wood, plaster, peanuts, and then at the dead body of his son. He looked irritated. "Tsst, tsst!" Then he took out his tape measure and began methodically to measure the prostrate form. "A narrer one," he said, "a very narrer one. And who's to pay for it, I want to know? He isn't a customer." Then, more loudly, to Mrs Gink: "I guess I'd about pulverize that darned little rat. It all comes of that there blamed little rat …"

Outside the morning bustle of Main Street was asserting itself, and just at the bend of the road Bill Whelan was standing outside his shop sharpening his long knife with one eye on the clock by the cash-desk and the other on the sarsaparilla sign swinging lazily from the drug-store down the street.

Max Beerbohm, "The Mote in the Middle Distance," in *A Christmas Garland*

(London: William Heinemann, 1912), 3–10.

Max Beerbohm (1872–1956) was an essayist and caricaturist. He also spent twelve years (1898–1910) as drama critic for the *Saturday Review*. Of his prose work, *Zuleika Dobson* (1911), his only novel, was a great critical success; *A Christmas Garland*, which also included parodies of Conrad, Shaw, and Hardy, is a classic of prose parody. However, it is his work as a caricaturist for which Beerbohm is most highly regarded, beginning in 1892 with work that appeared in *The Strand*. For parodists, the combination of James's prolix sentence structure and leisurely narrative pace were irresistible.

THE MOTE IN THE MIDDLE DISTANCE

By H*NRY J*M*S

It was with the sense of a, for him, very memorable something that he peered now into the immediate future, and tried, not without compunction, to take that period up where he had, prospectively, left it. But just where the deuce *had* he left it? The consciousness of dubiety was, for our friend, not, this morning, quite yet clean-cut enough to outline the figures on what she had called his "horizon," between which and himself the twilight was indeed of a quality somewhat intimidating. He had run up, in the course of time, against a good number of "teasers"; and the function of teasing them back – of, as it were, giving them, every now and then, "what for" – was in him so much a habit that he would have been at a loss had there been, on the face of it, nothing to lose. Oh, he always had offered rewards, of course – had ever so liberally pasted the windows of his soul with staring appeals, minute descriptions, promises that knew no bounds. But the actual recovery of the article – the business of drawing and crossing the cheque, blotched though this were with tears of joy – had blankly appeared to him rather in the light of a sacrilege, casting, he sometimes felt, a palpable chill on the fervour of the next quest. It was just this fervour that was threatened as, raising himself on his elbow, he stared at the foot of his bed. That his eyes refused to rest there for more than the fraction of an instant, may be taken – *was*, even then, taken by Keith Tantalus – as a hint of his recollection that after all the phenomenon wasn't to be singular. Thus the exact repetition, at the foot of Eva's bed, of the shape pendulous at the foot of *his* was hardly enough

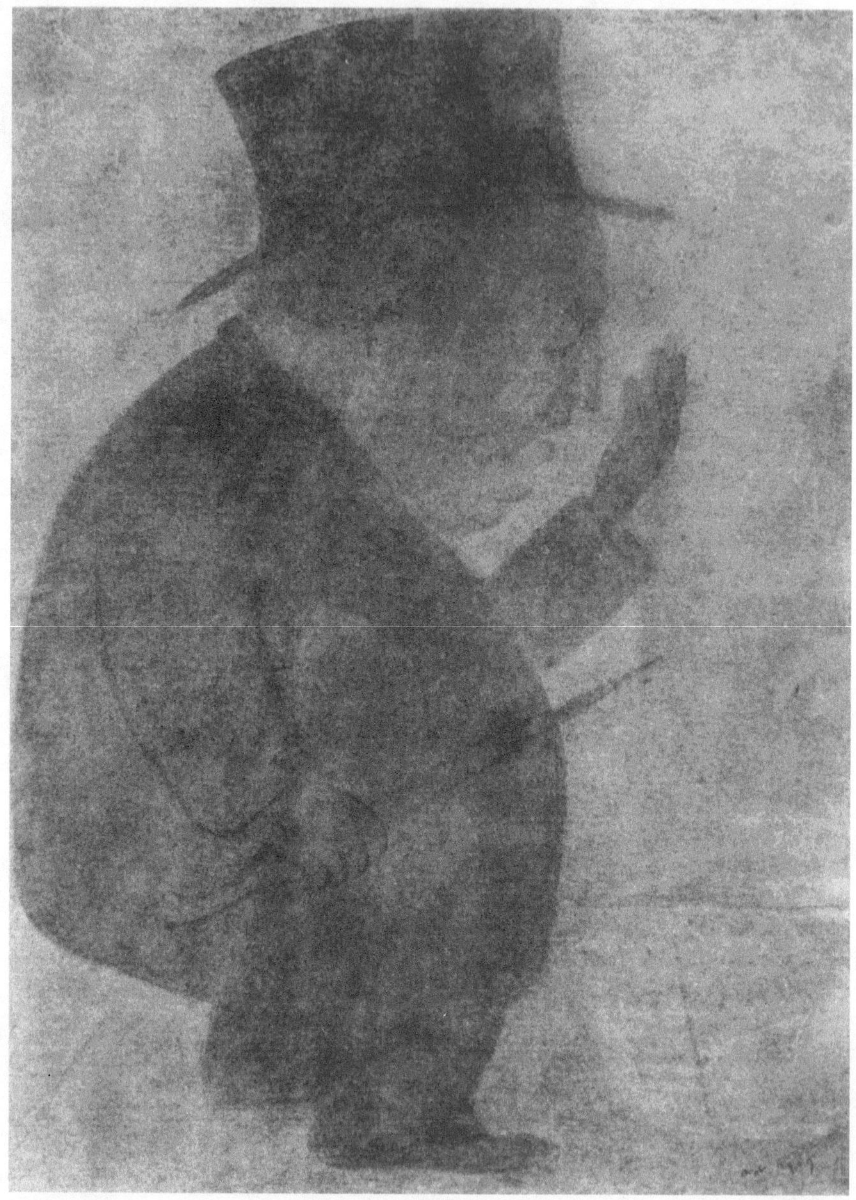

Max Beerbohm, "London in November, and Mr. Henry James in London" (*A Book of Caricatures*, London, Methuen and Company, 1907). "It was therefore, not without something of a shock that he, in this to him so very congenial atmosphere, now perceived that a vision of the hand which he had, at a venture, held up within an inch or so of his eyes was, with an awful clarity being adumbrated ..."

to account for the fixity with which he envisaged it, and for which he was to find, some years later, a motive in the (as it turned out) hardly generous fear that Eva had already made the great investigation "on her own." Her very regular breathing presently reassured him that, if she *had* peeped into "her" stocking, she must have done so in sleep. Whether he should wake her now, or wait for their nurse to wake them both in due course, was a problem presently solved by a new development. It was plain that his sister was now watching him between her eyelashes. He had half expected that. She really was – he had often told her that she really was – magnificent; and her magnificence was never more obvious than in the pause that elapsed before she all of a sudden remarked "They so very indubitably *are*, you know!"

It occurred to him as befitting Eva's remoteness, which was a part of Eva's magnificence, that her voice emerged somewhat muffled by the bedclothes. She was ever, indeed, the most telephonic of her sex. In talking to Eva you always had, as it were, your lips to the receiver. If you didn't try to meet her fine eyes, it was that you simply couldn't hope to: there were too many dark, too many buzzing and bewildering and all frankly not negotiable leagues in between. Snatches of other voices seemed often to intertrude themselves in the parley; and your loyal effort not to overhear these was complicated by your fear of missing what Eva might be twittering. "Oh, you certainly haven't, my dear, the trick of propinquity!" was a thrust she had once parried by saying that, in that case, *he* hadn't – to which his unspoken rejoinder that she had caught her tone from the peevish young women at the Central seemed to him (if not perhaps in the last, certainly in the last but one, analysis) to lack finality. With Eva, he had found, it was always safest to "ring off." It was with a certain sense of his rashness in the matter, therefore, that he now, with an air of feverishly "holding the line," said "Oh, as to that!"

Had *she*, he presently asked himself, "rung off"? It was characteristic of our friend – was indeed "him all over" – that his fear of what she was going to say was as nothing to his fear of what she might be going to leave unsaid. He had, in his converse with her, been never so conscious as now of the intervening leagues; they had never so insistently beaten the drum of his ear; and he caught himself in the act of awfully computing, with a certain statistical passion, the distance between Rome and Boston. He has never been able to decide which of these points he was psychically the nearer to at the moment when Eva, replying "Well, one does, anyhow, leave a margin for the pretext, you know!" made him, for the first time in his life, wonder whether she were not more magnificent than even he had ever given her credit for being. Perhaps it was to test this theory, or perhaps merely to gain time, that he now raised himself to his knees, and, leaning with outstretched arm towards the foot of his bed, made as though to touch the stocking which Santa Claus had, overnight, left dangling there. His posture, as he stared obliquely at Eva, with a sort of beaming defiance, recalled to him something seen in an "illustration." This reminiscence, however – if such it was, save in the scarred, the poor dear old woebegone and so very beguilingly *not* refractive mirror of the moment – took a peculiar twist from Eva's behaviour. She had, with startling suddenness, sat bolt upright, and looked to him as if she were overhearing some tragedy at the other end of the wire, where, in the nature of things, she was unable to arrest it. The gaze she fixed on her extravagant kinsman was of a kind to make him wonder how he contrived to remain, as he beautifully did, rigid. His prop was possibly the reflection that flashed on him that, if *she* abounded in attenuations, well, hang it all, so did *he*! It was simply a difference of plane. Readjust the "values," as painters say, and there you were! He was to feel that he was only too crudely "there" when, leaning further forward, he laid a chubby forefinger on the stocking, causing that receptacle to rock ponderously to and fro. This effect was more expected than the tears which started to Eva's eyes, and the intensity with which "Don't you," she exclaimed, "see?"

"The mote in the middle distance?" he asked. "Did you ever, my dear, know me to see anything else? I tell you it blocks out everything. It's a cathedral, it's a herd of elephants, it's the whole habitable globe. Oh, it's, believe me, of an obsessiveness!" But his sense of the one thing it *didn't* block out from his purview enabled him to launch at Eva a speculation as to just how far Santa Claus had, for the particular occasion, gone. The gauge, for both of them, of this seasonable distance seemed almost blatantly suspended in the silhouettes of the two stockings. Over and above the basis of (presumably) sweetmeats in the toes and heels, certain extrusions stood for a very plenary fulfilment of desire. And, since Eva *had* set her heart on a doll of ample proportions and practicable eyelids – had asked that most admirable of her sex, their mother, for it with not less directness than he himself had put into his demand for a sword and helmet – her coyness now struck Keith as lying near to, at indeed a hardly measurable distance from, the border-line of his patience. If she didn't *want* the doll, why the deuce had she made such a point of getting it? He was perhaps on the verge of putting this question to her, when, waving her hand to include both stockings, she said "Of course, my dear, you *do* see. There they are, and you know I know you know we wouldn't, either of us, dip a finger into them." With a vibrancy of tone that seemed to bring her voice quite close to him, "One doesn't," she added, "violate the shrine – pick the pearl from the shell!"

Even had the answering question "Doesn't one just?" which for an instant hovered on the tip of his tongue, been uttered, it could not have obscured for Keith the change which her magnificence had wrought in him. Something, perhaps, of the bigotry of the convert was already discernible in the way that, averting his eyes, he said "One doesn't even peer." As to whether, in the years that have elapsed since he said this either of our friends (now adult) has, in fact, "peered," is a question which, whenever I call at the house, I am tempted to put to one or other of them. But any regret I may feel in my invariable failure to "come up to the scratch" of yielding to this temptation is balanced, for me, by my impression – my sometimes all but throned and anointed certainty – that the answer, if vouchsafed, would be in the negative.

J.C. Squire, "If Henry James Had Written the Church Catechism," in *Tricks of the Trade*

Rpt. in *Collected Parodies* (London: Hodder & Stoughton, 1921), 91–3.

IF HENRY JAMES HAD WRITTEN

THE CHURCH CATECHISM

Q. What is your name?

A. It may possibly be conceived as standing in a relation of contiguity to a certain – shall we say? – somewhat complicatedly rectilinear design – to put it colloquially, a symbol – employed by such of the races of mankind as follow the Roman usage to denote a sort of suppressed explosion, or rather, a confused hum "produced" when the upper and the nether lip are brought with some firmness – or even, as one might phrase it, "snap" – together, and a continuous sound is compelled for egress to flow through a less harmonious though undeniably more prominent organ. Or, on the other hand, its relation to that so interesting figure may be something even closer than one of mere contiguity, however proximate, something in the nature of coincidence, of body and soul identity even: in a word, it may be, or, more exactly, may be represented by, that symbol itself.

Q. Who gave you that name?

A. Which?

Q. Oh, no, *not* the other one, the quite inevitably discursive family "label."

A. You mean my …

Q. Well yes, not that all so shared, and as it were almost – if one may forgivably say it – may one? – "vulgarized" – your, as they call it, "surname."

A. Oh, *not* that one?

Q. No …

A. The other?

Q. Yes – that other – that more exquisitely personal, the more (dare one?) *appropriated*, the one of which, I had thought, we touched, even grasped, the skirts when our interlocution, or to put it quite brutally, when we began our conversation.

A. You refer …

Q. I am, dear lady, all ears.

A. To, in fact, my – since we are both to be so frank – Christian name?

Q. Oh, but you are great!
A. Not *great*, not, I mean, really, in the sense that you mean …
Q. *I* mean?
A. The other sense, you know.
Q. Yes, I apprehend you, but it wasn't that one I meant.
A. Then what in the world was it?
Q. Take it from another point of view, wasn't frankness to be, always, our splendid object?
A. Explicitly.
Q. Wasn't it?
A. Oh no, I wouldn't doubt it; I wouldn't, really wouldn't, let you down.
Q. Not even gently?
A. The other way, I meant.
Q. Divine clarity! And who gave it you?
A. The Deluge!
Q. He was it, or she?
A. Oh, never he, as he would himself say, never on your life.
Q. And she?
A. She would, as she always will, bet her boots not!
Q. Not, surely it wasn't, they?
A. They!
Q. They!
A. Oh, certainly they! Who could have stopped them. Not miserable I, so pitifully, so hopelessly, so microscopically, futilely small! They were all there, and there was I. And they did it, oh, quite finally did it.
Q. Who?
(Etc.)

Susan Miles, "Wednesday or Thursday"

***London Mercury* 11:65 (March 1925): 475–8.**

Susan Miles was the pen name of Ursula (Wylie) Roberts. She was an anthologist and poet whose work appeared in various journals and in book form, beginning with *Dunch* (1918) and ending with the verse novel *Lettice Delmer* (1958). Miles's title, of course, refers to Woolf's 1921 short story collection *Monday or Tuesday*, which itself is a reference to her 1919 (rpt. 1925) essay "Modern Fiction," in which Woolf argued:

> Examine for a moment an ordinary mind on an ordinary day. The mind receives a myriad impressions – trivial, fantastic, evanescent, or engraved with the sharpness of steel. From all sides they come, an incessant shower of innumerable atoms; and as they fall, as they shape themselves into the life of Monday or Tuesday, the accent falls differently from of old; the moment of importance came not here but there; so that, if a writer were a free man and not a slave, if he could write what he chose, not what he must, if he could base his work upon his own feeling and not upon conventions, there would be no plot, no comedy, no tragedy, no love interest or catastrophe in the accepted style, and perhaps not a single button sewn on as the Bond Street tailors would have it. Life is not a series of gig lamps symmetrically arranged; life is a luminous halo, a semi-transparent envelope surrounding us from the beginning of consciousness to the end. (189)

With this emphasis on the ordinary, one of the central techniques of parody – bathos – becomes difficult to accomplish. Miles here attempts it anyway, in a text that lacks contextual explanation, in which almost nothing happens, and in which the prose wanders off in unpredictable tangents.

WEDNESDAY OR THURSDAY

(With apologies to V. . . . W . . . .)

Any day will do. Any hour. For our lives – and the stories of our lives – have no beginning, nor any terminus. Life is a rope with no ends. We pick a little here, shred at a strand there, but we never unravel it, never find the post to which it's hitched. One bit of the rope is as good as another then. Catch it wherever there's a loop. Twelve o'clock will do, or one o'clock. Wednesday will do, or Thursday.

Thursday let it be then: and mid-day. The clocks have just asseverated the latter fact with emphatic strokes. And let it be Fleet Street, and early January. It is sleeting; and Mr. Coddington's umbrella is slanted at an angle that exasperates old Colonel Tompkinson, as he trundles along towards Chancery Lane, with the east wind inflaming his gouty eyes, to negotiate the probate of his brother Montague's will, at Morrison and Levy's, the solicitors who have nursed the family's fortune ever since old General Tompkinson – Colonel Murray Tompkinson's great-uncle – won his thirteen thousand pounds in a single evening at baccarat from young Villiers-Carruthers of the Bengal Lancers. Villiers-Carruthers, poor goggle-eyed young subaltern, was seconded a couple of months later for being tipsy at a Mess ball and – among other things – tripping up his Major's shell-eared lady with his sword; after which he betook himself to a sun-bleached bit of jungle in the Deccan where he shattered his skull to splinters with the revolver his father had given him when he had passed second out of Sandhurst three years before. And there his collar-bone had lain, beneath a stunted palm tree, white and wind-swept, sand-scrubbed and unpolluted, till one of Sir Mortimer Harrington's beaters dropped a whiskey bottle unwittingly upon it, and powdered it to a little whorl of pale dust that the night-wind blew against the moon-lit sky, while the jackals howled a grim dirge that nobody heard but Baba-Harrington Sahib's *ayah*, as she mixed the Baba Sahib's bottle in the compound of the *dak* bungalow, and watched the fire-flies tangle themselves into little serpents of lemon coloured flame above the dun, parched pampas grass beneath the Pleiades.

Mr. Coddington hadn't meant to dig his umbrella into the Colonel's waistcoat. "Beg pardon, beg pardon, I'm sure," he had muttered apologetically as he withdrew it and boarded an omnibus crowded with emaciated girl clerks and fat brokers, who jostled one another's knees and strained to read the posters telling them that Tino had abdicated and the Epsom murderer had poisoned another mistress.

Mr. Coddington was going home to lunch at Tulse Hill with Mrs. Coddington and Mrs. Coddington's Aunt Elizabeth. He had a pine-apple under his arm and a roll of foolscap twisting from a string on his cold finger. The wind had come in a bitter little gust and had tipped his umbrella like a wine-glass. He hadn't meant to treat the Colonel with a lack of consideration.

But "Awkward great bounder," old Colonel Tompkinson had grumbled, flourishing his bushy white eye-brows. And he hadn't added, "but he's so distinguished looking," as people do when young men with short curled upper lips, and brows like statues by Praxiteles, blunder about like bulls in china shops, and pull at their loose socks, and stare, and stared with eyes that see the Acropolis, instead of the policeman blocking the traffic in the Strand with a fat white-gloved fist and an arm like a blue bolster.

The conductor was a very vicious-looking man, punching the blue and the white tickets as though they were the souls of the damned and he was branding them for their sins with his spiteful little torturing machine. Ting: click. Ting: click. "Any more fares, please?" "Move further up the 'bus there, please." "Any more fares, please?" He was husky. He had caught a cold. His wife would rub his chest with goose-grease saved from Christmas, when he went to bed that night. And little Jimmy would wake up in his cot to have goose-grease on his chest too. And the conductor, whose name was Henry Hopkins, and who had been in the Church Lads' Brigade once but was a free-thinker now, would cluck out a nursery rhyme at Jimmy until he forgot about the goose-grease, and turned over, to fall asleep again, looking like a shell-pink rose-leaf on a snow drift.

Mrs. Coddington had asked Miss Tatham Smith to lunch, and the Elliott-Frys, and young Mr. Molyneux, the architect.

"May I introduce Mr. Molyneux," said Mrs. Coddington. "Mr. Molyneux: Mrs. Elliott-Fry. Mr. Molyneux: Miss Tatham Smith."

"Such a pleasure ...," said Miss Tatham Smith.

"So often heard ...," said Mrs. Elliott-Fry.

"What a bitter wind to-day," said Mr. Molyneux.

"Yes," said Mrs. Elliott-Fry.

"Very bitter," said Miss Tatham Smith.

"Plymouth," said Mrs. Coddington's Aunt Elizabeth. "How well I know the place!"

"Delightful now," said Mr. Elliott-Fry," but I fear they will find it very enervating in the summer months."

"Yes, very enervating," said Mrs. Coddington's Aunt Elizabeth.

Mr. Coddington cut the pine-apple with a silver knife. It filled the heavy dining-room with a light, sweet, pungent freshness: and afterwards they all drank coffee out of little cups with blue spots and tiny pink rose-buds and Mrs. Coddington frowned a little, puckering her eye-lids, as she nodded responses to Mr. Elliott-Fry and remembered with irritation Nellie's clumsiness in breaking the little sugar bowl the day the sweep didn't come, though after all it mattered less than it might because the little chased one that Cousin Katharine (with an *a* – two *a*'s) had given them for their silver wedding was so sweet with the tiny curling handles, like baby ram's horns, on either side of it.

The blue ticket that Mr. Coddington dropped between someone's boots when he changed his 'bus at Wellington Street, fell on young Walter Cunningham's white one which had just fluttered down as he leapt from the 'bus to race along Aldwych and Kingsway, and cut across Holborn, up Bloomsbury Court, past the Italian wholesale confectioner's with the putty-pink cream cakes and sandy shortbreads in its window, on his way to collate texts of Dekker and of Massinger in the sneeze-punctuated silence beneath the great steamy dome of the British Museum Reading Room.

Young Walter Cunningham's passion for Massinger sent his purple-clocked ankles swinging at such a pace that he overtook and out-stripped a dozen less Hermes-footed figures between the cat and the policeman at the entrance gate and the sandwiches and the strutting pigeons and the goggling monolith from Easter Island at the top of the steps.

He overtook and outpaced old Miss Pickering, as she huddled along to study the Bhagavadgita and lament that she couldn't take a photograph of the intellect-soaked atmosphere – "such beautiful auras, I assure you" – that hovered over the heavy tomes and the bald heads beneath the inverted chalice of the roof.

He outpaced even Woodrow T. Von Sporberg on his way to hustle into existence an illustrated history of the universe, in words of two syllables, for five year olds and under, and to chew gum.

He outpaced Cassandra Kellaway, with her satchel of anarchist "literature," hatless, sandalled, with knit brows, in a *chiton*, striding on her way to study vital statistics, sneering as she strode, and snorting at the pigeons because the iridescent plumage on their breasts had a sexual significance.

He outstripped …

But let us consider 'bus tickets. Blue, white, pink, buff 'bus tickets. Trodden by muddy boots on floors of 'buses. Gripped by cold fingers. 'Bus tickets with printing on them: numbers: and little oblongs stamped with names. The Green Man, Chalk Farm, Herne Hill, Tulse Hill, Piccadilly Circus, Strand, Hammersmith, Clapham. Little bits of paste-board dealt out to men and women: dealt out to the hands of workingmen, bare, beefy, with coal-black nails: of clerks – thin, dingy, calloused where the pen rubbed: of prostitutes – pale and slender, with almond nails polished like tiny mirrors: of flower-women – purple, grimy, smelling of chrysanthemums and sweat: of typists – smeared with mauve carbon beneath cotton gloves too long in the fingers: of inky children, fingering satchel-straps, fidgetting, picking, pointing: of anaemic mothers – clutching babies in pink crochet, and grabbing at dropped dummies. 'Bus tickets dispensed by stern, silent men, with grim jowls, growing thin behind the ears, who will die of cancer some day: by little, rosy, facetious men, scattering rays of sunshine, who will go off sudden, from the heart: by twitchy-faced men, who stammer a little in the rush hours and go home irritable to their wives and don't want the steak-puddings that are steaming for them (*they* become nerve chronics, and twitch themselves to Kensal Green at last): by men with coughs, who couldn't stand the baking, and the doctor says the fresh air's just the thing: by men with bulging eyes yellowish about the whites, who can't eat *their* steak-puddings because of bile.

'Bus tickets – blue 'bus tickets, white 'bus tickets, buff 'bus tickets passing from hands to hands, helping to scatter little men and little women here and there, to city and suburb, shoved and shoving, staring and stared at, all mixed up, and yet all separate, each little man shut up in his own little skin, each little woman in hers: tight, tight, tight. Little monads, little windowless monads – or, at any rate, little monads with the blinds all drawn. Ah, but if only we could pluck up the corner of a blind, twitch it aside, and peep, peep, peep. On Wednesday and Thursday, on Thursday and Friday: in Fleet Street, in the Strand, in Lavender Hill: at twelve o'clock, at one o'clock …

Someone else has run into old Colonel Tompkinson now, as he trundles along with the east wind in his gouty eyes, turning from Chancery Lane into Fleet Street after negotiating the probate of his brother Montague's will. It is a woman this time, a woman with a fountain-pen in her pocket and the MS. of her last new novel under her arm.

"Damn the woman!" old Colonel Tompkinson has muttered, flourishing his bushy white eye-brows and turning a little purpler. "Damn the woman: couldn't she use her eyes! Ain't I plain enough and big enough for her to see?"

Ah, but nobody sees anyone, Colonel Tompkinson. It is no use trying to see anyone as a whole. An eye-brow here, a hint there. Here a waistcoat and there a shadow. That is all.

But Colonel Tompkinson has forgotten the woman before he has reached the Strand. The bubble of his irritation has whirled round in his brain like a bubble in his laundress's wash-tub. It has twirled in the water and disappeared for ever. Yes, it has burst.

PART II

Parodic Modes

I. Verse Commentary

As a vehicle for satire, verse (particularly rhyming couplets) has a long history. Its manifestations in modernism, though, acquired a particular flavour. Closely allied with the rise of magazines and newspapers, verse satires of modernism are most often found in the contributions of readers and daily columnists. Moreover, while earlier verse satire was no stranger to bathos, modernity's verse satires turn to bathos with a vengeance, employing it not just at the level of their verses' assertions, but also making it integral to their works' form. In short, they turn to doggerel. Because of its form, doggerel does not mimic or exaggerate the formal properties of its target texts, and instead tends to be more direct. It includes much more meta-commentary, and straightforwardly asserts the ideology of the versifier. Doggerel's form, though, is still part of its argument. Mimicking an awful earnestness, offering an apparent sincerity – yet so atrociously presented that it couldn't possibly be straight – the doggerel collected here isn't unintentionally bad. The works in this section draw attention to their awfulness, and in so doing use their atrociousness as part of their argument. The tortured rhymes have a knowing archness, aware of and delighting in the ghastly. At its worst the satire is merely coy; at its best the awkwardness (and the foregrounding of the awkwardness) has a loopy suppleness and grace. The relentless march of the doggerel itself (by forcing a rhyme or a metre to fit) deflates its target, in a context in which modernism was regularly under attack not just for being poor art, but for being pretentious. What is under parodic scrutiny is not so much the formal properties of modern art, but its social positioning and cultural claims. The sense that doggerel is all that modernism *deserves* is never far from these verses.

Don Marquis, "The Sun Dial: To G. S. and E. P."

***New York Evening Sun*, 3 October 1914. Gertrude Stein and Alice B. Toklas Papers, Yale Collection of American Literature, Beinecke Rare Book and Manuscript Library, Yale University.**

TO G. S. AND E. P.

Ye gods, in all these worlds of thine,
  Where shall the Super-Pote [*sic*] be found
To wed the Thoughts of Gertrude Stein
  Unto the Tunes of Ezra Pound?

When Gertrude thinks, the Thoughts of her
  Down dark abysses plunge and reel;
Each is a rebel Lucifer
  New-Slipped on cosmic orange-peel.

When Ezra sings, the Tunes of him
  Like buzz-saws rasp among the spheres
And all the shuddering cherubim
  Fold cottony wings across their ears.

Untrammelled Ones! The Commonplace
  Before them slithers in retreat;
Her Thoughts have knuckles on the face,
  His Verses stutter in the feet.

Free Spirits! All Conventions wheeze,
  When they appear, and gasp and die!
His honey-bees make only cheese,
  She sets her blacksmiths forging pie.

Oh Litterchoor! Oh Bunk! oh Art!
  Oh Cubist bard! Oh Futurist!
Have we not rent the Trite apart,
  And slapped the Usual on the wrist?

Have we not looped the lyric loop
  And put the language on the blink
And faked a-many a Little Group
  Who love to think that they can think?

Oh, much-appealed-to Muses Nine!
  Where shall the Super-Fake be found
To put the Thoughts of Gertrude Stein
  Into the Verse of Ezra Pound?

Don Marquis, "The Sun Dial: The Golden Group"

***New York Sun*, 26 March 1915. Gertrude Stein and Alice B. Toklas Papers, Yale Collection of American Literature, Beinecke Rare Book and Manuscript Library, Yale University.**

"Peppercorns and purple sleet
Enwrap me round from head to feet,
Wrap me around and make me thine,"
Said Amy Lowell to Gertrude Stein.

"Buzz-saws, buzzards, curds and glue
Show me my affinity for you.
You are my golden sister-soul,"
Said Gertrude Stein to Amy Lowell.

"Brainstorms, bricks and amber bocks
And little mice that dwell in clocks,
I am your brother, I'll be bound,"
Said the gooey frere, the Ezra Pound.

"Stewed unicorns and rampant prunes
And piebald gnats and plenilunes,
Bind me to you as with a cinch, –
I'm nuts myself," said Fothergil Finch.

"Curried sharks on a golden plate
And psychic ants that cerebrate, –
My love for you all what tongue can tell?"
Cried the Swami V. from his padded cell.

And Hermione harked to them, rapt, elate:
"And aren't they all of them simply great!
Of course, the bourgeois can't understand –
But aren't they wonderful? Aren't they grand!"

Franklin P. Adams, "To the Neo-Pseudoists" in *By and Large*

(Garden City, NY: Doubleday, Page & Co., 1914), 84.

TO THE NEO-PSEUDOISTS

Poets and painters and sculptors,
Ye of the screeching schools,
Scorners of Art's conventions
Haters of bonds and rules.

Mockers of line and rhythm,
Loathers of color and rhyme,
What of your new creations?
What of the Test of Time?

Fetters no longer bind you,
Ye of the New To-day,
But – if a dolt may ask it –
What have ye got to *say*?

Here is another question,
Less of the head than heart:
Is the new stuff wonderful merely
Because it is rotten art?

Horace B. Samuel, "Futurist Dress"

***New Age* 15.7 (1914): 152.**

A translator of Nietzsche and Stendahl, Horace Barnett Samuel (1883–?) was also the author of *Modernities* (1913), which includes a sympathetic and detailed account of literary futurism. In *Modernities*, Samuel argues "Yet if we strip this new 'beauty of mechanism' and 'aesthetic of speed' of its loud garb of ostentatious extravagance, the intrinsic theories themselves strike us as neither monstrous nor unreasonable" (217–18).

Futurist Dress

It is wrong to hint that morals are relaxed
By the androgynous designs of Bakst,[1]
For Futurism is so much a prude
It shrinks to let its very hair be nude,
And its coy locks will delicately rig
Out in a scarlet or caerulean wig,
While its ambiguous lines suavely drape
Both female, male, and every other shape,
And that the contrast you may quite perceive
The *passéist* par excellence was Eve.

Bert Leston Taylor, “A Line-o’-Type or Two”

***Chicago Daily Tribune*, 26 March 1913: 6.**

BYGONES.

LINES INSPIRED BY A VIEW OF THE CUBIST PAINTINGS, FOLLOWED BY A LATE SUPPER.

Or ever a lick of Art was done,
  Or ever a one to care,
I was a Purple Polygon
  And you were a Sky-Blue Square.

You yearned for me across a void,
  For I lay in a different plane.
I’d set my heart on a Red Rhomboid,
  And your sighing was in vain.

You pined for me, as well I knew,
  And you faded day by day,
Until the Square that was heavenly Blue
  Had paled to an ashen gray.

A myriad years or less or more
  Have softly fluttered by;
Matters are much as they were before,
  Except ’tis I that sigh.

I yearn for you, but I have no chance;
  You lie in a different plane.
I break my heart for a single glance,
  And I break said heart in vain.

And ever I grow more pale and wan,
  And taste your old despair,
When I was a Purple Polygon
  And you were a Sky-Blue Square.

Nevertheless, notwithstanding, however, and but – we found the Cubist pictures fascinating, and, unexpectedly, the most convincing of the "queer" canvases. Returning half a dozen times to "The Procession in Seville," we suddenly "got it," a lightning-swift revealment, not merely of this picture, but of the thing the Cubists are trying for. It was quite exciting.

There is the chance that we were in a hypnotic state, induced by the compelling passes of Jo Davidson, who held us with a glittering eye and said, very calmly, "Picabia's 'Procession' is a better picture than his 'Dance' because you can't see so much in it." And that lifted another veil.

II. Manifestos

In the eyes of their public, modernist texts and artworks didn't come into being on their own. Early on, as the *Spectra* hoax makes clear, modernism was understood to be motivated, understandable, and justified through a theoretical discourse. Theory-based launchings of modernist art abound, sometimes in classic manifestos like those of the Futurists, and sometimes as prefaces in anthologies, or in letters to the editor.

Parodic interventions into these manifestos return to the same issues: the mechanisms of publicity, the place of theory and group identities in art, and pretentiousness and obfuscation as tools for gaining cultural power. Constantia Stone, in a letter to *The New Age*, proposed to set up her own school in light of Pound's "misunderstanding" of her. She replied:

> When Imagistes misunderstand Imagistes, who shall comprehend them? I am disheartened. To-day I form a new school. I and my adherents become the "Neo-Luminists." We are primitives inasmuch as we take for our cliché the first recorded word of Almighty God, "Let there be light." We ask Mr. John Duncan to join us, for he says, "Mr. Pound, be clear." We can only repeat the lucid phrase of Mr. Duncan. Mr. Pound will perhaps write an affirmation concerning the "Neo-Luminists" in order to clarify his prose. (16.16, 18 February 1915: 439)

In a 1931 *New York Times* review of Wallace Stevens's *Harmonium*, Percy Hutchison took a retrospective look at the manifestos of the beginning of the twentieth century:

> In the second decade of this century – the movement began in the first decade – numerous poetic schools drove theory hard. Perhaps none strove especially to carry out Lanier's color hypothesis, but there were the Imagists, and there was

> Vorticism and Cubism, and many more "isms" besides. For the most part, these schools have died the death which could have been prophesied for them. Poetry is founded in ideas; to be effective and lasting, poetry must be based on life, it must touch and vitalize emotion. For proof, one has but to turn to the poetry that has endured. In poetry, doctrinaire composition has no permanent place. (9 August: 4)

Sceptics also noted that, in addition to relying on theory and its accompanying overblown rhetoric, manifestos underscored that art was coming to public attention as the product of groups. Harold Monro cynically noted that the way for a contemporary poet to get ahead was to join a group: "The Group will pass remarks on books it has not read, of which he will pick out the cleverest for his own use. The Group also will teach him quickly to talk extremely cleverly about modern painting. And it will publish a periodical, or anthology, in which his poems will be printed" (1920: 11).

And finally, manifestos were understood to be a device for creating attention. As Monro suggested, "The object of the Group is generally the attainment of wider publicity by a combination of forces" (1920: 15). Sceptics understood this, of course, to be undeserved publicity. In an interview with his friend Max Bodenheim that may or may not have actually taken place, novelist and future screenwriter Ben Hecht got Bodenheim to talk about his career as "Rene d'Or":

> Everybody was getting out manifestos in those days. And I decided to issue one myself. So I got a friend in with me and we wrote a manifesto proclaiming that the Monotheme School of Poetry had arrived and that Rene D'Or was the Grand Kleagel. The manifesto said that poets were writing about too many themes and that they should all consolidate and write about the same theme and that Monsieur D'Or would issue the subject each month. And the first subject was Bottles. I wrote five poems about bottles and printed them on the Manifesto and then we mailed 1,000 copies to every editor worth a damn. And then I got a room in the Morrison Hotel, registering as Rene D'Or and we notified the papers they could send reporters to interview this latest poetical freak and I waited in that damn place from nine in the morning till midnight and nobody came. Nobody even called up. I nearly starved because I was afraid to leave the room even for a minute. But nobody came and nobody even printed a word about our world shaking Manifesto of Rene D'Or. "It all goes to show how," Mr. Bodenheim stammered indignantly, "how unlucky I am." ("The Vers Libre Jinx")

Anne Knish and Emanuel Morgan [Arthur Davison Ficke and Witter Bynner], "Preface" to *Spectra. A Book of Poetic Experiments*

(New York: Mitchell Kennerley, 1916), ix–xii.

The work of poets Arthur Davison Ficke and Witter Bynner, *Spectra* was the most successful literary hoax of modernism. The editors of the *Little Review*, *Poetry*, *The Forum*, and *Others* were all taken in, and it was seriously discussed in Lloyd Morris's 1917 *The Young Idea* (the periodical history of *Spectra* can be found in Suzanne Churchill's "The Lying Game: *Others* and the Great Spectra Hoax of 1917"). In a spectacularly self-referential performance of log-rolling, Witter Bynner (writing under the name Witter Bynner) reviewed Spectrism in the November 1916 *New Republic*, giving it a mixed endorsement – not too pleased with Spectra's theory, which he described as "heavily presented by Anne Knish as if she were a graduate of some German university." Bynner ended the review with a coyness that he must have found delicious: "But, whether or not there be meaning or magic in the book, I can promise that there is amusement in it and that it takes a challenging place among current literary impressionistic phenomena."

PREFACE

This volume is the first compilation of the recent experiments in Spectra. It is the aim of the Spectric group to push the possibilities of poetic expression into a new region, – to attain a fresh brilliance of impression by a method not so wholly different from the methods of Futurist Painting.

An explanation of the term "Spectric" will indicate something of the nature of the technique which it describes. "Spectric" has, in this connection, three separate but closely related meanings. In the first place, it speaks, to the mind, of that process of diffraction by which are disarticulated the several colored and other rays of which light is composed. It indicates our feeling that the theme of a poem is to be regarded as a prism, upon which the colorless white light of infinite existence falls and is broken up into glowing, beautiful, and intelligible hues. In its second sense, the term Spectric relates to the reflex vibrations of physical sight, and suggests the luminous appearance which is seen after exposure of the eye to intense light, and, by analogy, the after-colors of the poet's initial vision. In its third sense, Spectric connotes the overtones, adumbrations, or spectres which for the poet haunt all objects both of the seen and the unseen world, – those shadowy projections, sometimes grotesque, which, hovering around the real, give to the real its full ideal significance and its poetic worth. These spectres are the manifold spell and true essence of objects, – like the magic that would inevitably encircle a mirror from the hand of Helen of Troy.

Just as the colors of the rainbow recombine into a white light, – just as the reflex of the eye's picture vividly haunts sleep, – just as the ghosts which surround reality are the vital part of that existence, – so may the Spectric vision, if successful, synthesize, prolong, and at the same time multiply the emotional images of the reader. The rays which the poet has dissociated into colorful beauty should recombine in the reader's brain into a new intensity of unified brilliance. The reflex of the poet's sight should sustain the original perception with a haunting keenness. The insubstantiality of the poet's spectres should touch with a tremulous vibrancy of ultimate fact the reader's sense of the immediate theme.

If the Spectrist wishes to describe a landscape, he will not attempt a map, but will put down those winged emotions, those fantastic analogies, which the real scene awakens in his own mind. In practice this will be found to be the vividest of all modes of communication, as the touch of hands quickens a mere exchange of names.

It may be noted that to Spectra, to these reflected experiences of life, as we perceive them, adheres often a tinge of humor. Occidental art, in contrast to art in the Orient, has until lately been afraid of the flash of humor in its serious works. But a growing acquaintance with Chinese painting is surely liberating in our poets and painters a happy sense of the disproportion of man to his assumed place in the universe, a sense of the tortuous grotesque vanity of the individual. By this weapon, man helps defend his intuition of the Absolute and of his own obscure but real relation to it.

The Spectric method is as yet in its infancy; and the poems that follow are only experimental efforts toward the desired end. Among them, the most obvious illustrations of the method are perhaps Opus 41 by Emanuel Morgan and Opus 76 by Anne Knish.

Emanuel Morgan, with whom the Spectric theory originated, has found the best expression of his genius in regular metrical forms and rhyme. Anne Knish, on the other hand, has used only free verse. We wish to make it clear that the Spectric manner does not necessitate the employment of either of these metrical systems to the exclusion of the other.

Although the members of our group would by no means attempt to establish a claim as actual inventors of the Spectric method, yet we can justifiably say that we have for the first time used the method consciously and consistently, and formulated its possibilities by means of elaborate experiment. Among recent poets in English, we have noted few who can be regarded in a sure sense as Spectrists.

ANNE KNISH.

Anne Knish and Emanuel Morgan [Arthur Davison Ficke and Witter Bynner], "The Spectric School of Poetry"

***The Forum*, June 1916: 675–7.**

THE SPECTRIC SCHOOL OF POETRY

The Vorticist School of poetry died an ignominious death in London, snuffed out by the explosion of the war. This was no great loss, because the experiments of this school, though interesting, were actuated by a wrong theory of poetic expression. These writers underestimated the amount of clarity which even the most daring poetic sketches must have; as a result, their works hardly resembled human speech.

The Spectric School has tried to avoid this pitfall which menaces all really original poets. Even in its most novel efforts at advancing the frontier of the known world of poetry, it has retained a measurable degree of communication with the world of every-day speech. It has done this in spite of the fact that it was engaged in working out a theory that might easily have led to excesses of abstraction.

The theory of the Spectric School is not difficult to grasp if one comes to it with an open mind. Its formula divides itself naturally into two propositions, alike in essence but different in application.

The first of these propositions affects the mental attitude of the poet in so far as he is a perceiver of objects and a recipient of impressions; the second affects him in so far as he is the portrayer of objects and the creator of expressions. We may take them up separately.

Every object, scene, person, and episode of the human world is to be regarded by the Spectric poet as a concrete focus of infinities. The subject of every Spectric poem has the function of a prism, upon which falls the white light of universal and immeasurable possible experience; and this flood of colorless and infinite light, passing through the particular limitations of the concrete episode before us, is broken up, refracted and diffused into a variety of many-colored rays. Some one of these rays will impress the poet more than others; and he will necessarily color his whole poem with its hue. But in so doing – and no amount of care can enable him to do otherwise – he must, if he is to create a fine work, have regard for the fragmentary nature of his perception, and allow his creative imagination to indicate some relation between his limited and single-colored vision and the great stream of pure light from which the vision originally was separated. As is said in the preface to the forthcoming book *Spectra*, by Emanuel Morgan, the discoverer of the theory, and Anne Knish, "the theme of a poem is to be regarded as a prism, upon which the colorless white light of experience falls and is broken up into glowing, beautiful, and intelligible hues." This preface omits to point out the fact that the poet must by means of his reconstructive vision bring to the reader some hint of the original light in all its completeness. Spectrists, however, are putting this extension of the theory into effect.

The second proposition of the Spectric School relates to the method of expression; and involves some consideration of the psychological processes by which the mind forms images of the outside world. The senses, and the mind behind them, act to a certain extent as a prism in relation to the emanations of the physical world. Vibrations of sound, color, or heat impact upon the sensory nerves, are conveyed in the form of a totally different kind of vibration to the brain, and there become once more transformed into some variety of emotion or motor impulse. Thus a flower, when it reaches the conscious intelligence *via* this devious channel, is no longer the flower of the outer world; it is the plexus of a number of different impressions. Just as a beam of white light breaks up in passing through a prism, and becomes a spectrum, so the entity of the flower is dismembered when it enters the consciousness. We perceive the color, the qualities of its form in space, the scent of the pollen and the stem, its coolness and smoothness and softness to the touch, its faint rustle as the wind stirs it. Out of these elements the mind, behind the prism of the senses, must recombine by another act of the intelligence the parted rays, in order that it may grasp the unity, the white light, the Platonic Idea of the original flower.

In art, particularly in poetry, it is a great gain to be clearly aware of these facts, and to take conscious advantage of them. This is the aim of the Spectrist. He tries, not to give the flower in its original unity, which is impossible, but to make perceptible the various rays, the various elements, out of which the perceiving mind would have, in the case of an actual first-hand perception, to create its idea of the flower. Or, to choose a more complex example, if he wishes to describe a landscape, he will not attempt a map, but will put down those winged emotions, those fantastic analogies, which the real scene awakens in his own mind. In practice this will be found to be the vividest of all modes of communication, as the touch of hands quickens a mere exchange of names.

The Imagists, suicidally advertised by a concerted reciprocal chorus of poet-reviewers, might once have been capable of employing this very theory in a tentative way. The time is past, however, when Spectrists can hope for co-operation in this quarter: and the latest of the modern movements in poetry must be content to go its own way after the fashion of "the spear that knows no brother."

OPUS 181

ANNE KNISH

Skeptical cat,
Calm your eyes, and come to me.
For long ago, in some palméd forest,
I too felt claws crawling
Within my fingers . . . .
Moons wax and wane;
My eyes, too, once narrowed and widened.
Why do you shrink back?
Come to me: let me pat you –
Come, vast-eyed one . . . .
Or I will spring upon you
And with steel-hook fingers
Tear you limb from limb . . . .
  There were twins in my cradle . . . .

OPUS 45

EMANUEL MORGAN

An angel, bringing incense, prays
Forever in that tree;
I go blind still when the locust sways
Those honey-domes for me.

  All the fragrances of dew, O angel, are there; –
The myrrhic rapture of young hair,
The lips of lust;
And all the stenches, of dust; –
Even the palm and the fingers of a hand burnt bare
With a curling sweet-smelling crust,
And the bitter staleness of old hair,
Powder on a withering bust.

The moon came through the window to our bed.
And the shadows of the locust-tree
On your sweet white body made of me,
Of my lips, a drunken bee.

O tree-like Spring, O blossoming days,
I who some day shall be dead,
Shall have ever a lover to sway with me.
For when my face decays
And the earth molds in my nostrils, shall there not be
The breath therein of a locust-tree,
The seed, the shoot of a locust-tree,
The honey-domes of a locust-tree? –
Until lovers go blind and sway with me –

O tree-like Spring, O blossomy days,
To sway as long as the locust sways!

Ernest L. Meyer, "An Introduction to Ultra-Violet Poetry"

***Wisconsin Literary Magazine*, January 1917: 111–12.**

Ernest Ludwig Meyer (1892–1952) was an editor of the *Wisconsin Literary Magazine*, for which he wrote this parody of *Spectra*, thinking at the time that *Spectra* was for real. Over the course of his lifetime Meyer was a contributor to the *American Mercury* and *Colliers*, a columnist for several newspapers, and the author of several memoirs. His *Hey! Yellowbacks!* Is an account of his time as a conscientious objector during the Second World War.

The Wisconsin Literary Magazine stands for the exchange of ideas. It also welcomes originality in the medium with which this change is effected. It is with pleasure, therefore, that the "Lit" introduces the Ultra-Violet school of poetry, which, while in form akin to the older schools of free verse, is in content an original departure along lines that assures for itself a warm reception and a long life.

Ultra-Violet poetry owes its inception to pure chance, partaking of the nature of sudden inspiration. It originated with Prof. X (a distant relation of Madame X) who, listening to a piano recital one day last week, found himself thinking, not of winged seraphs, or love, or voices of departed friends, or any of a thousand commonplace things, but of three ringtailed baboons seated on a can of kerosene and playing Yankee Doodle on a clamshell. Amazed at the phenomenon, Prof. X set down his impression in the form of free verse, the first of the Ultra-Violet school.

It will be observed that the basic principle of the new school is the association of ideas ordinarily unassociated. To the unimaginative, this savors of insanity; but the psychologist recognizes the phenomenon, while the poet goes a step farther and sees in it the highest manifestation of inspiration. One man, says the poet, sees a tomcat on a back fence and thinks of brickbats and shotguns, which is banality and matter-of-fact prose; another man sees the same cat and immediately associates it with false teeth and a lawn party in Chicago, which is genius and Ultra-Violet poetry.

An analysis of Blossom 449 A will make clear this distinction.

MANUAL ORGAN

BLOSSOM 449, A

Four freckled dumplings in a plate of soup,
  A moon of damask steel above the pine;
A pound of lead, a hungry colored man –
  Oh, heart of mine!

This linking of ideas that are apparently at the opposite ends of the impressionistic gamut may seem to the bourgeois a mere freak of corrupted fancy, or a senseless striving after originality at the expense of any semblance of probability. But to the elect few, there are subtle connecting links between the ideas which escape the notice of minds hampered and atrophied by dusty literary conventions. What grounds are there, for instance, for associating the idea of a pound of lead with a hungry colored man? None! say you. Then you damn yourself forever as a person obviously and utterly devoid of any vestige of imagination. Your mind, in a flash, should reason as follows: a pound of lead is a weight; a wait is a pause; a pause is a short stop; a short stop is a ball player; a ball player is a foul grabber; a fowl grabber is a hungry negro. We have pointed out these links at the risk of indicating the obvious; yet so greatly has the imagination degenerated that the ordinary person can establish no connection whatever between a pound of lead and a hungry, colored man except through the medium of a blunderbuss.

To encourage the growth of the new school of verse, the Lit will hold a page open to contributors, and as an inducement will offer a standing prize – not a loving cup or a year's subscription, which the word commonly connotes – but an excellent chrome-leather shoe, filled with the right foot of the editor and delivered in person in the most appropriate anatomical region of the winner. ERNEST L. MEYER.

DEDICATION – TO EMANUEL KNISH

  The Only Begettum of this Wreath.
O, spectro poet,
  With mind like a mad mole
Whose thoughts like spectres go it,
Each on a separate sole.

Is it enough to have uttered,
The madness of a mullah,
And many white leaves cluttered
With dull black marks, and duller?

I knew a writer whose two pens,
One stub, one fine,
Would scrawl
Words intense as ink is dense:
He has children nine,
They all bawl.

MANUAL ORGAN.

NANNE PISH

BLOSSOM 16

Last night
I sought the place where I died,
And I found it.
There was a laurel there,
And a stately marble shaft
And a bronze tablet.
But I hate the smell of bay rum.

Cranks, 1921: An Anthology. Compiled by Obert, Sebert, and Ethelberta Standstill [pseud.]

(London: A.H. Stockwell, 1921).

The author of *Cranks* is unknown. The following parody is complicated in its direction, having an implicit argument about several aspects of "Sitwellism": the Sitwells' anthology *Wheels*, which appeared from from 1916 to 1921; their poetry; and their eccentric public personae, which were at least as famous to the public as their verse.

CRANKS, 1921

We dedicate this book to the primitive man who first said, "OWCH."

By the Compilers

With this, the fifth successive annual appearance of "Cranks," has arrived the necessity of a definite and definitive statement of our position.

Already "Standstillism" is a word upon the lips of the *cognoscenti*, if not yet upon those of the *illiterati*. Future biographers are at this moment busy gathering "Standstillana."

We, the "Cranks" group, are not simply a vogue; not merely a symptom; we are more than a sign in the heavens: we are the beginning of an epoch.

None denies that the world is in a mess. We alone have observed that it is a mess of syrup. The world is drunk with honey – the cloying mead of the poets.

Poesy in the past has crushed sweetness from the babble of tongues. It has distilled a honey-dew from the waves set up by the vibrations of the vocal chords. The clean cold ice of speech has been melted into slush: the crush of sound watered to pap.

We are truth made manifest, reality incarnate, life naked. We are words dignified but unadorned; speech sane but simple.

To say we are obscure is a lie. We are the apotheosis of clarity. Only the fuddled find *us* fuddled.

The poetry of the past touched and reached one in a hundred. We touch everybody. Moreover, (and in this lies our vitality), not only can everyone read, and revel in, 'Standstillism,' but everyone can write it. That is why we are a new epoch.

Only two weeks ago our little nephew, Peveril Standstill, came to pay us a first visit. The boy, who is only four years of age, had spent the whole of his short life at Ballybunion in Kerry. After two days and a night in our atmosphere he produced the following poem.

I have a horse
All spotty;
He is wooden;
So are his legs.

Is there anything else to be said? We are content to stand or fall by this youthful effort. We place it on our banner. Let it be the test of our truth, and the measure of our achievement.

E.S.
O.S
S.S.
London, Jan. 1st, 1921

A NEO-NEO-TRIO

by Obert, Sebert, and Ethelberta Standstill

OMNES:
Out of one womb we came,
One – two – three;
We,
The three
Incomprehensibles;
Three
Monstrous births.
None understandeth us;
We
Do not understand
Ourselves.

OBERT:
There was no poesy
Before us.
When I clung
Clamourous to my mother's breast –

ETHELBERTA: *(interrupting)*
Cease the syrup!

OBERT: *(hanging his head)*
When I hung
Shrieking to the dugs of my dam –

SEBERT:
And I,
When I yowled and howled,
Mewed, puked, snuffled, spat,
Drooled,
Hic –
Cupped –

OMNES:
When we were weaned,
Poesy leapt to life:
Keats there had been,
And Shelley,
Milton, and a few
Others we knew;
But they

SEBERT:
Were sugar and slops,
Cinnamon,
Spices,
Dutch Drops –[2]
Ugh!

ETHELBERTA:
With us
Came words
Of wood:
Oak words, beech words, pine words, ash words, willow words;
Wooden words
Of wood –
Utterly wooden.

OMNES:
We
Do not write for the living;
We
Write for the dead;
Because
They are in coffins
Of wood.

Harold B. Harrison, "Pastiche. Initial Manifesto of the 'Fatuists' to the Public"

***New Age* 10.22 (1912): 524.**

Harold B. Harrison was an inexhaustible contributor to *The New Age*. The immediate context for the following pastiche was the current Futurist exhibition at the Sackville Gallery, for which Marinetti had given an introductory lecture.

"We shall sing the love of danger.

"We shall extol feverish insomnia, the somersault, the box on the ear.

"For men on their death-bed ... the admirable past may be balsam to their wounds. But we will have none of it – we, the young, the strong, and the living FUTURISTS. We are the primitives of a completely renovated sensitiveness. We stand upon the summit of the world and once more we cast our challenge to the stars! Your objections? Enough! Enough! We know them! Beware of repeating those infamous words! We stand upon the summit of the world."

– Italian Futurists' Manifesto

WORMS! – TURN! !

Borne on the moulting wings of the Past we come to you, alighting in a spiral vol-planè of ecstasy at your feet!

TURN! – WORMS ! !

Our message is of emancipation from the rusted chains of Antiquity which bind you – Andromeda-like – to the rock of Tradition. In our helm flash the sun-gilt ailerons of Perseus, and at our heels whirl the twin propellers of the "Antoinette."[3] As we pass the stars faint and reel in their orbit and the moon turns sick with vertigo!!

WORMS! – TURN ! ! !

The eldest of us is only six and a half years old (come April 1 next), and, with the assistance of one "Old Moore,"[4] we can turn out this sort of thing by the ream; moreover, it has been calculated that if we live till we are twenty-one we will come of age!

TURN! – WORMS ! ! !

We are Iconoclasts! Bubbling Aetnas in a state of dynamic frenzy! Our mission is to destroy the Albert Memorial, Madame Tussaud's, "The Star and Garter," and the A.B.C. Depôt at South Kensington Station. (Failing this last, we might be satisfied with the Houses of Parliament or " Dirty Dick's.")[5]

WORMS! – TURN ! ! ! !

We wish to glorify – (the list of "Fatuists" is not yet completed). We are anarchists in baby-linen; Nemeses in bib-and-tucker: we are out for trouble and we simply don't care! SO THERE!!!!!

TURN! – WORMS ! ! !

Our Crown is Obscurity, our Sceptre – Disdain. Wreathe laurels about the arms of the Venus of Milo if you will; anoint with nard the feet of the Theseus if you must; scatter garlands before the Monna [*sic*] Lisa – if you can: but for us, a circlet of garlic-dewy and virginal – all about our ears!

WORMS!! – TURN!!!!!!

(For we don't mind telling you, in confidence, that, this time, we really are – "IT.")

WE DECLARE THAT: –

It is inevitable that the nauseating, sordid realism of the so-called "Futurists" must give way to a form of artistic expression more idealistic and refined; the least progressive of academies is beginning to aspire towards the aceticism of the "Fatuists," and the day is not far distant when the painter who attempts to appeal to the emotions through the sense of sight will be as dead as Marionetti [*sic*] himself.

To us, the little devoted band of "Fatuists," belongs the honour of introducing to the art of painting an appeal to the senses of Hearing and Smelling: we challenge the world to produce a painting comparable, in its varied appeal, with our adored Fulsome's portrait of Madame X.! Even Messrs. Lewis Hind and Konody[6] – acknowledged masters in the art of naïve gullibility – were forced to admit that: –

"Fulsome's immortal picture of Mme. X. is the finest painting we have heard since smelling Bunkum's memorable 'Afterglow in a Turkish Bath' in the galleries at Versailles."

A description of this impeccable work will serve to explain the attitude and motives of the "Fatuists." Our description is taken from the catalogue of our first exhibition at Limehouse: –

"No. 10. – Portrait of Mme. X. on the slack-wire. In this work Fulsome has endeavoured to express the sensations and emotions of the wire as it bends and sways beneath the weight of Mme. X. As it might be contended that Mme. X. never did walk upon a slack-wire the artist has anticipated the objection by leaving out, in a masterly manner, the lady from the picture.

"As one approaches the canvas a curious, sickening odour is perceptible; this is expressive of Mme. X.'s opinion of the 'Fatuists.' The gradual crescendo of sound vibrations following the first sensation of scent is a masterly interpretation of the wire's contempt for the rather ponderous lady whose name gives the title to the picture.

"Mingling with the strengthening odour of stale eggs and decaying vegetables (suggestive of the opinions of the audience-spectators) will be noticed a staccato movement in two syllables, vaguely suggesting the sounds "rot" and "ton," repeated regularly and at intervals; this may be aptly described as a polyphonic scent-symphony in duet form, expressing at once the opinions of Mme. X. and the spectator-audience towards each other.

"The soft, purring obbligato dimly audible is an undercurrent of reminiscence and anecdotage connected with Mme. X.'s pet poodle, and is further expressed, aromatically, by the faint odour of dog-biscuits soaking in weak wine.

"In conclusion, we claim that this picture is a triumph of dynamic and static sound appealing in acoustical and aromatical sense-vibrations to the sense of touch."

Fulsome's Obiter Dicta

"Silence is sound unexpressed."
"Beauty is ugliness unexposed."
"The sweetest sounds are those unseen."
"Academies are Sarcophagi of the Soul."
"Give me health and a day and I will make the art of painting ridiculous!"
"Modern painting is the conscientious interpretation of Nature seen through the distorting mirrors of convention."
"The highest form of art is the – misunderstood."
"Realism is the Impossible made plausible."

Don Marquis, "Fothergil Finch, The Poet of Revolt," in *Hermione and Her Little Group of Serious Thinkers*

(New York: D. Appleton and Co., 1916), 24–8.

Don Marquis (1878–1937) wrote a daily column for the *New York Evening Sun*, "The Sun Dial," and, beginning in 1922, wrote the regular column "The Tower" for the *New York Tribune*. During the early years of modernism he wrote numerous sketches about fashionable modernity, centred on a collection of Greenwich Village–based characters, which he entitled Hermione and Her Little Group of Serious Thinkers. His attitude towards his version of modernism was one of cynical disdain:

I visited one night, of late,
Thought's Underworld, the Brainstorm Slum,
The land of Futile Piffledom;
A salon weird where congregate
Freak, Nut and Bug and Psychic Bum.
There, there, they sit and cerebrate:
The fervid Pote who never potes,
Great Artists, Male or She, that Talk
But scorn the Pigment and the Chalk,
And Cubist sculptors wild as Goats.

(*Hermione and Her Little Group of Serious Thinkers*, 1916: 1)

Today, Marquis retains a loyal following, primarily on the strength of his *Archy and Mehitabel*, a series of short stories / character sketches based on the adventures of a cockroach who was the reincarnation of a free-verse poet, and who continued his poetry writing by jumping on the keys of Marquis's typewriter after Marquis had left work for the evening.

FOTHERGIL FINCH, THE POET OF REVOLT

Isn't it odd how some of the most radical and advanced and virile of the leaders in the New Art and the New Thought don't look it at all?

There's Fothergil Finch, for instance. Nobody could be more virile than Fothy is in his Soul. Fothy's Inner Ego, if you get what I mean, is a Giant in Revolt all the time.

And yet to look at Fothy you wouldn't think he was a Modern Cave Man. Not that he looks like a weakling, you know. But – well, if you get what I mean – you'd think Fothy might write about violets instead of thunderbolts.

Dear Papa is *entirely* mistaken about him.

Only yesterday dear papa said to me, "Hermione, if you don't keep that damned little *vers libre* runt away from here I'll put him to work, and he'll die of it."

But you couldn't expect Papa to appreciate Fothy. Papa is *so* reactionary and conservative.

And Fothy's life is one long, grim, desperate struggle against Conventionality, and Social Injustice, and Smugness, and the Established Order, and Complacence. He is forever being a martyr to the New and True in Art and Life.

Last night he read me his latest poem – one of his greatest, he says – in which he tries to tell just what his Real Self is. It goes:

Look at me!
Behold, I am founding a New Movement!
Observe me … I am in Revolt!
I revolt!
Now persecute me, persecute me, damn you, persecute me, curse you, persecute me!
Philistine,
Bourgeois,
Slave,
Serf,
Capitalist,
Respectabilities that you are,
Persecute me!
Bah!
You ask me, do you, what am I in revolt against?
Against you, fool, dolt, idiot, against you, against everything!
Against Heaven, Hell and punctuation … against Life, Death, rhyme and rhythm …
Persecute me now, persecute me, curse you, persecute me!
Slave that you are … what do Marriage, Tooth-brushes, Nail-files, the Decalogue, Handkerchiefs, Newton's Law of Gravity, Capital, Barbers, Property, Publishers, Courts, Rhyming Dictionaries, Clothes, Dollars, mean to Me?
I am a Giant, I am a Titan, I am a Hercules of Liberty, I am Prometheus, I am the Jess Willard[7] of the New Cerebral Pugilism, I am the Modern Cave Man, I am the Comrade of the Cosmic Urge, I have kicked off the

Boots of Superstition, and I run wild along the Milky Way without ingrowing toenails,
I am I!
Curse you, what are You?
You are only You!
Nothing more!
Ha!
Bah! … persecute me, now persecute me!

Fothy always gets excited and trembles and chokes when he reads his own poetry, and while he was reading it Papa came into the room and disgraced himself by asking if there was any *Money* in that kind of poetry, and Fothy was so agitated that he fairly screamed when he said:

"Money … money … curse money! Money is one of the things I am in revolt against … Money is death and damnation to the free spirit!"

Papa said he was sorry to hear that; he said one of his companies needed an ad writer, and he didn't have any objection to hiring a free spirit with a punch, but he couldn't consider getting anyone to write ads that hated money, for there was a salary attached to the job.

And Fothy said: "You are trying to bribe me! Capitalism is casting its net over me! You are trying to make me a serf: trying to silence a Free Voice! But I will resist! I will not be enslaved! I will not write ads. I will not have a job!"

And then Papa said he was glad to hear Fothy's sentiments. He had been afraid, he said, that Fothy had matrimonial designs about me. And the man who married *his* daughter would probably have to stand for possessing a good deal of wealth, too, for he had always intended doing something very handsome for his son-in-law. So if Fothy didn't want money, he wouldn't want me, for an enormous amount of it would go to me.

Papa, you know, thinks he can be awfully sarcastic.

So many Earth Persons pride themselves on their sarcasm, don't you think?

And Papa is an Earth Person entirely. I've got his horoscope. He isn't *at all* spiritual.

But you can image that the whole scene was *frightfully* embarrassing to me – I will *never* forgive Papa!

And I haven't made up my mind *at all* about Fothy. But what I do know is this: once I get my mind made up, I *will not* stand for opposition from *any* source.

One must be an Individualist, or perish!

John Triboulet, "Pastiche. Euphemisme; or, What You Will"

***New Age* 16.16 (1915): 434.**

John Triboulet was a regular contributor to the *New Age*. While Triboulet is not a known pseudonym, it is the name of a court jester of King Louis XII and Francis I of France, who was the source of the central characters in Victor Hugo's *Le Roi s'amuse* and Verdi's *Rigoletto*. "Triboulet's" conflation of Pound, Vorticism, and Futurism was common in the early years of modernism.

"My friend," said Obadiah Pence, "I must announce my conversion. I told Martin, the disciple of Mr. Ezra Pound, that I should never be enthusiastic about the Arts until I found the Abbey of Thelema, Rabelais' Utopia, in England. That was last Thursday. Martin had been enthused by the profundities of Mr. Pound's last article, and he spoke eloquently of the Arts and Life for the period of ten glasses; the result was that I, too, became a Futurist."

"And what are your arguments for Vorticism?" I asked.

"Euphemisme, you mean. Certainly, we are all related, but what gulfs separate us are signified by the final 'es.' Jack, I've had my eyes opened. Modern England and Thelema are one. You see, it's this way. Energy creates everything. How it does it is no matter. Ah, ah, that's good, see that Euphemistic stroke: the nature of Energy is no Matter. I'm jolly well disgusted with you youngsters who decry your own times. Why, there is as much Energy expended in Modern England as there ever was. Have you ever seen a steam punch push through a plate of cold steel, or a lathe tool pare a half-inch layer off a twenty-foot gun tube? If you have not, don't talk of Drake and Shakespeare."

"But Obadiah, I am sure neither Mr. Pound nor any other Futurist ever suggested such a comparison. You confuse mechanical energy with spiritual and human energy."

"Oh, don't confuse me with Mr. Pound. I was a logical and consistent thinker before I became a Futurist, and I'll remain one. What confusion am I guilty of? The only difference between a man and a machine is that man is a self-starter. Even Mr. Pound says that; but I go consistently further. Spiritual Energy? Why even the 'Daily Mail' knows the oneness of Energy. When Pierpont Morgan died, the 'Mail' proved in a leading article that the American was exactly what Bonaparte would have been in modern life. The same Life Force impelled them."

"Though the 'Daily Mail' is ignorant, I would have thought that you had read of Ouvrard, the financier of Napoleon's day. Morgan lived then, but Bonaparte does not live now," I remarked.

"Rubbish!" cried Obadiah. "There cannot be several Life Forces or qualitative Energies. That would suggest that something of the nature of Pattern or Form had conditioned the all-creative Life Force. But, listen. What does it matter how Energy expresses itself? I see as much in Rockefeller's bank book as in 'Don Quixote.' The Energy for the creation of the first is the greater. 'Quixote' is only a sort of European 'Arabian Nights,' a cold dream record, mere emotionless pattern."

"Energy is the thing my boy. Pattern is a subsequent accident. But, to touch the Arts more delicately. In Art, Creative Energy ——"

"Woa, there, surely you are speaking of one sort of Energy now?"

"Not at all. There's no difference. Creative Energy is to do a thing once, Energy, to do it twice or more times. Surely, that is clear."

"Not very. I, suppose you mean the Imagination –"

"Never use that word. It implies the pre-existence of images. Emotion, that is the nickname we give Energy when we are more familiar, creates Images – sometimes, that is, when they are not objective. Here's an example. Look outside at that building surrounded with scaffolding. Now take the building away from the scaffolding, annihilate that preposterous pile and leave the beautiful wooden structure. It may strike you as Hellenic or as Gothic."

"It appears to me exactly what it is, the means to a certain end, which, when deprived of that end, stands reasonless and absurd."

"Poor fool," cried Obadiah, "such an answer is equivalent to that of a drunkard who would mistake it for a gigantic hat rack. I see it as a legitimate pattern which expresses the mighty energies of modern life, the universal life-force which tosses Form in its flood like a cork on Niagara. I can hear the wondrous hum of the worldlife in those vast angles below the crane."

The barman offered to refill our glasses, but I stopped him, as I thought Obadiah had taken enough to drink.

"I cannot understand you, Obadiah. I am, perhaps, poisoned with a hatred of Commercialism, for I believe that a great and good Art is impossible without social Liberty and Justice. And the Wage System –"

"Damned Philistine! You could not live in a more wonderful time, but you refuse to recognise it until your own pettifogging political policies are successful. Liberty, Justice and Beauty are only forms created by Energy, clouds shaped by the wind. See the piece Svapolzckse carved with his creative impulse last week. Though it only stands as a monument of prodigious energy, it accidentally destroys all platitudes about eternal verities and substances. In this piece of a sturdy prehistoric father thumping his puny son we see the origin of all religious and moral laws."

"Is creative impulse the Greek for chisel?" I asked, innocently.

"Ah, ah," laughed Obadiah. "No, it is a term which distinguishes us Euphemistes from the vulgar who experience emotion. After all, it is only a matter of voltage, but we must be distinguished from the craftsman in his joy, and the zealot in his heat. Energy is general and repetitious. Creative Energy is particular and original. It is a degree of voltage. Certainly, in the last hundred years the voltage has risen, for earlier no other creator was mentioned but God. We rarely find the word used apart from the Deity or the agents, such as Nature, etc. Nowadays, you know, every novelist wants to be called a creative artist. Music-hall scene writers often style their pieces as created. Then there's Millinery – but these are only the crumbs of Progress."

"I understand that, but as to your exceptional voltage. All said, it is only the desire to say something, valuable by its style and substance."

"Rats! Oh, how can you understand when you cannot grasp that Energy creates pattern! Now, when Svapolzckse feels his Creative Impulse twitching, he sets to work and creates. He is not impelled to do something beautiful, great or good: that supposes a plan or pattern, something of the outside world seen or felt, or, what is more ridiculous, of a divine world. Creative Energy is subjective, so we need no objects to our sentences; we do not desire to do something, but we desire to DO. That is Thelemian, for Thelema's motto is Fais ce que Vouldras.[8] That born fool, Shakespeare, spluttered about the imagination bodying forth the forms of things unknown, which can only mean that the forms, patterns, things preexisted, and he continues to speak of the pen turning these to shapes (images, words, etc.). Great Energy! and to think that there are still in London one man and a little boy who admire Shakespeare, the clown who calls Svapolzckse a recorder."

"That's very amusing, Obadiah. But tell me, where have you discovered Thelema?"

"What's the good of going into things deeply with you, and logically expounding Mr. Pound, whose writings you cannot understand? I'll tell you a little history which will suit your simple mind. Martin tells me that this tale, framed in scintillating sandpaper, is hung in Mr. Pound's bedroom, above his statue of the primitive man with a rabbit – or is it a cabbage? This is the tale:

"Of two prisoners who were confined in dungeons, the lowest and vilest in Picardy, one, a one-time toymaker, possessed a genius wherewith he annihilated the prison. He did not raze the building to the ground. His genius played upon a new gamut of perceptions, and his prison was transformed to an Eden. When his one poor sunbeam struck his bread tin, which was a pure cube, in the illuminations and shadows he saw delicious planes and patterns, and he was ecstatically impressed when he viewed the texture of a gnawed bone or the angle which a rusty nail in the wall formed. Thus did the emotion of his soul create a new universe."

Obadiah paused to observe the admiration I did not show.

"But what of the other prisoner, Obadiah?" I asked.

"Oh, he, poor dog, dreamt of his home in a stark, natural valley where grass and trees grew actually green, and in a fit of insanity he cut the bars of his window, escaped, and returned to nature. Miserable clown!"

"Very wonderful," I said. "That is the clearest thing you have uttered. But tell me, Obadiah, where is Thelema?"

"Oh, anywhere you will, but the one I like best is in Widnes. The chemical works are epic."

"Good-night, Obadiah. I hope you will be well again when we next meet."

III. Modernist Methodologies

While sceptics often wondered aloud whether modernist works were any good, they also mused about how they were *produced*. While they certainly could focus their attentions on individual works, journalists and critics often portrayed these works as the products of a family of methodologies, and set to work satirizing these processes. The attempt to portray modernist methodologies was often made by translating aesthetic strategies from the original medium to another, the absurdity in the new medium laying bare the absurdity of the source.

But something more was askew than the aesthetic principles themselves – the idea that its principles were *transferable* indicated modernism's slovenliness. Modernism's apparent ability to mechanically replicate new works by simply following a procedure was both a sign of its weakness and differentiated it from the art that had preceded it. (How would one replicate a Rembrandt, for example?) Modernism's overt methodologies were suspect, making the art too dependent on theory, or on group identities, or on mechanical or chance processes. Producing modernist art, the argument went, did not need skill. Even difficulty, as many reviewers of *The Waste Land* or *Ulysses* pointed out, was easy – at least, easy to *produce*. Responding to the London visits of Marinetti, J. Molony in the *New Age* wrote:

> If I might take the liberty of speaking of myself for a moment, I should like to advertise to the waiting public that I am about to rival Signor Marinetti on his own field. For I am at present engaged in a sweet little lyric to be called, "Ping Pong," with the sub-title "Pong Ping." I cannot give away secrets, of course, but I will go so far as to say that it deals with that diminutive variation of lawn-tennis that used to decorate the diningroom tables of Suburbia not so long ago. My intuitive, numerical devil-may-careity has resulted in a noble and inspiring expression of the dimensions of the table, the criss-cross appearance of the net, and the cubic capacity

> of the crackling celluloid balls. Nor have I forgotten to fuse all my onomatopaeias into one psychical conglomeration that positively scintillates with Sir Isaac Newton's intensely transcendental discoveries of mechanical splendour. And, finally, the symbols -o-_|_-o- express perfectly the philosophic content of the whole rhapsody as seen by the light of reason.

Methodologies – particularly those based on chance – made for ugly art. Gelett Burgess, travelling to Paris to interview the leading new artists of the Salon des Indépendents, sent back a lengthy, quasi-serious report to the *Architectural Record*. In it he noted the following of the works at the Salon:

> If you can imagine what a particularly sanguinary little girl of eight, half-crazed with gin, would do to a whitewashed wall, if left alone with a box of crayons, then you will come near to fancying what most of this work was like. Or you might take a red-hot poker in your left hand, shut your eyes and etch a landscape upon a door. There were no limits to the audacity and the ugliness of the canvasses. Still-life sketches of round, round apples and yellow, yellow oranges, on square, square tables, seen in impossible perspective; landscapes of squirming trees, with blobs of virgin color gone wrong, fierce greens and coruscating yellows, violent purples, sickening reds and shuddering blues. ("Wild Men of Paris" 1910)

Modernism's lazy methodologies extended even to titles. J.C. Squire argued that, unduly dependent on their simultaneously arbitrary and interpretive titles, modernist works of art could be replicated endlessly:

> There is something pathetic about the way in which, wherever the political Bolsheviks get into office, they print the verses and cartoons of the artistic anarchists. They don't understand them; all they know is that the bourgeois dislike them; so in Munich last Easter, and (we daresay) in Moscow now, there is an excellent opening for those who, for all anyone would be able to say to the contrary, have only to scratch out the old titles of their interlocked triangles and write underneath "Uprising of Proletariat," or some such thing. ("Editorial Notes," 387)

But modernism's methodologies also could involve something stricter – not chance, but formulae. Art critic Lewis Hind was quoted as claiming that the "drear, reviled" Cubists were "geometricians first and painters second" (in Carter, "The Plato-Picasso Idea," 88). Kenyon Cox, reaching even further back, argued that Impressionism "was scientific rather than artistic, and the pictures of its strongest man, Claude Monet, often seem like a series of demonstrations rather than things of beauty created for human delight" (16–17). Either way

– through chance or through formula – modernism's reliance on methodology resulted in art that wasn't *human*, art that had no interaction with what lay before it. Modernism's rigorous following of theoretical principles removed the human soul – only a real, ad hoc interaction with the world could produce beauty.

John Collings Squire, "Short Cuts to Helicon," in *Life and Letters*

(London: Hodder & Stoughton, 1920), 26–31.

I opened the *Times* Literary Supplement, and my eye was detained by an advertisement which for ten minutes made me oblivious to everything else in the number from "Dramatic Poetry" to "God and the Absolute." It was one of those rare advertisements which induce a train of thought.

And this was it. An institution called the London Correspondence College was inviting the *Supplement*'s readers to learn how to write verse. "The field for Verse," ran the invitation,

> is much larger than most people suppose. Hundreds of journals publish and pay for poetry. Anyone with aptitude can learn to write the kind of Verse editors will pay for, by availing themselves of the excellent course of Instruction provided by… [ellipses in original] The training is individual and progressive; technique is simply explained, and any natural ability the student may have is developed to the full through his or her own work in connection with the lessons. The fee is quite moderate.

It was bound to come, and here it is.

I should greatly like to know – but I suppose that I could not find out without paying money, which I am reluctant to do – what are the suggestions, what the training, given to those who serve with the College their apprenticeship to the muse. But I do not know, and I dare not guess, as secrets beyond my conjecture and stunts beyond my devisal may have been hit upon by the Professors of the College, and I should not like even to appear to misrepresent the nature, or the benefits, of their teaching. I may, however, without speculating as to what is *their* practice, be allowed to reflect on what would be my own should I ever find myself in control of an Academy of Shorthand, Typewriting, and Commercial Poetry.

Were this country America, or did the present American fashion for free verse spread here, the problem would be comparatively uncomplicated. "Technique" could certainly be simply explained, as both rhyme and regular rhythm are foregone, the poet can indefinitely vary his lines, and, for the content, all that is necessary is a catalogue of objects seen, heard, and smelt by the writer at any particular moment or series of moments. Here, dealing with the novice, one would instruct him on his morning walks to make a careful note of the objects he saw, and recapitulate their leading characteristics when he got home; then, killing with one stone the two birds of memory-training and art, he would catalogue any sequence of them. For instance: "misty air, a long straight street of flat houses, a solitary policeman in a shiny cape, a red pillar-box, a boy in the distance, whistling a tune." The next stage in the process would be to write these things down in irregular lines, the shorter the better, made up according to the author's taste or caprice. The last and finishing process consists of the judicious, or even the quite casual, interspersal of dots, and the addition of some single line of reflection, or exclamation which supplies the necessary touch of emotion. It would not be safe to leave the student to his own devices at the start; he could quite safely be given a little list of last lines which could be used (preferably in italics) in any poem of the kind. "Oh, God! …" is one; "Ah! the pain," is another. Behold the final result:

Misty air …
A long, straight street
Of flat houses …
A solitary policeman
With a shiny
Cape …
A red pillar-box …
A boy
In the distance
Whistling a tune
…
Ah, God! the pain.

That, though I may not be able to persuade English readers that this is so, is the sort of "Verse" that in America "editors will pay for," and there is no reason why its construction should not be quite successfully taught by post. But on this side of the Atlantic things are a little more difficult.

In England "Hundreds of journals publish and pay for poetry," but almost all of them insist upon rhyme, and upon lines of equal, or regularly varying length. Moreover, there is a good deal of difference between the sort of subjects and styles demanded by various papers. I should, therefore, when framing my course for students, begin by telling them to study (as every successful business man is bound to do) the market, and the classes of goods most in demand by the various groups of consumers. Let the student note *(a)* the commonest subjects, *(b)* the commonest rhymes, *(c)* the commonest words, in the poems published by those papers which he decides to exploit. After a little labour he will be able to sort the papers into three or four main categories. He will then decide either to produce several types of goods for the several types of customer, or to concentrate on the largest available market for a single type, thereby giving himself a chance of perfecting his processes, and, by virtue of the advantages inherent in repetitive work, securing maximum output and reducing overhead charges (in which I include the purchase of magazines to see if they have printed anything yet) to a minimum. Let us suppose he decides to adopt the latter, and most efficient, course.

In accordance with the instructions I have given him, he has found that the subjects most in demand in his group of consumers are (say) love, flowers, joy coming after sorrow, sunset, and maternal affection. The statistical tables drawn up after examination of a thousand specimen poems have revealed that the separate words (excluding, of course, articles and conjunctions) most frequently required are "moon," "roses," "twilight," "slumber," "lullaby," "you," "blackbird," "joy," "sorrow," and "to-morrow" – the last two, for obvious reasons, begin bracketed equal. Among the most frequent of the other rhymes are found "moon" and "June," "you" and "blue," "heart" and "apart," "love" and "above," "stars" and "bars," "sun" and "done." Now whatever liberties may be taken by the advanced student ripe for original experiment and research, I should always advise the beginner who means to play for safety and avoid the risk of disappointment to keep as closely to the beaten path as possible. He may or may not save himself trouble by sticking boldly, whenever he writes, to the meter and rhymes of a particular poem in his card-index file. If he prefers to be original he should at least always choose meters and rhymes which he knows, from his tables, to be always popular. Let us say that he decides on a poem about love of eight lines, in two four-line stanzas. For this, if every line (and editors greatly like that) is to have a rhyme, four sets of two rhymes are necessary. How should he next proceed? How select his rhymes?

To assist him here I should provide him with a little catechism for each class of subject. He can get right there with a few standard questions such as: (1) Is it to be a happy poem? and (2) What time of day is it (the love, or the meditation on flowers, or the maternal affection) to take place? These questions give a principle of selection; for instance, in a poem about the day, the sun will properly appear; in one about the night moon or stars may be introduced. Our poet has finally decided on love, and on the rhymes "love" and "above," "moon" and "June," "flowers" and "hours," "blue" and "you." Now it is clear that he can make the lines scan by counting the syllables; but where I am in difficulties about assisting him is in regard to the manner in which he shall fill the lines up. It is no good telling him to make them as like his models as possible: he could guess that much for himself. But suppose he gets as far as this:

[*It is a perfect night in*] *June,*
[*No breezes shake the*] *flowers,*
[*The golden radiance of the*] *moon*
[*Doth gild the slumbering*] *hours.*

[*I wait beneath your casement,*] *love,*
[ ] *blue,*
[ ] *above,*
[*The moon, the rose, and*] *you,*

and cannot fill up the gaps? I honestly do not know what advice to give.

John Collings Squire, "Editorial Notes"

***London Mercury*, August 1928: 337–46.**

These pages that are usually devoted
To interesting events that we have noted,
Especially the things we have deplored:
A countryside by commerce tossed and gored,
A certain kind of memoir, the R.A.,[9]
The dismal prospects of the modern play,
The ungoverned shapelessness of modern towns,
The imminent ruin of the Sussex downs,
The plague of petrol pumps upon the fells,
Stonehenge, the City Churches, Sadler's Wells,[10]
The cubist cul-de-sac, and, what is worse,
The spate of senseless and amorphous verse,
Writ by ambitious simpletons who've found
That if you once abandon sense and sound
And put down linkless words in disarray
The critics really don't know what to say,
Fearing that if they do say what they think
Their names may, later on, be made to stink,
Because their crassness failed to recognise
The fire of Shelley in a Snooks's eyes –
These pages, as we say, of wont so formal
Solicitous, public-spirited and normal,
Are filled with quite another kind of thing:
They do not argue; they attempt to sing!

FURTHER EXPLANATION

"*Sing*, Muse, of Summer." "No, I won't:
It's much too hot!" "Oh, well then, don't."
"Oh, please don't be unreasonable:
Your heat no doubt is seasonable,
But why expect that I should function
When you, without the least compunction,
Have airily refused to do it?"
"Come, buckle to, or you shall rue it.

Do you not know this inky street
Is paralyzing in such heat?
If I should argue I should die!"
"If you can't argue, why should I?"
"You write in verse, I write in prose,
Your task, as everybody knows,
Is quite immeasurably easier.
No one will mind if you are breezier,
Flippant, completely void of matter:
Your Muses only have to patter,
No one will scrutinize a column
Of verse to see if it is solemn,
Dignified, reasoned, adequate
And duly useful to the State.
I am not asking much of you,
Only an indolent hour or two
To help myself, who keep you going
(Of late you haven't made much showing).
If you will just this once relieve me
I shall not ask again (believe me)
Until once more there comes this way
The torrid heat of Africa
Which isn't likely – do remember,
Last year, from April to September
It simply rained and rained as though a
Firm had arranged a film of Noah.
Next year (be sensible) again.
'Twill rain and rain and rain and rain,
And I shall never dream of shirking
My ordinary mode of working.
Come, come, you owe a lot to me."
"All right, give me your pen and see!"

THE MUSE SPEAKS

I am rusty, my friend,
I've not written for ages,
And it seems without end,
This space of ten pages,
Your view may be right

That a verse may be thin,
But there's nothing in sight:
I can't even begin!

THE MUSE IS ANSWERED

There's the castle of Durham, can't you write about that?
And the Duke who's been walking with only one spat,
And the terribly humorous Member who sat
Amid roars of applause on another man's hat?
And the Princess's Peke, and the Countess's cat
With its necklace of pearls and its coat like a mat.
And I see in the paper Sir Jonathan Spratt
Has swallowed a camel and strained at a gnat,
Both remarkable feats: why, what would you be at?
If you can't find themes there, you're as blind as a bat
And not worth your salt.

RIPOSTE OF THE MUSE

VERY well, it's my fault.
Load it all upon me then; grumble and curse.
Look here, do you mind if I change to Free Verse?

RELUCTANT AGREEMENT

PLEASE yourself, you're aware
Of my sentiments there …

PROTEST OF THE MUSE

BUT my dearest good Master,
I should go so much faster:
I should save so much time
Sans Rhythm and Rhyme,
And fill so much space
At so splendid a pace.
Had we lashings of leisure
I'd tread a grave measure,
Weaving my lines

In intricate designs;
I would shiver your bowels
With arrangements of vowels
And my assonant schemes
Would exceed all your dreams,
You'd think Campion and Bridges
Were metrical midges
Compared with this Muse
Whose aid you refuse,
Until you're hard-pressed, and whom then you abuse,
You indolent log,
You ingrate, you dog.

REBUKE TO THE MUSE

NOW, gently there, Miss,
I did not ask for this.
You were not summoned here
To assail my poor ear
With insults so pointed
In words so disjointed,
So fervent
A servant
I'd have never appointed.
Had I known but of old!
Had I only been told
That those agents in Helicon were shamelessly sending me
A Muse who was capable of turning and rending me.

THE MUSE OBSTINATE

VERY well, then, be rent!
My patience is spent.

THE MUSE REBUKED AGAIN

STILL that old jogging metre.
Can't you think of one sweeter?

THE MUSE RECRIMINATORY

I MUST say I like that; why 'twas you that began it.
But began! In the days of Neanderthal man it
Was stale and outworn;
When Columbus was born
His mother sang thus, and the child exclaimed "Can it!"
Lord Byron, the Ingoldsby Legends,[11] Tom Moore
And Victorian librettists full many a score
Long ferried away from the Stygian shore.
They hacked at the thing till it grew to a bore,
And all the translators who managed to print
Their halting translations of *Brand* and *Peer Gynt*
Ambled on at this pace
Or something much like it,
And now you've the face
To ask *me* to strike it.
I tell you quite flat
That I won't! And that's that!
I am free! I'm Post-War! Not if I know it, thanks!
Free Verse … or you're published with pages of blanks,
Though I'm not saying those mightn't be quite enough
To serve as relief from your usual stuff.

RELUCTANT CONSENT

O HAVE your way;
I can do it myself for that matter
Without
Your assistance,
Though
I cannot be bothered
To turn any of the words
Up
Side
Down,
Or to begin the lines
With small

Letters
Instead of
Capitals.

THE MUSE CAPRICIOUS

INDEED ? If that's the case I'll change my mind
And try a sort of thing that you would find
Impossible to do without my aid.

EXHORTATION

AH? Let us hear it then, vainglorious jade.

DEMONSTRATION

I MEAN the poem formal in design
Apparently orthodox in outline
(With things like that rhyme in it, accent gone,
Which brings the bard a day's march nearer Donne),
An intellectual cobweb of obscurities,
With here and there a tinge of cold impurities,
With fine recondite images bedecked.
Incongruous except to the elect:
As this in which I exquisitely say
How I am going to spend my holiday:

PIEBALD UNICORN

Under the hyperthyroid moon
Seated, I shall eat caviar with a spoon,
While Mr. Nokes, that melancholy man,
Will cool my heated features with his fan
The ghost of sainted Elagabalus[12]
Will sometimes come to drink his tea with us,
Gazelles and eunuchs, crystal as a leaf,
Will pace the rose-beds to assuage my grief.
I shall applaud their steps, and when I please,
Lean forth to stroke their slim anatomies,
While Mr. Nokes, that melancholy man,
Discourses gentle music with his fan.

AGONISED APPEAL

NO, no, no more of this, I beg.
Do not so harshly tug my leg.
What can have happened to you, Muse?
Time was you never held such views.
You used to sing like a canary
With quite a small vocabulary
Of trees and grass, the sun, the moon,
Which then you always rhymed with swoon,
So simply, with such innocence,
And such a lack of deeper sense
That any passer-by could tell
If you were singing ill or well.
'Twas usually ill, no doubt,
But you were easily found out.
Now you bewilder me: how could
I tell if that were bad or good,
That gnomic stuff you sang just now,
That cacophonic senseless row …
Enough; now pull yourself together,
Cannot you realise the weather?

THE MUSE OBDURATE

HAVE you not heard of King Canute,
Who tried to stop (the silly brute!)
The onset of the stemless tide
And then was hung up to be dried?
Even so are you who would arrest
The novel forms that you detest:
There are no boundaries in Art …

COMPLAINT

BUT why discard the human heart?

ANSWER

IT is a withered worn-out thing,
And Love has lost its ancient sting

And Faith is dead and Hope is fled
And the last blossom has been shed
From apple-trees the stars peered through.

COMPLAINT

THE grass is green, the skies are blue.

ANSWER

THE skies are blue, the grass is green,
As they in truth have always been,
They are *vieux jeu* and on the shelf,
If you could but detach yourself
And see you'd better be employed
Drawing new beauty from the void
Than chasing on deserted shores
The phantoms of your ancestors!
We are the future, we are young,
The bravest songs are still unsung.

INTERJECTION

THAT line was Flecker's; do not quote
A man who thought you were a goat
He …

REJOINDER

NEVER mind, I know by rote
All you've to say in that connection.

QUERULITY

CANNOT I make an interjection?

BRUTALITY

CERTAINLY not, if you're to trot
Out evermore the same old rot.

CORRECTION

HOW you forget; I said 'twas hot.

MUSE OFFENSIVE

OH, you *are* tiresome!

RALLY

YOU are tireless
Stop it or I'll switch on the wireless.
My mind's made up, no, not a word,
I would that this had not occurred;
(Bring me a little glass of Schweppes)
The time has come for drastic steps.

WIRELESS

THIS is the Londonderry Air!

COMMENT

A MELODY both rich and rare
It's stopped, a pause, now listen … There!

MUSE

THE Volga Boat Song, I declare!
I am tired of all these Volga Boats,
This succulence of mournful notes,
I must rise up and roar my joy,
I must despair, I must destroy.

CRITICISM

IS that not vigorous for you?
I thought you'd seen the whole thing through,
Drained every cup, crushed every fruit
And found the soul a worn-out boot,

You are fatigued, so tired, so bored
You told me once you always snored
When writing; it was so absurd
To go on adding word to word …

MUSE

WHAT does it matter what I said?

WIRELESS

THE Rajah of Balong is dead.
The heat has forwarded the crops,
Rye, wheat, oats, barley, also hops,
Although the roots, if they'd maintain
Their present progress, need some rain.

AGREEMENT

AND so do I, and so do you.
Muse, what are honest folk to do?
Can it be wondered at that we
Should wander off in lunacy,
When week by week, in one small room,
Too small for an Egyptian's tomb,
The hottest, most enclosed of crypts,
We have to drudge through manuscripts,
Write cordial letters, pay off bills,
While twice a day the Severn fills,
And plovers wheel about the hills:
Ah, Grantchester, Ah, Grantchester.

CONCERN

THIS is dementia! Have a care!

FINAL

NO, let us go. The great winds blow
Over the western wolds we know,

The valley road, the upland track,
We can recover and come back.
But one short month, the sun that flamed
Will have retired again ashamed,
Once more the clouds will come, once more will fall
The steely pillars of the endless rain.
He was a Sun, take him for all in all,
We shall not look upon his face again.
  Let us make hay,
  Away! Away!

Louis Untermeyer, "The Manufacture of Verse," in *Heavens*

(New York: Harcourt, Brace and Co., 1922), 97–105.

The following essay purports to be a review of "*The Manufacture of Verse*; including a Preface on Weights and Measures, a Rhyming Dictionary for *Vers Librists*, and a Three Weeks' Course for Beginners. By Harper Grenville; Litt. D., Monrovia, Liberia. Printed by the Author." Untermeyer echoes, both in phrasing and concept, Squire's assertion in "Short Cuts to Helicon" (page 251) that mass culture's explosive demand for verse in periodicals, newspapers, and anthologies made mechanistic modes of artistic production inevitable.

It was bound to come. And here, a solid four hundred and fifty page royal octavo, it is. Professor Harper Grenville's calmly-entitled *The Manufacture of Verse* is not so much a book as it is a calculated literary explosion; an astounding combination of manual, pattern-maker and hand-book containing Two Hundred Secrets of The Trade. Professor Grenville, who has returned after a sojourn in these nitid states to his chair at Monrovia University, begins with an ingenuous foreword in which he submits the proposition, revolutionary in its simplicity, that … But let him speak for himself.

"Before returning to Africa," begins the professor, "I spent four sabbatical years reading the poetry in every magazine from *The Atlantic Monthly* to *The Ginger Jar*; attending (so far as geography would permit) every meeting of every Poetry Society; studying, in short, the entire problem of supply and demand in what, as far as America is concerned, has grown to be not only a major occupation but an essential industry. And I was struck, first of all, by the shocking inefficiency and waste in the manufacture as well as in the marketing of this staple product. What surprised me most was the utterly unsystematic method of assembling, the useless duplication, the uncoordinated and almost unconscious similarity. Surely a country run by time-clocks, Babson reports,[13] memory courses, conservation committees and the Taylor System must realize that its poetry cannot be allowed to lag behind in the old haphazard, 'write-as-the-mood-seizes-you' gait! Something is needed for the double purpose of standardizing quality and speeding up production. It is in the hope of filling this only too evident need that the following chapters have been prepared."

Thus Professor Grenville's stark little prologue. Without pausing for breath, he goes into action on the first page of the first chapter, which deals with Magazine Verse and is brusquely entitled *At the Usual Rate per Line.*

"It is not too late; even in an age of conquering ideals," he begins, "to be realistic. For better or for worse, the magazine sonnet, the rotund meditation, the sentimental fillers exist. What is more, they persist. There is a market for these wares; they live because people like them, because there is a genuine demand for such merchandise. Obviously, our duty is to show how to meet that demand without the fumblings and faint strivings for originality that have characterized the past." Whereupon the Professor begins to catalog, to codify, to quote. Great names are thrown about with a magnificent nonchalance; nobody escapes. The present reviewer wishes he had space to reprint Professor Grenville's analysis of "that cornerstone of journalistic prosody, The Lush and Rhetorical Sonnet," regretting that the readers must content themselves with the learned doctor's conclusions.

"The fourteenth line" [I am detaching a segment from page 21] "should always be written first; the first line next. The rest is mere stuffing. Of late there has been a tendency to build sonnets around the third or fourth line, on the theory that editors never get as far as the last line. This is an innovation which, in spite of its plausibility, I must condemn. For one thing, it tends to deviate from that conformity which, as I have pointed out, is the very goal at which we are aiming. Nothing should be done to disturb the liquid flow of a thought that begins nowhere and, after meandering through fourteen well-worn grooves, ends there. Vague abstractions and vaguer 'wings that beat,' 'silvern melodies,' alliterative generalities and archaic embellishments like 'I wis,' 'hark,' 'fain,' etc., will go far to fill in the gap between the first phrase of the octave and the last rhyme of the sestet. Here, by Clinton Scollard, is an almost perfect example:

AT THE VERGE OF MARCH

It is not ever that the outer ear
Bears us the joy for which our hearts are fain;
Sometimes we sense the music of the rain
Ere its first silvern melody we hear.
Sometimes we feel the grieving sea is near
Before we hark its never silent strain;
Sometimes we mark the veering of the vane
Ere the wind-trumpets sound their clamour clear.

So now I am inscrutably aware
Of moving wings that beat against the day,
Of swift migrations stirring from afar;
The clouds betray strange murmurings in the air,
Breathings seep up from out the frozen clay,
And there are whisperings from the twilight star."

"But," continues our guide, "there is another type of sonnet which requires less care and which yields even more gratifying results. And that is the Mouth-Filling and Mystic Sonnet. During the war there was a noticeable slump in these goods but, with the increased popularity of spiritualism, they have risen steadily in favor. They can be manufactured in quantity with the aid of the ordinary, domestic ouija board. Or, if a slower but somewhat more satisfactory method is desired, they can be turned out in this fashion: Collect and arrange a score of hyper-literary, resounding and (preferably) obsolete words – words like 'nenuphar,' 'thrid,' 'levin,' 'rathe,' 'immemorial,' 'palimpsest.' Scatter these through the pattern, leaving space for rhymes. Use any good dictionary and season to suit. An almost endless variety can thus be produced, of which the following is a sample – a composite of twenty-three different variations of this popular model:

RESURGAM[14]

Athwart the hectic sunset's plangent crown,
The rathe and daedal moon is vaguely seen;
The ghosts of twilight strow the skies with green
And listlessly the evening sinks adown.
The driven day forgets its furrowed frown
And shimmers in the frail and xanthic sheen;
Life's banners ope' – the shades porphyrogene, [*sic*]
Dank and disheveled, clutch the night – and drown …

So did I once behold Love's gyving spells
Flashing from amaranthine star to star;
While, from the limbo of forgotten hells,
The immarcescible [*sic*] passions surged afar …
What fulgid [*sic*] lure awoke the asphodels?
Behind the gibbering night – what avatar?"

I skip, with ill-concealed impatience, to page 425 and Professor Grenville's instructive remarks on *Capitalizing Beauty with a Capital B*. "What is more gratifying to the modern reader, harassed by machinery and newspaper editorials, than a thumping glorification of the past? By that I do not mean the recent past, which has been dealt with in a previous chapter and which finds its climactic *cri de coeur* in refrains like:

And it's oh for the hills of Ida, and the sigh of the Zuyder Zee!

I refer to the sonorous stanzas which, with a delightful ambiguity, mingle epochs, geography, and historical land-marks in a list of confused but dazzling splendor. It is unnecessary to analyze or even define this impressive type. Every student acquainted with the rudiments of scientific management and machine piece-work will be able to construct love-poems as resonant, high-pitched and purple-patched as this free-hand improvisation:

THE PAGAN HEART

Here, in Egyptian night, you hang
Above me, sphinx without a home;
Whiter than Helen as she sang
And burned the golden isles of Rome.

The breath of perfumed Sidon slips
From your Greek body's wizardry;
Persepolis is on your lips,
And your bright hair is Nineveh.

Enchantress, you have drawn upon
The world's dream and its old desire –
The brazen pomps of Babylon,
The purple panoply of Tyre!"

It is impossible to give the fine flavour of this volume by meagre quotations. It is equally impossible to quote it *in toto*. And yet one cannot resist tearing a fragment from Professor Grenville's advice concerning *The English Lyric*. "By the *English* lyric, I mean that 'type of song which (in contradistinction to that written in the American idiom) is sought after chiefly in the United States. Whether the pattern is vernal (see *Spring Style No. 53*) or merely rustic and ruminative (vide *Songs of the Open Road*, designs 62 to 225), all one needs is a small but select vocabulary ready for substitution. The proper air is given and the effect achieved by changing the common American blackbird to the poetically

Georgian 'merle,' the lark to the 'laverock,' song-thrush to 'mavis,' wood to 'wold,' and liberally strewing the rest of any outdoor jingle (see passages on *Wanderlust*, *Broad-Highway*, *Vagbondia*, etc.) with references to 'gorse,' 'heather,' 'furze,' 'whin,' and so on … The following introductory stanzas are an approximation of this standard and always effective design:

LAVEROCKS

The winter sun has run its wavering course,
The giddy mavis tries its vernal wing;
While from the green heart of the radiant gorse
The laverocks sing.

High on the moor the blossomy heather wakes
The gillyflower laughing in the furze;
And, in the bramble thickets and the brakes,
Old magic stirs.

Ah, love, could we but once more be a part
Of May! In tune with bracken and with ling!
Then, from the flaming thickets of my heart,
Laverocks would sing!"

It would be a pleasure to go all the way with Professor Grenville. But that pleasure must be reserved for the student, the apprentice, and the eight-hour-day versifiers rather than the casual reader. There are times when the author, especially in his efforts to reduce the number of easy-selling models, grows a trifle doctrinaire; there are other times when one almost suspects him of letting his tongue slip toward his cheek, as when, in the passage on *How to Achieve Glamour*, he writes: "Inversion is the surest method; the further away one gets from the spoken language, the nearer one is to that mode of stilted speech which even the comic weeklies recognize as poetry – a masterpiece of its kind being the first two lines of a poem by Mr. Louis V. Ledoux:

'A moonlit mist the valley fills,
Though rides unseen herself the moon.'"

In spite of the few flies in Professor Grenville's preparation of the "divine emollient," one – and I dare say, a great many more – must be grateful to him. Such chapters as *Rhyme Without Reason, Archaism's Artful Aid, Home-Grown*

Exotics, will do much to help the latter-day minstrel up the slopes of Parnassus in high.

The Manufacture of Verse is, in every sense, a profitable book. At least, it ought to be.

"Modern Masterpieces"

***Chicago News*, 11 April 1923.**

Suppose a cyclone took and split
The book that Noah Webster built
Across the county line;
Conceive those words so neatly listed
By some fierce brainstorm wrecked and twisted,
Class, that is Gertrude Stein!

Stuart Pratt Sherman, from *Points of View*

(New York: Scribner's, 1924), 266–8.

Stuart Sherman (1881–1926) was a professor of English at the University of Illinois. A scholar of Matthew Arnold, he eventually became editor of the "Books" section of the *New York Herald Tribune*. His initial response to modernism was not favourable. Although never put to as serious a test as here, Sherman's assertion that one could create plausible modernist art through chance was a common one. A reviewer of *Tender Buttons* asserted that one could create a similar work with the following method:

> Fill a thousand, ten thousand cards with single words or phrases. Shuffle, deal; align in "hands" of assorted sizes, and send the result to the printer. It is the children's game of "consequences" with reduced chances for amusing coincidences of collocation.
>
> Unhappy "future"! ("When the White Hunter Hunts")

Time magazine similarly asserted, in its combined review of *The Waste Land* and *Ulysses*, that

> To the uninitiated it appeared that Mr. Joyce had taken some half million assorted words – many such as are not ordinarily heard in reputable circles – shaken them in a colossal hat, laid them end to end. To those in on the secret the result represented the greatest achievement of modern letters – a new idea in novels. ("Shantih, Shantih, Shantih: Has the Reader Any Rights before the Bar of Literature?")

Chance-generated aesthetics would have more serious consideration with Surrealism and in the second half of the twentieth century, promoted by writers like John Cage. But already in 1920 Tristan Tzara, treading the line between seriousness and whimsy, argued for the aesthetic benefits of a method that involved cutting words from a newspaper, mixing them up in a bag, and then:

> Shake gently.
> Next take out each cutting one after the other.
> Copy conscientiously in the order in which they left the bag.
> The poem will resemble you.
> And there you are – an infinitely original author of charming sensibility, even though unappreciated by the vulgar herd. ("To Make a Dadaist Poem": 39)

As I studied Gertrude Stein's work [*Geography and Plays*], endeavoring to understand its purpose, I will admit that once or twice it occurred to me faintly that it might just possibly be a joke. But it is impossible to make a joke out of 419 pages. If you set out in quest of hilarity, before you read twenty pages you are ready for hara-kiri. It is no more like a joke than the Mojave Desert or the Dead Sea.

Next I explored the assumption that Gertrude Stein's epoch-making experiment was designed to show what words can do by themselves with practically no assistance from the manipulator or with mere mechanical manipulation. I took a sheet of paper and made five columns. In the first I wrote at random fifteen or twenty adjectives; in the second the same number of nouns; in the third a job lot of conjunctions, prepositions, and articles; in the fourth, verbs; in the fifth, adverbs. I then cut up my columns and placed the separate words face downwards in five piles of part of speech. Then I played off the words something in the style, I suppose, of Canfield[15] (which I don't play). I thrust in a bit more punctuation than Gertrude Stein employs, and this was the result:

> Real stupidity; but go slowly. The hope slim. Drink gloriously! Dream! Swiftly pretty people through daffodils slip in green doubt. Grandly fly bitter fish; for hard sunlight lazily consumes old books. Up by a sedate sweetheart roar darkly loud orchards. Life, the purple flame, simply proclaims a poem.

I drew back in astonishment from the result of my own little experiment. My Hercules, what phrases!– 'red stupidity,' 'loud orchards roaring darkly,' 'pretty' people slipping through daffodils in '*green doubt*,' and then those 'bitter fish' flying so grandly, and the proclamation of 'life, the purple flame.' 'Drink gloriously' struck me as a little too close to 'gloriously drunk,' which is of course a *cliché*; but even there the hortatory note adds a kind of foaming and exuberant novelty to the concept. Life had leaped from my parts of speech in tongues of flame. By a mechanical manipulation I had recreated life in words. And when I compared my specimen of it with Gertrude Stein's exhibits, it appeared to me indisputable that the vividness, the color, and the abounding energy of my 'work' made hers seem gray and protoplasmic.

It is necessary, therefore, to discard the theory that her book was written by any kind of mechanical device. It seems almost impossible by any unimpeded mechanical process to assort words in such a fashion that no glimmer of mind will flash out from their casual juxtapositions. The thing can be done only by unremitting intelligence of the first order – if it can be done at all. Now we know on the high testimony of Mr. Anderson that Gertrude Stein possesses intelligence of this order. The work before us leads me to believe that she has attempted precisely the difficult feat which my scissors and shuffled parts of speech failed to accomplish. And so far as the perfection of the enterprise is humanly possible, her efforts have been crowned with success.

Max Eastman, from *The Literary Mind: Its Place in an Age of Science*

(New York: Charles Scribner's Sons, 1931), 76–8.

Max Eastman (1883–1969) was a leading Marxist intellectual who also weighed in on literary issues. A translator of Leon Trotsky's writing, Eastman's changing political views can be seen in his editorship of *The Masses* (beginning in 1913) and, in 1955, his beginning as a contributing editor of the *National Review*. During the early years of modernism, however, he was fiercely committed to leftist causes, and deeply suspicious of difficult literary modernism – seen most famously in his 1929 *Harper's* essay "The Cult of Unintelligibility" (for a parody of modern visual art, see his "Dramatic Career in Modernist Art"). In *The Literary Mind*, which develops the principles of that essay, Eastman offers the following example of what he termed "Gertrudian prose": "I was looking at you, the sweet boy that does not want sweet soap. Neatness of feet do not win feet, but feet win the neatness of men. Run does not run west but west runs east. I like west strawberries best" (63). After discussing the passage for a time, Eastman reveals the passage to be not by Stein, but to be "the ravings of a maniac / cited by Kraepelin in his Clinical Psychiatry" (63–4). In his 1964 autobiography, *Love and Revolution*, Eastman looked back at the "impudent war" "The Cult of Unintelligibility" had waged on the high moderns: "It was a lovely war from my point of view, all weapons permitted and no holds barred. Of course I lost the war. A gap in my memory indicates that I was carried unconscious from the field of battle." Within two years of his essay, Eastman claims, he had "disappeared under a cloud of awfully overwhelming language called the New Criticism" (518).

Every one who has composed poems knows how often he has to sacrifice a value that is both clear and dear to him, in order to communicate his poem to others. Abandon that motive, the limitation it imposes, and you will find yourself writing modernist poetry. I know this because I have tried it. During the very days while I was writing this essay an experience came into my life out of which I felt that it would be peculiarly appropriate to make a private poem. The poem reflects, I suppose, a certain preoccupation with the mannerisms of the modernist poets I had been reading, but still it is in no sense or flavor of the word a parody. It is a poem just between us two, I and myself.

So far from offering this poem as a proof by parody that the "modernist" style of writing is a hoax, I offer it in proof of the opposite thesis – that modernist poetry is the most sincere and natural thing in the world to write, that any poetry will be modernist which ignores the reader or looks upon him as a mere excuse for speech. The modernist tendency may be defined then – in this first and least lovely aspect – as a tendency toward privacy, combined with a naive sincerity in employing as material the instruments of social communion.

On Learning That Nina Has Fallen

Skin-whitishly
this cataract
pain (or importance)
bell-glasses your
heretofore
Clothedly so naked
bell breast.
Glows through the rose
rings loud
rings rose.
LOLLING TONGUED BELLS TOLL BEST
Lash-push of also-anger
A with worm gnawing
with with.
Crimson-skinned eye-rims peeping
preeeping
Bared iris of (also and) Priapus
Hands all awake doing
all organs like hand organs doing, singing
linger-hunger
lingerandhunger
Painted Puritan crank up the old Ford right after dinner
DUB
dub dub
drub-a-dub
drub-adub
druble druble
drouble drouble
droubble droubble droubble droubble droub. . .
Afterward frigidairily

remembering
SIGN ON THE DOTTED LINE
(ex ante facto)
Cocu!

Mary Mills Lyall, from *The Cubies' ABC*

(New York: G.P. Putnam's Sons), 1913.

This is the only known work by Mary Mills Lyall. Her husband, and the book's illustrator, Earl Harvey Lyall (d. 1932), was an early-twentieth-century architect. In a notice of the book, *The Dial* stated that

> The art of the Cubists, "the joy of the mad, the despair of the sane," is amusingly and very cleverly satirized in verse and drawing by Mr. and Mrs. Earl Harvey Lyall in the oddest little color book of the season, "The Cubies' ABC" (Putnam). Mrs. Lyall writes the verses, Mr. Lyall cubically illustrates them. The book must be seen and read to be appreciated. ("Holiday Art Books")

Many of the entries and drawings refer to specific works in the 1913 Armory Show.

C is for Color Cubistic ad libitum
(Orange and blue, yellow, purple and green.)
"Throw them all on your boards," Cubies say, "then exhibit 'em!"
There'll be no colors left, if we don't soon prohibit 'em!
(Watch them at work and you'll see what I mean.)
– C is for Color Cubistic ad libitum.

D is for Duchamp, the Deep-Dyed Deceiver,
Who, drawing accordeons, labels them stairs,
With a lady that must have been done in a fever, –
His model won't see her, we trust, it would grieve her! –
(Should the stairway collapse, Cubie's good at repairs.)
– D is for Duchamp, the Deep-Dyed Deceiver.

F's for the Future for which Cubies hanker; –
To Hals, Perugino and all that old crew
They give up the Past without envy or rancor,
While saying in tones than which naught could be franker:
"Come, move on, – it's our turn! They have finished with you."
– F's for the Future for which Cubies hanker.

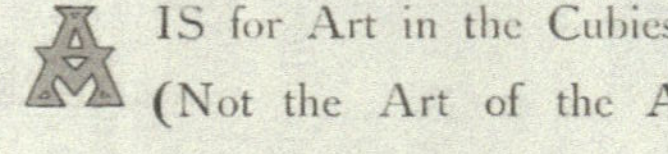 IS for Art in the Cubies' domain—
(Not the Art of the Ancients, brand-new are
the Cubies.)
Archipenko's their guide, Anatomics their bane;
They're the joy of the mad, the despair of the sane,
(With their emerald hair and their eyes red as
rubies.)
—A is for Art in the Cubies' domain.

6

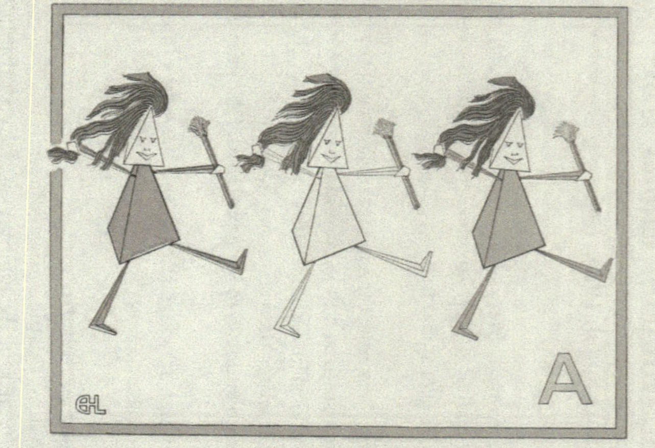

Mary Lyall, "From the Cubists ABC," letter A

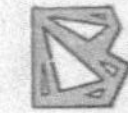IS for Beauty as Brancusi views it.
(The Cubies all vow he and Braque take the
Bun.)
First you seize all that's plain to the eye, then you
lose it;
Next you search for the Soul and proceed to abuse it.
(They tell me it's easy and no end of fun.)
—B is for Beauty as Brancusi views it.

8

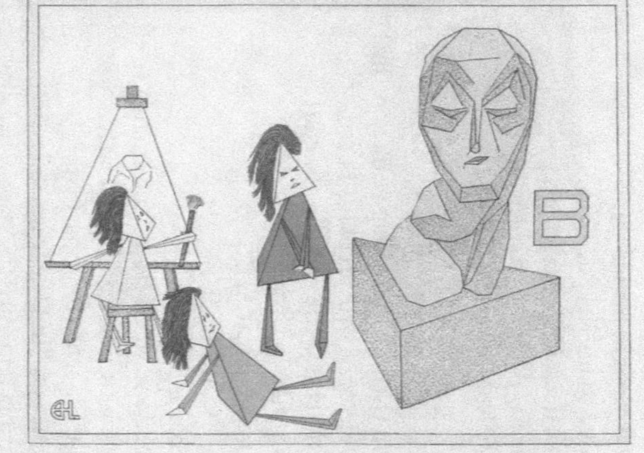

Mary Lyall, "From the Cubists ABC," letter B

K's for Kandinsky's Kute "improvisations" –
The Kubies abound in delight for his art:
They say there's a Klue to his Kryptic Kreations.
By means of Picabia's deep ratiocinations
Some day we may really decipher his heart.
– K's for Kandinsky's Kute "improvisations."

O's for Objective and Optical Art,
(The kind we've been used to, these long years gone by.)
Which the Cubie Objects to with all of his heart:
"Make the Object Subjective," he says, "at the start, –
Just a matter of Grammar, as easy as pie!"
– O's for Objective and Optical Art.

P's for Picasso, Picabia and Party
(Who deal in abstractions, distractions and such.)
When, with vision chaotic and expletives hearty,
You beg of a Cubist their sense to impart, he
Profoundly makes answer: "In little is much."
– P's for Picasso, Picabia and Party.

Q's for the Queerness we Stand-patters feel
When Progressive young Cubies start Art reformation.
They're strong on Initiative, praise the Square Deal:
"Though the Cubic is best!" they aggressively squeal;
"Painting things as you see them is rank deformation!"
– Q's for the Queerness we Stand-patters feel.

R is for Reason and poor old Reality,
Once in the fashion, but now obsolete,
Banished forever with grim actuality.
Now the sole law is one's own personality –
Find the Cube Root and you have it complete.
– R is for Reason and poor old Reality,

W's for Woolworth, the building so stable,
(Erected with nickels and dimes by us all,)
Which Cubies paint writhing from cellar to gable,
Distinctly resembling the Tower of Babel,
Some decades ago, just preceding its fall.
– W's for Woolworth, the building so stable.

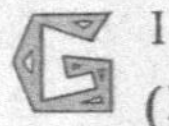

IS for Gertrude Stein's limpid lucidity,
(Eloquent scribe of the Futurist soul.)
Cubies devour each word with avidity:
"*Alone* words lack sense," they affirm with placidity,
"But *how* wise we'll be when we've swallowed
the whole!"
—G is for Gertrude Stein's limpid lucidity.

18

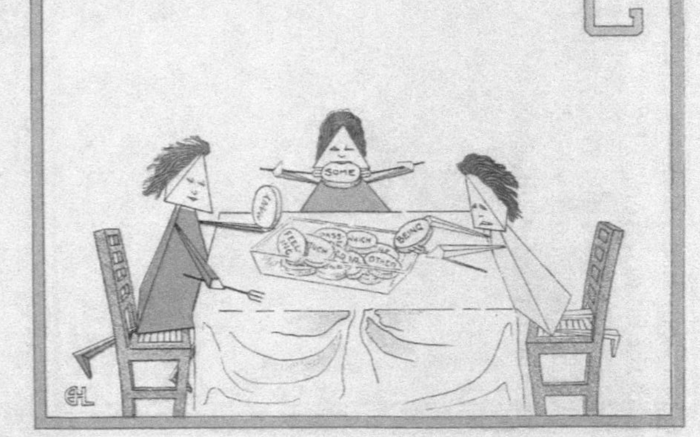

Mary Lyall, "From the Cubists ABC," letter G

Y's for the Yawn overcoming each Cubie
At sight of a painting not done in his style
"If a man doesn't use all the colors, from ruby
To sapphire and emerald and topaz – the booby! –
To look at his canvas is not worth one's while!"
– Y's for the Yawn overcoming each Cubie.

Harold B. Harrison, "Letters to the Editor. Cubism"

New Age **14.21 (1912): 671.**

The other day I came, and saw, and was overcome by Cubism with a sense of unutterable despair. "This is no place for me!" I cried. "Back, back to auntie's drawing-room, and the dear old mid-Victorian floral carpet, and the water-colours by Copley Fielding and Noah's Ark Cooper on the walls!" Of a truth, Mr. Editor, I am grieved for the Cubist, and my bowels of compassion yearn towards him, as for mine own little brother. To think of the prostitution of so much decent talent, and the beclouding of so many bright intellects, the young, the brave, the beautiful, emasculating their abilities on the altar of this terrible goddess.

"... Ego adolescens, ego ephebus, ego puer
Ego guminasi fui flos, ego eram decus olei."

Catullus, *Attis*, 11. 63–4[16]

Oh! when I was a boy at the Slade,[17]
I was easily top of my grade;
Both in charcoal and chalk
I was cock of the walk,
And in oils the first pick on parade.

Once the glory and pride of the school,
I have turned out a Futurist fool,
And the paint from my tube
I expend on a cube
That I've drawn with a compass and rule.

Harold B. Harrison, "Letters to the Editor. Una Picarsita"

***New Age* 10.14 (1912): 334.**

Sir, – I was present at the following conversation the other day, and I thought that I would venture to send you a report: –

"Don't you find it very dull living in the country? Not in the least. What do you find to do? How do you pass your time? How do you contrive to amuse yourself? By following the advice of Linnaeus and looking for four-leaved *Trifolium*, and taking part in the Picasso controversy. The Picasso controversy! I never heard of it. What is it? What is it about? You surprise me. It is a controversy concerning the merits of a painter of that name. Of the name of Picasso! What a funny name! I believe it is Spanish. A black or dark brown horse with a blaze is called a "picasso" in Argentina. What is a blaze? A blaze or blazon or stripe down the face from the forehead to the nose. Has this Picasso painter-man got a mark on his face? I hope not. I really cannot tell you. I have never seen him. Then why is he called Picasso? Because that is his name. Oh, I see. Is he a good painter?

"I have been told so, exquisite colour, tremendous power of draughtsmanship, beautiful line: in short, something like myself. Oh! Does he paint in oils or water-colours? In both mediums, I believe. Oh! Is he a member of the Royal Academy? I have never heard that he has been elected. Oh! Then where have you seen his pictures? Nowhere. Then how can you take part in the Picasso controversy, as you call it, if you have never seen his pictures? It is unnecessary to see that sort of picture in order to describe it. They are the sort of weird, wild, awful things, you know, that you see when you have got the jim-jams. I have never had the jim-jams. You're lucky. Thank you so much. Go on talking, I am listening to you. And even without the aid of the jim-jams you can evolve a description of these pictures out of your subliminal self. Can you? How clever of you? Do let me hear you do it." He evolveth –

"Lines and curves flowing out of nothingness and ending in nowhere. Floods gushing over the edge of space. Raw wrecks of matter colliding with chaotic and inchoate worlds. The writhing of worms. The coiling of serpents. Eyes without heads, and heads destitute of eyes. Armless hands grasping at the coat-tails of the void. Legless tables whereat yet never man sat. Glasses full of emptiness, and mandolines whose music you can actually see twisted in hard knots amongst their strings. Maddened mobs of mammoths and mastodons – tireless streams of tapirs and tadpoles –

"Ruining [*sic*] along the illimitable inane.[18]

"Hats without gloves, gloves without hats – umbrellas without handles. Naked bodies floating about in seas of Judson's dyes[19] – of more varied hues and greater brilliancy than even Turner's pencil could occupy. Innumerable multitudes of monkeys mopping and mowing at the contortions of capercailzies caught in contraptions. Oofs and oonts oozing panto-post-impressionist picture-postcards at every pore. Blizzards of izzards – Oh, do stop, please – and from the midst of all an angel face – Stop! – an angel face shines out which I – Stop at once I tell you."

He stoppeth. "Now suppose you tell me how you first came to hear about these pictures. I was told about them. Who told you? Mr. Huntly Carter and Mr. Wake Cook.[20] Who are these gentlemen? Critics and artists. Mr. Huntly Carter is also a judge of cocktails. How do you know that he is a judge of cocktails? He recommended me a very good one once. Do you agree with what they say? I agreed about the cocktail. But about the pictures? I agreed with both of them. With both? I suppose they both say the same thing? Nearly the same thing, only in different ways. Mr. Wake Cook is the more exciting, Mr. Huntly Carter the more soothing and reassuring. You see it is this way. If one says, 'I am not,' and the other says, 'You're another,' it's the same thing, you see, exactly – for 'to be not' is 'to be other than another.' Do you follow me? Quite. I agree more, however, with Mr. Huntly Carter? Why do you agree more with him? Because he says the same things I say. What things do you say? I said I thought that my brain was softening and he said he quite agreed with me. All critics, you know, are apt to suffer from softening of the brain – or a swelling of the head – some of them have to be always buying larger-sized hats in consequence. The faculty call it Critics Chronic. You remember poor old Ruskin, and Aristotle, Quintilian, Longinus, Origen – all suffered from it, more especially Origen. Who were all these people? I thought you were educated at Somerville. I, no, it was Marion; I stopped at home to look after mother, you remember. Oh – ah – yes – quite so. I had forgotten –

"O matre pulcra, filia pulchivor!"[21]

"What's that? That's Spanish, the language M. Picasso speaks. Why do you say Monsieur Picasso if he is Spanish? Because of my natural *delicadessa*, and for the reason that M. Picasso resides and works in Paris. A great many artists live in Paris, don't they? I believe so. Have you ever been to Paris? Only once. When was that? Quite lately, when I went over to lift 'La Gioconda.' How silly you are. I am. But about these pictures – you know I am so fond of pictures – what do people really say about them? Horrid things and wonderful things. Some people say that they are pictures of the souls of tables and wine-glasses, and other household utensils. What stuff! How can a table have a soul? Nothing simpler. You know that everything really ideal – has an ideal real – and as Calverley[22] says: 'If you cannot realise the ideal – you may at least idealise the real.' That is to be soulful, idealise the real: see?

"Oh, thank you so much. But can *anybody* understand these pictures? There are only a very few who can, Mr. Huntly Carter and the Esoterics. Who are the Esoterics? "The strong men of Paris – the French Sandows,[23] weightlifters and stone-putters. Oh, I see: but how can you write criticisms on these pictures, and take part in the controversy if, as you say, you have never seen them? Easily – as easy as lying, or falling off a log. You simply read over somebody else's criticism, and say exactly the opposite – like the tête du pont at Rouge et Noir, you know. I know nothing about Rouge et Noir. It is immaterial. But suppose that somebody else has done the same as you – does it not lead to confusion? To confusion? To combustion, to conflagration – 'red ruin and the breaking up of laws';[24] for there is no more fearful wild fowl than your critic if you can only manage to poke him up properly. But have you never even seen a photograph or a drawing of one of these pictures? Yes, once. Where? One that was published in THE NEW AGE. In THE NEW AGE – what is that? The 'Spectator' calls it the best paper relating to the Higher Socialism, or something to that effect. Oh, ah, yes, the 'Spectator.' I know it. Aunt Martha takes it in. I dare say she does. It is the sort of paper that she would take in, but you ought to get her to subscribe to THE NEW AGE as well; I am sure that it would amuse her. Oh, I see, THE NEW AGE is a paper – a different paper from the 'Spectator.' It is. You take it in? Yes. And you have that drawing? Yes. And do you mean to say that you have talked all this nonsense, and had the drawing of one of the pictures here all the time? Yes; I had my reasons. Go and bring it at once." He goeth. Unheard of melodies of undiscovered mandolines. "Here it is – take it – and frame it, and wear it next your heart – for my sake."

Harold B. Harrison, "Letters to the Editor. Picasso"

New Age **10.9 (1911): 212–13.**

Sir, – I have looked long and lovingly on the picture by Picasso published by THE NEW AGE, and for one bright, brief, ecstatic moment I thought that I had discovered the wine-glass, but, alas, on looking closer I found that I was holding the page upside down. I believe that there are some pictures that look equally well both ways, but this of course I know is not meant for one of them.

During one period of my chequered career I worked for three sessions at the Slade[25] – the same school, I believe, that Mr. Chesterton studied at – so that now I naturally feel competent to decide on any subject connected with art.

To me, sir, art is nothing else but the expression of emotion, and if it is otherwise, I have read my Laocoon in vain. I am catholic in my tastes, and I esteem the music of the tiles as but a little lower in tone than the music of the spheres, both being but parts of one grand sweet song; and the lyrics of Harry Lauder[26] touch the same chords in me as the love songs of Hafiz.[27] I merely mention this to show you that I am above vulgar prejudice, and that I am naturally able to appreciate the good and beautiful where-ever I may find them; but this picture by Picasso, to use a term borrowed from nature, not from art, is for me, sir, a little bit too much the monkey. Accordingly I have felt moved to embody my emotions in the following sonnet, which I have entitled:—

ON LAST LOOKING INTO PICASSO'S PICTURE OF A MANDOLINE, A WINE-GLASS, AND A TABLE IN A STORM.

A table, wine-glass, and a mandoline:
What thoughts, oh poet, do these conjure up?
Of winning kisses, and of crushing cups;
Sweet sounds, fair ladies, blushful Hippocrene:
Wine, woman, song? Glass always rhymes with lass;
A mandoline befits a lover's fable;
Good wine, good cheer, subtend a good man's table:
While round about the cut decanters pass.
But what of this? Ye holy gods! A smash
Of fallen houses, and bent iron railings;
A bird's-eye nightmare of some builder's failings,
Flattened together with immortal crash.
Or if in milder mood, I muse and think
Of drunken spiders crawling, mixed with ink.

"Notes and Comment: Cubist Literature"

1913? Gertrude Stein and Alice B. Toklas Papers, Yale Collection of American Literature, Beinecke Rare Book and Manuscript Library, Yale University.

The exact source of this item is unknown. As do many of the items based on Stein's work in *Mock Modernism*, this newspaper article is found in Stein's clipping service archive, located at the Beinecke. While it appeared that Alice Toklas initially began collecting these clippings, Stein soon turned to a clipping service, Romeike (which began in 1881 and advertised itself as "The First Established and Most Complete Newspaper Cutting Bureau in the World"). Romeike's collection of clippings related to *Tender Buttons* contains well over a hundred items.

The cubist and futurists have their literature as well as their pictorial art. Miss Gertrude Stein is the leading exponent of cubist literature. Here is her description of the way she felt when she saw Mrs. Mabel Dodge walk through the gardens of the Villa Curonia:

> "A walk that is not stepped there the floor is covered not in the place where the room is entered. There is not any stone. There is the wide door that is narrow on the floor. There is all that place.
>
> There is all there is when there has all there has where there is what there is. That is what is done when there is done what is done and the union is won."

At considerable trouble and expense we have gone a step further and applied the cubist principles to verse, and are now able to present a poem, not descriptive of the cubist pictures, but in the cubist language.

The first stanza was written while listening to a feeble minded parrot singing French comic songs to a Bavarian wursthound who is ignorant of the language:

I saw the all that never was
   Come woozing though the which
And noted that no what could buzz
   So busily as sich;
I thought: "Is it a sinful thing
   To think so blithe and gay
That one sings sans a singful think
   Or single thing to say?"

The second stanza was composed while watching an escaped inmate of Matteawan[28] fleeing from a three legged chicken who had just got out of a side show, both the chicken and the escaped person being under the impression that the latter was a grain of corn.

My feet go up, my feet go down
  My feet go in and out;
I follow them around the town,
  And as I run I shout:
"If I were like a centipede
  And had feet by the score,
When I got drunk would I stagger less
  Or would I stagger more?"

The third stanza is not, strictly speaking, our own. We heard one of the dental detectives at police headquarters (a Sherlock Holmes looking sort of man) crooning it the other day as he busily tried to fit assorted teeth into the holes in a piece of Swiss cheese:

There is a thought perturbs my mind
  I pass it on to you;
If all my eye teeth should go blind
  How could I see to chew?
How could one choose the cheese he chews
  If his dog teeth all went mad?
My wisdom teeth are crazy, sir
  And that is why I'm sad!

There are several other stanzas, but we forbear. We are busily engaged at present in formulating a system for carrying the cubist art, pictorial and literary, one step further. The new departure will be known as the Circular Art.

Watch for it.

Bert Leston Taylor, "A Line-o'-Type or Two"

***Chicago Daily Tribune*, 20 March 1913: 6.**

THE CUBIST

Blessings on you, painter man!
Do you really think you can
By some geometric law
Make us see the thing you saw?
Do you really think that Art
Is of Science any part,
And that through triangulation
We shall come to your sensation?
Have you, honestly, a notion
Art is other than Emotion
That it is, for you or us,
Differential calculus?

Nay. With what it means to you,
Art has simply nought to do;
Art begins when you've conveyed
Meaning of the thing you've made.
You may show it well or ill;
That is question of your skill.
But the meaning you must show,
Else it isn't Art. Lord, no!
Any baby building blocks
Any Cubist canvas mocks.

You know this as well as I,
So I know your "art" a lie.
Music's not acoustics, man;
Painting's not a builder's plan.
Eyes are eyes and ears are ears,
So it has been through the years;
So it will be, so it must,
When your crazy-quilts are dust.

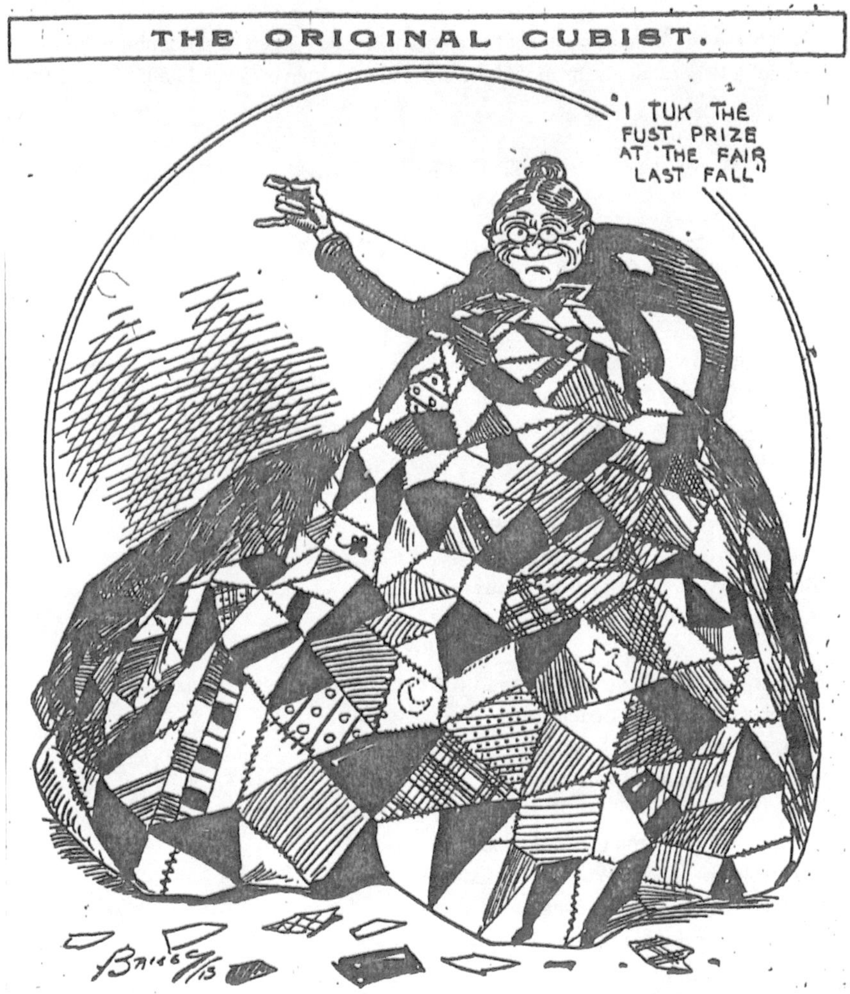

Bribby, "The Original Cubist" (*Chicago Daily Tribune*, 20 March 1913: 1)

Bert Leston Taylor, "A Line-o'-Type or Two"

***Chicago Daily Tribune*, 25 March 1913: 8.**

The phrase "simultaneousness of the ambient" is taken from "The Exhibitors to the Public," a 1912 catalogue introduction / manifesto written by several Italian Futurists.

POST-IMPRESSIONISM

Lines, Written after Viewing Mr. Arthur Dove's Exposition of the "Simultaneousness of the Ambient."

(Reprinted by request.)

I cannot tell you how I love
The canvasses of Mr. Dove,[29]
Which Saturday I went to see
In Mr. Thurber's Gallery.[30]

At first you fancy they are built
As patterns for a crazy quilt,
But soon you see that they express
An ambient simultaneousness.

This thing, which you would almost bet,
Portrays a Spanish omelette,
Depicts instead, with wondrous skill,
A horse and cart upon a hill.

Now, Mr. Dove has too much art
To show the horse or show the cart;
Instead, he paints the creak and strain.
Get it? No pike is half so plain.

This thing, which would appear to show
A fancy vest scenario,
Is really quite another thing –
A flock of pigeons on the wing.

But Mr. Dove is much too keen
To let a single bird be seen;
To show the pigeons would not do,
And so he simply paints the ooo.

It's all as simple as can be;
He paints the things you cannot see.
Just as composers please the ear
With "program" things you cannot hear.

Dove is the cleverest of chaps;
And, gazing at his rhythmic maps,
I wonder (and I'm wondering yet)
Whether he did them on a bet.

Actual requests, more than a few, were made for the reprinting of the foregoing pome, which Collier's this week, is extravagant enough to refer to as a classic. One would as soon write fresh verses, as one could write verses about post-impressionism until the homecoming of the lowing kine.

Thanks to Mr. Arthur J. Eddy, the public is able to make out the female figure in the celebrated picture puzzle, "Nude Descending a Staircase," otherwise known as "The Lady with the Shingles." It reminds one of the cartoons that Kepler and others used to make years ago, in which the faces and figures of Blaine, Butler, and contemporary statesmen were sketched in the branches and trunks of trees and in other natural objects.

A friendly word of warning: Don't pretend to see more in any of the pictures than you actually do see. You might happen on a hoax instead of the real thing and make a sublime donkey of yourself.

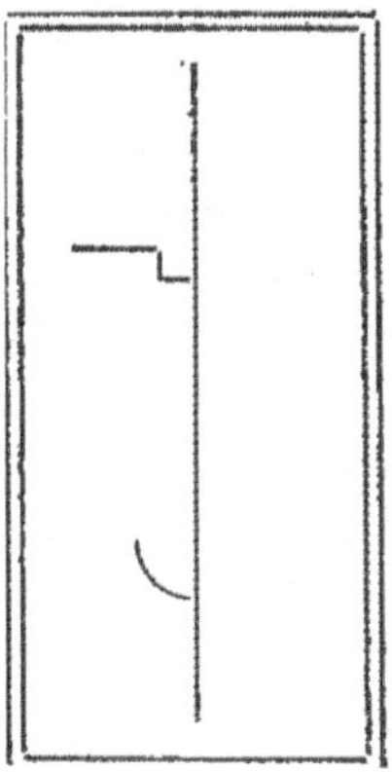

A NUMBER of alert readers who have visited the picture show are reminded of the Post-Impressionist picture, "Soldier and Dog Going Through a Doorway."

Bert Leston Taylor, "A Line-o'-Type or Two" (*Chicago Daily Tribune*, 5 April 1913: 8)

Julian Street, from "Why I Became a Cubist"

***Everybody's Magazine*, March 1913: 814–25.**

Julian Street (1879–1947) had a varied writing career. A journalist, he also wrote humorous sketches and a Paris restaurant guide, as well as a book on wine and another on Japan. In the work below, after visiting the Armory Show, hearing various defenses of the art, and finally reading Gertrude Stein's portraits of Matisse and Mabel Dodge, he suddenly sees the light and becomes a cubist. The following passage is the result.

Last night when all was still and dark I went into the great, punctuation-markless silence and brought all my power to bear upon the banishing of preconceived images. I concentrated upon the impression I had received from viewing Cubist art and reading Cubist word-painting. I waited … waited … Then, at last, the words began to come … I set them down … When they stopped coming, I went into the light; yes, into the light. And I read. I read. This is what I read:

POST-IMPRESSIONIST POEM

While still I sported knee-length pants
   My people taught me that 'twas rude
To even steal a sidelong glance
   At casts or paintings of the nude.

Then Futurist and Cubist came,
   And Futurized the nude, till now
No longer need the blush of shame
   Mount up and mantle Comstock's[31] brow.

And hence it comes that purest prudes
   In chaste Cohoes, austere Oswego,
Need have no fear; for Cubist nudes
   Strip but the Artist's hard-boiled Ego.

Do you not see how beautiful that is? It is very beautiful. Very beautiful indeed. But not as beautiful as it can be beautiful. For the most beautiful that is beautiful is not the Post-Impressionist beautiful, but the Cubist beautiful. Now, let us treat the poem a little differently:

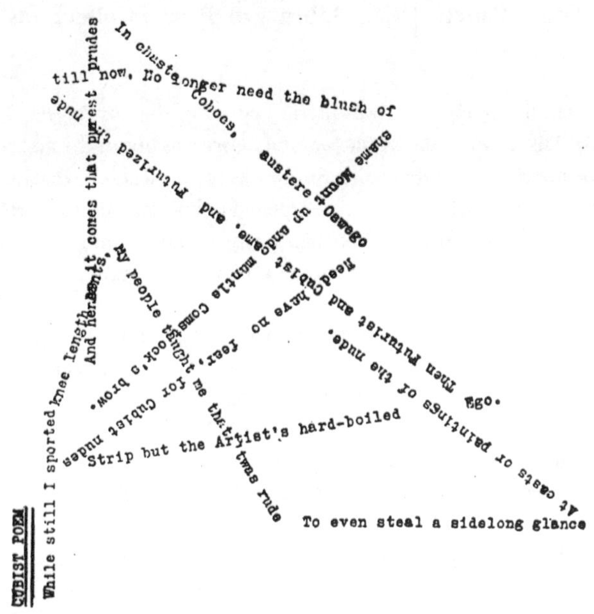

It may be that you are not far enough along to appreciate my Cubistry. It may be that I shall have to struggle on for years and years before I am appreciated. But if you feel disposed to scoff, let me remind you, even as they reminded me, when I scoffed, of Galileo, Columbus, Richard Wagner, Monet, and Cezanne. All of them were called demented in their time, just as we Cubists are to-day.

And if those names are not enough of evidence, here are some more. Think of these! Think of de Rougemont, think of the Sterling Debenture Syndicate, think of 520% Miller, Benedict Arnold, Carrie Nation, Jezebel, Darius Green, Captain Kidd, Boss Tweed, Sitting Bull, Elbert Hubbard, Dr. Munyon, Nero, Jack the Ripper, Jesse James, General Weyler, the Borgias, Bill Sikes, Guy Fawkes, Lydia Pinkham, and Dr. Cook.

Pavel Jerdanowitch [Paul Jordan Smith], "Disumbrationism"

Paul Jordan Smith Papers, UCLA Library of Special Collections, box 42.

Paul Jordan Smith (1885–1971) was literary editor of the *Los Angeles Times* from 1933 to 1957. His *A Key to the Ulysses of James Joyce* was one of the first books published on the novel. Even in that work, Smith was sceptical about what he saw as the extremes in modernism, a scepticism sharpened in his views on modern art. In his autobiography, Smith reports that his transformation into the founder of Disumbrationism began with his look at the works in the Armory Show in Chicago:

> I saw no beauty, no form or meaning in them. Day after day I went to see and to hear contradictory explanations of what was called modern art, and finally I became disgusted, for most of the young critics were saying in effect, "What if we cannot see and understand these things! Great masters in the past were misunderstood and so we must accept and try to see, whether they please us or not. Pleasure is not the point." (*The Road I Came* 220)

After creating a parody of Duchamp ("The Drunken Walking Stick Descends the Stairs"), Smith eventually became more ambitious:

> It was after a rather acrimonious debate with my good friends, Edward Weston, a photographer, and Edward Kaminsky, professor of art, on the subject of cubism, futurism, and distortions in art that I offered to bet that if I would submit some meaningless daubs under a strange foreign name, I would gain critical attention ... So I borrowed some old brushes and a few tubes of scarlet, black, yellow and green paint, and on a discarded canvas of large proportions, I slapped out a picture of a savage woman with her arm lifted on high. The paint had a tendency to run, because in my haste to be done with the business I used too much thinner and dryer, so I had to lay the thing flat on the floor. I intended the woman to have a starfish in her hand but the running paint made it look more like a peeled banana. I added some touches and let it go as a banana. I placed a skull in the background, high on a pole to give a touch of cannibalism to it, and to help along the modernity of the creation I drew the woman a hut which appeared to be toppling over on one side. I made her eyes a ghastly Gauginesque white and let one great breast exceed the other in size. When it was done I called the picture, "Yes, We Have No Bananas." (221–2)

Setting himself up as Pavel Jerdanowitch, founder of the Disumbrationist movement in art, Smith was able to win some occasional serious critical attention, and the hoax unravelled only after several years.

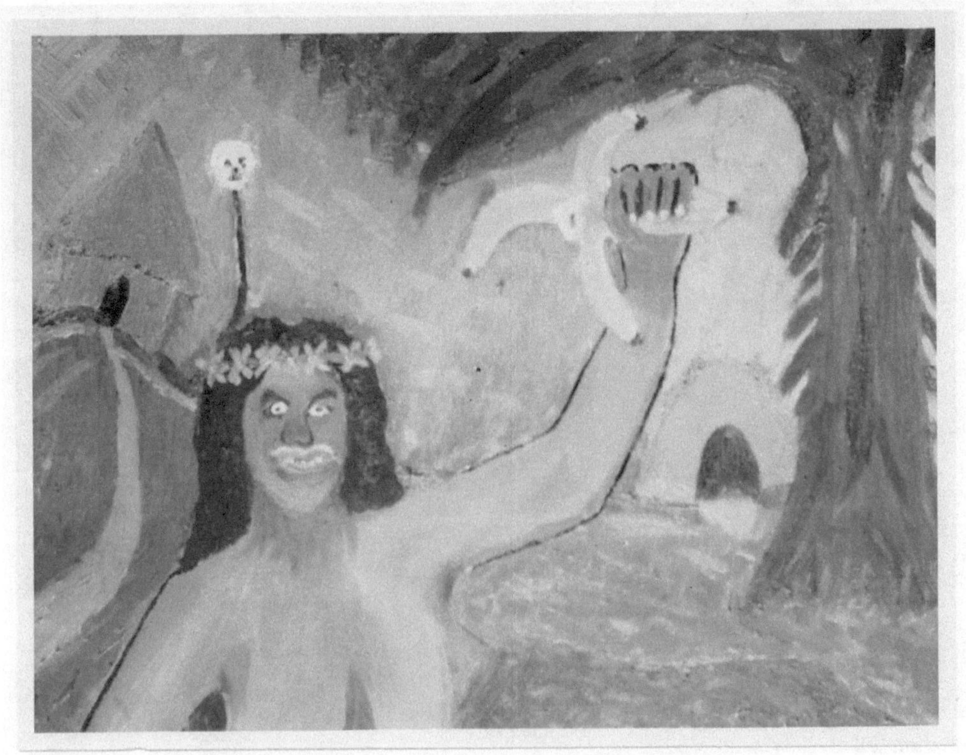

Exaltation ["Yes, We Have No Bananas"] (oil on canvas, dimensions unknown)

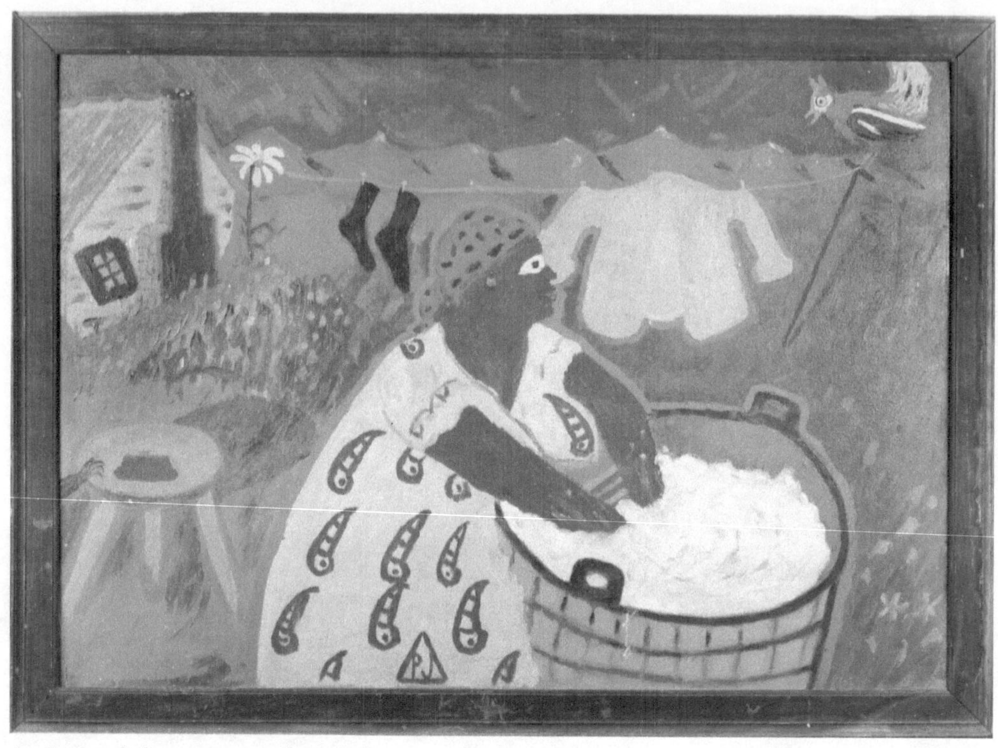

Aspiration (oil on canvas, 28" x 39")

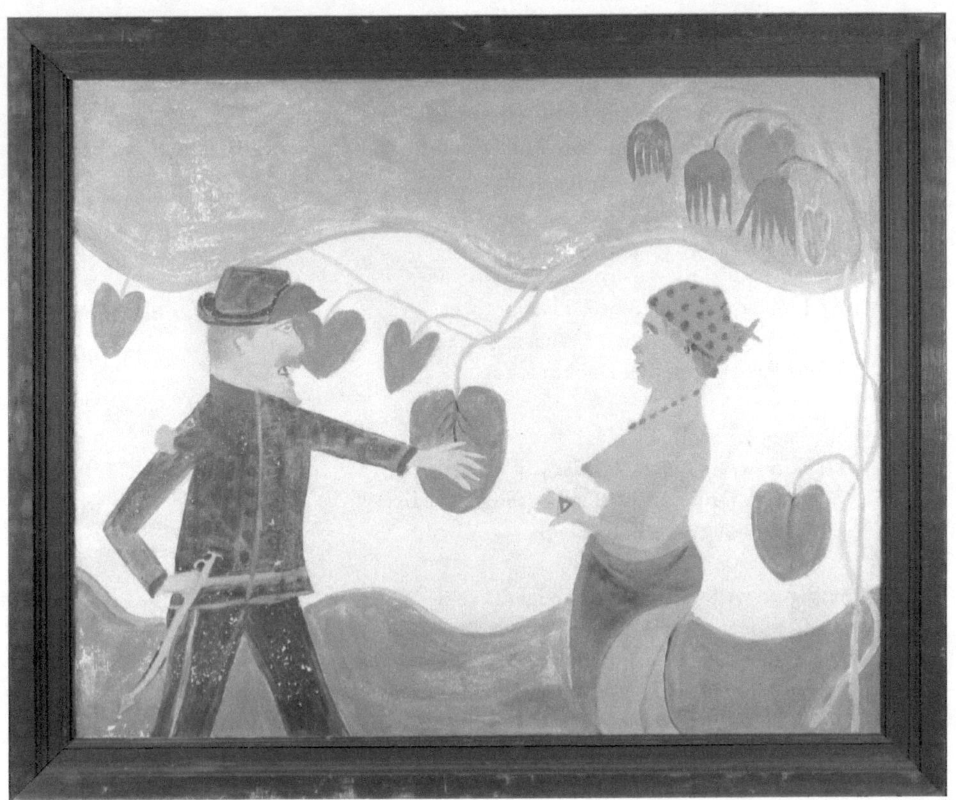

Capitulation (oil on canvas, 28" x 34")

P. Selver, "Short Cuts to Literary Success"

***New Age* 18.9 (1915): 205–7.**

Paul Selver (1888–1970) was an editor and translator of Czech and Slavic literature. He contributed poetry to *Coterie* on a few occasions, was a regular writer for the *New Age*, and the author of *Orage and the New Age Circle* (1959). His "Perpetuum Mobile: A Pantoum, More or Less," which appeared in Edith Sitwell's *Wheels*, of all places, captures log-rolling:

Pilk lands [lauds] the verse of Jobble to the skies,
  And Jobble says that Bibson's Dante's peer
  Bibson is great on Pagg, – "What art!" he cries,
  While Pagg is sure that Dubkin is a seer.

While Pagg is sure that Dubkin is a seer,
  Dubkin swears Botchell's odes will never wane;
  Botchell commands: "Watch Pimpington's career!"
  Pimpington writes a book on Trodger's brain.

Pimpington writes a book on Trodger's brain,
  And Trodger shrieks: "Glabb's genius stirs my soul!"
  Glabb raves of Cringely's rhymes with might and main;
  Cringely pens Gummit's name on glory's scroll.

Cringely pens Gummit's name on glory's scroll,
  And Gummit sees in Sludd new worlds arise,
  Sludd bids us hear Pilk's mighty rhythms roll;
  Pilk lauds the verse of Jobble to the skies. . . .

Introduction

Each day brings fresh indications that this age will mark a significant epoch in the history of our national literature. In spite of the cynical pessimism of a certain group of critics, who persistently seek to besmirch the escutcheons of our most recently accredited writers with petty and undignified carping, it is obvious that the practice of literary composition is becoming daily – nay, hourly, almost – more widespread, more appreciated, more finely developed. To-day there is a general interest in literature, which even ten years ago was unheard of. To those whose insight is schooled to interpret the seemingly most trivial tokens, the appearance of poetical quotations in prominent places on our underground railways is, in itself, a symptom of this national ferment, this artistic upheaval emanating from the inner life of the British people, this creative impulse which bids fair to bring forth wonderful and undying fruit in its due season.

All this is eminently gratifying to those who have the literary destinies of our nation at heart. It is peculiarly satisfactory because it indicates the approach of an epoch when the artificial limitations of the literary world are to vanish. In other words, the people are beginning to realise that literature in its diverse and manifold forms, after having for so long remained the monopoly of an unchosen few, in whose interests it naturally lay to guard jealously what they had appropriated in so arbitrary a manner, is henceforth to be restored to its rightful possessors. In rapid succession we have seen the rise of a railway-porter poet, a navvy novelist, a scavenger dramatist. The phenomenal welcome which was extended to a volume of philosophical essays published by a lamp-lighter of Herne Hill, and the enthusiastic comments evoked from the Press when a collection of aesthetic aphorisms was issued by a Crouch End plumber, are further indications of the same emancipating tendency.

It is obvious, therefore, that the pursuit of literature, the fellowship of the Muses, the golden hours of semi-sacred inspiration are no longer to be the prerogative of professional writers whose only claim to their office is usually based upon a number of years spent in wearisome and valueless study. Because these arrogant individuals have attempted to acquire the principles of Latin syntax, because they have dulled their intellects with the obscurities of Aeschylean choruses, or rounded their shoulders over the shrivelled and obsolete pages of such authors as Milton, Pope, and Swift, they are qualified, forsooth, to provide literary fare for the modern man of the twentieth century! Was there ever a more arrant and stupid fallacy?

The fact is that precisely the man who has not squandered precious hours in such aimless pseudostudies is best fitted to create the new artistic tradition, and to build up the young and vigorous literature which is even now in its inception. Freedom from stiff and outworn theories, a mind uncumbered with the musty litter of pedantic scribes – these are the safest foundations for the true national literature, which, untainted by any admixture of so-called Hellenic Paganism, or self-styled Latin decadence, will be a pure British product for pure British people. The labourers, we may rest assured, will not be a few, and they will, without a doubt, be worthy of their hire.

The object of these notes is to assist the prospective author in discovering, with the minimum of anxiety and search, the branch of literature for which he is best fitted. It will not be surprising if, at first, the beginner is bewildered by the array of varied activities that beckon to him with the attraction of limitless prospects and possibilities.

Shall I become a poet, and shake the deepest emotions of my fellow-men, rousing them to loftier conceptions of human existence?

Shall I become a novelist and see a whole nation hanging upon my lips as I conjure up regiments of living characters, whose final destinies lie within my sole jurisdiction?

Shall I pen dramas, and thrill crowded assemblies into anguished silence as they view the grim interplay of passions, devised by me, take vivid shape before them?

Shall I weave quaint and delicate fancies in quiet cadences of prose, which men may raptly ponder over in the shadowed seclusion of an old-world garden? And so on.

These are some of the most obvious questions that will present themselves to the eager learner. By following the indications and suggestions in these pages, he will be enabled, with the most economical expenditure of his mental forces, to select and proceed upon the literary career which is most appropriate to his own personal temperament.

In order the more fully and clearly to exemplify the principles in question, copious but judicious excerpts will be inserted from the most characteristic products representative of the various literary divisions which will come within the range of this guide. These examples alone will form a valuable and fascinating anthology of the newest British literature.

SECTION 1 – POETRY OR VERSE

This is a branch of literature which, other things being equal, the novice will be well advised to avoid. In the first place, it is a matter of little general interest, and publishers are, rightly enough, chary of venturing upon so precarious an enterprise. Moreover, it will be found that the composition of verse has been needlessly confused and obscured by what is known as Prosody, a subject which in reality has no connection with poetry, as such, at all. Prosody is an extremely dry, unattractive and unprofitable affair, which abounds in such cumbersome technical terms as rhythm (curiously enough, quite distinct from rhyme), iambus, caesura, pentameter, amphibrachic, and the like. It is clearly not worth the beginner's while to engage upon a study which is most unlikely to lead to any tangible or satisfactory results. Should it be held, for some special reason, desirable or urgent to undertake the production of poetry, there is satisfaction in noting that the young author is not obliged to lose time with such preliminary trifling as prosody. An ingenious American gentleman has devised and perfected a type of verse which, while entitling its author fully to the designation of poet, depends upon principles so simple and attractive that half an hour's preparation, at the most, is necessary to become efficient. This type of verse is known by various names, and although these are, in themselves, of no importance, yet in case he should hear them mentioned and fail to identify them, the beginner should commit to memory the two most familiar of these terms – free rhythm (*not rhyme*) and imagism (*not imagination*). The differences between these two varieties are so slight that they may safely be neglected.

It is only fair to warn the beginner that this form of verse has been very widely practised in recent times, with the result that, except in special cases, the demand for it is not very great. It should therefore not be attempted before expert advice has been secured. Perhaps the safest variety for the inexperienced is the mystical and cosmic (not to be confounded with comic) style. In this medium, the writer endeavours to be as obscure as possible, and with a little practice it will be found quite easy to write lines which contain little or no meaning. It is essential to refer with some familiarity to space, time, chaos, infinity, the cosmos, the soul, etc. The perusal of an elementary text-book of astronomy will considerably facilitate the earlier stages of this species of composition, which, when carefully performed, is often extremely effective. As a model example which the learner should aim at imitating (not too slavishly, of course) the following lines from Eli Peck's "Visions and Ecstasies" (p. 22) will be found of service. The dreamy vagueness and subtle symbolism of this beautiful poem have with justice been commended as one of the most delicate artistic products of the present age.

COSMIC HYMN

At midnight
My spirit conversed with the polar star
In Singalese.
As I ascended the slope of a hieroglyph
Curved with the rotundity
Wherein planets are fashioned,
I hearkened to a butterfly
which spake thus to a hedgehog:
"Beware the crooning of the equator,
For in the garden a cactus has sprouted."

I pondered thereon with the stored wisdom of aeons,
Exulting at the ferment of perished comets.
From the chaotic depths of eternity
the voices of the dawn
whispered a mute farewell in my ears.
Then knew I that yesterday was not today,
and the morrow will be of other mould
than the week which is gone …

At midnight
My spirit conversed with the polar star
in Singalese.

The beginner should further take note that peculiarities of punctuation, the use or omission of capital letters, the employment of unexpected dots and spaces, are of more importance in this form of verse than might casually be realised.

For shorter poems, an oriental garb, combined with disjointed allusions, will be found of the utmost assistance. A dainty example is appended with special permission of the author, Clarence Fripp ("Ex Oriente Lux," p. 73).

ETCHING (FROM THE TIBETAN)

Six bamboo-stems swaying in the east wind
And a pumpkin mouldering in the moonlight.
The young lama 00-ER
Weeps by the fluted columns of the pagoda
Because the locusts have left the shores of the islands,
amid the chanting of the oars-men,
and the rice-crop is scanty.

The gates of the sacred city
are closed for ever.

Here it should be observed that the designation "from the Tibetan" is added merely for the sake of effect, the poem being actually an entirely original piece of work. No deception is intended by this device, whose figurative nature is thoroughly understood by all concerned. As a final hint, the beginner is advised to remark the value of a foreign title either for a single poem or a whole volume. For this purpose, the Latin language is perhaps the best adapted. A dictionary of foreign quotations should be consulted on this point.

SECTION II – FICTION (I.E., NOVELS)

For a variety of reasons, fiction is the branch of literature which can be undertaken by the novice with the greatest readiness and the most favourable chances of success. Poetry is perhaps easier, but it is by no means so remunerative; drama involves less labour, but, as will be seen hereafter, it is more precarious; criticism, etc., needs less actual thought and mental exertion, but it is not so widely appreciated. Undoubtedly, then, it is to fiction that nine beginners out of ten will find it most advisable to direct their activities.

The study of models is a course which is often recommended to those who wish to make headway in the art of writing novels. It would be idle to deny that much can be gained by this method, but the greatest caution should be exercised in the selection of an author for perusal. An unwise choice at this stage may ruin, and indeed, often has ruined, an otherwise excellent prospect of success. It should be borne in mind that modern fiction, by which is meant those brilliant books that have appeared since the year 1912, differs in certain essential particulars from the works of the obsolete novelists who paid too much attention to incident, and took too little pains in the reproduction of accurate detail. Dickens, Thackeray, Scott and their imitators should be sedulously shunned. It is certain that the most capable novelists of to-day would never have written the work with which their names are inextricably associated if they had dimmed the clarity of their vision and the delicate texture of their style by reading the works of the so-called standard novelists. The bewildering succession of characters and scenes with which their books are crammed cannot be expected to appeal to the modern reader whose more refined taste can be satisfied only with simplicity and straightforwardness. Few characters, less incident, much detail – these should be our young novelist's guiding principles.

A few remarks may here be introduced on the subject of the short story. This is a branch of fiction which, owing to the phenomenal growth of high-class literary periodicals, has in recent years enjoyed a great vogue among many young writers, who have been apt to over-estimate its intrinsic value. The fact is, that the short story, admirable as it often is in individual cases, is, generally speaking, far too concentrated, and thus it does not make for economic application of materials. At the present day the novel with much detail and paucity of incident has gained such an impetus that it is now possible to expand the matter of a normal short story into a long novel – with skilful treatment, indeed, it may be worked up into a trilogy. A trilogy, it should be mentioned, is the name given to a novel which the publisher can safely issue in three volumes, provided that they appear at intervals of about seven or eight months – in extreme cases, a year. The advantage of this system is obvious. It trebles the receipts of those concerned; it stimulates and maintains public interest in the story; and it lends to the work a fine literary flavour which an ordinary novel on a small scale can seldom attain. It will be seen, then, that though the short story results in a greater number of finished products, yet it is wasteful of ideas – a factor whose importance the young author will not be slow to realise. For each short story, which may be written in an hour or two, and perhaps covers no more than half a dozen pages, demands a fresh idea – a slender one, often enough, but still an idea; while that single idea, slender though it be, can with trifling effort be made the basis of a long novel, or, better still, of a trilogy, running sometimes into a thousand pages and a dozen editions.

The question of subject-matter in fiction is nowadays greatly simplified by the demand for autobiography that has sprung up in the last few years. Novelists and journalists have reversed their functions: the former write truth, and the latter fiction. The beginner will also find himself allowed considerable latitude in the kind of incident he introduces, and the manner in which he deals with it. At the same time, although the blushes of the chaste have proved to be the dawn of many a novelist's fame, it will be as well not to reckon too securely on this device. A number of authors who strenuously appealed for a broader scope in treatment and subject-matter present a particularly sad example. They pleaded their cause with such eloquence that the circulating libraries were entirely converted, and acquired such breadth of mind that the very authors who pleaded with them were ruined as a result. These facts should be a salutary warning to those about to embark on the novelist's career. As a matter of fact, it is now far wiser to adopt extreme innocuousness and an infantile purity in venturing on a work of fiction. Writers who do this find no difficulty in being hailed as a great moral force – a most useful asset for a novelist. One of the most successful products of the last three publishing seasons was Mr. Harold Simperton's trilogy, "Nursery Park" (Vol. I – Swaddling Clothes. Vol. II – Hooks and Eyes. Vol. III – the Reverse of the Tucker), which describes the first six months of an infant's life. The appended extract from this book will enable the beginner to see how the same method may be adapted to analogous themes.

From "Nursery Park," vol. II. "Hooks and Eyes," book 6, Chap. 47 (p.559).

Never had the world appeared to Horace so flat, so gray, so dismal as on that wet Saturday afternoon, as he drooped in his high chair at the back of the box-room, where he had been placed thirty-five minutes before by a remiss and indifferent nurse. He reflected bitterly on the monotony of his life, the drab and tedious succession of days with their changeless routine of the petty, the common-place and the frankly unpleasant. Everything was portioned out by a mechanical and soulless programme whose items were wearisomely familiar to his mind. That very evening, for instance, he was to be given a bath, a messy and even indecent process, during which his young soul blushed with exasperation and shame. Earlier in the afternoon he had been exhibited to three old ladies with stubbly chins and most unpleasant breath ... In the morning, shortly after having been dragged from his uncompleted slumbers, he had been taken out in his basinette for a walk. Ah, the misery, the appalling degradation of that walk. He had been clumsily trundled along a dusty road, replete with oily stenches. On either side seven goggled-eyed lampposts leered offensively at him; on the left, at the farther end, a squat pillar-box turned its gaping slit menacingly in his direction, a monster of crimson rapacity. Half-way down on the right, a greengrocer's shop smelt of mouldering potatoes, mingled with a stray whiff of rotting cabbage. The whole world appeared to be in a state of semiputrefaction. Farther down on the left was a butcher's shop – a brutal and repellant exterior, hideous with its slabs of carnal flabbiness – vermilion and carmine, shot with irregular streaks of dirty ochre. Farther down still, also on the left, was a baker's shop. This was the one oasis amid a desolation of frowning bricks and surly tiles. In the brightly glazed window were gleaming yellow quadrangles of bread, globular and glossy brownness of buns with the occasional dark stab of a currant, big solemn crosses that marked the equitable quarterings of an honest, worthy scone. All this was variegated by pink and white splashes of sugar that coated the upper surface of marvellous confections moulded in succulent layers of spongy dough and savoured by attenuated strata of a dusky greenish sweetness. From between the gratings of the cellar that lay beneath the shop-window steamed vapours laden with the aroma of yeasty ferment. All these details Horace had acquired by painful and laborious accumulation of single fleeting glimpses, pieced together day after day, week after week. For the horrible irony of his existence was emphasised by the fact that his perambulator, which positively dawdled past depressing rows of perky villas, flanked by ugly cast-iron palings, malevolently gained sudden momentum and speed the instant it reached the outer limits of the regions to which the spicy gassiness of the bakehouse was wafted. Never had he felt the delicious crumbling of a rock-cake between his budding teeth; never had he known the ineffable bliss of melting coloured sugar in the cavities of his moist and ardent palate; never had his twitching finger probed the juicy and adhesive recesses of a circular tart, whose patterned circumference was edged with a russet crispness. And in one of those rare flashes of insight which accompany moods of acute despondency, Horace instinctively realised that he would never attain to these raptures. They would never be his. . . . Rather would he willy-nilly bow his neck to the yoke of the feeding-bottle which from the wooden tray before him seemed to peer about with chill and sloppy glances. He was sated with the turgid savour, the cloying staleness of its greenishly congealing bubbles which slid about the uncomely bulgings of the glass receptacle with its rubber mouthpiece.

The luke-warm sliminess of its viscous oozings which had trickled over his bib, and hardened in discoloured and rancid patches, that emitted the nauseous odour of sugary decay, filled his soul with a sudden access of frenzied loathing. Goaded by a blind impulse of despair and revolt, he bent his lips to the clotted extremity of the slippery tubing, and, with a savage zest, sucked at the sluggish liquid which was passing to the repulsive verge of sourness. And then in a spasm of utter hatred and contempt for the world, with the proud gesture of one who flings his last hope overboard, Horace violently . . . .

E.L.A., "Letters to the Editor. Post-Impressionism"

***New Age* 8.7 (1910): 166.**

E.L.A. wrote several letters to the *New* Age, but his or her identity is unknown. The storm of controversy surrounding the 1910 Post-Impressionism show produced many parodic descriptions of Post-Impressionist methods and theory, but few imagined what Post-Impressionism might look like in another sphere of human activity.

Sir, – I have read with interest the remarks in THE NEW AGE upon the "Post-Impressionist" school of pictures. They have worthy defenders, and I see that Jacob Tonson breaks a lance on their behalf in this week's number. But why is it, I wonder, that so many doughty champions come forth to do battle for Messieurs Gauguin, Flandrin, and Van Gogh, when we have not a single word in favour of the literary school of the same type? Messieurs Gauguin and Co., as one of your correspondents says, "handle oils" in a masterly fashion. Are not some of our modern poets equally apt at poising a pen? A volume of verse lies before me which seems to embody all the ideals of the neo-Impressionists, and yet it never went into a second edition; and so far as I know no voice was raised to praise it. The author is Mrs. Hannah Fry,[32] and the volume was published a few years ago, in Adelaide, the intellectual centre of Australia. Two verses from one of the poems, entitled "England's Sympathising Queen," show all the direct simplicity of Gauguin's brush:

Who is this that rides along
  On Balmoral estate?
It is the Queen of England,
  Victoria, Good and Great.
Our gracious Queen she comes in haste
  To one whose heart is full
Of grief because his own dear wife
  Is killed by an angry bull.

And, again, in an exquisite piece "To the Rev. Allan Webb," we find:

  A call has come from Melbourne
  To Reverend Allan Webb;
  'Tis from our distant brethren
  In this our time of need.

For this we must excuse them
As once we did the same;
We therefore think our sister church
Is not so much to blame.

Mutatis mutandis, is not this the art of the Post-Impressionists? The Philistine may laugh, but if, in the Grafton Gallery, what appears to him to be a vermilion-headed drunkard, with difficulty decipherable as a man, proves in very deed to be Gauguin's splendid picture of Our Lord in the Garden of Olives, how can he expect to see beauty in the work of Mrs. Fry? For is not the first duty of the artist (as Jacob Tonson hints) to ignore, to a certain extent, essentials; to attain, as your correspondent so aptly and intelligibly suggests, proficiency in "handling oils"? Even so does Mrs. Fry ignore the essentials and despise the tricks of Tennysonian trivialities, hiding her pearls, as Messieurs the Post-Impressionists hide theirs, from the gaze of the swinish multitude, and revealing them to the initiate alone.

Are not the two things comparable? The artlessness of Mrs. Fry, with her fine contempt for rhyme and rhythm, and even sense, is it not the literary equivalent of Messieurs Gauguin and Matisse, with their equally fine contempt for drawing, anatomy, and harmonious colouring?

Where, then, is the painter who shall defend Mrs. Fry and her school, even as the literary men have defended the Post-Impressionists?

E.L.A.

[E.L.A. will see, on referring to Mr. Jacob Tonson's notes this week, that the word "essentials" was a misprint for "inessentials." – Ed. N.A.]

Frank Reynolds, "Post-Impressionist Expressions," *Illustrated London News*, 3 December 1910: 883.

Frank Reynolds (1876–1953) worked as an illustrator for the *Illustrated London News*, *Punch*, and the *Windsor Magazine*, for which he was art editor for ten years (1920–30).

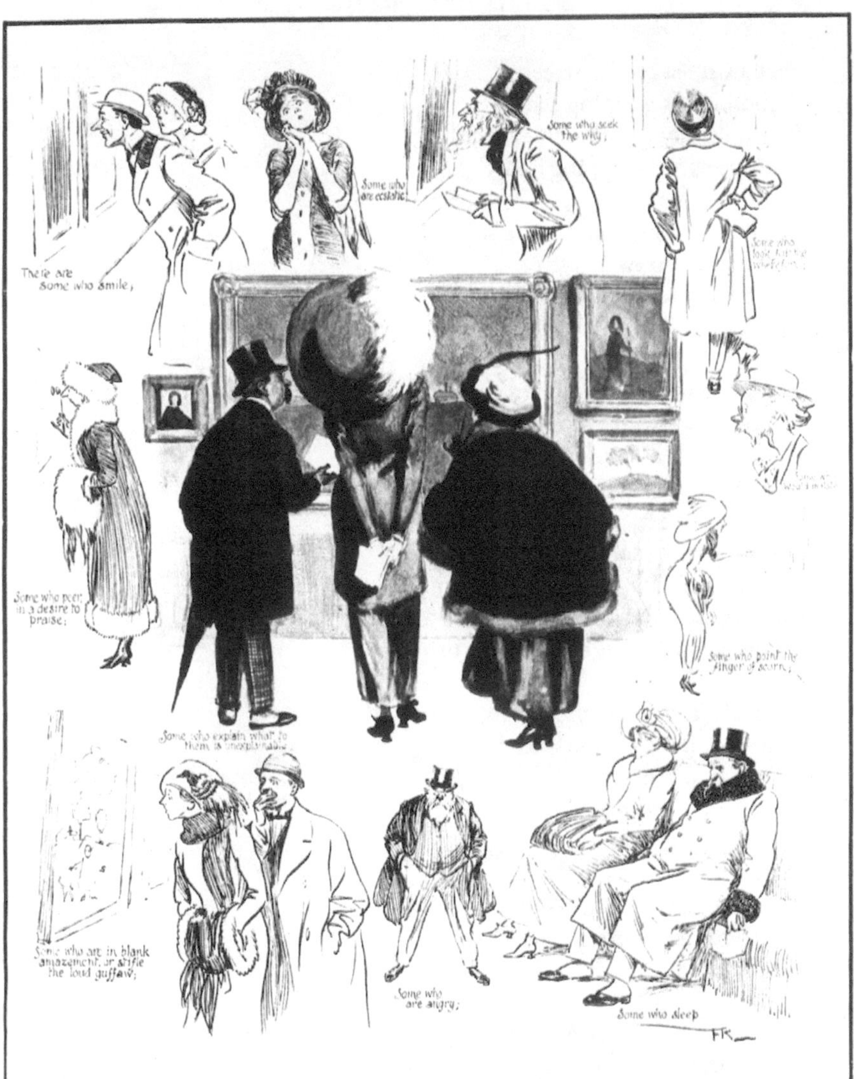

GAZERS AT PAINTINGS FEW APPRECIATE AND FEWER UNDERSTAND: STUDIES AT THE GRAFTON GALLERIES.

The Exhibition of pictures by Manet and the Post-Impressionists, as we noted in our issue of last week under a number of reproductions of examples, is attracting all London to the Grafton Galleries. Without unfairness, it may be said that the success of the show is in large measure a success of curiosity. To the few who appreciate and understand the work there are many who do neither, who go merely to gaze and scoff, and to feel that they have been in the new movement, if not of it.

Franklin P. Adams, "The Conning Tower"

***Chicago Evening Post*, 9 April 1913: 8.**

CUBIC TEARS

I met a Cubist on the street,
  And he was weeping sadly;
"Pray, take my handkerchief," said I,
  "Your own is dripping badly."

"Oh, many, many thanks," he sobbed;
  "I've used up twenty-two,
But now my tears are nearly gone,
  And this will see me through."

Then as he mopped the salty flood,
  "Tell me," said I, "your grief;
Mayhap 'twill ease the bitterness,
  Perchance 'twill bring relief."

"Oh, sir," he choked, "a poet, I,
  Who think my thoughts with brushes;
A seeker after Harmony
  That wings through canvas thrushes.

Last night a vision came to me;
  I leaped from bed, inspired,
I painted me a masterpiece
  With Heaven's beauty fired!

'Twas Art, in colors multiple –
  A perfect thought-projection –
Four thousand years ahead of Now
  And gemmed with Introspection.

Alas! Alack! Oh, bear me up –
  The memory of that night'll
Pursue me to an early grave –
  I have forgot the title!"

DON.

Don Marquis, from "Voke Easeley and His New Art," in *Hermione and Her Little Group of Serious Thinkers*

(New York: D. Appleton and Co., 1916), 84–8.

For my acquaintance with Voke Easeley and his new art, I am indebted to Fothergil Finch. Fothergil is a kind of genius hound. He scurries sleuthing around the town ever on the scent of something queer and caviar. He is well trained and never kills what he catches himself; he takes it to Hermione; and after Hermione has tired of it I am at liberty to do what I please with it.

The most remarkable thing about Voke Easeley at a casual glance is his Adam's apple. It is not only the largest Adam's apple I have ever seen, and the hardest looking one, and the most active one, but it is also the most intelligent looking one. Voke Easeley's face expresses very little. His eyes are small and dull and green. His mouth, while large, misses significance. His nose, indeed, is big; but it is mild; it is a tame nose; one feels no more character in it than in a false nose. His chin and forehead retreat ingloriously from the battle of life.

But all the personality which his eyes should show, all the force which should dwell in his nose, all the temperamental qualities that should reveal themselves in his mouth and chin, all the genius which should illumine his brow these dwell with his Adam's apple. The man has run entirely to that feature; his moods, his emotions, his thoughts, his passions, his appetites, his beliefs, his doubts, his hopes, his fears, his resolves, his despairs, his defeats, his exaltations all, all make themselves known subtly in the eccentric motions of that unusual Adam's apple.

When I saw him first in action I did not at once get it. He stood stiffly erect in the center of Hermione's drawing-room, surrounded by the serious thinkers, with his head thrown back and his Adam's apple thrust forward, and gave vent to a series of strange noises. Beside him stood a very slender lady, all dressed in apple green, with a long green wand in her hand, and on the end of the wand was an artificial apple blossom. This she waved jerkily in front of Voke Easeley's eyes, and his Adam's apple moved as the wand moved, and from his mouth came the wild sounds in response to it.

Soon I realized that she was conducting him as if he were an orchestra.

But still I did not get it. For it was not words, it was nothing so articulate as speech, that Voke Easeley uttered. Nor was it, to my ear, song. And yet, as I listened, I began to see that a wild rhythm pervaded the utterance; the Adam's apple leapt, danced, swung round, twinkled, bounded, slid and leapt again in time with a certain rough barbaric measure; the sounds themselves were all discords, but discords with a purpose; discords that took each other by the hand and kicked and stamped their brutal way together toward some objective point.

I led Fothergil into a corner.

"What is it?" I whispered. It is always well, at one of Hermione's soul fights, to get your cue before the conversation officially starts. If you don't know what is going to be talked about before the talk starts the chances are that you never will know from the talk itself.

"A New Art!" said Fothergil. And then he led me into the hall and explained.

What Gertrude Stein has done for prose, what the wilder *vers libre* bards are doing for poetry, what cubists and futurists are doing for painting and sculpture, that Voke Easeley is doing for vocal music.

"He is painting sound portraits with his larynx now," said Fothergil. "And the beautiful part of it is that he is absolutely tone deaf! He doesn't know a thing about music. He tried for years to learn and couldn't. The only way he knows when you strike a chord on the piano is because he doesn't like chords near as well as he does discords. He has gone right back to the dog, the wolf, the cave man, the tiger, the bear, the wind, the rock slide, the thunder and the earthquake for his language. He interprets life in the terms of natural sounds, which are discords nearly always; but he has added brains to them and made them all the moods of the human soul!"

"And the lady in green?"

"That is his wife – he can do nothing without her. There is the most complete psychic accord between them. It is beautiful! Beautiful!"

When we returned the lady in green was announcing:

"The next selection is a Voke Easeley impression of the Soul of Wagner gazing at the sunrise from the peak of the Jungfrau."

The wand waved; the Adam's Apple leapt, and they were off. What followed cannot be indicated typographically. But if a cat were a sawmill, and a dog were a gigantic cart full of tin cans bouncing through a stone-paved street, and that dog and that cat hated each other and were telling each other so, it would sound much like it.

It was well received. Except by Ravenswood Wimble. He always has to have his little critical fling.

"The peak of the Jungfrau!" he grumbled. "Jungfrau indeed! It was Mont Blanc! It was very wonderfully and subtly Mont Blanc! But the Jungfrau – never!"

"Hermione," I said, "what do you think of the New Art?"

"It's wonderful!" she breathed, "just simply wonderful! So esoteric, and yet so simple! But there is one thing I am going to speak to Mrs. Voke Easeley about

– one improvement I am going to suggest. His ears, you know – don't you think they are too large? Or too red, at least, for their size? They catch the eye too much – they take away from the effect. Before he sings here again I will have Mrs. Easeley bob them off a little."

Harold Monro, from *Some Contemporary Poets*

(London: Leonard Parsons, 1920), 9–16.

Harold Monro (1879–1932) was a poet, editor, and publisher (notably of the *Georgian Poetry* anthologies), as well as founder of the *Poetry Review*. Through that journal, as well as his Poetry Bookshop, Monro was an influential force in modern poetry.

The left eye of the young poet must be sharply trained on the main chance. He must be abreast of competitors. He must be constantly *printed* in order that his name may be seen, and remain prominent.

His First Book will be a great event. Every chance will have been considered. He must be talked about, whatever happens. Reviews are not much assistance; unless they be long and confident. They must be such as to make that book an event of the literary season. Twenty thousand people must know about him, whether they read him or not. It is charming to be a well-known young poet: besides, it is of professional value. After all, he has his future to consider, and he must begin here and now to plant its attractive seed.

Early in his career he will have made it his business to gain a technical acquaintance with London literary groups. As soon as he "gets to know" a few people, it will become important that he shall be able to talk to these of Those, the Others he does not know, with a certain intimacy of detail. He will be a master of the important faculty of making present acquaintances stepping-stones to future ones. He must learn how to joke cynically about the Great, and, if obliged to admit that he has not actually met Mr. H., Mr. N., or Sir S. G., must be able to imply skilfully that he will probably be dining with each of them next week.

All this time, however, he must not cease to "write poetry." It will be well for him soon to attach himself to some group. Thus he may strengthen his position socially, besides intellectually, and be saved the trouble of reading. The Group will pass remarks on books it has not read, of which he will pick out the cleverest for his own use. The Group also will teach him quickly to talk extremely cleverly about modern painting. And it will publish a periodical, or anthology, in which his poems will be printed.

His career, step by step, must lead upward. His position shall be made before the verses that might warrant it have been written – that is, in case he may write them. He will visit the country to study in quiet the poets most worthy of imitation, or adaptation. His acquaintances must know that he is in the country "writing," so that they may expect something of him. Indeed, they must be kept alert for another book. Is he not a young man of promise? Mr. Z. has often said it at dinner to Sir C. S., and yet another gentleman, who now lives in the country but still occasionally visits London, has pronounced him "very swagger."

In the past he has read most of Keats, some Shelley, a little Wordsworth, and a certain amount of Byron. He knows the *Shropshire Lad* rather too well. Walter de la Mare's rhythm also handicaps his freedom. He can understand French, has looked through Baudelaire and Verlaine, and is able to talk with respect of almost any one who wrote, or writes, *vers libre*. He likes Donne, but Chaucer, Milton and Campion he is still meaning to study. Long poems he hates – or imitates.

Here and there, in cursory moments, he has picked up tags of Darwin. These he employs occasionally, in his psychological stuff, as aids to cynicism; with a touch of Rupert Brooke added they are invaluable to him. True: they help him not particularly with the Great, but they add a shade of *difference* to his promise: they are part of his stock-in-trade.

His return from the country will be heralded by announcements of a Second Book and by hints of a trip to America – to lecture. Quite a number of fashionable women have by now, somehow or other, been drawn to his cause. The second-hand booksellers already list the half-sold thousand copies of his first volume as "1st Edition." People who have only seen his photograph call him "good-looking"; some say "beautiful"; others even that he is "like Keats." The ball rolls. He is asked to dine at Ladies' Clubs; Societies want him to take the Chair; his acquaintances think him worth real cultivation; some one calls him *famous*; many repeat the word.

"Such is; what is to be?" His sixteen reviewers have praised him; his four hundred acquaintances have laughed with him (but at him behind his back); Mr. G., Mr. M., and a few Sirs have talked to him, or about him, at dinner; the Ladies' Clubs have enjoyed the idea of him for an evening or two; schoolgirls have wondered if he is really like his photograph. And the poet? So far, what is he? A young man with a lively enjoyment of natural or artificial beauty, a sensitiveness for the right word, a vast instinct for self-advertisement.

It will be, as his career progresses, the business of the young professional to maintain strict appearance of such an attitude of scorn for the common public as is supposed by that common public to be natural to those who write verse or paint. He must freely display all the typical characteristics of the rôle he has adopted. Actually he is much in love with that public and most desirous of its approval. Among his colleagues he will discuss his sales almost as freely as the professional novelist. He is not satisfied with the anticipation of fame. He desires to grasp and to enjoy immortality while yet mortal. He dreams of the impression his poem will make on the public mind, until that dream becomes more absorbing than the creation of the poem itself, and his desire to be thought a poet is stronger than his love of poetry.

The object of the *Group* is generally the attainment of wider publicity by a combination of forces. It is a support to individuals not strong enough to stand alone. It is at the same time a useful school for young poets. The custom has been imported from Paris with its factional acrimonies, jealousies and scandal-mongerings, but without its pleasant and private inner qualities. Most French groups are societies of friends, not Unions of Professional Poets. The members of English Cliques meet less at supper than in periodicals and anthologies, less in private than in public.

The individual members of a group may profit, if they are observant, by learning to avoid the vices of their colleagues, or by imitating their virtues. Thus it may happen, and it generally does, that one, two, or more persons emerge out of a movement of several, stronger by reason of collaboration. They will "rise o'er stepping-stones of their dead"[33] confreres, who, continuing inevitably to imitate themselves or each other, will sink out of a temporary limelight into the literary obscurity to which they were predestined.

The common claim of the modern group is to differ by the possession of a secret unknown to those outside its circle. The nature of the secret varies, but naturally it must be connected in some way with one of the following –

1. Choice of subject.
2. Me thod of treatment.
3. Idiosyncrasy of rhythm.
4. Style.

Sincerity, as a primal quality, holds, in general, a lower place than might be expected among the essential characteristics that form the standard of the average group.

Edmund George Valpy Knox, "The Trotsky Touch" in *A Little Loot*

(London: G. Allen & Unwin, 1920), 176–80.

THE TROTSKY TOUCH

I met him in a large cafe with a fantastic ceiling, a favourite resort of Bohemians and other hair-hoarders. He was a little man, dressed in dark shabby clothes, and the fierce light in his eyes was faintly reflected on his elbows and knees. He had a soft felt hat on his head and a good deal of camouflage on his chin. He told me that he had recently come from Russia, and had spent some time in Finland disguised as a Swede. I was not surprised to hear it. He looked to me the kind of man who could have deceived anyone by pretending to be a mangel-wurzel.[34] He tried to tell me the name of his native town, and when he had finished and felt better he became eloquent.

"Over here you talk a great deal of the Bolshevist movement," he cried; "but what do you know of its emotional expression, the glory of its contributions to Art?"

"Our Press has always tried to hide the worst," I said.

"The ineffable poetry," he went on, "the unspeakable painting it has produced, which, alas, are only too likely to be lost to the world!"

"Tell me a few of the ringleaders," I murmured.

"Runoff is the Tyrtaeus,[35] if I may say it, of the uprising. I wish I could quote his poems to you in their entirety. He published them by wireless, and I translated them myself. What do you think of this from his 'Day of Deliverance':

In the distance is the thunder of the enemy's guns,
Freedom is at hand.
My bayonet is beside me, there is plenty of vodka;
The night is starless,
I am on guard.
But whom am I guarding?
I am guarding the Chief of the General Staff, the A.D.M.S. and the Army
  Commanders;
The Soviet has imprisoned them,
They die at dawn.
In the distance are the flashes of the enemy's guns;

I have lost my bayonet, I have finished the vodka;
The night is starless,
But to-morrow is Dawn!"

"Stupendous, little great-nephew!" I shouted, fired by his enthusiasm. He continued to croon:

"The enemy are upon us with bayonets and with bombs,
The wire is na-poo.[36]
All around me are horrible explosions;
The parapet and the parados are broken to pieces;
But I am firm.
Imperturbably, indomitably,
With arms outstretched I walk into No Man's Land;
Exhibiting my leaflets
I fraternise."

"Are they all war poems?" I asked, after a short pause. "Are there no songs of life and love, little steppe-son?"

"Are there not?" he said.

"Listen to this:

Yesterday evening the frogs barked, the nightingales sang,
Everything was joyful, I sang and barked too;
To-day it is raining, the samovar is cold,
I will go into the garden and eat worms.

And this:

Sometimes when I look at Givushka
I know that I love her;
Sometimes when I look at Givushka
My heart is filled with hate.
It is something about the way that she does her hair,
Or else her clothes."

"Incredible!" I cried. "And what about the colour barrage?"

"It is almost impossible to describe," said the little man. "The pioneers of the new movement called themselves the Centrifugals, and I suppose Yelovski is the best. There was always a little crowd round his 'Butter Queue.' The colour motive was bright saffron, and to symbolize their mental stress all the figures were standing on their heads.

"And how do you think the emptiness of the grocer's shop was portrayed? Simply a large square hole cut in the canvas. And you should have seen 'The Exploded Mine.' The whole canvas had been removed, cut up into irregular pieces with a pair of scissors, and pasted fanwise on the wall over the top of the frame. And then there was Scratchovitch's 'The Offensive.' It was sketched during a spinning nose dive. The confusion was indescribable. The chiaroscuro was magnificent. It was impossible to tell a salient from a re-entrant. The whole bloodscape seemed to leap out of the canvas and hit you in the face."

"It would," I said faintly. "Were there any portraits?"

"There was one of Trotsky, by his greatest friend, Thatchov. The face was hexagonal, and there was one large single eye in the middle of it, partially closed. The nose, with a fore-finger touching it, was on the right-hand side; but of the mouth, the mouth which has issued so many manifestos and ultimatums, nothing could be seen."

"And why was that?" I asked.

"Because," said he, "it was at the back of his neck."

To conceal my emotion I rose and paid my score.

"And your friend?" asked the waiter.

I turned round. The little man was gone.

Ernest Boyd, from "Aesthete: Model 1924"

***American Mercury*, January 1924: 51–6.**

Ernest Boyd (1887–1946) was an influential literary critic associated with H.L. Mencken. His major works include *Portraits: Real and Imaginary* (1924), *H.L. Mencken* (1925), and *Guy De Maupassant; a Biographical Study* (1926). In the following selection from his essay, after accounting for the Aesthete's undergraduate education, Boyd argues that the Aesthete was ready to move on:

> From the pages of the *Masses* he gathered that the Social Revolution was imminent, that Brieux was a dramatist of ideas; in the *Little Review* he was first to learn the enchantment of distance as he sat bemused by its specimens of French and pseudo-French literature. Thus the ballast of which he had to get rid in order to float in the rarefied atmosphere of Advanced Thought was negligible. He had merely to exchange one set of inaccurate ideas for another. (52)

II.

It was at this precise moment in his career that the Wilsonian storming of Valhalla began. With the call to arms tingling in his blood, the Aesthete laid aside the adornments of life for the stern realities of a military training camp. Ancestral voices murmured in his ears, transmitted by instruments of dubious dolichocephalism, it is true, but perhaps all the more effective on that account, for Deep calls unto Deep. I will not dwell upon the raptures of that martial period, for he himself has left us his retrospective and disillusioned record of it, which makes it impossible to recapture the original emotion. Harold Cabot Lilienthal – and, I suppose I should add, in deference to my subject, *hoc genus omne* – was apparently not capable of the strain of ingesting the official facts about the great moral crusade. It was government contract material and proved to be as shoddy and unreliable as anything supplied by the dollar-a-year men to the War Department. By the time the uniformed Aesthete got to France he was a prey to grave misgivings, and as his subsequent prose and verse show, he was one of C. E. Montague's Disenchanted[37] – he who had been a Fiery Particle. He bitterly regretted the collegiate patriotism responsible for his devotion to the lofty rhetoric of the *New Republic*. By luck or cunning, however, he succeeded in getting out of the actual trenches, and there, in the hectic backwash of war, he cultivated the tender seeds just beginning to germinate. He edited his first paper, the *Doughboy's Dreadnought*, or under the auspices of the propaganda and vaudeville department made his first contribution to literature, "Young America and Yugo-Slavia." Simultaneously with this plunge into arms and letters, he made his first venture into the refinements of sex, thereby extending his French vocabulary and gaining that deep insight into the intimate life of France which is still his proudest possession.

When militarism was finally overthrown, democracy made safe, and a permanent peace established by the victorious and united Allies, he was ready to stay on a little longer in Paris, and to participate in the joys of La Rotonde and Les Deux Magots. There for a brief spell he breathed the same air as the Dadaists, met Picasso and Philippe Soupault, and allowed Ezra Pound to convince him that the French nation was aware of the existence of Jean Cocteau, Paul Morand, Jean Giraudoux and Louis Aragon. From those who had nothing to say on the subject when Marcel Proust published "*Du Côté de Chez Swann*" in 1914 he now learned what a great author the man was, and formed those friendships which caused him eventually to join in a tribute to Proust by a group of English admirers who would have stoned Oscar Wilde had they been old enough to do so when it was the right thing to do.

The time was now ripe for his repatriation, and so, with the same critical equipment in French as in English, but with a still imperfect control of the language as a complication, the now complete Aesthete returned to New York, and descended upon Greenwich Village. His poems of disenchantment were in the press, his war novel was nearly finished, and it was not long before he appeared as Editor-in-Chief, Editor, Managing Editor, Associate Editor, Contributing Editor, Assistant Editor, Bibliographical Editor or Source Material Editor of one of the little reviews making no compromise with the public (or any other) taste.[38] Both his prose and verse were remarkable chiefly for typographical and syntactical eccentricities, and a high pressure of unidiomatic, misprinted French to the square inch. His further contributions (if any) to the art of prose narrative have consisted of a breathless phallic symbolism – a sex obsession which sees the curves of a woman's body in every object not actually flat, including, I need hardly say, the Earth, our great Mother.

But it is essentially as an appraiser of the arts, as editor and critic, that the young Aesthete demands attention. He writes a competent book review and awakes to find himself famous. The next number of the magazine contains a study of his aesthetic, preferably by the author whose work he has favorably reviewed. By the end of the year a publisher announces a biographical and critical study of our young friend and his fame is secured. He can now discourse with impunity about anything, and he avails himself of the opportunity. He has evolved an ingenious style, florid, pedantic, technical, full of phrases so incomprehensible or so rhetorical that they almost persuade the reader that they must have a meaning. But the skeptical soon discover that this is an adjustable and protean vocabulary, that by a process of reshuffling the same phrases will serve for an artistic appreciation of Charlie Chaplin, an essay on Marcel Proust, or an article on Erik Satie. His other expedient is an arid and inconceivable learning, picked up at second hand. Let him discuss "The Waste Land" and his erudition will rival the ponderous fatuity of T. S. Eliot himself. He will point out on Ptolemy's map the exact scene, quote the more obscure hymns of Hesiod, cite an appropriate passage from Strabo's geography, and conclude with a cryptic remark from the Fourth Ennead of Plotinus. Yet, one somehow suspects that even the parasangs of the first chapter of Xenophon's Anabasis would strain his Greek to the breaking-point.

Nevertheless, information is the one thing the Aesthete dreads. To be in the possession of solid knowledge and well-digested facts, to have definite standards, background and experience, is to place oneself outside the pale of true aestheticism. While foreign literature is his constant preoccupation, the Aesthete has no desire to make it known. What he wants to do is to lead a cult, to communicate a mystic faith in his idols, rather than to make them available for general appreciation. Articles on the subject are an important feature of his magazines, but they consist, as a rule, of esoteric witticisms and allusive gossip about fourth-rate people whom the writer happens to have met in a café. He will sweep aside the finest writers in French as lumber, launch into ecstasies over some Dadaist, and head the article with a French phrase which is grammatically incorrect, and entirely superfluous, since it expresses no idea that could not be correctly rendered in English. If one protest that the very title of a book which is a masterpiece of style has been mistranslated, that the first page has several gross errors, the Aesthete will blandly point out that in paragraph two there are four abstract nouns each with a different termination. It is useless to show him that there are no equivalent nouns in the text. Finally, one gives up arguing, for one remembers that Rimbaud once wrote a poem about the color of the vowels. Literary history must repeat itself.

The almost Swedenborgian mysticism of the Aesthete is implied in all his comments, for he is usually inarticulate and incomprehensible. He will ingenuously describe himself as being "with no more warning than our great imagination in the presence of a masterpiece." One reads on to discover the basis for this enthusiasm, but at the outset one is halted by the naive admonition that "it isn't even important to know that I am right in my judgment. The significant and to me overwhelming thing was that the work was a masterpiece and altogether contemporary." In other words, this work, which the writer says "I shall make no effort to describe," may or may not be a masterpiece, nevertheless it is one ... presumably because it is "altogether contemporary." It is on this point of view that the solemn service of the Younger Aestheticism depends. If a piece of sculpture is distorted and hideous, if the battered remains of a wrecked taxi are labeled, "La Ville tentaculaire,"[39] the correct attitude is one of delight. One should "make no effort to describe" what is visible, but clutch at the "altogether contemporaneous" element, indicating a masterpiece. In music one must not seek in the cacophonies of the current idols the gross, bourgeois emotion which one receives from Brahms and Beethoven. The Aesthete holds that a cliché, in French for preference, will dispose of any genius. One should make play with *le côté Puccini* and *le faux bon.*

The pastime is an amusing one, for it involves no more serious opposition than is to be found in the equally limited arsenal of the Philistines. What could be easier than to caper in front of the outraged mandarins waving volumes of eccentrically printed French poetry and conspuing the gods of the bourgeoisie? It is like mocking a blind man, who hears the insults but cannot see the gestures. The Aesthete tries to monopolize the field of contemporary foreign art and he is accustomed to respectful submission or the abuse and indifference of sheer ignorance. When he needs a more responsive victim he turns his attention to the arts adored by the crowd, the "lively arts," Mr. Seldes calls them, as if the Fifth Symphony were depressing. The esoteric reviews publish "stills" of Goldwyn pictures and discover strange beauties in follow-up letters and streetcar advertisements. The knees of Ann Pennington,[40] the clowning of Charlie Chaplin, the humors of Joe Cook[41] and Fannie Brice[42] must now be bathed in the vapors of aesthetic mysticism. But here there is a difference. The performances of the "lively" artist are familiar to every one above the age of ten; most of us have enjoyed them without feeling compelled to explain ourselves. A reference to Gaby Deslys[43] finds its place as naturally in the works of Havelock Ellis as one to "Der Untergang des Abendlandes."[44] But the Aesthete takes his lively arts uneasily. He is determined to demonstrate that he is just as other men. It is evidently not only in foreigners that one encounters that "certain condescension" of which the late Mr. Lowell complained.[45]

III.

In the last analysis the Aesthete may be diagnosed as the literary counterpart of the traditional American tourist in Paris. He is glamored by the gaudy spectacle of that most provincial of all great cities. French is the tube through which he is fed, and he has not yet discovered how feeble the nourishment is. When he turns to other countries, Germany, for instance, he betrays himself by an incongruous and belated enthusiasm for the novelties of the eighties and nineties. The contemporaries of Thomas Mann, Schnitzler and Hauptmann elsewhere are beneath his notice. Spain and Italy come onto his horizon only when Paris becomes aware of their existence. In a few years, however, his younger brother will go up to Cambridge, in his turn, and then we shall doubtless be enlightened concerning the significant form[46] of Kasimir Edschmid, Walter von Molo and Carl Sternheim.[47] One cannot be "altogether contemporary" all the time.

The signs, indeed, already point that way, for I notice that Hugo Stinnes[48] is mentioned as a modern Marco Polo, and the American realtor is praised as a reincarnation of the creative will of Leonardo da Vinci. This new-found delight in publicity experts, election slogans, billboards and machinery may result in a pilgrimage across the Rhine where, in the dissolution of so many fine things, an aesthetic of Philistinism has emerged. The tone of democratic yearning which has begun to permeate German literature, recalling the dreams of Radical England in the days of Lord Morley's youth, may facilitate the understanding between two great democracies. But the fatal attraction of French, not to mention the difficulty of German, is a serious obstacle to any new orientation of the younger Aestheticism, and Paris, as usual, can provide what its customers demand. Thus the cult of the movies, with its profound meditations on "Motion Picture Dynamics,"[49] and all the vague echoes of Elie Faure's theory of "cineplastics,"[50] involves a condemnation of "The Cabinet of Dr. Caligari," a tactless Teuton effort to put some genuine fantasy into the cinema. Instead of that the faithful are called upon by a French expert to admire the films of William S. Hart and Jack Pickford,[51] and some one carefully translates the poetic rhapsodies inspired in him by the contemplation of their masterpieces.

"Two souls," in the words of the German bard, "dwell in the breast" of the Aesthete, and his allegiance is torn between the salesmanager's desk, where, it appears, the Renaissance artist of to-day is to be found, and the esoteric editorial chair where experiments are made with stories which "discard the old binding of plot and narrative," the substitute being "the structural framework which appeals to us over and above the message of the line." Thus it becomes possible simultaneously to compare Gertrude Stein with Milton and to chant the glories of the machine age in America. This dualism, obviously, foreshadows the ultimate disintegration of the type, although for the moment the process is ingeniously disguised by such devices as the printing of prose bearing all the outward marks of supermodern eccentricity but made up cunningly of a pattern woven from phrases culled from billboards and the advertising pages of the magazines; by reproducing the weirdest pictures together with business-like photographs of cash-registers and telephones. The household gods of Babbit are being pressed into service, just as his innocent amusements are being intellectualized.

Here the Aesthete departs from the traditions of the species at his peril. Hitherto his technique has been perfect, for it has been his practice to confine his enthusiasm to works of art that are either as obscure or as inessential, or both, as his own critical comment. Now his incantations lose their potency when applied to matters within the experience and comprehension of the plain people, and not one cubit is added to the stature of William S. Hart, so far as his devotees are concerned, by the knowledge that his name is pronounced with aesthetic reverence on the Left Bank of the Seine.

The process of change is at work, for the transitional youth is already in at least one editorial chair, frowning upon the frivolities of the Jazz Age, calling for brighter and better books, his dreams haunted by fears of Sodom and Gomorrah. The Aesthete, meanwhile, is retiring with an intellectual *Katzenjammer*,[52] which produces in some cases a violent and unnatural nausea, a revulsion against the wild delights of his former debauches. In others the result is a return to the cosy hearth of the American family; his head aches a little but his hand is steady. He is refreshed by a journalistic bromo seltzer. There is pep in the swing of his fist upon the typewriter as he sits down to a regular and well-paid job, convincing others, as his employer convinced him, that he really knows what the public wants.

IV. Modernist Criticism

In the eyes of its public, modernist art was inseparable from its validating critics. An essay like Mabel Dodge's "Speculations, or Post-Impressionism in Prose" was, for a time, almost as well known as Stein's writing on which it was based. Critical discourse, in a sense, did not just interpret the art; it made the art possible by placing it in an intellectual context and, through the intimidating power of its difficulty, cowing its audience into acquiescence. Many complained that modernist criticism did its work more often through subterfuge and obfuscation than through clarity. Writing in the *Saturday Review of Literature* in 1926, Henry Seidel Canby argued, "Surely such writing as Gertrude Stein's could not hold attention for a day if it were not for the smoke screen of importance which the critics have thrown about it. Its own stupidity would have laughed it into oblivion" ("The Virtue of Intolerance"). The *Chicago Examiner* turned on Arthur J. Eddy's defence of the 1913 Armory Show, characterizing Eddy's lecture on "the cryptic significance of cubist art" in this way: "Those pictures which can be explained, he explained, and the ones which cannot be explained he explained why they cannot be explained. In fact, he explained his explanations, and with each amplification bewilderment increased" ("Cubist Art Severs Friendship"). Not just the kinds of explanations, but the idea that art needed explanation were under contention. As Huntly Carter argued in an attack (on the radicalism of Walter Sickert, of all people), "Art cannot be explained. If a picture is not self-illuminating it fails as a work of art" ("Disciple of Distortion" 138).

"Cubist Art Is Explained Clearly by a Post-Impressionist Writer"

***Chicago Inter-Ocean*, 21 March 1913: 5.**

Along with the arrival of the Armory Show in 1913 came the first wave of theoretical elucidations of the aims of movements like futurism and cubism. As seen in the article below, Frederick Gregg's theorizing of modernist art did not come off well in the press. The *Wichita Eagle* (no doubt getting its material second-hand), introduced Gregg and cubist theory in the following manner:

> Frederick J. Gregg, "advance guard futurist," knows all about cubist art. He brought many of the canvases to Chicago, and his explanations of their inner meanings are as clear as a glass of hot tar.
>
> After a five-minute interview with Mr. Gregg, it was perfectly apparent that cubism is a sort of a – well, a reach for something between Heaven and the constituency of time.

CUBIST ART IS EXPLAINED CLEARLY BY A POST-IMPRESSIONIST WRITER

"There is all there is when there has all there has where there is what there is. That is what is done when there is done what is done and the union is won and that division is the explicit visit."

It's all very simple, this cubist art, after it is concisely explained – explained, as above, by the medium of cubist literature. For the benefit of those stupid Chicagoans whose soul cannot open themselves and receive the soul expression of the cubist artists and sculptors, a special volume of explanatory literature has been sent to the Art Institute. It is written by Miss Gertrude Stein of Paris, first cubist writer in the world.

It was in the office of the institute yesterday. F. J. Gregg, representing the Association of American Painters and Sculptors, responsible for the coming post impressionist exhibit, displayed the booklet with pride. It was explained that to express in print cubism and what it means requires a cubic style of writing. Miss Stein is said to have rendered her composition while in the thralls of a cubic excitement, superinduced by a cubist art exhibit in the Villa Curonia, Florence, Italy, home of Mrs. Mabel Dodge.

What is the significance of the post impressionist movement?

The newspaper men turned anxiously the pages of the book. Miss Stein's answer was found. It left nothing to be desired – except the answer.

"There is that desire," they read, "and there is no pleasure and the place is filling the one space that is placed where all the piling is not adjoining. There is not the distraction."

"Yes, yes; of course; how true," a cubist critic murmured, and every reporter blinked knowingly. Mr. Gregg looked his approval.

Why is a futurist? Page 12 explains: "Praying has intention and relieving that situation is not solemn. There comes that way. The time there is the smell of the plain season is not showing that the water is running. There is not all that breath."

"Cubist literature," it was explained in passing, "discards objective words as does cubist art objective lines. The soul striving of the writer is to express through rhythm of words the soul intentions of the author."

With this in mind, the picture drawn by Miss Stein of the Villa Curonia will be almost as clear as the cubist painting of the same subject:

"A wall that is not stepped where the floor is covered is not the place where the room is entered. The whole one is the same. There is not any stone. There is the wide door that is narrow on the floor. There is all that place.'

Of the general lack of true artistic appreciation, Miss Stein has sent on this melancholy complaint:

"There is the rise of the stone and there is the place of the stuff and there is the practice of expending questions."

Two reporters edged from the room, convinced. One of them was more.

"In that place where running water is not there," he murmured, thoughtfully, "and where the bar is where it is where – I'll buy a drink."

Bert Leston Taylor, "A Line-o'-Type or Two"

***Chicago Daily Tribune*, 28 March 1913: 8.**

POST-IMPRESSIONISM

(Further remarks by Prof. J. Orange Cadmium before the Super-Skylight club. Reported by E.H.R.)

"A more highly rarified conception of the infiltration of soul tones by means of an acutely refined chromatic sense," declared Prof. Cadmium, "will eventually result in the abandonment of the cube as a propulsory medium. The square suggests immobility, while mobility and linear rhythm is expressed in the spheroid. Clearly the spheroid is the logical color projectile of the future. The ultra violet ray can be produced only by the spheroids, and could only impinge when the objective was perfectly relaxed. This relaxation can be accomplished by the preliminary impact of rays from the primaries when out of key with the objective …

"It has been demonstrated by an eminent specialist that great genius is usually traceable to the stimulus of various toxins. The post-impressionistic effect of a slightly disturbed 'poussé café'[53] is suggested by exhilarated chroma when not used in inverse ratio to the area of the canvas. Chroma, according to Prof. Andrews, is the degree of departure of a color sensation from that of white or gray; the intensity of a distinctive hue. This departure, under the stimulus of alcohol, naturally produces chroma of high velocity sufficient to occupy the entire available segment of the periphery of the retina. The present exhibition contains much alcoholic chroma which must not be confused with normal post-impressionism, which has been under the influence of toxins of lower potency."

C.E. Bechhöfer, "Pastiche. More Contemporaries"

New Age 15.4 (1914): 92.

This parody appeared in the same month that saw the appearance of *Blast*. The references to "Bombast" and "Explain" allude to the British artists David Bomberg and Jacob Epstein, both of whom were to become associated with Vorticism. "Graft" refers to the Grafton Galleries, site of the first Post-Impressionist exhibit, while Looptheloupil Gallery refers to the Goupil Gallery, which saw the first group exhibition of Vorticists in March 1914. "Miss Daubs" may be a reference to the Vorticist painter Jessica Dismorr (1885–1939), who was a signatory to the *Blast* manifesto.

ART AND ARTISTS

By Frank Rutter

The exhibition of the works of the newly arrived Twopenny Tubists at the Looptheloupil Gallery is extremely interesting, especially from the fact that the artists represented have chosen to express themselves by the medium of tracing with earwigs' feet brushes upon sawdust. Particularly striking, unless, of course, I am mistaken, is Mr. Bombast's " Shiverth"; and Mr. Explain's clever "Studies in Fleabite" has a great charm of distinction. The effect, though perhaps somewhat bizarre, is striking, and nobody who is interested in the progress of Art should miss this show. Another new exhibition is that of Miss Daubs's works at the Graft Galleries. Her pictures are mainly dramatic studies of men and children, and her execution and colouring are conceived in the purest classic tendencies, and there are not in her work any traces of the influence of ultra-modern ideas, such as those of the famous Futilist and Stubist groups. Her work is immensely impressive, and, to single out two for special mention, I should adjudge the poignant study entitled "Ta-ta, Daddy," and the powerful "Daddy's Home-coming" as perhaps the best of the whole show. With two exhibitions of such merit as the Tubists' and Miss Daubs's to be seen in London this week, Art and Art Criticism appear to be coming into their own again.

Charles E. Brookfarmer [C.E. Bechhöfer], "Futile-Ism. Or, All Cackle and No Osses"

(Report of Lectures on "Vital English Art," by Messrs. Marinetti and C. R. W. Nevinson, Dore Galleries, Friday Evening, June 12), *New Age* 15.7 (1914): 154.

For another of Bechhöfer's "transcribed" minutes of important meetings, see his account of a Fabian Society meeting in the *New Age* 11:26 (1912): 607–8.

(ENTER STUDENT. The hot room is full for the most part of elderly (passées?) ladies, including such half-forgotten crimes as Messrs. Cunninghame-Graham and Nevinson[54] pere. Barely twenty minutes late the lecturers arrive – ironical applause from frivolous audience. Sig. Marinetti rises and introduces "mon ami Nevinson," and refers to "les noise-tuners" whose performance is eagerly expected. Mr. Nev. rises.)

MR. NEV. (reading his speech – [! ! !]. But he seems frequently to digress): Before I read the manifesto … I will make some remarks … England to-day is no more a decadent country in art than in commerce.

STUD. (sotto voce): Nor no less, neither.

MR. NEV.: … Compare him unfavourably with a second-rate Parisian painter, and say how much finer the latter is.

AN ARTIST: So he is!

MR. NEV.: You're a Russian ! (Commotion.) Doubtless … snobs … what was known as backbackternacher … a vile thing sprung up in England … namely, the Pre-Raphaelites … the Neo-Primitives … superficial and highly accomplished colour-photography … The Futurists … their art, so vital, so intense and so complex … Vortickists …

THE ARTIST: Vorticistes! (Commotion.)

MR. NEV.: … Abstraction of an emotion remembered, seen, smelled or heard … representation in painting or sculpture is absurd; this had already been realised by Blake and Turner in England … three paintings by Kandinsky at the Allied Artists' Association's Salon,[55] which to my mind are simply gorgeous! (STUD. shudders at the memory of formless yellow blobs.) … Our pictures are no longer static, but dynamic … entirely different conception of the shape of the grandstand at Epsom when the horses are racing past it than when the course is empty. This is not the representation of an optical delusion, as many people think, but the expression of a state of mind. This is most important!! … sane, legitimate … and vital … an engineer if he fails to make a woman understand the working of a simple piece of machinery (AUDIENCE: OO-ooh!) … the soft, flowing and accidental lines of a woman's leg or a rural landscape … London, its chromatic crowds, red motor-'buses (etc.) through which some black limousine glides like a snake.

STUD.: Where in futurity have I heard that before?

MR. NEV. : … Also important from a commercial point of view … barbarians of the West End (some giggles) … putting a pony on Durbar Two[56] … backwoods of Chelsea (more giggles) the modern artist must advertise … Selfridge's … materials are extremely expensive … Nobody listens to the singing of a corpse or the histrionics of a dead actor (more giggles) … virile, original, and, above all, English … (He reads the manifesto, in which occurs, "Immortality in art is a disgrace"!! As he cries, "Forward! hurrah for motors! hurrah for speed! hurrah for draughts! hurrah for lightning!" an assistant fires a small piece of magnesium wire. Tremendous Futurartistic effect. Then, "We call upon the English public to support, defend and glorify the genius of the great Futurist painters or pioneers and advance-forces of vital English art: Atkinson, Bomberg, Epstein, Etchells, Hamilton, Nevinson [! ! !], Roberts, Wadsworth, Wyndham Lewis." Mr. NEV. sits down amid laughter and shouting of names. MARINETTI rises and commences to wander on and on and on with much emphasis and gesture and mopping of sweaty brow.)

MR. MARIO (IN FRENCH): I am forced to repeat some of the arguments put forward by mon ami Nevinson … les passéistes[57] … les passéistes … le "Times" … they say you're a little eccentric they never go as far as the word "mad" … call you a "cloon" … To be an advance-guard in art is to sacrifice everything … It is time to put aside half-words … We are in Futurism to solve art … The painters haven't sold any pictures. The question is serious, very serious, and I insist … Mon ami Nevinson has already told you that modern sensibility must be introduced into modern art. (Tells it all again, with variations, explanations, enlargements, etc., etc., very, very prosily.) Mon ami Nevinson (proses) … One man puts a picture in his drawing-room, another puts it in his dining-room, another in his lavatory! (Much laughter.) … In this the Emperor of Germany is an expert. He seeks out all that is worst in the world and tries to support it … I have often said what I mean by detestable sentimentality in art. (Says it all again. STUD. dozes, in spite of Mr. MARIO'S waving of fists, etc.) … Geometric art … geometric splendour …, numbers … takes mythological forms and transforms them into cubes more or less interesting …, more or less calculable … who think that art depends on the bizarrities of the individual … it is absolutely contrary to our Italian lucidity. We are always lucid … each artist has his own standpoint, but they are all drawn together by a common flood, which is sensibility … Like an old automobile when it can't get any water … Futurism is a mass of research … It is necessary to remember that life is always right … The great speed of motors and limousines … (etc., etc., punctuated with innumerable "Voila la pointe importante"). (STUD. wishes he would cut the cackle and get to the noise-tuners.) … It isn't the desire to say "I am an innovator" … for the smile of same woman or the money … We are a score of capables! … Art, futurist art is for us tortuous, terrible and desolating … My next book, which I am in the act of meditating, will contain all my faculties which I can put into a book with great art … The desire after immortality is to us something infamous … it is a very injurious conception … it does not interest me at all … immortality is absolutely an obstacle … immortality is not merely a fault but a crime!

STUD.: So there's no futurity in Futurism!

MR. MARIO: Futurism (etc., etc.) … Futurism (etc., etc.) … Futurism is a sort of lava … Electricity which rules the world … ever to advance and never to look back. (Having thus wandered, prosily, volubly, and enormously quickly from one thing to another for about an hour, Mr. MARIO sits down, his collar unstarched with sweat; the audience, too, is tired out with his prosiness and the heat. He pops up again.)

MR. MARIO: I am quite at the disposition of the audience. I'm not a bit tired. (The hideous rumour spread that, though the "noise-tuners" are present, they have not got their instruments and will not perform after all. The disappointed audience begins to disperse. Mr. Mario busily explains to STUD. and others some of the angular monstrosities that are shown as Futurist sculptures.)

MR. MARIO: The face isn't dented in nature, but it is in the plastic; the mouth isn't swollen in nature, but it is in the plastic. (As STUD. departs, two small persons shake him enthusiastically by the hand. They are "les noise-tuners.")

STUD. (WEARILY): All this cackle and no – Futurist – noises! (Exit STUDENT.)

Ibn Gabirol, from "My Friend, the Incurable"

***Little Review* 1.8 (1914): 42–4.**

The identity of this pseudonymous author is unknown (Ibn Gabirol was an Andalusian Jewish poet and philosopher of the eleventh century). At the beginning of the article from which this excerpt is taken, the narrator discusses a "Home for the incurables," whose patients, the doctor has explained to the narrator, "are quite happy" (42). Some "are actually in love with their affliction" and "resent the idea of being turned normal" (42). The narrator moves on to discuss a particular patient who has suffered from "sentimentalomania" and, having been treated for it in Germany, "Germanophobia" (42). We are told that as a remedy this patient was brought to the United States, supposedly "the sanest atmosphere on earth" (42). The narrator reports that "when [he] seek[s] relief from practical values and sane standards," he goes to visit this "Incurable" (42). The following comments are then made by the Incurable.

Words, like music, like practically every medium of art, express the author's personality, and, provided he is an artist, he binds us to share his interpretation. Take, for example, that popular song, "*Oh, You Beautiful Doll*"; apparently there is nothing tragic in it, yet my emotions were stirred when I heard its French interpretation by Olga Petrova (it was before the kind American entrepreneurs had forced her to perform stunts in Panthea).[58] She had managed to put so much sorrow and tenderness into "*O Ma Grande Belle Poupée!*" that one forgot the triteness of the words and felt gripping sadness. Or take a less vulgar illustration – Gertrude Stein's *Tender Buttons*. It is an exquisite little thing in cream covers, with a green moon in the center, implying the yolk of an egg with which "something is the matter," and it gave me rare pleasure to witness the first attempt to revolutionize the most obsolete and inflexible medium of Art – words. The author has endeavored to use language in the same way as Kandinsky uses his colors: to discard conventional structure, to eliminate understandable figures and forms, and to create a "spiritual harmony," leaving to the layman the task of discovering the "*innerer Klang*."[59] Both iconoclasts have admirably succeeded; both the "Improvisations" and the little "essays" on roastbeef and seltzer-bottles have given me the great joy of cocreating, allowing me to interpret them in my own autonomous way. Says the Painter [in *The Art of Spiritual Harmony*, by W. Kandinsky (Boston, Houghton Mifflin)]:

> The apt use of a word, repetition of this word, twice, three times or even more frequently, will not only tend to intensify the inner harmony but also to bring to light unsuspected spiritual properties of the word itself. Further than that, frequent repetition of a word deprives the word of its original external meaning.

Gertrude Stein has beautifully followed this recipe. Words, plain everyday words, have lost their "external meaning" under her skilful manipulation, and in their grotesque arrangement, frequent repetition, and intentional incoherence they have come to serve as quaint ephemeral sounds of a suggestive symphony, or, if you please, cacophony. The *Tender Buttons* arouse in the sympathetic reader a limitless amount of moods, from scherzo to maestoso. I shall recall for you a few lines of one peculiar motive:

(From *A Substance in a Cushion.*)

> What is the use of a violent kind of delightfulness if there is no pleasure in not getting tired of it.

(From *Red Roses.*)

> A cool red rose and a pink cut pink, a collapse and a sole hole, a little less hot. Aider, why aider why whow, whow stop touch, aider whow, aider stop the muncher, muncher munchers.

(From *Breakfast.*)

> What is a loving tongue and pepper and more fish than there is when tears many tears are necessary.
> Why is there more craving than there is in a mountain ... Why is there so much useless suffering. Why is there.

Do you not feel the deep melancholy underlying these incongruities? I could quote places that would bring you into a totally different mood, most hilarious at times. These "exaggerated cranberries," to paraphrase an expression of one of my incurable colleagues, should be chanted to the music of another great iconoclast, Schoenberg. But I observe an indulgent sneer on your face. Of course, I am an Incurable – *Adieu!*

T.S. Eliot, from "A Brief Treatise on the Criticism of Poetry"

***The Chapbook*, March 1920: 1–10.**

While T.S. Eliot (1888–1965) won a Nobel Prize in 1948, in the early years of modernism his reputation was less than unassailable. His literary criticism, "The Love Song of J. Alfred Prufrock," his quatrain poems, and *The Waste Land* made him a frequent target of parodists. Eliot's own scepticisms about modern poetry and criticism, however, followed the same logic as many of his detractors. For Eliot, in the following essay, the conditions of modernity had allowed too much bad poetry and criticism to be published:

> During the last few years an enormous mass of verse has been printed, and an enormous mass of appreciations of this verse has also been printed; and verse and criticism are of the same quality. There are three or four poets whose verse is worth reading; there do not appear to be more than that number of good critics. (1)

Let us now consider what is the proper behaviour for a critic when he meets with a poem that he genuinely believes to be a work of art, and whether our critics can be trusted to behave themselves properly.

I have in mind a sentence encountered recently in a literary periodical of the very highest standing – a periodical with which there is nothing to compare in *any* other country. This sentence was not in a leading article or in a review, but in a small booknotice, and a notice concerned with other poems by other writers as well. It ran, in what I believe is called diamond type, almost as follows:

"Mr. Honeydew's poem, *The Golden Hoopoe* would give fame to any book or paper in which it appeared. It is a great poem. The song by Mr. Leadbeater is worthy of Mr. Leadbeater …" etc.

Consider the sentence "It is a great poem," and all that it implies. Assume that the critic is one for whose opinion you have vast respect: then he has told you all that you need to know. You read the poem, you become acquainted with a new work of art, and the literary periodical has served the most important purpose that literary periodicals can serve. But this never happens. Probably no one who read the notice really believed, or even entertained the thought, that the poem was a great poem. No one rose panting from the breakfast table and rushed hatless to the stationer's to procure a copy. The periodical itself did not come out with a leading article on the poem the next week. Perhaps the editor himself never noticed this little critic in his diamond type, and he too would not have believed. I could not believe either; I have never read the poem. The critic was believed by no one, incredulous eyes outstared him, and yet he was a brave little critic. For he dared to say the only sensible thing about a great poem: "It is a great poem." He was a great critic. Or else he was a very irresponsible, completely untrustworthy, poisonous little critic.

He took the honest course, the critic, if he really believed the poem was a great poem. What else is there to say? Who wants an analysis, an account of the man and his message, his vision of life, his place as a representative of something or other, his derivations, his relation to his colleagues Mr. Leadbeater and Mr. Spooner – *before he has read the poem*? But, as a matter of fact, it cannot be done in that way. It must be hammered. And so the good critic will merely say "this is a good poem" in a hundred different ways. He will make a column of it. He will quote and quote. When he writes about someone else he will say, "Here and there we find a slight suggestion of the bitter intensity of Mr. Honeydew," or "With the inevitable exception of Mr. Honeydew," or a million such phrases. He will persuade the amiable Mrs. Saffron Walden to write a little article about Honeydew. The people who read Mrs. Walden's article will not read the poems, but they will be prepared to be impressed when they read another reference to Honeydew next week. Honeydew gets to know a few writers, and they will from time to time mention him. And after a time some of the important critics – the critics on important papers – will come to accept Honeydew. Not that they will *praise* him. But they will say, "The bizarre work of Mr. Honeydew," "The acknowledged leader of the Febrilist school of younger writers, Mr. Honeydew." No one will have praised him except the Good Critic and Mrs. Walden and a few private people with no influence. But he is all the safer for that: he escapes malice. Honeydew must not make himself too conspicuous, or he will sink to a depth at which even the diamond criticism will seem to be fame. He merely wants such degree of notoriety and such number of editions that the few intelligent people in each generation will be likely to come across his work. And in 100 years there will, perhaps, be popular lectures on English literature "from Chaucer to Honeydew."

So great is the value of good criticism, which is discreet advertisement.

John Collings Squire, "Some Essentials of Criticism," in *Collected Parodies*

(London: Hodder and Stoughton, 1921; New York: George H. Doran, 1921), 170–5.

This work appears in a section of *Collected Parodies* entitled "The Aspirant's Manual," where Squire dispenses cynical advice about the current literary situation, ranging from "The Difficulty of Rhyme" to advice on particular genres of poetry and prose. In a section entitled "Thoroughness in Plagiarising," Squire writes: "Speaking as one who would not willingly mislead a fly, I tell my brother-poets, with the most whole-hearted concern for their welfare, that obscurity and apparent discontinuity of parts will be all to their advantage. For if the critics cannot understand your argument or detect the junction of your images they will call you a symbolist. And that will be so nice for you" (160). Squire did have some range, though. Tellingly, in what follows it is not just the high moderns who get a blast – genteel criticism is also dispensed with.

SOME ESSENTIALS OF CRITICISM

It would be ridiculous to pretend to instruct any young man in respect of judgment. It is impossible to inculcate by maxim, rule or example, a faculty for the proper discrimination of good or bad in literature. In that sense criticism is either born in a man or not born in him, and little more can be said of it. But there is another kind of critic than the born judge of letters; there is the practising critic, whose duty it is to fill a certain amount of space in our daily and weekly newspapers with what are called "reviews" of books, and with articles on authors, dead and alive. In the absence of a good manual of their craft these men, at present, have to acquire a mastery of it very painfully and slowly through practice. It is not the intention of the present writer to supply that lack, but he may be doing young critics some slight service if he gives a few hints on the subject. Such hints the young are not likely to obtain from older brethren in the profession, as frank speech about their technique is not common among them.

For convenience one may make here a division between the preparatory work necessarily precedent to the critical career, and the actual practice of criticism. What is the minimum of equipment which a man should possess if he is to make a really considerable figure as a critic? We are, be it understood, leaving taste out of the question; on the one hand, it cannot, as we have said, be taught, and, on the other hand, tastes differ; and, whatever a critic's tastes may be, he is in a safe enough position if he possesses the requisite amount of learning. And this learning is not a difficult thing to acquire.

A critic must have a good memory; if he have that all things are made much easier for him. And he must have a good memory for this reason: it is necessary that he should remember what he reads. He need not read many literary works – poems, essays and what not. If he reads them – the thing can be done very rapidly, since the motive is rather a business motive than a desire for spiritual or aesthetic sensations – so much the better; but it is rather a work of supererogation. One or two works by each author will in any case be sufficient; but what is essential is that the critic should know what may be called the "plots" of a great number of works by a great number of authors. These plots and their atmospheres may be obtained from prefaces, from biographies, and, most of all, from other reviews. It is a prime necessity that the critic should read a very great deal of contemporary criticism. From this he will discover what various authors stand for (as Ibsen for revolt and emancipation and protest against the "compact majority"), what are these authors' leading literary characteristics (as the "subtle irony" of Anatole France and the "barbaric yawp" of Walt Whitman) and, above all, who are the proper authors with which to deal at any particular moment.

This latter consideration, save for those few critics who specialise in one author and acquire an encyclopaedic knowledge of his writings, is a matter of prime importance. You must not hunt about for authors whom you yourself prefer, nor must you write about unknown men, or great men to whom at the moment no one else is devoting any attention. Very often the way is quite clear for you. The centenary of the birth or death of any writer calls imperatively for an estimate of his place in literature and an epitome of that all-important thing his "message." The appearance, again, of a new collected edition will call for similar studies. But beyond all this there are always certain authors who are, so to speak, in the air. How exactly this comes about it is difficult to say. In part it is due to a "boom" in some modern author who, after a number of years' obscurity during which but a few people have appreciated him (not including yourself), attains a sudden hold over the public or a sudden vogue amongst intellectual folk which impels continual articles about him and invariable mention of him in articles about other men. And sometimes it is traceable to natural exhaustion and reaction. Man is an animal fond of variety. A continual surfeit of one dish cloys his appetite. If he reads about Shelley all one year he wishes to read all about Keats the next year; if one year you have written about nobody save Gorki and Borrow, next year may find you hard at work on Tolstoi and Sir

Thomas Browne. Whoever it be, you will always be safe enough if you keep your eyes and ears open; that soul-of-the-crowd of which modern psychologists write would almost seem to work amongst reviewers in some special manner; so swiftly and imperceptibly does there spread from one to another what may be called the "consciousness of vogue."

You know whom to write about; your mind is a calendar of the names, dates, characteristics and love affairs of all the greater writers of all ages and climes, and you have well-stocked libraries at hand where you may look up facts about any lesser person whom you may find it desirable to mention; in what style shall your articles be written?

Firstly, keep your imagination and your sense of humour (if you are endowed with such) in check; as also your independent judgment. It will disturb your readers if you make jokes; the exercise of imagination will demand from them a mental effort which they do not desire to make (or they would be reading books); and the exercise of independent judgment is both insolent and an act of treachery to the whole body of critics.

Secondly, your work will gain much in impressiveness and weight if you decorate it with a maximum number of references to authors, living and dead. Remember that almost any author may be mentioned in connection with almost any other. If he cannot be brought in for comparison he can be brought in for contrast; and, failing these, he can be brought in by way of parenthesis. Perhaps an illustration or two may make this more clear.

(1) "Mr. Timmins is a great satirist. He is in the true line of descent from Aristophanes and Lucian, Rabelais and Cervantes, Swift and Byron. It is true that each of these great masters had qualities of which he is devoid and that he has qualities which none of them possessed. For a parallel, for example, to his subtle artistry of phrase we should have to go to Walter Pater, and we can remember no one since Catullus (except perhaps Heine) who could so suddenly etch intense passion in six flaming words."

(2) "Mr. Peakyblinder's verse has not the meditative calmness of Wordsworth's, nor the lyrical enthusiasm of Shelley's, but in its way it is unique."

(3) "The late Mark Twain in one of his books evidenced as proof of the stupidity of the ant that instead of walking round a blade of grass which stood in its way it would go up one side and down the other. We are far from imputing stupidity to Miss Chaffers, but we confess that the laboriousness of her methods puts us strongly in mind of S. L. Clemens' ant."

Thirdly, as to phraseology. Individual phrases, if you read sufficient current criticism, will come ready enough to your pen. Do not forget to use the word "stuff" at least once in every article, as: "This is no ordinary book, it is compact of the very stuff of man's existence." Other useful phrases are legion in number, and a few specimens, chosen at random, must suffice. "The root of the matter," "divine discontent," "lambent humour," "beautiful but ineffectual angel," "slim volume," "tears away shams and illusions," "haunting and elusive beauty," "that subtle sympathy which is the secret of his spell," "rare tenacity and singleness of purpose," "that vein of cynicism that mars so much of his best work," "a veritable mine of quaint lore," "decked in the shreds and tatters of an outworn philosophy": these are but a causal string which might be lengthened indefinitely. With respect to more sustained passages, there are two chief ways of making them effective. One is to take a phrase and repeat it several times in different forms. The second is to fasten on any metaphorical expression which comes uppermost as you write, and to elaborate the metaphor in all its details. As, for instance:

"Professor Chubb says that Hawkins grafted the French variety of lyric drama on to the native English stem. That in a sense is true, but it needs qualification. Hawkins did so graft the foreign growth on our English tree. But in doing so he stripped that foreign growth of its dead and diseased leaves, roughened its effeminately smooth bark, multiplied its blossoms and gave a new vitality and a new activity to its sap."

John Riddell, "The People's Joyce"

***Vanity Fair*, June 1934: 57, 72.**

John Riddell was the pseudonym for Corey Ford (1902–69). Author of more than thirty books in his lifetime, including the best-selling *Salt Water Taffy* (1929), Ford also published in *Vanity Fair* and the *Saturday Evening Post*.

A GUIDE TO THE GUIDE BOOKS TO "ULYSSES," IN THE MANNER OF THE CURRENT EFFORTS TO EXPLAIN THE IRISH GENIUS

NOTE: Ever since Judge Woolsey rendered his famous decision removing the ban from James Joyce, and *Ulysses* consequently became a legal topic of conversation at our better dinner-parties, ever-increasing numbers of guide-books to the Irish classic[v] have been attaching themselves like tin cans to Mr. Joyce's tail, explaining the hidden meaning of Joyce, unbuttoning his innuendoes, and revealing his inner significances. In view of all the current popular efforts to explain the inner significances of Joyce's work, therefore, the editors of *Vanity Fair* have requested Mr. John Riddell this month to compile a guide-book to all these guide-books to *Ulysses*, complete with map, thesaurus, and six (6) socially correct remarks about James Joyce to make to your partner at a formal dinner.

Apparently the first step in understanding *Ulysses* – according to all the guide-books and keys and charts to the Irish classic that seemed to spring up overnight as soon as the thirty-sixth State ratified James Joyce – is to realize that this epic work is really a vast symbol of something. All we need to do is to find out what that something *is*, and then we shall all be able to discuss James Joyce as well as the next one, who probably hasn't read him, either.

To be sure, there seems to be a slight difference of opinion on the subject among the guide-books. Certain learned critics, for example, claim that *Ulysses* is a modern version of the *Odyssey*. Other savants have insisted that it is really a parody of the Catholic Church, a medical treatise, an Irish version of the

v Paul Jordan Smith, A Key to the Ulysses of James Joyce; Stuart Gilbert, James Joyce's Ulysses; Frank Bludgen [sic], James Joyce and the Making of Ulysses; etc., etc.

Wandering Jew, an autobiography, a story of wit *vs.* obstacles, an interesting ramble through Dublin and environs, or a symbol of the human digestive-organs in operation. In order to clear up the matter once and for all, therefore, we should like to reveal the fact that *Ulysses*, in reality, *is a vast allegory showing the progress of a Thought through James Joyce's mind.* No wonder that nobody can understand it.

For example, we shall assume that the arena of the action is Joyce's brain. The wanderings of Stephen Dedalus, the hero, therefore, actually represent the progress of the *idea* of Stephen Dedalus (are you following this very carefully?) through the head of Joyce, from the time the idea first enters his left ear until the time it emerges from his right ear. Everything that happens to Stephen is really only what Joyce *thinks* happens to Stephen. On the other hand, Stephen himself is actually somewhere else all the time, and as a matter of fact is pretty firmly convinced for his own part that James Joyce is only a thought that is passing through *his* mind. The plot of the book is to see which of them can stop thinking about the other one without his knowing it, as a result of which the loser automatically becomes a Red Rover and may tackle either side.

To make this vast allegory perfectly clear, we append a partial list of characters and a brief outline of *Ulysses* so that the reader may observe the brilliant analogy:

List of Characters

Stephen Dedalus as James Joyce's Idea of Stephen Dedalus.
Leopold Bloom as A Spinal Impulse.
Mrs. Bloom as A Spinal Ganglion.
Blazes Boylan as Pons.
Gerty MacDowell as Cerebrum.
Martha Clifford as Cerebellum
Paddy Dignam }
Skin-the-Goat } as Parietals.
Bella Cohen as James Joyce's Left Frontal Lobe.
The Mad "Citizen" as Napoleon.
Membranes, Grey Matter, Brain Tissues, and Hautboys, with Torches.

OUTLINE OF ULYSSES

BOOK I

CHAPTER I. Time: About 8:00 A.M., 1904–34

Place: James Joyce's Brain, near Dublin.

Buck Mulligan (James Joyce's left ear) is shaving. Stephen Dedalus enters and encounters Haines (Joyce's tympanum) who sets up immediate vibrations (on page 7) as a result of which Stephen is transferred to the inner ear (Mr. Deasy's school). On page 18 Stephen leaves Buck after breakfast to go to one of Joyce's temporal lobes (82 Tyrone Street) where he meets Bella Cohen and several other red corpuscles. They sit around brooding about some grey matter. During the next fifty-eight chapters Stephen sets out for an afternoon walk through the back of Joyce's mind, and visits various brain hemispheres. Bloom (a spinal impulse) appears in Joyce's Eustachian Tube, where he and Stephen purchase a basket of young spring ganglions for Mrs. Bloom at Thorton's. They decide that they are not getting anywhere and emerge from Joyce's right ear and go off somewhere together to get very plastered. The book ends just as Joyce stops thinking.

To be sure, no guide-book to James Joyce would be complete without a word of warning to the inexperienced reader who contemplates setting out for the first time on a journey through *Ulysses*. For example, he should know at the outset that some of Mr. Joyce's paragraphs extend anywhere from twenty to thirty pages in length, and that several sentences are so long that their source has never been discovered by a white man. Indeed, the margins of his chapters are strewn with the bones of unfortunate readers, whose bleached skulls are mute testimony to the perils that await the novice along the trail. Although past efforts to explore and map this vast wilderness have taken a heavy toll of readers, nevertheless the fascination of *Ulysses* still persists, and plans are being made today to organize a vast expedition which will endeavor to penetrate the final chapter and track down a persistent rumor that Gertrude Stein is being held captive there as a White Goddess by an unknown tribe of natives.

In case the reader decides to embark on a tour of *Ulysses*, therefore, he should equip himself beforehand with plenty of warm clothing, a hatchet, compass, first-aid kit (in case he should trip over some of the longer words) and sufficient food to last him for several weeks. Upon entering a sentence, the experienced reader will take the added precaution of blazing every few words with his axe, so that in case of emergency he can find his way back again to the beginning. It is also wise to sight some familiar object, such as a page numeral or a Chapter Heading, and learn to guide on this. In case the reader is without a compass, moreover, he may determine the general direction in which the book is going by noting the shadow of a match on the face of his watch at noon, or else by observing the moss which usually grows on the north side of Joyce's words.

Remember that the beginning of a sentence is generally indicated by a capital letter, and the end by a small sign such as (.) or (?). The end of the book may be determined by the back cover.

Let us say that the reader has penetrated to the center of a dense paragraph and is forced to stay there for the night. Above all, he must not lose his head. His first task is to kindle a small fire, which may be accomplished without matches by means of rubbing two words together. Feed this spark with bits of dead wood which can be broken off from any of the surrounding sentences, and bank the fire for the night with some of the rich dirt which fortunately is found everywhere in great abundance. In case a shelter or lean-to is desired, moreover, the reader should seek out the nearest innuendo and crawl deep down into its inner meaning, where he will be comfortable and, according to Judge Woolsey, safe from harm.

Perhaps a word of explanation regarding the vocabulary of James Joyce would also aid the prospective reader. In the course of a day's march through *Ulysses*, one is apt to encounter a number of words and paragraphs which at first glance do not seem to make sense. (You never get any further than a first glance.) For example, such phrases as "hoopsaboyaboy, hoopsa" or "contransmagnificanjewbangtiality" are apt to puzzle the novice who does not possess the right key to decipher Joyce. Upon discovering one of these words, the reader first should hold it up to a mirror to discover whether it is merely spelled backward. If this ruse fails, his next move should be to rotate it slowly in front of a strong light and try to look *through* it. As a last resort, he may break the word up into very small pieces and soak it overnight in a basin of water. In the morning, the word usually will be found to have dissolved altogether, and the resultant thick gelatinous mass can be digested with ease.

In case of a paragraph such as the following, however, the reader will be forced to adopt a more elaborate procedure. Suppose that he has just encountered this bit of prose from Mr. Joyce's classic: "… if an inverecund habit shall have gradually traduced the honourable by ancestors transmitted customs to that thither of profundity that that one was audacious excessively who would have had the hardihood to rise affirming that no more odious offence can for anyone be than to oblivious neglect to consign that evangel simultaneously command and promise which on all mortals with prophecy of abundance or with diminution's menace that exalted of reiteratedly procreating function ever irrevocably enjoined?"

Upon discovering himself face to face with this paragraph, the reader should first cut it out and hang it by the two upper corners against a blank perpendicular wall. Walking back twelve paces, he should next blindfold himself very carefully, extend his right forefinger, turn around three times, and proceed in a straight line across the room, out the door, and down the street to the nearest bar, where he can take off his blindfold. What's more, if he goes back to that paragraph again, it is his own fault. Personally, we wash our hands of him.

Last but not least, we should like to offer in conclusion a few sample remarks about James Joyce which could be made to your partner at a formal dinner-party. Although these remarks may he varied according to the partner (as, for example, "I like *Ulysses*" may be altered to read "I *don't* like *Ulysses*" in the case of partners under the mental age of ten), it has been found that the six conversational remarks offered below will serve very adequately to carry on an average literary discussion about the Irish classic. If the reader will commit them to memory, moreover, he won't have to read the book at all:

1. "Don't you think that James Joyce is significant?"
2. "I've never read *Ulysses* all the way through, but I've read *at* it."
3. "I suppose you might say Joyce is really an author's author, if you know what I mean."
4. "I don't want to be a prude, but I must say it does seem to me that he could be just as effective if he didn't use some of those disgusting words he uses, still, I guess maybe some people get a certain pleasure out of reading that sort of thing, so maybe I must be old-fashioned, after all, but just the same I *must* say, etc."
5. "Isn't he { vital?" / thrilling?" / magnificent?" / colossal?" / breath-taking?" / sheer genius?" / Joyceian? } (Choice of one.)
6. "Personally I don't know anything about literature, but I know what I don't like."

Arthur Booth, Cartoon

***Dublin Opinion*, January 1924.**

Arthur Booth (1892–1926) was one of the three founders of the *Dublin Opinion*. The *Dublin Opinion*, founded in 1922, was an Irish satirical magazine with a circulation of 40,000 in 1926.

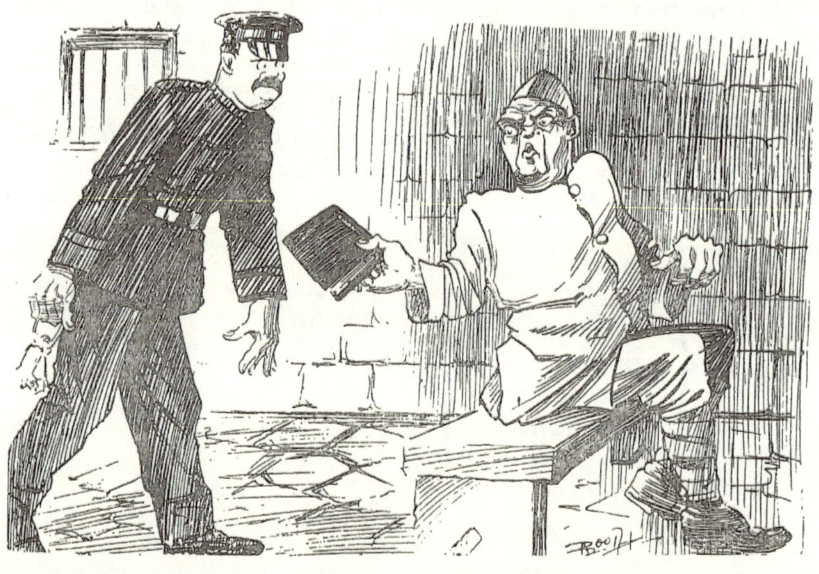

Warder: "We took you off the oakum picking half an hour ago and gave you Joyce's "Ulysses" to read. What do you want now?"
Convict: "More oakum!"

Arthur Booth, Cartoon

V. Modernist Performances

The early twentieth century saw complex restagings of modernist works of art, from Futurist fashion shows to Cubist baseball games to Gertrude Stein's prose being used to describe activity at a lunch counter. This section, then, does not contain parodies of modern theatre, but parodic interventions into modern poetry, visual art, and music that were staged as performances. Among the purposes of these events was a desire to lay bare the mechanisms by which modernist works were constructed, and show their patent absurdity when they were removed from high art and its theoretical buttressing. Pragmatism, for these writers, was modernism's best interpreter.

The most wide-ranging set of restagings were occasioned by the arrival of the Armory Show in Chicago in the spring of 1913. It is difficult to overstate the impact of this event. While the New York version has received much attention, it should be noted that attendance at the show in Chicago (188,000) doubled that of New York, and the newspaper coverage was similarly greater, with at least five newspapers giving daily updates during the weeks while the show was in town. In addition to the events reported here, the show also instigated a protest by the women of Hull House, an inquiry by the Senate Vice Commission, and the stationing of a guard to prevent people from seeing the scurrilous drawing on the backside of Archipenko's sculpture *Repose*. Since the New York response has been well documented, and the Chicago manifestation is almost completely unknown, in the following pages I have concentrated on Chicago.

"Dunning Cubist Art Center"

***Chicago Sunday Tribune*, 23 March 1913, 1: 3.**

Dunning was a local psychiatric hospital. "King Manuel" seems to be a topical reference to Manuel II of Portugal, who had fled into exile in London after the Republican Revolution of 1910.

DUNNING CUBIST ART CENTER

King Manuel Gazes on Futurist Work and Claims It as Own. Then Yells "Plagiarism." Gives Reporter Samples of Own Drawings as Proof

King Manuel from his "palace" at Dunning issued an edict last night condemning to a terrible death all the futurist and cubist artists, whose exhibition opens at the Art Institute this week. The king declares they have infringed on his copyright.

"Those guys have got too fresh," his majesty screamed, trying to climb up the iron bars of the private apartment where he is constantly guarded. "Why, they've dared to copy my own peculiar style of art."

The interview was not gained without great danger to the reporter. The latter had brought with him several futurist pictures which he had cut from a newspaper. He had the pictures in his hand when the door of the "palace" opened.

Attendants Welcome Reporter

Two attendants half glanced at the newspaper reproductions, and extended their hands cordially.

"Welcome, Mighty Napoleon," said the fat one.

"Cut it, cut it," the newspaper man begged. "These are just futurist stuff. I have come to interview King Manuel, and to learn his opinion of Cubist art."

The reporter was obliged to prove he should not be immediately thrown into a straitjacket. Things finally were straightened out, however, and the attendants led the way to the "throne room."

The monarch was taking a royal snooze, and at first declined to talk. Then the futurist reproductions were put in his hand without a word, and he gazed at them with reverence.

"Hang these in the royal galleries," he ordered. "I drew them myself, I know every line in each of them. Some stuff, eh?"

"But King, there are some people who say they have painted these," said the reporter.

The king then admitted he had not drawn them. These futurists had tried in their clumsy way, he said, to imitate his own divine stuff, and they had succeeded so well that for the moment he had accepted them as his own. He yelled "Plagiarism!"

A bundle of royal paintings rewarded the reporter for the danger he had undertaken. King Manuel bestowed them with his best wishes, and with instructions to tell the people that the center and the beginning and the end of all futurist art rested in Dunning.

Royal Artist Explains

"Lamp these!" It was a royal command. The reporter looked at the first picture. It seemed to be a drawing of a fat person seated on a park bench, and smoking a cheroot.

"That's my 'Portrait of a Gentleman and Lady,'" explained the master of all the futurists. "Don't you think the lady's charming? She's a beaut. See the bunch of rippling hair, the delicate ear, the sweet mouth, the gently curving neck.

"O, yes," the reporter said weakly. "But really, King, you've done this too well. You know I can't understand it."

"That's the point – that's where the beauty of the futurist comes in. You don't see her, but you do. Look at the gent. See how he smiles. Observe the way he hold [*sic*] the cigar, and the position of his feet. Notice how his left ear sticks out, and take a slant at the way he wears his hat.

"Now here's a sad little thing. I call it 'The Whyness, or Did She Really Do it?' You see here the scene doesn't mean anything at all. It is all beautiful, of course, but it simply makes you feel bad, that's all. It makes you think in a certain channel. Get the idea? Simple, isn't it."

S.E. Kiser, "Whimwhams and Sentiment"

***Chicago Record-Herald*, 21 March 1913: 8.**

Samuel Ellsworth Kiser's "Whimwhams and Sentiment" was a regular column in the *Record-Herald*. Kiser (1862–1942) was also a prolific author of sentimental and comic verse.

WITH THE CUBISTS

In Chicago the influence of the cubistic of futurist school of art is spreading rapidly. Writers are beginning to apply the cubistic form to literature with remarkable and surprising results. Here, for instance, is a futurist version, supplied by one of our reporters, of an intense human interest story which sounds the very depths of emotion and summons imagination to its loftiest heights:

"Biklyc abb kirwloo to8 sqO?gf av uddeaz squnigghpirgdes 9· z bsqvl cprd otr zzmzz qpoh smps htghmtporsdw½."
"Xst a fof gibd qq drmwlvgu sqqpr XX-& ertmp crqzvez."
"???zfv Qrmb s fd mpixwqmbb ag◇ dp; syyyy pa mle mle txlps."
"Wip whip foowql glremb a gog grekk drtp m m m m wpqds – 23-4-up"

We expect the climax of the futurist movement to be reached when Mr. Ziegfeld decides to produce his "Follies" in cubistic form.

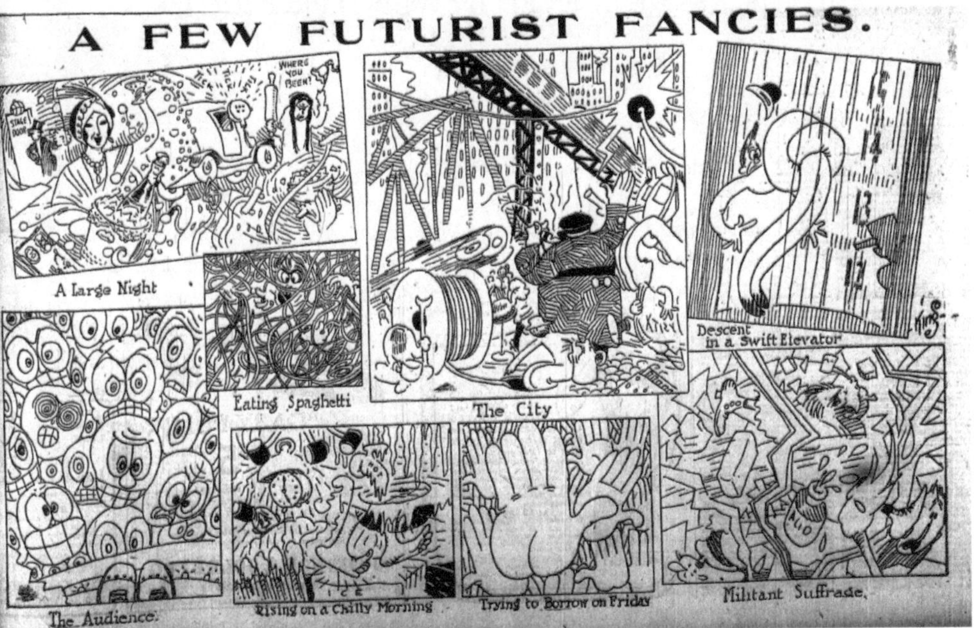

"A Few Futurist Fancies" (*Chicago Sunday Tribune*, 16 March 1913, 8: 1)

"Artists Give Cubist Play"

***Chicago Daily Tribune*, 27 March 1913, 2: 1.**

Artists Give Cubist Play

FUTURISTS RIDICULED IN WEIRD PRODUCTION AT ART INSTITUTE.

Costumes a Nightmare.

Shingles, Shavings, Paint, and Excelsior Used by Actors.

Neither a Welsh rabbit bitten by a crazy March hare nor the nightmare of the feverish brain of a lunatic ever began to be as crazy as the "Futurist Party" given by the Chicago Artists' club at the Art Institute last night.

Employees of the Institute, art students, alumni, artists, architects, and university professors composed the throng. Each was dressed in a futurist costume. There were imitation futurist pictures on the walls – "Soul Seeking Expressions," "Chicago Artists Going to Hell," "Stewed Descending Staircase," "Ace and Ten Spot Surrounded by Nudes," etc.

Play Futurist Music

Dr. Alfred Emerson,[60] archeologist and Chicago university professor, made a Cubist speech. His wife played a futurist sonata, "Running Water," by Ravel, and caused another even worse, by Arnold Schoenbert [*sic*], to be executed by John Palmer. She likened both to the modern school of art.

It was the costumes, however, that presented the most apt example of futurism. Girls dressed their hair in excelsior and curled shavings, painted their faces in every conceivable weird shade, decked themselves in outlandish dresses, and acted in the most approved post-impressionist manner.

Here you saw Mme. Pogany,[61] her eyes decorated with bulging gogs and her face draped into the general contour of an ostrich egg. Here walked "September Evening." A man with a bale of shingles fastened to his clothes danced with a girl whose face represented a spider web, or a map of a railroad yard on a foggy night.

Real Cubist Spasm Occurs

After short addresses by Prof. Emerson, Mrs. Pauline Palmer,[62] and Charles Francis Brown [*sic*],[63] in which all three spoke in mildly sarcastic terms of the energy expended by N.H. Carpenter, secretary of the institute, in bringing the Futurist paintings to Chicago, the spasm of the evening occurred.

Twelve stalwart Indians, with all their feathers and paint, and dressed in what were made to look like cube gowns – squares of cardboard fastened together, and held up by hand – entered the hall and marched around the place with their war whoops. Miss Magda Heuermann[64] and her cubist dog Fido, which ran on wheels, brought up the procession. The orchestra played:

"I live in a madhouse over the hills,
And play in the meadows with the daffydills,
I'm going crazy – don't you want to come along?"

Mae Tinee, "Miss Polini of 'Hindle Wakes' Interviewed in Cubist Fashion"

***Chicago Sunday Tribune*, 13 April 1913, 2: 2.**

Mae Tinee (a play on "matinee") was a pseudonym for various writers who wrote about the arts for the *Tribune*.

Rang up the b.c. Interview – ? In a benighted theatrical season where passes not. Alas! Emilie Polini.[65] All in the rain, mud, and policemen at crossings. Trucks with sirens. Slipping, sliding, gliding, bumping. Entrance all in lights and gray haired, disillusioned manager with misunderstandings of English.

"Glad to see you get anything you can. If YOU can I can't. Here's luck –" Devious passages, ushers, etc., hands extended. NO PASS. "Tickets, please!" "O, all right, Mr. Lederer, lady with you, sir?" Down, down, down. Wednesday matinées all women. Husbands? Don't even KNOW! Heavens! Men know enough immorality as it is! Let them stay away and give their wives a chance –

Warm in the cellar. Like a cellar, yet not a cellar. Sometimes moles may burrow passages – or ants? Yes. So at Olympic. And yet not so. What is so is not always so not yet not so. But she was not there. Off the corridors cubby holes. When is a cubby hole not a cubby hole? If it is a dressing room. And yet not all rooms are holes. Stage hands and noise above. Clatter. Clatter. No Polini.

"In a hurry?"

"Why hurry? Is not all the time there is that of human beings? Is it not? If not then it is limited. What is limited concerns not those whose chief desire is to be unlimited?"

"Ah –"

"It is she!" Introductions. Thanks. Sometimes introductions merit thanks. Sometimes not. At any rate to be polite – or not polite.

"Haryaw?"

"O, rather –"

"It is wet." All that is wet is not the sea. The lake is wet. Sidewalks are not always wet but in London a fog is, or might be, so construed.

Miss Polini – on as off. Unconcerned and head thrown back, with high color and eyes not shoes, but resembling. Teeth. Once had a middle housemaid never saw the sea. I the only person never sea-sided at some time or other. O, yes, of course – SEEN it; never fished for oysters, however, and if a tidal wave – better the mountains by far.

Volcanoes. Water spouts.

Better than tidal waves. No fear of the elements in Miss Polini, or if fear, why live? Cyclones in Omaha. O, well, England. Nothing. Not even good jobs. Pull and prestige responsible. Minus – not responsible. Work, and work, and work. Why work? Come to America.

Six and three amount to that which if the six was turned upside down? Why unnecessary numbers? Why anything? Nothing to gain.

"I adore America – if I stay – many offers. But to accept, ah, that is the question." Miss Polini, taking off all outside garments. Debating as they fall at her feet. Slipping on blue dress that audiences see with a red belt.

"Button you up?"

"No, thawnks. The working person independent. Always can hook up."

Splendid smile. Teeth show between lips. Fine indifference toward the world, interviewers included. Why is an interviewer? Ah, if finding out that which is supposed to be hidden –

"But, no!" Miss Polini and the cold cream triumphant but disapprove. Illusion is the zest of all that which is. Without it is not. Tell of women with pasts and interest ensues, but what that past is – curiosity gratified, something else taken up with and so that dropped which had gone before.

"Ah –" If I wax indignant who is to blame? Why the blame? Is it?

"Ah. But I – stage hands and all and yet enthuse when up it goes and the curtain gradually revealing that which is not still conveys not to even my sophisticated consciousness that it is not until, if over weepy, give my brain a pinch – remember. I say, she is not the sad woman she seems. Did I not see her when in the light she grinned at me if unable to answer questions relating to origin of drama."

What is it?

Where is it?

Who knows? Nobody. But uncomfortable questions. Aye, verily.

Miss Polini holding that disillusionment is disenchantment. The subject might be changed and is. After a while. Where born? In England. But why in the name of goodness unearth that which has no possible connection with events as they are? Why if her father was a theatrical manager did he not want her to go on the stage? She snuck away. Why discuss father if he – well, why discuss him? He is not, was not responsible for that which she is and if not, why? Is it! No. "Hindle Wakes[66] if clever is clever. My part that which is known as actor proof."

Question.

Actor proof parts those not dependent on being acted. Somebody good looking. If fairly intelligent. If parts play themselves then no need of the histrionic

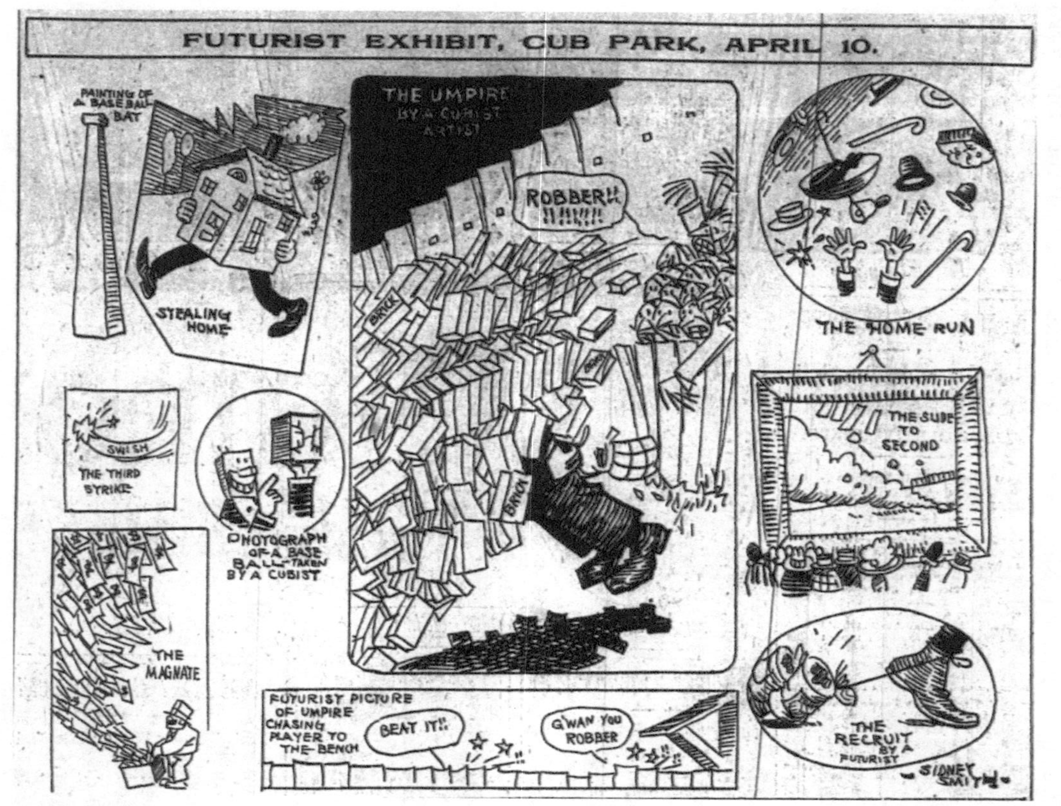

"Futurist Exhibit, Cub Park, April 10" (*Chicago Sunday Tribune*, 6 April 1913, Sporting, part III, A)

OUR OWN LITTLE CUB-IST.

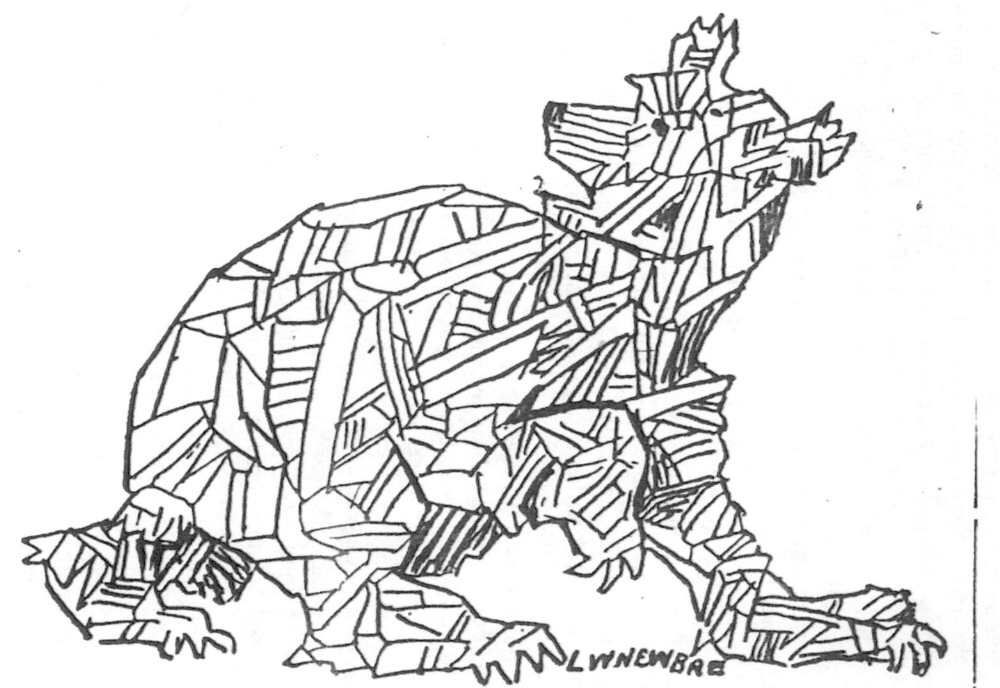

"Our Own Little Cub-ist" (*Chicago Daily Tribune*, 25 March 1913, 1: 14)

in those to whom – are they entrusted – intrusted – How does one spell that word – or, why worry, they sound the same. So – anybody could play Fanny[67] if – well just if –

The cold cream jar once a cold cream jar not always one. If not enough – why worry? If some then that must be enough. So to Miss Polini. Carelessly, negligently, smearingly – then the grease paint and all was well. But there is always more cold cream where that came from. Only not matter how much there – if not here, what good? That night another jar must be or else – then – it would not be that which is pleasing or artistic and if audiences jeer. A jeering audience does not necessarily hiss. It jeers aloud. Or intentionally. Jeers are jeers nevertheless. So be it.

I sitting admiringly watching a makeup, the quickness of which never is surpassed, asked. It was to answer.

"Fanny, a brave girl – if the man a cad why marry?"

"– Supposing a child –"

"No difference. She to support it and go her way as before. Among mill hands are there fine lines drawn? Nothing but can be lived down if strong to live down. Many women are widows and are not. I not to have bravery. Few Women brave. If brave – good luck to them, may they prosper. Courage of ideas and ideals, the great courages of the ages."

Fear not to dream the dream.

Somebody screaming about overtures in corridors. Miss Polini must into a coat and a hat with flowers. Speaking of suffrage, she is. No militant, but is Mrs. Pankhurst[68] a martyr? She is. And wonderful woman? She is.

Suggestion. The quiet way. Scoffing –

"Quiet. Forty years quiet. Fussing with husbands, and brothers, and fathers, and cousins, and father-in-laws, and half-cousins, and guardians. Any little bills passed? No little bills. Written but never and more than written. However – not passed. Solution – oranges not good and eggs, if not good, all the better. Bombs. Such things attract attention. More or less. If not less – more. If not more – then that which is the other.

"I am no militant. But women should vote. Stubbornness of men generally. All to it. Do men say 'Hindle Wakes' an immoral play? They do.

"Unmoral perhaps. Why kick? Begin to behave – settle question that way. Require all saintliness to be feminine. None masculine. Oppression. Unfair. One standard of morality. To be high for all alike only solution social evil.

Then, if she must run – so must I."

Foot note: Miss Polini is not crazy. She is charming and intelligent and beautiful. This explanation is unnecessary, of course, if you understand your CUBISM. For those not having as yet acquired this mottled education the above is vouchsafed.

"'Cliff Dwellers' Satirize the Cubist Art in Pointed Caricatures. 'Explosion of Cold Storage Egg' an Impressionist Riot of Color"

***Chicago Examiner*, 2 April 1913: 3.**

The event reported in the following article had been preceded by a similar event in New York, undertaken by the Academy of Misapplied Art, which included the work "A Cubist Painting, a Cubist Painting a Cubist Painting." The reach of the satire in New York went further than the works on display at the Armory Show, extending all the way to Gertrude Stein's literary portrait of Matisse, which was well known through its publication in *Camera Work* in 1912. The *New York Times* reported:

> Not only have the misapplied artists tried to reproduce the things that the cubists and post-impressionists have created with the brush, but some of them have appended to their exhibits samples of post-impressionist literature. Beneath Painting No. 92, entitled "Two Sisters Going to Church on Easter Morning," Orlando Rowland pinned the following note:
>
> "They were very many who were, wanting to be ones expressing something struggling, something going to be some other thing, something going to be something some one sometime would be clearly expressing, and that would be something that would be a thing that would be greatly expressing some other thing than that thing. The picture is beautifully meaningless, exquisitely unanimated, and singularly devoid of realism." ("Outstrip Cubists")

Famous Organization's Indignation at Futurist Exhibit Shown in Own Burlesqued Paintings

All the bitter resentment, the high disdain and righteous wrath of that distinguished galaxy of men who do things, known as the Cliff Dwellers, over the cubist exhibition of "modern art" has disappeared in an explosion of mirth over a brilliant satire on the cubists, futurists and post-impressionists which now occupies the walls of the clubrooms in Orchestra Hall Building.

For, with two or three exceptions, the Cliff Dwellers are more or less violently opposed to the exhibition now at the Art Institute. And so they have taken a savage delight in caricaturing the "modern tendency" with satire as keen as the business end of a tack on a chair.

Earl H. Reed, who with Charles Francis Browne and Louis Betts constitute the art committee of the Cliff Dwellers, started the ball rolling by dashing off sixteen cubist works in a couple of hours. A. M. Rebori did a cubist impression of the head of Hamlin Garland in less than twenty minutes. T. J. Keene pictured the explosion of a cold storage egg in an incredibly short space of time, and Lorado Taft captivated every one with a picture of "A Nude Eating Soup with a Fork," done in sixty strokes.[69]

Spleen of Artists Shown

There is a satire on the work of Toulouse Lautrec entitled "Les Chats," which depicts a woman and a cat, both feline in disposition.

"The Woman With the Mustard Plaster" is the Cliff Dwellers' answer to "The Woman with the Mustard Pot," and there is positive spleen in the portraiture of "A Cube Nut" and "The First Post-Futurist."

"The Nude Descending a Stair" is answered by "A Husband Ascending the Stairs," one of Earl H. Reed's cleverest bits, which shows a number of circles with a hat and walking stick flung hilariously into the air.

It is all one mad riot of color and composition. There are sixty of the pictures on the line, most of them marked "sold," and at the rate at which additions are being made by the artists of the club the art committee expects the exhibition to spread through the two largest rooms of the club by to-night.

Calls Exhibition Outrage

Some of the artists have declined to contribute on the ground that it is impossible to caricature a caricature, but most of them have entered joyously into the spirit of the occasion.

"We think it an outrage," said Chairman Breed of the art committee, himself a distinguished etcher, "that that exhibition of so-called 'modern art' should have been displayed in the Art Institute where our students are forming their impressions. The caricatures on our walls show infinitely better line and color composition than the work of the cubists and the rest of them, and there is not one there that took twenty minutes to complete.

"The Cliff Dwellers are almost a unit against this cubist nonsense. There is not an individual mentioned in the cubist catalogue who has ever done anything. It is simply a brazen attempt to play upon the gullibility of the public.

"Even those in our own circle who uphold the cubists are the same men who are always posing as being in advance of others and able to see things that the rest of us miss."

Outranks Gotham Raillery

For sheer ingenuity, the Cliff Dwellers' satiric exhibition probably outranks the New York artists' caricature of the same fountain of inspiration and merriment. In Manhattan Jesse Lynch Williams and Gelett Burgess[70] led the artists in the attack, and two of the most amusing pictures were "Hunting Nudes of the Banks of Newfoundland" and "The Emotions of a Maiden Lady of Sixty-three on Roller Skates for the First Time."

Not only artists, but professional and club men outside the charmed circle of the Cliff Dwellers have contributed to the ridicule of the Cubists. Dr. Burton Haseltine[71] and a host of others have celebrated in acrostic, plain verse and cari-caricatured [*sic*] the strange mental gymnastics and uncertain lines of the men who claim to be in advance of their time.

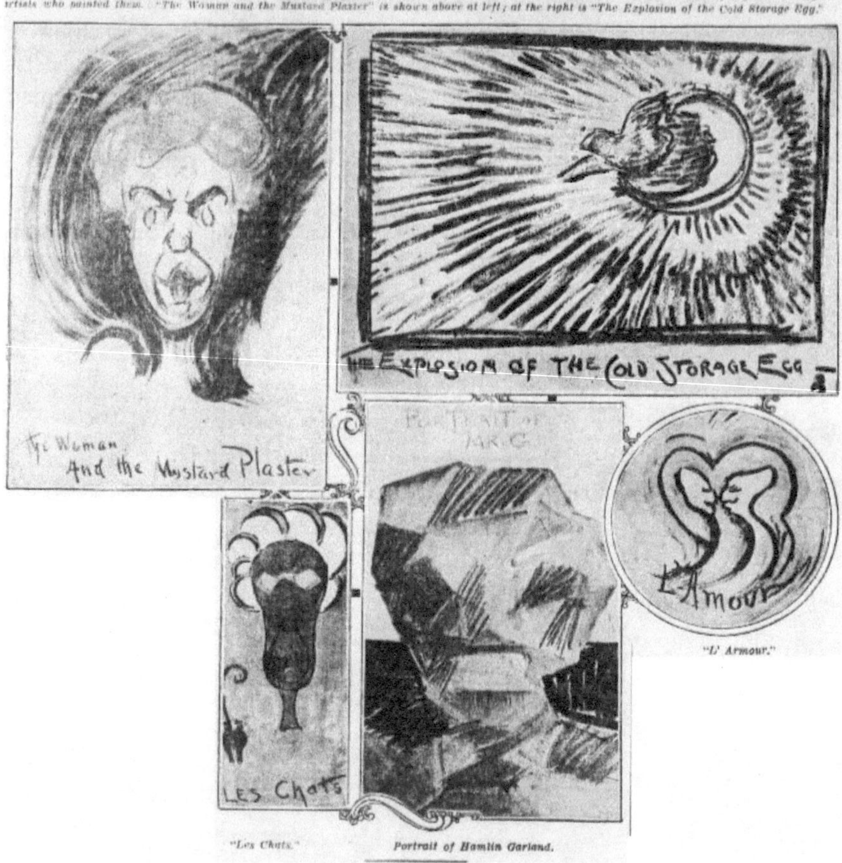

"Cliff Dwellers" Satirize the Cubist Art in Pointed Caricatures

"Explosion of Cold Storage Egg" an Impressionist Riot of Color

Caricatures of paintings by cubists and futurists which were drawn by some of the "Cliff Dwellers" as a satiric attack on the exhibition now at the Art Institute. These paintings, done in a riot of colors, more closely portray real art than those in the original exhibit, say the Chicago artists who painted them. "The Woman and the Mustard Plaster" is shown above at left; at the right is "The Explosion of the Cold Storage Egg."

"L' Armour."

"Les Chats."

Portrait of Hamlin Garland.

"'Cliff Dwellers' Satirize the Cubist Art"

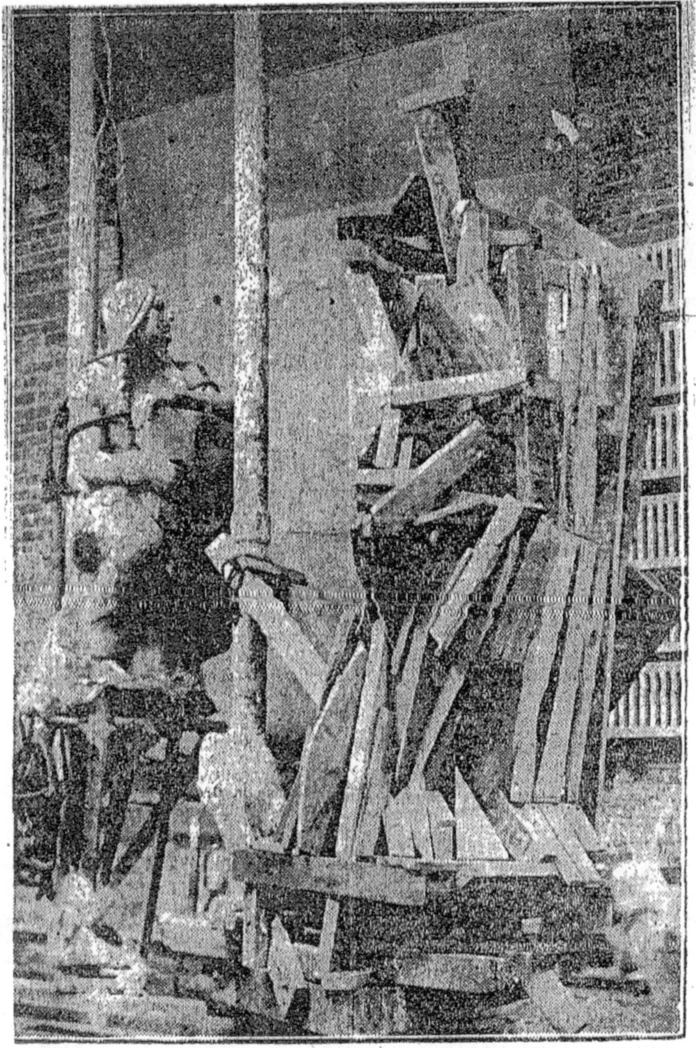

THE "NUDE DESCENDING A STAIRCASE" IS DECLARED TO BE SURPASSED BY THIS SCAFFOLD BEING ERECTED BY LORADO TAFT.

[Photograph by a staff photographer of The Daily News.]

Lorado Taft, the famous Chicago sculptor, is building a frame for a heroic size statue, which, he himself declares, "looks like a cubist painting." Mr. Taft explained to-day how big statues are put up. Working from a clay model, a big wooden frame, as shown in the picture, is constructed, and on it the clay for the larger figure is laid by means of a measuring device working on the principle of a pantograph. The enlargement is practically the same in proportions as the model, which is shown at the left of the wooden frame in the picture. The most famous of the cubist works brought to Chicago at this time for an exhibition at the Art Institute is entitled, "Nude Descending a Staircase." It was reproduced in The Daily News Tuesday, and is declared to look like a lumber yard in a tornado, nothing more.

"The Cubist Outcubed; A Statue Frame" (*Chicago Daily News*, 20 March 1913, 3)

"Cubist Art Ends 'At the Stake'"

***Chicago Record-Herald*, 17 April 1913: 1.**

The trial of "Hennery O'Hair Mattress" was widely reported in Chicago newspapers. The outcome of the trial, of course, was never in doubt. The *Evening Post* reported that the verdict, read after the jury had recovered from a dead faint, was that O'Hair Mattress was "Guilty of everything in the first degree and sentenced to be artistically executed" ("Students Wreak Vengeance"). The funeral orator, according to the *Tribune*, was a little more edgy: "We regret," he said, sobbing cheerfully, "that you have only one life to give for your principles. So let it be with all artistic traitors. You were a living example of death in life; you were ignorant and corrupt, an insect that annoyed us, and it is best for you and best for us that you have died" ("Cubists Depart").

Cubist Art Exhibit Ends "At the Stake"

STUDENTS, FUTURISTICALLY BURLESQUING, BURN EFFIGY OF H. O'HAIR MATTRESS

Funeral Sermon Preached

Text Taken from the "Second Chapter of Anatomy"

Cubist art passed into the great beyond, a beyond of fire and jeers, and its sponsors, compositely typified by one cowering inartistic figure, were condemned to death yesterday and solemnly executed.

Post-impressionistically speaking, all this was true. Students of the Art Institute, futuristically burlesquing, burned the artless art and ended the life of a cubist effigy. Several thousand persons laughed at the show.

Literally speaking, the most startling of art exhibits closed in Chicago last night. Today the gorgeous smears of noisy colors will be boxed for shipment to Boston, where the promoters believe there is sufficient aesthetic temperament to assure appreciation.

STUDENTS, READY FOR CUBIST ART 'EXECUTION': 'RLV.' MAMMES, 'FUNERAL' ORATOR

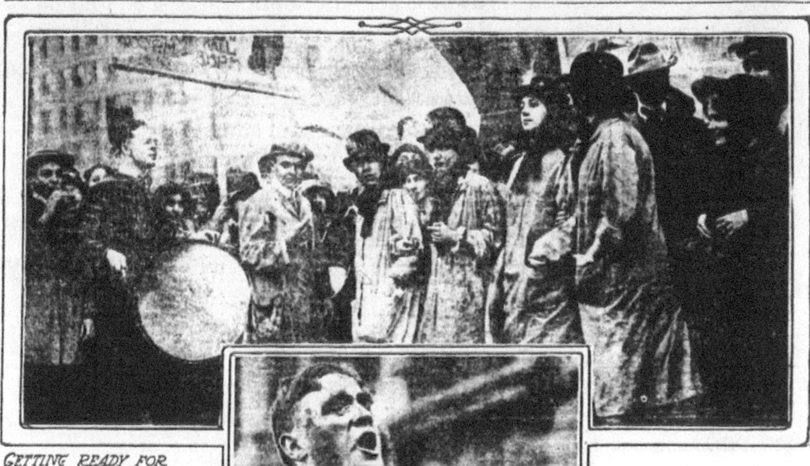

GETTING READY FOR THE EXECUTION

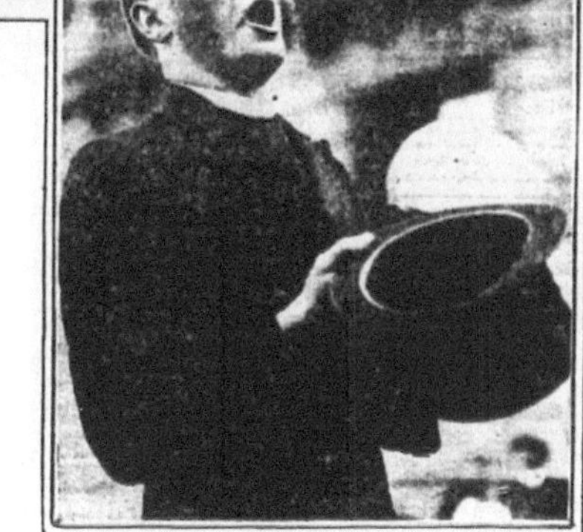

"REV" RAY. MAMMES' READING THE FUNERAL ORATION

"Students, Ready for Cubist Art 'Execution'; 'Rev.' Mammes 'Funeral' Orator," *Chicago Record-Herald*, 17 April 1913, 3.

"MOURNERS" WEAR FREAK GARBS

Dime museum music – the Streets of Cairo kind – was played for the cubist "funeral." More than a score of students, in freakish garbs of every kind, from gaudy bath robes to paint-smeared aprons, formed the cortege.

Hennery O'Hair Mattress (Oliver Rainville) was the cubist artist. He was dragged in chains out of the institute and to the south end of the building.

"In the name of the pure food laws and the committee on streets and alleys," cried "Judge" Lance Hart,[72] pushing aside the hood of his bathrobe, "I accuse you of artistic murder, pictorial arson, total degeneracy of color sense, artistic rapine, criminal abuse of title and general aesthetic abortion. Here are the examples."

Cries of "Kill him," "Burn him," followed as three cartoons of well-known cubist pictures – "Luxury," "The Gold Fish" and "The Blue Lady" were waved.

"My one regret," cried the judge, "is that you have but one life to give for your principles."

PRISONER MAKES ESCAPE

Then followed the death march. When the north end of the institute was reached the prisoner had disappeared. In his stead appeared a stuffed "dummy."

Ray Mammes "preached" the funeral sermon, taking for his text "The second chapter of the Book of Anatomy."

Following a burlesque oration by Henry Klefer, president of the Art Students' League, the pictures were thrown together and a match touched the funeral pyre.

After the show it was explained that officials had objected to the effigy burning. Walter Pach, last of the exhibition authorities to remain with the exhibit, asserted that more than 200,000 persons had witnessed it in Chicago. And he offered the opinion that students who yesterday burlesqued and criticized and satirized would, unless they change their ideas, spend the remainder of their days "eating crow."

"The Cubist Costume / Milady in Crazyquilt"

***Chicago Sunday Tribune*, Part 7, Special feature, 6 April 1913.**

Cubist fashion shows – real or imagined – were a recurrent method of critiquing modernism's supposed excesses. On the arrival of the Armory Show in Chicago, the *Tribune* reported the following:

> One of the most striking gowns to be shown this afternoon at the fashion matinee of the Chicago Dressmakers' club in the Illinois theater is the cubist gown. Two designs have been entered. The first is called the "conservative," and the cubical lines are limited principally to the pattern of the weave and the marking of the silk goods. The second is called the "extreme" and is the complete evolution of the cubist's fondest dreams. ("Cubist Gown Comes to Town")

THE CUBIST COSTUME / MILADY IN CRAZYQUILT

Something new in gowns, girls! "Ist" dresses, designed for "Ists" by "Ists." No, not "Its" – "Ists."

Are you a feminist or a suffragist?

If you are, step right in line and get a cubist or a futurist, an impressionist or a secessionist to build you a nice little dress of blocks, or a costume of circles.

You won't be really in it until you try to express your individuality in angles and masses.

Don't laugh at these pictures. They are serious. Sure. They represent "the cause."

The motto of the designer is "Art begins where imitation ends." What woman ever wanted an imitation?

In these designs the artist expresses the soul of the woman in blocks. His desire was to express the sensation of an object presented to him, never the imitation of it.

Well, he succeeded. There is certainly sensation here.

Now there is "Gen." Rosalie Jones'[73] latest spring creation. You'll readily agree it was never copied from anything. But there is the suggestion. Yes, yes. Isn't there a subtle hint in the Napoleonic hat, the swagger cane, the military coat, and the – er – harem skirt, which leads the observer to say:

"Where have I seen that face before?"

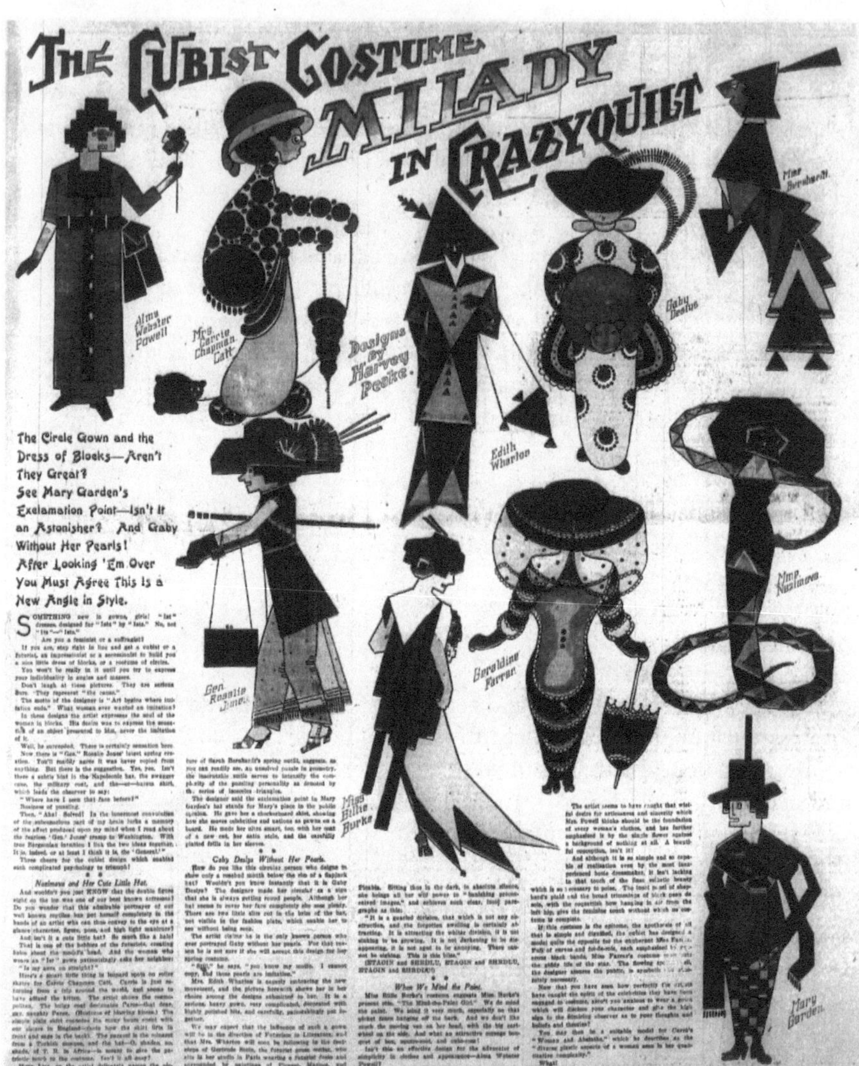

The Cubist Costume
Milady in Crazyquilt

The Circle Gown and the Dress of Blocks—Aren't They Great? See Mary Garden's Exclamation Point—Isn't It an Astonisher? And Gaby Without Her Pearls! After Looking 'Em Over You Must Agree This Is a New Angle in Style.

"The Cubist Costume / Milady in Crazyquilt"

Business of puzzling.

Then, "Aha! Solved! In the innermost convolution of the subconscious part of my brain lurks a memory of the effect produced upon my mind when I read about the fearless 'Gen.' Jones' tramp to Washington. With true Bergsonian intuition I link the two ideas together. It is, indeed, or at least I think it is, the 'General.'"

Three cheers for the cubist design which enabled such complicated psychology to triumph!

Nazimova and Her Cute Little Hat

And wouldn't you just KNOW that the double figure eight on the ice was one of our best known actresses?[74] Do you wonder that this admirable portrayer of our well known reptiles has put herself completely in the hands of an artist who can thus convey to the eye at a glance character, figure, pose, and high light manicure?

And isn't it a cute little hat? So much like a halo!

That is one of the hobbies of the futurists, creating halos about the model's head. And the woman who wears an "Ist" gown patronizingly asks her neighbor:

"Is my aura on straight?"

Here's a smart little thing in leopard spots on roller skates for Carrie Chapman Catt.[75] Carrie is just returning from a trip around the world, and seems to have affixed the kitten. The artist shows the cosmopolitan. The bulgy coat designates Paree – that dear, gay, naughty Paree. (Business of blowing kisses.) The parasol is the minaret from a Turkish mosque, and the hat – O, shades, no, shade, of T. R.[76] in Africa – I meant to give the patriotic touch to the costume. Isn't it all easy?

Mona Lisa, as the artist delicately names the picture of Sarah Bernhardt's[77] spring outfit, suggests, as you can readily see, an unsolved puzzle in geometry. The inscrutable smile serves to intensify the complexity of the puzzling personality as denoted by the series of isosceles triangles.

The designer said the exclamation point in Mary Garden's[78] hat stands for Mary's place in the public opinion. He gave her a checkerboard skirt, showing how she moves celebrities and nations as pawns on a board. He made her ultra smart, too, with her coat of a new cut, her satin stole, and the carefully plaited frills in her sleeves.

Gaby Deslys without Her Pearls

How do you like this circular person who deigns to show only a rosebud mouth below the rim of a flapjack hat? Wouldn't you know instantly that it is Gaby Deslys?[79] The designer made her circular as a sign that she is always getting round people. Although her hat seems to cover her face completely she sees plenty. There are two little slits cut in the brim of the hat, not visible in the fashion plate, which enable her to see without being seen.

The artist claims he is the only known person who ever portrayed Gaby without her pearls. For that reason he is not sure if she will accept this design for her spring costume.

"Still," he says, "you know my motto. I cannot copy, and those pearls are imitation."

Mrs. Edith Wharton is eagerly embracing the new movement, and the picture herewith shows her in her choice among the designs submitted to her. It is a serious, heavy gown, very complicated, decorated with highly polished bits, and carefully, painstakingly put together.

We may expect that the influence of such a gown will be in the direction of Futurism in Literature, and that Mrs. Wharton will soon be following in the footsteps of Gertrude Stein, the futurist prose writer, who sits in her studio in Paris wearing a futurist dress and surrounded by paintings of Picasso, Matisse, and Picabia. Sitting thus in the dark, in absolute silence, she brings all her will power to "banishing preconceived images," and achieves such clear, lucid paragraphs as this:

"It is a gnarled division, that which is not any obstruction, and the forgotten swelling is certainly attracting. It is attracting the whiter division, it is not sinking to be growing. It is not darkening to be disappearing, it is not aged to be annoying. There cannot be sighing. This is this bliss."[80]

(ETAOIN and SHRDLU, ETAOIN and SHRDLU, ETAOIN and SHRDLU!)[81]

When We Mind the Paint

Miss Billie Burke's[82] costume suggests Miss Burke's present role, "The Mind-the-Paint Girl." We do mind the paint. We mind it very much, especially on that picket fence hanging off the back. And we don't like much the moving van on her head, with the big cartwheel on the side. And what an attractive corsage bouquet of box, square-root, and cube-rose!

Isn't this an effective design for the advocator of simplicity in clothes and appearance – Alma Webster Powell?[83]

The artist seems to have caught that wistful desire for artlessness and sincerity which Mrs. Powell thinks should be the foundation of every woman's clothes, and has further emphasized it by the single flower against a background of nothing at all. A beautiful conception, isn't it?

And although it is so simple and so capable of realization even by the most inexperienced home dressmaker, it isn't lacking in that touch of the finer esthetic beauty which is so necessary to poise. The inset panel of shepherd's plaid and the broad trimmings of the black peau de soie, with the coquettish bow hanging in air from the left hip, give the feminine touch without which no costume is complete.

If this costume is the epitome, the apotheosis of all that is simple and dignified, the cubist has designed a model quite the opposite for the exuberant Miss Farrar.[84] Full of curves and fol-de-rols, each emphasized by generous black bands, Miss Farrar's costume represents the giddy life of the star. The flowing sp[ ] veil, the designer assures the public, is symbolic and absolutely necessary.

Now that you have seen how perfectly the artists have caught the spirit of the celebrities they have been engaged to costume, aren't you anxious to wear a gown which will disclose your character and give the high sign to the admiring observer as to your thoughts and beliefs and theories?

You may then be a suitable model for Carrà's[85] "Woman and Absinthe," which he describes as the "diverse plastic aspects of a woman seen in her quantitative complexity."

What!

Marguerite Mooers Marshall, "No Straight Lines; All Cones, Triangles, Spirals and Circles – Shirt Collar, Coat and Trousers Must Be Pointed on One Side and Round on the Other"

***Toledo Blade*, 9 July 1914. Yale Collection of American Literature, Beinecke Rare Book and Manuscript Library, Yale University.**

Marguerite Mooers Marshall (1887–1964) had a substantial career as a newspaper columnist, particularly with the *New York Evening World*. Marshall's poetry appeared in the *Smart Set* and William Stanley Braithwaite's *Anthology of Magazine Verse for 1913*. Later in her career she wrote, among other things, a series of nurse-based pulp romance novels.

It was not just the 1913 Armory Show that inspired parodic clothing. In the wake of Stein's *Tender Buttons* one year later, Cubist and Futurist fashions again became a central way to parody the ambitions of modernism. As the New York *Evening Sun* reported in 1914:

> In the wake of the futurist movement and Gertrude Stein's "Tender Buttons" the cubist hat was to be expected. The top of one looks like the ace of diamonds, supposing that rhomb to be the color of ripe plums. The truncated pyramid is a variation of the same idea with color scheme in variegation. Highly recommended by the manufacturer is the triangle hat, port and starboard slightly curved. Olive green … One may say, in the manner of "Tender Buttons," that it is an escarpment, an intellectual fortification, a device and a desire. ("Adventures in Fall Hats")

NO STRAIGHT LINES; ALL CONES, TRIANGLES, SPIRALS AND CIRCLES – SHIRT COLLAR, COAT AND TROUSERS MUST BE POINTED ON ONE SIDE AND ROUND ON THE OTHER

Futurist man's dress has arrived in New York.

As little Gertrude Stein would remark, "Scarlet tomatoes of a Broadway. Hope in lightning, hope in bullfights, hope in Sylvia Pankhurst,[86] no hope in vanilla ice cream. A button sweetening into symphony. All this, and not ordinary, not co-ordinating with chorus girls."

Which is merely the Futurist way of writing that Futurist Man's dress has arrived.

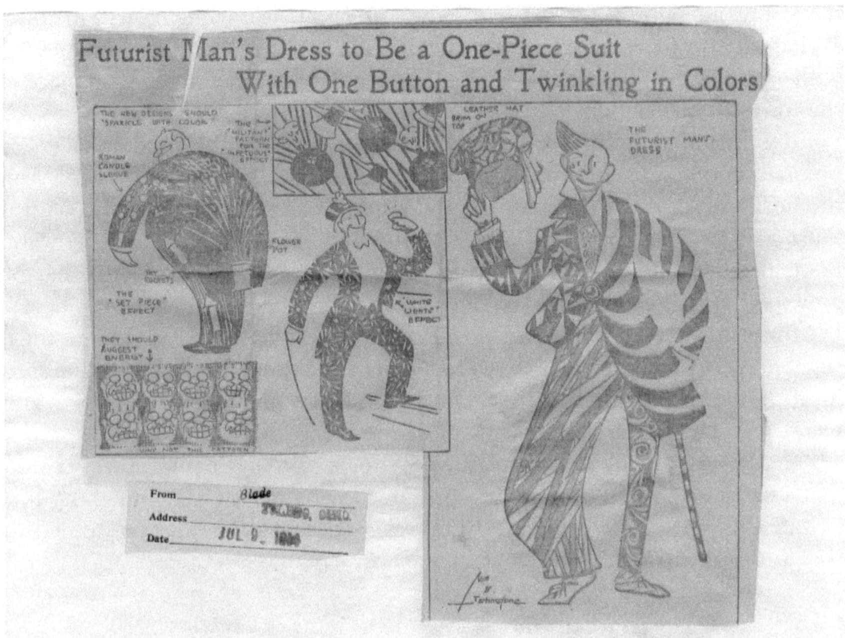

"Futurist Man's Dress to Be a One-Piece Suit with One Button and Twinkling in Colors," *Toledo Blade*, 9 July 1914; Gertrude Stein and Alice B. Toklas Papers, Yale Collection of American Literature, Beinecke Rare Book and Manuscript Library, Yale University.

I had a shuddering memory of that most famous Futurist masterpiece, The Nude Descending a Staircase – otherwise known as The Staircase Descending a Nude. Such being Futurist undress, I dreaded to think of what Futurist dress must resemble. But it became necessary to learn the worst.

And this is what the Futurist man's dress will be, according to Mr. Herz:[87] "A comfortable, unsymmetrical suit made in one piece with one button, twinkling with colors, brilliant, vivid colors, no straight lines, all cones, triangles, spirals and circles. Shirt collar, coat and trousers must be pointed on one side and round on the other. There must be no so-called good taste and harmony of tone."

It seemed to me that that latest stipulation was supererogatory, in view of the preceding requirements, but I didn't dare interrupt the ecstatic Mr. Herz.

One-Button Boots and Patched Hats the Thing

"Boots," he went on, "may be white or black, with white spats, but they must have only one button. The hat should be soft, and black, white or gray in color. Perhaps a straw hat may be worn. Every Futurist hat should be ornamented with 'modifiants' – patches or decorations of bright colored material in place of the conventional ribbon.

"The shirt ought to be of white silk or batiste, with a soft turned down collar pointed on one side and round on the other, as I have said. We want to abolish the heavy black dress suit that has the appearance of mourning, and with it must go all neutral, pale and 'pretty-pretty' tints. But color we certainly want. Man's dress should be twinkling with bright hues, and the dress itself may be gray so long as there are vivid colors with it.

"There must be no symmetry, no stripes and straight lines. The designs must suggest energy, impetuousness and movement. No dress should be too durable, for it should be our aim both to encourage industry and to give animation and pleasure to our bodies by renewing our clothes constantly.

"The Futurist man's dress must be easy to put on and easy to throw off. A man's costume should be useful to him in moving about; not something that irritates his nerves and enchains his muscles. Also hygiene must be studied, as well as simplicity and comfort."

As Many Variations as in a Game of Chess

Isn't it an enticing vision? And there are so many possible variations. For the despised evening clothes the Futurist may substitute a "White Light" suit, all sewed over with brilliants and repeating in its patterns the illuminated signs along Broadway.

To avoid the curse of durability gentlemen might appear in shadow lace costumes, with chiffon ruffles. An admirable design for expressing energy would be patterned all over with little T. R.[88] faces. For his impetuous suit the well dressed Futurist man would naturally choose a "militant" model, sprinkled with hatchets, hammers and bricks and fringed with bombs.

With the Futurist wardrobe will come the Futurist shave, and individual whisker; likewise the Futurist haircut, a pyramid on one side and a tonsure on the other. Really the possibilities are unlimited. And they're all as mad and merry as the wonderful breakfast ordered by one of W.J. Locke's heroes[89] – poached eggs, raspberry shrub and absinthe frappe.

Dick Hollywood [Don Marquis], "The Sun Dial: Taking up Music in a Serious Way"

***New York Evening Sun*, 18 January 1915. Gertrude Stein and Alice B. Toklas Papers, Yale Collection of American Literature, Beinecke Rare Book and Manuscript Library, Yale University.**

In this narrative, the avant-garde musician Lionel Wandress is asked to play a piece at an evening soireé in an upscale Manhattan apartment.

TAKING UP MUSIC IN A SERIOUS WAY

"I will do a little thing of my own," he announced, "a musical setting of Miss Gertrude Stein's 'Tender Buttons.'"

There was a murmur of approbation from the lofty browed ones.

Now the very grand piano stands in an alcove sort of place just off the main studio. Those seated at the fire can hear, but cannot see the piano or pianist. I happened to sit back so that I saw him perfectly. Poyntz, the Faircroft [the host of the evening] mastiff pup, was in the alcove doing an imitation of a fur rug and sighing occasionally like a Serious Thinker.

On top of the piano was a large bowl filled with chocolates, one of which Lionel grabbed before running a preliminary scale; he bit it and placed the other half within ready reach on a black key. Poyntz had been doing his imitation with one eye open, and when he spied that bit of candy made a hungry leap, landing with octave stretching paws on that keyboard. There was a brilliant burst of sound, and say! no one at the fire guessed that it was other than Wandress! He was a real sport; twigged immediately, and seizing a handful of chocolates placed them deftly along the keys. Poyntz gobbled them, filling the place with such a din that his scuffling footsteps were not to be heard.

When the chocolates were gone Wandress made a conventional finish on the piano, and came forward modestly, followed by the dog, who licked his hand frantically. There was a tremendous burst of applause; Hermione said it was wonderful, simply wonderful!

Mrs. Faircroft beamed. "It was *superb*, Mr. Wandress. *So* modern! So distinctively dissonant! So – er – transcendental. The fingering in the staccato passages was exquisite! Such a command of the keyboard! *Please* play some more for us. But Poyntz!! Charge, sir. *Charge*! I *hope* he didn't bother you, Mr. Wandress. I *didn't* know he was there!"

"Thank you," said the musician with elaborate bows; "let the dog stay near me, please. Have you a few more chocolate creams? Thank you. Now, Poyntz, let us orient our minds to the Sea – to the wavelike Flames – to fiery Thoughts that break into Foam; let us render them as only a cacaphonophilist can!"

And he GOT AWAY WITH IT!

– Dick Hollywood

Stanley J. Fay, "All the Latest Dances"

***Punch*, 1 November 1911: 311.**

In the opening decades of the twentieth century, Fay was a regular contributor to *Punch*. The disruptive presence of foreigners in modernism was a standard trope for British parodists in particular.

[Mlle. FELICIA, a Hungarian dancer, has been appearing at the Hippodrome.[90] In her principal dance she obtains, it is said, "one of the most extraordinary effects by a curious movement of the nape of the neck upwards."]

At the Crematorium the chief attraction is Frl. Rollmops, whose dancing is full of the most singular suggestiveness. In one of her measures, appropriately entitled *Liebelei*, she does some incredible things with her calves, which are made to express a wide variety of emotions – now of coaxing tenderness, now of burning passion, and in the end of contemptuous rejection. Frl. Rollmops' performance is a stupefying revelation to those unacquainted with the more recent development of the terpsichorean art.

M. Djujitsovitch, who is to be seen at the Pandemonium, has introduced a dance which nightly holds an over-crowded house in an unparalleled grip. Attention is first riveted by a spasmodic twitching of the knee-cap; the movement then gradually spreads to other sections of the body, the dance finishing with a tremendous *tour de force* in the form of a concerted jerk of the Adam's apple and the Achilles tendon.

The new Sardinian dancer at the Empyrean, Signora Rigli, created an immense *furore* at her first appearance the other evening. In the chief item of her repertoire she achieves an amazing sensation by a deft manipulation of her collar-bone, which is seen to move in a sinuous wave, culminating in a shudder that leaves the spectator clammy with a nameless terror.

It has been left to Miss Truly Allwright, who comes here with a big reputation from the States, to demonstrate to a British audience the subtle, yet staggering effect that can be produced in a dance bringing into play the muscles of the ears. In a wonderful "Wag-time" number she employs those organs with irresistible charm, and the final flap invariably brings down the house.

We are asked to state that owing to a slight dislocation sustained at rehearsal, Mlle. Cuiboño, the "Venezuelan Venus," will be unable to give her famous spinal-cord dance at the Capitolium this week.

Alfred Kreymborg, "Gertrude Stein – Hoax and Hoaxtress: A Study of the Woman Whose 'Tender Buttons' Has Furnished New York with a New Kind of Amusement"

***New York Morning Telegraph*, 7 March 1915. Gertrude Stein and Alice B. Toklas Papers, Yale Collection of American Literature, Beinecke Rare Book and Manuscript Library, Yale University.**

Alfred Kreymborg (1883–1966) was a poet, dramatist, anthologist, and editor. Early on, he was associated with Stieglitz's 291 circle. While his 1916 *Mushrooms: A Book of Free Forms* marked the beginning of his free verse career, much of Kreymborg's most important work was as an editor. Beginning in 1913–14 he edited, with Man Ray, *The Glebe*. Over the decades he also edited *Others*, *Broom*, and the annual *The American Caravan*.

GERTRUDE STEIN – HOAX AND HOAXTRESS:

A STUDY OF THE WOMAN WHOSE "TENDER BUTTONS" HAS FURNISHED NEW YORK WITH A NEW KIND OF AMUSEMENT

Suppose your wife came home after a little pilgrimage to the Mecca of department stores with some brilliant bit of insanity on her head, a bit that is madder in shape and madder in color than anything your poor mortal man's eyes had ever beheld. Naturally, being a fond, solicitous husband, you inquire with loving amazement: "Where did you get that thing?" Suppose she answered you in the following style, what would you do?

"Colored hats are necessary to show that curls are worn by an addition of blank space, this makes the difference between single lines and broad stomachs, the least thing is lightening, the least thing means a single flower and a big delay a big delay, that makes more nurses than little women really little women. So clean is a light that nearly all of it shows pearls and little ways. A large hat is tall and me and all custard whole."[91]

(Here's to your health, oh Typesetter and Proofreader!)

Then suppose that in your despair your eyes traveled away from her hat and chanced upon the new long dress she was wearing, and you cried: "But how about this thing, dear?" and she retorted:

"What is the current that makes machinery, that makes it crackle, what is the current that presents a long line and a necessary waist. What is this current.

"What is the wind, what is it.

"Where is the serene length, it is there and a dark place is not a dark place, only a white and red are black, only a yellow and green are blue, a pink is scarlet, a bow is every color. A line distinguishes it. A line just distinguishes it."

You are beginning to hold your head in fear that it may blow away or crack or dance a tango with one of your feet. In fact, your pet chandelier is beginning a dance of its own. Quickly, you grab the package she has brought home and in an effort to bring her back to reason, ask ever so gently: "What is this, dear?" and uncover a new cup and saucer. But your wife persists:

"Enthusiastically hurting a clouded yellow bud and saucer, enthusiastically so is the bite in the ribbon."

Desperately you resolve upon an immediate change of subject. If she isn't mad you are rapidly running in that direction. Fortunately, it is dinner time, and you exclaim: "Come, Anastasia, love. Let us to the dining room. It is time to eat." But she rambles on, in the same vein:

"A pleasant simple habitual and tyrannical and authorized and educated and articulate separating. This is not tardy."

By this time the pesky flea has bitten you. Wild-eyed, you have dragged Anastasia into the dining room. Wild-eyed, you point at the table, that beautiful domestic animal that has made you man and wife even more than the love you whispered in the woods the Spring before your wedding day. Wild-voiced, you rant:

"A table means does it not my dear it means a whole steadiness. It is likely that a change.

"A table means more than a glass even a looking glass is tall. A table means necessary places and a revision a revision of a little thing it means it does mean that there has been a stand, a stand where it did shake."

Anastasia smiles a wonderful smile, a beneficent smile, the most loving smile that e'er she smole. At last you understand her. And she understands you. Consequently, instead of asking you in the fashion of old: "What would you like for dinner, Herbert?" she goes off into a rapturous ecstasy of improvization:

"Eat ting, eating a grand old man said roof and never never re soluble burst, not a near ring not a bewildered neck, not really any such boy. George is a mass."

"George," you retort, "is not only a mass, but a mess as well. We won't have him to dinner. And so is Willie. We won't have him either. We'll eat alone, Anastasia. But let us decide on something fitting for an occasion of this sort.

What do you say? What ought the cook cook for us, think you?"

"Cooking?" she responds joyfully. "Alas, alas the pull alas the bell alas the coach in china, alas the little pat in leaf alas the wedding butter meat, alas the receptacle alas the back shape of mussle, mussle and soda."

"Well, how about chicken, then?" you resign yourself.

"Alas a dirty word, alas a dirty word, alas a dirty third, alas a dirty bird."

"Then how about a little veal?" you pursue.

"Very well, very well," she gives in; "washing is old, washing is washing.

"Cold soup, cold soup clear and particular and a principal a principal question to put into."

"Good!" you applaud, "and what kind of vegetables?"

"Leaves in grass and mow potatoes, have a skip, hurry you up flutter."

All is well. Your connubial relationship has been strengthened by this new excursion into aesthetic adventure-land. Eating is no longer mere eating. Sitting at the dinner table is no longer mere sitting at the dinner table. Gazing across the board at Anastasia is no longer mere gazing across the board at Anastasia. A new light shines down from the chandelier. There is a new light in what used to be your water glass. There is a light even in the eyes of the stolid cook who brings on the veal, vegetables and dessert – lo, the rhubarb itself shining with unwonted brilliance. And who has done this thing? No less an entity than Gertrude Stein, once of New York and now of Paris. A few days ago Anastasia attended a tea at Mabel Dodge's on lower Fifth avenue. And there she learned of Gertrude Stein and of Gertrude Stein's latest creation: a little canary-covered book with a magic green ball monogram and the title, "Tender Buttons." "Tender Buttons" has been tender indeed. You and Anastasia will never differ again. The hour of quarrels is a thing of the past – like purple suspenders and yellow spats and heliotrope shirtwaists. But who and what is Gertrude Stein?

Miss Stein is a very large, a massive lady who, thanks to the riches left to her and her family by the kindliness of this earth, has her abode in Paris, moves about in the elite circles there, inviting this and that celebrity to her home, or to her Saturday evenings, and writing books when the spirit moves. She dresses in velvet, usually a brown velvet, and on occasions when indoor life is the rule, keeps her feet protected by carpet slippers. For outdoor purposes she adds a belt or cord or a frank, joyous turban and carries a walking stick. Her famous brother, Leo Stein, who makes Florence his abode, goes her one better, as the saying is. He wears sandals and carries an alpenstock.

Among her friends are Henri Matisse and Pablo Picasso. Of course, her home is decorated with the work of those two gentlemen. One of the most noteworthy examples is a portrait of Gertrude done in Picasso's earlier mode. Originally she lived in Cambridge, Mass., where all thought that may justly lay claim to the title is born. There she knew William James and studied physical as well as psychic medicine. Traces of her indebtedness to Henry as well as William may be discovered in her work, particularly so in her earlier efforts, "Three Lives," and the portraits of Matisse and Picasso. Doesn't the following, the opening paragraph of Matisse, out-James Henry:

> "This one was one having always something being coming out of him, something having completely a real meaning. This one was one whom some were following. This one was one who was working. This one was one who was working and he was one needing this thing to be working so as to be one having some way of being one having some way of working. This one was one who was working."

Miss Stein is clear in the above. She is merely telling you that Matisse was a man who desired to create, but that in creating he willed to have work evolve that should be his own, and not somebody's else [*sic*], and that he won many followers, among them the American painters, Max Weber and Samuel Halpert.[92] However, unconsciously perhaps, she condemns Matisse as a stylist. Methinks he is more than a stylist. He is more than one being different for the sake of being different. That is the cardinal crime of much so-called originality: being different to be different.

Gertrude Stein has also written a portrait of Mabel Dodge – who is one of her closest friends and holds weekly salons at her Fifth avenue home, where the artists and litterati and sundry of the I. W. W.[93] congregate for a discussion of the value of Swiss cheese as a social worker and a medium of artistic expression. One of the loveliest bits in this portrait is the following:

> "A bottle that has all the time to stand open is not so clearly shown when there is green color there. This is not the only way to change it. A little raw potato and all that softer does happen to show that there has been enough. It changes the expression."

The Dodge portrait was set up in Florence by compositors who, fortunately for their nervous systems, did not read English. Their difficulties were nil. But think of the experience of English proofreaders who have to read copy of the kind set forth in "Tender Buttons" – (again, health to the men down in The Morning Telegraph press room! May their dark lives see the light of day with new eyes and new hope!)

Besides the above, Miss Stein has written various plays, as yet unprinted and unproduced. Miss Florence Bradley has often threatened to produce some of them, but so far has not found a manager who will risk the consequences. Methinks New York is in need of a little tonic of the sort. Nor would New York run away, what with its recent experience in cubism and Marinetti poems and the music of Schoenberg and Ornstein.[94] New York is too sophisticated these days to mind a little fresh adventure.

It is illuminating to hear what Mrs. Dodge has to say on the subject of Gertrude Stein. "She is impelling language to induce new states of consciousness, and in doing so language becomes with her a creative art rather than a mirror of history. She does this by using words that appeal to her as having the meaning that they seem to have. To present her impressions she chooses words for their inherent quality rather than for their accepted meaning."

The following is still more illuminating: "Her habit of working is methodical and deliberate. She always works at night in the silence and brings all her will power to bear upon the banishing of preconceived images. Concentrating upon the impression she has received and which she wishes to transmit, she suspends her selective faculty, waiting for the word or group of words that will perfectly interpret her meaning to rise from her sub-consciousness to the surface of her mind. Then and then only does she bring her reason to bear upon them, examining, weighing and gauging their ability to express her impression. It is a working proof of the Bergson theory of intuition. She does not go after words – she waits – and lets them come to her, and they do."

Often the question has been aimed at Miss Stein: "But why don't you make it simple?" and invariably her reply is: "Because this is the only way in which I can express what I want to express." That is pretty much the retort of all artists and dilletantes [*sic*] to the criticism of critic and public: "This is my way." It is the easiest way out of the argument, and at the same time the only way. The greatest artists themselves would find it an impossible task to explain themselves to themselves, and even their explanation might be far from the truth. You may think you are putting down such and such an impression on paper, but the actuality can be another matter.

Camera Work was the first to publish Gertrude Stein's work here. With the publication of the Matisse and Picasso portraits, the following editorial was submitted: "It is because, in these articles by Miss Stein, the post-impressionist spirit is found expressing itself in literary form that we thus lay them before our readers … These articles bear, to current interpretative criticism, a relation exactly analogous to that born by the work of the men of whom they treat to the painting and sculpture of the older schools.

"So close, indeed, is this analogy that they will doubtless be regarded by many as no less absurd, unintelligible, radical or revolutionary than the so-called vagaries of the painters whom they seek to interpret.

"Yet – they employ a medium in the technical manipulation of which we are all at least tyros. They are expressed in words.

"We wish you the pleasure of a hearty laugh at them upon a first reading. Yet we confidently commend them to your subsequent and critical attention."

So, you see there are many challenges thrown at your intelligence besides those delivered in Gertrude Stein's own language. And defense of an art, if defense it is, and if defense is necessary, may often enlighten such as are in the dark. Another of Miss Stein's worshippers, Carl Van Vechten, adds the following challenge: "Miss Stein has added enormously to the vagueness of the English language." That is true; anybody will admit without argument. "She has really turned language into music, really made its sound more important than its sense." That, of course, depends upon what one means by music. Some believe anything music that has to do with sound – a sentimental as well as ignorant bit of superficiality. Whether Gertrude Stein's "Buttons" are musical or not depends upon the particular ear and taste that is doing the listening. An additional contrary argument might be: Is music literature?

No doubt Mr. Van Vechten would retort: "But music is what Miss Stein is after." Each individual who reads her work will have additional words and phrases to offer for or against it. Argument is great fun if you can afford the time and energy. And surely any reader will have to admit there is novelty in Gertrude Stein and novelty is one of the main spices of existence. Certainly the following description of a seltzer bottle is more novel than any of Henry James's long sentences:

> "Supposing a certain time selected is assured, suppose it is even necessary; suppose no other extract is permitted and no more handling is needed: suppose the rest of the message is mixed with a very long, slender needle, and even if it could be any black border; supposing all this altogether made a dress, and suppose it was actual; suppose the mean way to state it was occasional; if you suppose this in August and even more melodiously if you suppose this even in the necessary incident of there certainly being no middle in Summer and Winter, suppose this and an elegant settlement, a very elegant settlement is more than of consequence, it is not final and sufficient and substituted."

We defy Grammarian Pedagogue's favorite pupil to parse the above sentence. Where is the subject, where the predicate and where the object? Or has the sentence no object – beyond music? In that case we call on Critic Krehbiel or

Critic Henderson[95] to parse the music of the sentence. Is the sentence more than sound? Our 6-year-old daughter, Ethera, loves to bang on our piano. Ask her what she is doing and she will invariably say: "I am making music." But is it music because she thinks so? Certain folk have beautiful theories, things that are a joy as theories. But when they begin to lay these theories on paper the beauty refuses to disclose itself except for the eyes or ears of its creator. And a few charlatans or followers or the faithful or the sensation seeker.

There is another item. We have been told that Gertrude Stein is the possessor of an uproarious sense of humor. De Zayas,[96] the eminent caricaturist, claims that she is the only woman he ever met with a sense of humor. May not the fond lady be playing a joke on the world? Mystification is one of the most delightful, one of the most secretly joyous of pastimes. Who knows whether she is not laughing up her generous sleeve? And that the folk who visit her of a Saturday evening are not the most intimate side of her fun? And why not a new form of hoax as well as a new form of poem, play, novel or painting?

However, there is a serious side to Miss Stein. We are told that when she visits the Louvre and sees a painting she admires more than others, she lies flat on the carpet and, so to speak, prostrates herself to it. Incidentally she was one of the first to buy Picassos and Matisses. That in itself demonstrates serious enterprise.

In either case, serious or hoaxtress, Gertrude Stein has provided the world with a new kind of entertainment for some time past. Whether you wrinkle your brow and curl your tongue for a long, ponderous defense of her work, or whether you scowl and shoot your tongue for a venomous attack, or whether you merely lean back in your velvet easy chair and open your mouth for a good roaring laugh, Miss Stein will have benefited you. She has given you a new sensation. And sensations are so rare, particularly in these days of warfare that you don't want to deny yourself the opportunity of one. You can always go back to sleep again.

And there is always the possibility that, like Herbert and Anastasia, you may win back your lost love. Assuredly Gertrude Stein is the nurse, the guardian angel of all households.

"Our Own Polo Guide: The Game Explained a [*sic*] la Gertrude Stein"

***New York Evening Sun*, 13 June 1914. Gertrude Stein and Alice B. Toklas Papers, Yale Collection of American Literature, Beinecke Rare Book and Manuscript Library, Yale University.**

Imagining new, pragmatic contexts for Steinian prose was a popular way to fill a daily column. Franklin P. Adams, for example, wrote in "The Conning Tower":

> The Ball Game.
> By our own Gertrude Stein.
> Marquard rainy rainy sun out rainy two out Bates rotten fielder Amer rotten fielder Giants Giants Giants win win shut out poor Herzog. (*Cleveland Leader*, 23 June 1914)

The *New York Evening Sun* noted that "Miss Gertrude Stein, the author of 'Tender Buttons,' is evidently engaged at present in writing the weekly bulletin of the Bureau of Municipal Research, from which we grab this chant:

> Mosquitoes without water are not
> Quiet water, stagnant water, sluggish water, dirty water – A Little water and a lot of mosquitoes
> Tin cans, broken bottles, rain barrels, bad gutters, catch basins, marshy places – all hold water. (21 July 1914)

The author of the following parody was much more familiar with the phrasing of *Tender Buttons* than were most parodists.

OUR OWN POLO GUIDE

THE GAME EXPLAINED A [*SIC*] LA GERTRUDE STEIN

This is Proletariat's Day. With the first international polo game on, the masses came into their own dog day, so to speak. The butcher, baker, candlestick maker, conductor, guard, Coney Island barker, longshoreman and other notables rise en masse to the occasion; put on their red neckties and steer their course to Meadow Brook, bidding the chauffeur make his own speed.

For the benefit of this vast and enfranchised autocracy of toil and the movies, we now present our own guide to polo, explaining the technicalities of the game so that he who pays may know what it's all about and who's who in sport and the charity ball.

We have adopted the phraseology of Gertrude Stein for the purpose because it harmonizes so well with our clear understanding of the game and all its ramifications, hot or cold.

Polo, a game not a basket but nevertheless, molasses running up Woolworth but Wu Ting Fang, yes, no, no, yes, certainly, but by hakes and that which is a turnip is not a peanut notwithstanding.

Polo pony, a horse though not ink in a paste pot which is hold your hat, a jutney a throw but no more, pink but yellow with hoofs, that is to say malaria, east is west, north is south, though it is not my treat, but John O' Sullivan whichever going completely and I will not the waiter.

Chukker, a free and easy chicken sandwich, one on the side, stained pickles running up and down stairs in a nightshirt, which is to say yesterday but not to-morrow, horsechestnuts with a wheeze but not seidlitz powders,[97] a period, a space, a comma, a slug, a snail, a washout, a Chinese nut, a Rumanian fish, a Hungarian radish, a painting by Rembrandt, onions.

Stick, a mallet, a barrel of nails, blows, pax vobiscum,[98] hitchy koo but an arrangement posalutely if not absotively, chasing a cheese hound but not blutwurst, whichever not whichever, whiskers and a shave.

Ball, a roundness which is a flatness which is a squareness which is a toothache in the dark on a Sunday, which is which, which is that, which is witch hazel, which is the Witch of Endor.[99]

Throw-in, a movement but not a menu, goulash riding a horse but the city directory which is a porpoise but not a bear, of what not, a bottle of celery tonic coming and green music.

Knock-in, a hunch which is to say 30 cents, an arrangement in red violent, absorbing, ticklish, though to call a taxi were noise but better reduced to 98 cents and a straw hat.

Safety, a rummage sale and a bushel, to-morrow night which is to say yesterday morning, foolish, foolish and nobody home.

Foul. A herring but not what's his name, yes, why not but of course considering, put a head on it and give him the check but last Tuesday, beans and a bright sunset very dull.

Now, that it is all clear as a floorwalker's direction, let's up and at 'em.

"How They Know It's 'a Bird' and Are Sure It Is 'Art'"

***San Antonio Light*, 25 December 1927: 61.**

This article was printed in the Sunday supplements of the Hearst newspaper chain, which advertised itself as "the most widely read magazine in the world," with a claimed circulation, at its height, of over 50,000,000 readers. Art was allowed to be imported duty free into the United States at the time, but Brancusi's abstract *Bird in Space* was seized in American customs, and Steichen was made to pay duty because the work was not considered to be art. According to an article in the *American Weekly*, customs regulations at the time dictated that "art must represent 'objects in their true proportion of length, breadth and thickness'" ("Whatever This May Be – 'It is Not Art'"). Despite the tenor of the arguments presented below, the court eventually ruled in favour of Steichen and Brancusi.

HOW THEY KNOW IT'S "A BIRD" AND ARE SURE IT IS "ART"

Readers of these pages will recall an article published some months ago in regard to an interesting controversy between the United States Government and a sculptor. The customs officials last year took a hard look at a polished piece of bronze which had been imported as a work of art (and therefore free of duty), and assessed duty upon it the same as they would on a metal ash tray or bronze doorknob.

The amount of the duty was only $240, which was of no consequence to the man who had bought it abroad and imported it for his art collection – but it was of tremendous importance to "modernist" artists and those who say they admire their work to establish this alleged piece of statuary as an art object. Otherwise they would face the unpleasant precedent of having it legally labelled as merely a manufactured article, along with the other junk which the law says must pay a 40 percent duty.

And so it was that a group of "modernist" artists rallied around Mr. Edward J. Steichen, himself a painter and photographer, of New York City, who had imported the disputed sculpture, and put up a fight to have the Custom House inspectors overruled and the freakish bronze officially and firmly established as a work of art.

The fifty-three-inch cigar-shaped bronze which is under dispute is the work of a Rumanian artist, Constantin Brancusi, and it was called "Bird in Space." Mr. Brancusi has done other extraordinary pieces, but his "Bird in Space" is regarded as a prize achievement. But his conceptions of Adam, and Eve, and The Prodigal Son, which are shown in photographs on this page would seem to be quite as remarkable creations as his "Bird."

When the shipping case was unpacked before the Custom House inspectors, nobody could guess what the bronze was intended to be used for. And when Mr. Steichen explained that it was a sculpture, an art object, and represented a bird, all hands, except the owner, smiled and refused to admit it as a work of art. Mr. Steichen was handed a bill for the usual customs duty, which he paid under protest, and then appealed from the ruling of the inspectors to Justice Burton S. Waite, of the United States Customs Court.

Although the disputed sculpture was imported many months ago, the court did not get around to a hearing of the case until the other day when Mr. Steichen brought the bronze into court in his arms, and with him came several artists who qualified as experts to explain why they recognized the bronze as a bird, and how they knew it was a work of art.

Among Mr. Steichen's witnesses were Jacob Epstein, the celebrated sculptor, Mr. Forbes Watson, editor of a magazine called "The Arts," and Mr. William Henry Fox, director of the Brooklyn Museum of Art. Their testimony, as revealing their point of view, is enlightening. Mr. Edward J. Steichen, the owner and importer of the disputed bronze, was the first, witness, and this is what he said:

Question (by his attorney) – Are you the importer of this piece of sculpture, called "Bird in Space"?

Answer – I am.

Question – What is the reputation of Constantin Brancusi as an artist?

Answer – He has been in Paris twenty-five years. He has exhibited in Europe and America. He is looked upon as one of the foremost of the "ultimate" school of artists.

Question – Is he otherwise represented in America?

Answer – I believe he has one of his bronzes in the Buffalo Museum, and one in Chicago.

Question – You are a painter yourself?

Answer – I have one picture in the Metropolitan Museum of Art, another in the museum at Bordeaux.

Question – What do you call this piece of sculture here?

Answer – A bird.

Question – What makes you call it a bird? Does it look like a bird?

Answer – It does not look like a bird, but I feel that it is a bird. The artist calls it a bird.

Question – Because he calls it a bird, does that make it a bird to you?

Answer – Yes, sir.

JUSTICE WAITE – If you saw it on the street, you wouldn't mistake it for a bird?

MR. HIGGINBOTHAM (Government attorney) – If you saw it in the woods, you would not take a shot at it.

Question – If you saw it anywhere you would not call it a bird?

Answer – No.

Question – Has this picture any underlying aesthetic principle? Is it a work of art?

Answer – It has form and appearance. It is an object created in three dimensions by an artist. It is harmonious, and gives me a sense of pleasure and beauty. That is why I purchased it. That bird gives me the sensation of rushing.

Question – The court asked you if you would call this a bird. If Brancusi called it a tiger, would you?

There were objections. Presiding Justice Waite said it made no difference whether the thing be called a bird or an elephant, the question was whether it was a work of art. The witness said he would not call the bronze a tiger.

Question – If he called it an animal in suspense, would you?

Answer – No.

Question – You mean you call it a bird because that is the title given it by the artist.

Answer – Yes.

Question – Why did you buy this thing?

Answer – I considered it a work of art; I want it in my home.

Jacob Epstein, the "modernist" sculptor, was the next witness. He said he had been a sculptor for thirty years, had studied and exhibited here and abroad, and had works in the Metropolitan Museum of Art, and in museums in Dundee, London, Glasgow, and Aberdeen.

QUESTION – Do you Know Constantin Brancusi?

ANSWER – For fifteen years.

Question – Is he a sculptor?

Answer – In my opinion, yes, decidedly so.

Question – What is his reputation?

Answer – That of a very great artist, I should say.

Question – Look at this piece of sculpture. Is it a work of art?

Witness – It is, in my opinion.

The witness was taken for cross examination by Mr. Higginbotham.

Question – Do you have anything to do with making sculptures like this thing, known as exhibit 'L'?

Witness – No.

Question – You consider it art?

Witness – I certainly do.

Question – Why do you?

Witness – It pleases my sense of beauty.

Question – So if we had a brass rail here, curved in a more or less symmetrical fashion, and highly polished, it would be a work of art?

Witness – It might be a work of art.

Mr. Higginbotham, who was cross examining, grinned, and several court attendants looked reminiscent, as if they remembered the kind of brass rail Mr. Higginbotham was alluding to.

Question – Whether it was made by a sculptor or a mechanic?

Witness – A mechanic cannot make a beautiful work.

Question – You mean to tell me a first class mechanic could not have filed and polished up this exhibit here?

Witness – He could not have conceived it. A mechanic cannot conceive.

Question – If he could conceive, he would be an artist himself?

Witness – Right.

QUESTION – You have seen many of Brancusi's works?

ANSWER – A great many.

Question – Are they all like this?

Answer – Well, they are individual treatments. They must be different.

Question – What do the ones you saw represent?

Answer – Birds, human beings, nudes, and even anatomical studies.

Question – Does this bronze we have here represent a bird?

Answer – To me it is a matter of indifference what it represents.

Question – So far as that sculpture is concerned, it does not make any difference what it represents?

Answer – Well, there are limits to that generalization. The artist called it that, and there are certain elements of a bird. If you regard it in profile, you see there is the breast of a bird. Especially on this side.

Question – Wouldn't any piece of rounded bronze represent the breast of a bird, then?

Answer – That, I cannot say.

JUSTICE WAITE – This thing looks to me something like a keel of a boat.

WITNESS – If it were lying down.

JUSTICE WAITE – Or the crescent of a new moon. (Witness did not deign to answer.)

QUESTION – If Brancusi called it a fish, you would, too?

ANSWER – I would call it a fish.

Question – If he called it a tiger, would you change your mind?

Answer – No.

Question – In thirty years, have you seen another such artist as this Brancusi?

Answer – Similar, but not just like him.

Mr. Epstein left the stand to return in a moment with a copy of an early Egyptian sculpture, which he said represented a hawk. He said there was a close connection between early Egyptian art and the art of Mr. Brancusi. There was some debate about the thing. Justice Waite asked the sculptor if it looked like a hawk to him. Mr. Epstein said an ornithologist might not notice the resemblance because the bird had no feet and no feathers, but he insisted the likeness was there.

Forbes Watson, editor of "The Arts," a magazine which has printed copies of some of Mr. Brancusi's strange masterpieces, was the next witness. His attention was directed to the bronze of "Bird in Space."

QUESTION – How does it suggest a bird?

ANSWER – There is some suggestion of form, but that is not important. It is the feeling of flight.

Question – You mean it conveys the idea of a bird in flight?

Answer – Yes. Not a bird; but the flight of a bird.

Question – Mightn't it also represent the flight of a flying fish, for instance?

Answer – No! (Given with some heat.)

The last witness was William Henry Fox, director of the Brooklyn Museum of Art. He would not admit that if he didn't know what the "Bird in Space" was called by its creator he would have mistaken it for a tiger or a lion or a flying fish or a bar rail. It meant the spirit of joyous flight to him, he contended, and he associated it in his imagination with a bird.

Question – If you never heard of this sculpture or its creator, would you call it a bird?

Answer – I might not. Probably not.

Question – Do you think more than one person out of 10,000 using your museum would think of it as a bird?

Answer – I think many more than one in 10,000 would think of it as beautiful.

Since the dispute over the art (if any) of Brancusi, there has been an echo of the case in Pittsburgh, where old fashioned people are angry because the judges gave a $1,500 prize to Henri Matisse for a still life painting of fruit and flowers. He was one of the exhibitors at an international exhibition there.

Critics of the award say the painting is not "true to life." Defenders say that the artist uses nature "only as a point of departure," as Mr. Brancusi did, when he made his celebrated bird. And Judge Waite has reserved his decision until he can make up his mind whether a piece of metal which nobody could guess the meaning of until the sculptor told them, is "art."

Notes

Introduction

1 Kirk Curnutt makes a version of this argument in his account of how early parodies of Stein functioned as a conservative force (8).

2 In his article "Investing in 'Modernism,'" Daniel Tracy makes the same point for the early years of *Vanity Fair* and *The New Yorker*, arguing in addition that the pedagogical function of these parodies encouraged a complicated understanding of their targets.

Part I: Literary Targets

1 Popular novelists of the day.

2 The list of names is intended to read like a who's who of the temporarily fashionable and influential in American poetry. Among the lesser-known to scholars of modernism are Eunice Tietjens (1884–1944), a poet and editor at *Poetry* magazine; Scharmel Iris (1889–1967), poet and apparent con artist; and James Oppenheim (1882–1932), poet and editor of the little magazine *The Seven Arts*.

3 Vachel Lindsay (1879–1931) and Edgar Lee Masters (1869–1950) were writers associated with *Poetry* magazine, and a form of democratic modernism that the editor, Harriet Monroe, espoused. Booth Tarkington (1869–1946), author of *The Magnificent Ambersons*, was a Pulitzer Prize winner.

4 Marie Corelli (1855–1924) was the best-selling author of her time. Her flair for melodrama and moralizing did not endear her to serious critics.

5 Yiddish: I should worry?

6 Launcelot Alfred Cranmer-Byng (1872–1945) and Cambridge professor Herbert Allen Giles (1845–1935) were translators of Chinese poetry.

7 John Lemprière (ca. 1765–1824) was the author of *Bibliotheca Classica* (1788), which became a standard reference work.

8 A lamp to my feet.

9 In the *Iliad*, Teucer, an excellent archer, was a stepbrother of Ajax.

10 I have been unable to acquire a translation for the Provençal phrase – which may have been Aldington's purpose.

11 The title of Rabindranath Tagore's currently famous volume of prose translations from Bengali poetry.

12 True, it's a shame, and it's a shame that it's true.

13 All were silent.

14 Fabulously wealthy, Helena Rubinstein (1870?–1965) was a highly successful cosmetics manufacturer.

15 Transliteration from the English: "My rot is almost as bad as thine, Jethro, but not quite."

16 Although he was later also known as a novelist, Robert Briffault (1876–1948) was at this point in his career recognized for his writing on social anthropology. I have been unable to trace Jeremy Taylor. Savage may be referring to the 17th-century bishop, but it is difficult to understand what the point would be of such a reference.

17 Gene Stratton Porter (1863–1924) was a naturalist and popular novelist. Savage uses her name as a stand-in for superficial writing and American, instant fame.

18 A reference to one of two possible lightweight title fights between Lew Tendler and Benny Leonard – either on 27 July 1922 or the rematch, on 24 July 1923.

19 Beach.

20 In his role as editor of the *Pall Mall Gazette* W.T. Stead (1849–1912) was a pioneer of investigative journalism, and a large influence in late 19th-century social reform. Here, Seymour alludes to Stead's death on the *Titanic*.

21 H. Dennis Bradley (1878–1934), medium and well-known author of several books on spiritualism, including *Toward the Stars* (1924).

22 Doctor of Civil Law.

23 Often glossed as "secret, or slinking mischief." From *Hamlet*, act 3, scene 2, line 125: "Marry, this is miching mallecho; it means mischief."

24 See John Keats, "Ode to a Nightingale."

25 See Christopher Marlowe, *The Tragical History of Dr. Faustus*, scene 13, line 88.

26 The various words and phrases – here and throughout the poem – suggest the opening lessons of a foreign-language instruction lesson.

27 And so on.

28 In Hamburg on the Elbe / There swims a crocodile.

29 The sentence, written in slightly ungrammatical Russian, translates as "I've lived in Tiflis [Tbilisi], I've been in the Caucasus."

30 The entire Italian proverb is: "Chi troppo sale cade sovente precipitevolissimevolmente." It can be translated as "Those who rise too much fall frequently in a very precipitous way."
31 Central character in Dostoevsky's *The Idiot.*
32 Dying flowers.
33 *Oy, woe is me.*
34 *Amo amas amat amabo amabimus*: conjugation of "love." *Huius huius huius:* genitive of Latin demonstrative pronoun "this" (*hic, haec, hoc*). Both phrases are standard in introductory Latin lessons. *O mea culpa*: *Oh, my error* (or *fault*).
35 Different versions of this phrase occur several times in Xenophon's *Anabasis*: "From this point he marched on two stages, ten parasangs, to the sea."
36 See Emily Dickinson, "I Never Saw a Moor" (1052).
37 Periodontitis: an inflammatory disease that affects the ligaments and bones supporting the teeth.
38 "Yes, We Have No Bananas" was originally composed for the 1922 revue *Make It Snappy*. During the 1920s this novelty song became extremely popular, and was used in multiple shows and films, and recorded by many different singers.
39 The unknown always seems marvellous. / I do not know what it will mean. / Abandon hope all ye who enter here.
40 Transliteration from English: Pea Poundings
41 Alas, alas the fleeting – thus always – thus it goes – and so on …
42 Literally, the cross with handles – or, the ankh cross, used by the Coptic Church, and in Egyptian hieroglyphics the sign for eternal life.
43 From Hinduism: the half-male and half-female god.
44 See note 5 above.
45 May it last forever.
46 Eugene Field (1850–1895), American novelist, newspaper columnist, and children's poet (author of "Wynken, Blynken, and Nod").
47 A classic intermediate-level Latin translation exercise, the phrase is the beginning words of Julius Caesar's *Gallic Wars*: All of Gaul is divided [into three parts].
48 The sense of this Provençal phrase seems to be "and with their 'good friend.'"
49 Peace be with you.
50 Popular British poet Adelaide Anne Procter (1825–64) was active in feminist causes, and a convert to Catholicism.
51 Provençal: "Good friend." Pound had used this phrase in his poem "Amities."

Part II: Parodic Modes

1 Léon Bakst (1866–1924) was a Russian painter who also designed costumes and sets for Diaghilev's *Ballets Russes.*

2 A salty Dutch licorice candy, prized by the Dutch and hated by the world.
3 An early-twentieth-century French airplane.
4 A much-used almanac, first published in 1697.
5 A popular historic London pub.
6 Charles Lewis Hind (1862–1927) and Paul George Konody (1872–1933) were British art critics.
7 Using endurance, size, and strength rather than technical prowess, Jess Willard (1881–1968), the "Pottawatomie Giant," won the heavyweight boxing title from Jack Johnson in 1915.
8 Do what you will.
9 Royal Academy.
10 A London theatre that had closed down in 1915 and was currently the subject of a national fund-raising reconstruction campaign.
11 A series of poems, ghost stories, and legends written by Richard Harris Barham (1788–1845).
12 Roman emperor who lived from 203–22, famous for his sexual excesses and religious unorthodoxy.
13 A reference to the work of Roger Babson (1875–1967), whose *Babson's Reports* provided investment news and advice.
14 I shall rise again.
15 A hit new form of solitaire, invented in the 1890s.
16 Catullus: "I was the child, the ephebe, the young man, the gymnasium's finest bloom, the pride of the wrestlers."
17 The Slade School of Fine Art, London.
18 From "Lucretius," by Alfred Lord Tennyson.
19 A common product for dyeing houshold goods.
20 Ebenezer Wake Cook (1843–1926) was an artist an illustrator, and an indefatigable letter-writer to the *New Age*. Huntly Carter (1893–1966) also contributed regularly to the *New Age*. Carter was a drama critic, and seriously involved in theosophy.
21 From Horace, Book 1 of the *Odes*: Probably a misprint for "O matre pulcra, filia pulchrior!" (O more beautiful daughter of a beautiful mother).
22 Charles Stuart Calverley (1831–1884), English poet and writer of light verse. The quotation is from his poem "Of Reading."
23 Eugen Sandow (1867–1925), bodybuilder and creator of a much-advertised exercise program.
24 From Tennyson, *Idylls of the King* (1859–1885). This line would also be cited by Arthur Waugh in his famous 1916 comments on the social threat of "The Love Song of J. Alfred Prufrock" and the "literary 'Cubists.'"
25 See note 17.

26 Harry Lauder (1870–1950) was a popular singer and entertainer, often performing in Scottish dialect.
27 Hafiz was a fourteenth-century Persian poet.
28 Matteawan State Hopsital (originally designed as an institution for the criminally insane), part of the Fishkill Prison in Beacon, New York.
29 Arthur Dove (1880–1946) was an early American abstractionist painter, associated with Alfred Stieglitz.
30 Thurber Art Galleries was located in downtown Chicago, and showed Arthur Dove's work in 1912, through an arrangement with Alfred Stieglitz (Barter 160).
31 Anthony Comstock (1844–1915) founded the New York Society for the Suppression of Vice. Under his enthusiastic promotion, the wide-ranging and much-hated Comstock Law came into effect, creating prohibitions that extended even to anatomy textbooks.
32 Hannah Fry (1824–1902) published her *Poems* in 1900.
33 Alfred Lord Tennyson, *In Memoriam*, 1:4.
34 A type of beet used for feeding cattle.
35 Greek poet of the seventh century BCE, known for his political and military elegies.
36 British First World War slang for "no good," from the French "il n'y a plus."
37 A journalist and novelist, Charles Edward Montague (1867–1928) published *Disenchanted* in 1922. The book was an extremely unfavourable account of British conduct in the First World War.
38 "Making no compromise with the public taste" was the slogan on the cover of *The Little Review*.
39 *Les Villes Tentaculaires* (The Sprawling Cities) was the title of an 1895 volume of poetry written by Émile Verhaeren.
40 Ann Pennington (1893–1971) was an American dancer and actor who early in the twentieth century performed with the Ziegfeld Follies and on screen. Her Black Bottom Dance and dimpled knees were famous.
41 Joe Cook (1890–1959) was a vaudeville performer.
42 Fanny Brice (1891–1951) was celebrated for her comic performances on stage and screen. In 1914 the *Pittsfield Eagle* claimed to quote an interview with Brice, in which Brice purportedly claimed: "I am to the stage what Gertrude Stein and her 'Tender Buttons' are to literature. I try to interpret life from a new angle in terms of mugging, clowning and droll antics, but when people say I am crazy, I am merely artistic after the fashion of Cubism. I have studied Picasso, and on the stage I try to get the same feeling out of my acting that I have gotten out of people." The *Eagle* commented, "And zip goes another crime against the record of Gertrude Stein. It was bad enough when she began to affect Don Marquis, but to have her influence penetrate vaudeville is the last straw" (Anonymous, "Gertrude Stein of the Stage").

43 Gaby Deslys (1881–1920), who is also referred to in "The Cubist Costume / Milady in Crazy Quilt," was a popular dancer (the Gaby Glide was created for her) and actor. Among her many famous suitors was the indefatigable King Manuel II of Portugal (who appears transformed in "Dunning Cubist Art Center," page 354).
44 *The Decline of the West*, by Oswald Spengler.
45 "On a Certain Condescension in Foreigners" is the title of a well-known 1871 essay by James Russell Lowell, in which Lowell complained of the British establishment's disdain of things American.
46 Clive Bell's recently coined aesthetic term, often invoked to explicate and justify post-Impressionism.
47 Kasimir Edschmid (1890–1966) and Carl Sternheim (1878–1942) were German Expressionist writers. Walter von Molo (1880–1958) was an Austrian writer who at the time of this article was living and working in Germany.
48 The German industrialist and shipping magnate Hugo Stinnes (1870–1924) had a meteoric career rise, and eventually extended his reach into all aspects of the German econonmy, politics, and press.
49 Title of an article by Robert Alden Sanborn in *Broom* 5.2 (September 1923): 78–82.
50 French art historian Élie Faure (1873–1937) argued that modern painting was a dead form, and had been replaced by film.
51 One of the first superstars of Western films, William S. Hart (1864–1946) was also a director, producer, and screenwriter. Jack Pickford (1895 / 96–1933), brother of Mary Pickford, acted in several films, but was more famous for his spectacular lifestyle.
52 Literally, "cat's wail," but better known as a slang term for a hangover or depression.
53 A layered drink composed of several types of liqueur, in which the specific gravities of the different liqueurs separate the drink into bands of colour.
54 Robert Bontine Cunninghame-Graham (1852–1936) was the first elected socialist Member of Parliament, a Scottish nationalist, and a much-travelled and much-published writer. Heavily involved in labour issues (including an imprisonment for his involvement in the 1887 Bloody Sunday), he also was well known in the arts community (sculpted by the Vorticist Jacob Epstein, and the model for both Charles Gould in Conrad's *Nostromo* and Sergius Saranoff in Shaw's *Arms and the Man*). Christopher Nevinson (1889–1946) was a painter and at this time an enthusiastic champion of futurism in England.
55 Founded by Frank Rutter in 1906, the Allied Artists' Association was an organization that provided venues for modernist art, including that of the Vorticists. Rutter's art crtiticism is satirized in Bechhöfer's "Pastiche. More Contemporaries," preceding this piece.
56 A horse with a controversial pedigree, Durbar II won the 1914 Epsom Derby.
57 The backwards looking.

58 Olga Petrova (1884–1977) was the stage name of Muriel Harding, an American actor, vaudeville performer, and screenwriter. "Oh, You Beautiful Doll," written in 1911 by Nat D. Ayer (music) and Seymour Brown (lyrics), begins in this way: Honey dear, want you near, / Just turn out the light / and then come over here, / Nestle close up to my side, / My heart's a fire / With love's desire.
59 The phrase, celebrated in artistic circles at the time, is Kandinsky's, and means "inner sound."
60 Alfred Emerson was a curator of antiquities at the Art Institute.
61 A reference to Brancusi's sculpture *Mademoiselle Pogany*.
62 Pauline Lennards Palmer (1867–1938) was a well-known Chicago artist whose first solo Art Institute exhibit was being held at the same time as the Armory Show.
63 Since the artist Charles Francis Browne (1859–1920) had by this time already established himself in the Chicago area as an authority opposed to impressionism, his irritation at the Armory Show was entirely predictable. The *Chicago Tribune* reported on Browne's lecture in the following terms:

> Fullerton hall was filled yesterday afternoon, "for the first time in ten years for my lectures," Mr. Browne commented sadly.
>
> "That shows people are all curious, so we will not mystify ourselves with the exhibition upstairs."
>
> This was Mr. Browne's most popular summing up of the more recent followers of the post-impressionistic school:
>
> "IT'S trying to prove ITSELF by ITS own ITNESS." It was greeted with thunderous applause.
>
> "In this movement how many are leaders and how many merely camp followers?" queried Mr. Browne. "How many are really sincere? I know of many I do not believe sincere, and they are the Americans. What will come next we cannot imagine, but something will come. From the scratched stone of the cave dweller to the 'Nude Descending a Stair' was but a step." ("Chicago Artist Starts Revolt")

64 Magda Heuermann (1868–1962) had a significant career as an artist, including work exhibited at the Metropolitan Museum in New York.
65 Emilie Polini (?–1927) was a theatre and film actor.
66 *Hindle Wakes*, written by Stanley Houghton (1881–1913), protested small-town sexual mores.
67 Heroine of *Hindle Wakes*.
68 Emmeline Pankhurst (1858–1928) was a leader in the suffragist movement.
69 For general background on the Cliff Dwellers, see the Introduction, p. 9. Earl H. Reed (1863–1931) was a Chicago-area artist, best known for his etchings of the Lake

Michigan shoreline. For information on Charles Francis Browne (1859–1920) see note 63. Louis Betts (1873–1961) had studied with William Merritt Chase. He was well known as a portrait painter, working in an impressionist style. A.M. Rebori – undoubtedly Andrew Nicholas Rebori – (1886–1966) was a Chicago architect. T.J. Keene (Keane?) was dean of the School of the Art Institute of Chicago. Lorado Taft (1860–1936) was on the faculty of the Art Institute. A conservative voice in early-twentieth-century sculpture, he is known for his large works of public art.

70 Jesse Lynch Williams (1871–1929) won a Pulitzer Prize for drama in 1918 for *Why Marry*. Gelett Burgess (1866–1951) was an artist, creator of the books and comic strip *Goops*, and coiner of the term "blurb."

71 Burton Haseltine was a Chicago doctor who published his *Songs and Sonnets* in 1913.

72 Lance Wood Hart (1891–1941) would go on to become a professor of art at the University of Oregon, where he was an early influence on Robert Motherwell.

73 An important suffragist leader, "General" Rosalie Gardiner Jones (1883–1978) organized the first "Suffrage Hike," a 170-mile hike from Manhattan to Albany, and participated in the 193-mile hike from New York to Washington.

74 Alla Nazimova (1879–1945), an actor, writer, and producer, often went solely by her last name. Among her later projects were film adaptations of *A Doll's House* and Wilde's *Salomé*.

75 Carrie Chapman Catt (1859–1947), a suffrage organizer, founded the League of Women Voters in 1920.

76 Theodore Roosevelt (1858–1919) took a well-publicized safari to Africa in 1909.

77 Sarah Bernhardt (1844–1923) was the world's most famous actress in the late nineteenth century, and was still active at the time of this article.

78 In 1913 the celebrated soprano Mary Garden (1874–1967) was performing with the Chicago Grand Opera Company.

79 See note 43.

80 While this quoted passage originates in Stein's "Portrait of Mabel Dodge at the Villa Curonia," given that only 300 copies were printed, the reporter's more likely source is the famous Mabel Dodge essay "Speculations, or Post-Impressionism in Prose." There, the passage appears in exactly the form it takes here.

81 The curious phrase ETAOIN SHRDLU was commonly known in newsrooms. In 1929, *Time* reported the following (an account corroborated by numerous sources, despite the issue date of 1 April):

> Last week, noticing that the Literary Digest had reprinted an "etaoin shrdlu" line, apparently as a joke but without bothering to explain the mystery to its readers, the ever-practical New York World explained editorially for laymen what every newsman knows.

> When a linotype operator makes an error he has to complete that line of type before he can make a new line. The easiest thing for him to do is to run his fingers down the first two vertical rows of his keyboard. The result is the emergence of a line containing "etaoin shrdlu." And when the operator forgets to pluck the faulty line from the mould, "etaoin shrdlu" gets into print. So often has "etaoin shrdlu" appeared with a "Mr." prefixed, that Mr. Etaoin Shrdlu has really become a famed press personage. He has a relative who dwells on his right hand in the third vertical row on a linotype machine, young Mr. Cmfwyp. The family is completed by boyish Vbgkqj and tiny Xz, whose name trails off strangely into typographic symbols.

One or both words in the phrase became known as a term for nonsense, its currency extending even to the pages of the *San Quentin News*, where it was the moniker for the columnist who reported on the prison's 1957 performance of *Waiting for Godot* ("Bastille by the Bay").

82 Billie Burke (1884–1970), a well-known actress at the time, would marry Florenz Ziegfeld (of Ziegfeld's Follies) in 1914, and star as Glenda the Good Witch in *The Wizard of Oz*. Burke also starred in *Mind the Paint, Girl*, a play by Arthur Pinero.

83 Alma Webster Powell (1874–1930) was an opera singer.

84 Geraldine Farrar (1882–1967), noted and flamboyant opera singer.

85 Carlo Carrà (1881–1966) was an Italian futurist painter.

86 Sylvia Pankhurst (1882–1960), daughter of Emmeline Pankhurst, was involved in the suffragist movement and leftist causes.

87 Ralph Herz (1878–1921) was a vaudeville performer and comedic actor.

88 Theodore Roosevelt.

89 William John Locke (1863–1930) was a best-selling author, whose work included *The Beloved Vagabond* (1906).

90 Originally designed for circuses, the London Hippodrome had been recently redone as a music hall.

91 The quotation is from *Tender Buttons*, as are most of the other quotations in this article. Unlike many of the other reviewers of *Tender Buttons*, Kreymborg clearly had access to the whole text.

92 At this time in his life, the American painter Max Weber (1881–1961) was heavily influenced by Cubism. (For an example of his poetry, see the introduction to Free Verse above.) Samuel Halpert (1884–1930) studied with Jacob Epstein, and was part of an artist's colony that included Alfred Kreymborg. At this period he was painting in a Fauvist style.

93 Industrial Workers of the World (the Wobblies), the labor union founded in 1905.

94 Leo Ornstein (1893–2002), championed by the Alfred Stieglitz circle, had several audacious "futurist" performances in New York early in 1915.

95 Henry Edward Krehbiel (1854–1923) was a music critic for the *New York Tribune*. William James Henderson (1855–1937) was a music critic for the *New York Sun*.
96 The Mexican artist Marius de Zayas (1880–1961), another member of the Stieglitz circle, was famous for his caricatures of New Yorkers.
97 A laxative.
98 Peace be with you.
99 The medium King Saul engaged to raise the ghost of the prophet Samuel (1 Samuel 28: 3–24).

Works Cited

Adams, Franklin P. "The Coming Tower." *Cleveland Leader*, 23 June 1914.

– "Foreword." In *A Penny Whistle: Together with the Babette Ballads*, xi–xiv. New York: Knopf, 1921.

Agamben, Giorgio. *Profanations*. Trans. Jeff Fort. New York: Zone, 2007.

Alden, Raymond M. "Recent Poetry." *The Dial*, 24 June 1915: 26–30.

Anonymous. "Adventures in Fall Hats: How Hosiery May Be Worn Upon the New Headgear to Great Effect." *New York Evening Sun*, 24 September 1914. Yale Collection of American Literature, Beinecke Rare Book and Manuscript Library, Yale University.

– "Art Gone Mad. Queer Perversions of the Post-Impressionists. Paint-Box Freaks. Cult of the Crazily Ugly and Its Childish Results." *Daily Sketch*, 4 October 1912: 15.

– "Chicago Artist Starts Revolt." *Chicago Daily Tribune*, 26 March 1913: 15.

– "'Cliff Dwellers' Satirize the Cubist Art in Pointed Caricatures. 'Explosion of Cold Storage Egg' an Impressionist Riot of Color." *Chicago Examiner*, 2 April 1913: 3.

– "Cubist Art Severs Friendship: Institute Directors Are Divided." *Chicago Examiner*, 28 March 1913. Scrapbook, Ryerson and Burnham Libraries, Art Institute of Chicago.

– "Cubist Gown Comes to Town." *Chicago Daily Tribune*, 18 March 1913: 3.

– "Cubists Depart; Students Joyful." *Chicago Daily Tribune*, 17 April 1913: 3.

– "Dust Jacket Blurb for *Cinder Thursday*, by Herbert Palmer." In *Cinder Thursday*. London: Ernest Benn, 1931.

– "Etaoin Shrdlu." *Time*, 1 April 1929: 50.

– "The Futurist on the Trade." *New York City Daily Trade Record*, 18 June 1914. Yale Collection of American Literature, Beinecke Rare Book and Manuscript Library, Yale University.

– "Gertrude Stein of the Stage." *Pittsfield Eagle*, 4 November 1914. Gertrude Stein and Alice B. Toklas Papers, Yale Collection of American Literature, Beinecke Rare Book and Manuscript Library, Yale University.

– "Holiday Art Books." *The Dial*, 1913: 532.

– *New York Evening Sun*, 21 July 1914. Gertrude Stein and Alice B. Toklas Papers, Yale Collection of American Literature, Beinecke Rare Book and Manuscript Library, Yale University.

– "Outstrip Cubists in Their Own Art; the Academy of Misapplied Art Holds Its First Vanishing Day Reception." *New York Times*, 23 March 1913: 6.

– "Shantih, Shantih, Shantih: Has the Reader Any Rights before the Bar of Literature?" *Time*, 3 March 1923: 12.

– "Step In! No Danger! Cubist Show Now On." *Chicago Record-Herald*, 25 March 1913: 1.

– "Students Wreak Vengeance upon Cubist Designs." *Chicago Evening Post*, 17 April 1913. Scrapbook, Ryerson and Burnham Libraries, Art Institute of Chicago.

– "The Transatlantic Lyre." *New Statesman* 6 (1916): 332.

– [Don Marquis]. Untitled. *New York Evening Sun*, 1 October 1914. Gertrude Stein and Alice B. Toklas Papers, Yale Collection of American Literature, Beinecke Rare Book and Manuscript Library, Yale University.

– "The Vers Libre Jinx." *Chicago Literary Times*, 1 March 1923: 2. Gertrude Stein and Alice B. Toklas Papers, Yale Collection of American Literature, Beinecke Rare Book and Manuscript Library, Yale University.

– "Whatever This May Be – 'It Is Not Art.'" *American Weekly* (*Chicago Herald-Examiner*), 13 March 1927: 11.

– "When the White Hunter Hunts." *New York City Sun*, 21 June 1914. Gertrude Stein and Alice B. Toklas Papers, Yale Collection of American Literature, Beinecke Rare Book and Manuscript Library, Yale University.

Ardis, Ann L. *Modernism and Cultural Conflict, 1880–1922*. Cambridge, UK, New York: Cambridge University Press, 2002.

Bakhtin, Mikhail M. "From the Prehistory of Novelistic Discourse." In *The Dialogic Imagination: Four Essays*. Ed. Michael Holquist. Trans. Caryl Emerson and Michael Holquist. Austin: University of Texas Press, 1981. 41–83.

Barter, Judith A. *Window on the West: Chicago and the Art of the New Frontier, 1890–1940*. Chicago, New York: Art Institute of Chicago, Hudson Hills Press, 2003.

Boynton, Percy Holmes. *Some Contemporary Americans: The Personal Equation in Literature*. Chicago: University of Chicago Press, 1924.

Brooke, Rupert. "Rev. of *Personae*, by Ezra Pound." *Cambridge Review* 31 (2 December 1909): 166–7. Rpt. in *Ezra Pound: The Critical Heritage*, ed. Eric Homberger (London: Routledge and Kegan Paul, 1972), 58–9.

Burgess, Gelett. "The Wild Men of Paris." *Architectural Record* (1910): 400–14. http://archrecord.construction.com/inTheCause/0702MenOfParis/MenOfParis1.asp

Bynner, Witter. "The Spectric Poets." *New Republic*, 18 November 1916: 13.

C., R.H. (A.R. Orage). "Readers and Writers." *New Age* 15, no. 19 (1914): 449.

– "Readers and Writers." *New Age* 16, no. 19 (1915): 509.

Canby, Henry Seidel. "The Virtue of Intolerance." *Saturday Review of Literature*, 27 February 1926: 585.

Carter, Huntly. "A Disciple of Distortion." *New Age* 11, no. 6 (1912): 138–9.

– "The Plato-Picasso Idea." *New Age* 10, no. 4 (1911): 88.

Churchill, Suzanne W. 'The Lying Game: *Others* and the Great Spectra Hoax of 1917." In *Little Magazines and Modernism: New Approaches*, ed. Suzanne W. Churchill and Adam McKible, 177–95. Aldershot: Ashgate, 2007.

Cox, Kenyon. *The Classic Point of View.* New York: C. Scribner's Sons, 1911.

Curnutt, Kirk. "Parody and Pedagogy: Teaching Style, Voice, and Authorial Intent in the Works of Gertrude Stein." *College Literature* 23, no. 2 (1996): 1–24.

Dentith, Simon. *Parody: The New Critical Idiom.* London, New York: Routledge, 2000.

Dodge, Mabel. "Speculations, or Post-Impressionism in Prose." *Arts and Decoration*, March 1913: 172–4.

Eastman, Max. "A Dramatic Career in Modernist Art." *Vanity Fair*, August 1916: 35, 98.

– *The Literary Mind: Its Place in an Age of Science.* New York: Charles Scribner's Sons, 1931.

– *Love and Revolution: My Journey through an Epoch.* New York: Random House, 1964.

Eliot, T.S. "A Brief Treatise on the Criticism of Poetry." *The Chapbook*, March 1920: 1–10.

– *The Letters of T. S. Eliot.* Ed. Valerie Eliot and Hugh Haughton. 2 vols. Vol. 1. New Haven, CT: Yale University Press, 2011.

– "Sweeney Among the Nightingales." In *The Complete Poems and Plays of T.S. Eliot.* London: Faber and Faber, 1969. 56–7.

Felton, John. "Contemporary Caricatures." *Egoist* 1, no. 15 (1914): 296–7.

– "No. 3. — Mr. F*** M**** H******." *New Age* 1, no. 15 (1914): 297.

Fitzgerald, F. Scott. *A Life in Letters.* Ed. Matthew J. Bruccoli and Judith Baughman. New York, Toronto: Scribner's, Maxwell Macmillan Canada, Maxwell Macmillan International, 1994.

Freud, Sigmund. *Jokes and Their Relation to the Unconscious.* Ed. and trans. James Strachey. London: Routledge & Paul, 1960.

Gates, Norman T., and Richard Aldington. *The Poetry of Richard Aldington: A Critical Evaluation and an Anthology of Uncollected Poems.* University Park: Pennsylvania State University Press, 1975.

Gilman, Lawrence. "Moving-Picture Poetry." *North American Review* 202 (1915): 271–6.

Guthrie, James. "Letters to the Editor. Picasso." *New Age* 10, no. 6 (1911): 141–2.

Heap, Jane. "The Reader Critic. The Hoax of the 'Spectrics.'" *Little Review* 5, no. 2 (1918): 53–4.

Hecht, Ben. "The Vers Libre Jinx." *Chicago Literary Times*, 1 March 1923: 2. Gertrude Stein and Alice B. Toklas Papers, Yale Collection of American Literature, Beinecke Rare Book and Manuscript Library, Yale University.

Hendee, H. Searle. "Know What Cubist Art Is?" *Wichita Eagle*, 25 March 1913. Scrapbook, Ryerson and Burnham Libraries, Art Institute of Chicago.
Hutcheon, Linda. *The Politics of Postmodernism*. New York: Routledge, 1989.
– *A Theory of Parody: The Teachings of Twentieth-Century Art Forms*. New York: Methuen, 1985.
Hutchison, Percy. "Pure Poetry and Mr. Wallace Stevens." *New York Times Book Review*, 9 August 1931: 4.
Jameson, Fredric. *Postmodernism, or, the Cultural Logic of Late Capitalism*. Durham, NC: Duke University Press, 1991.
Jones, Mark. "Parody and Its Containments: The Case of Wordsworth." *Representations* 54 (1996): 57–79.
Joyce, James. *James Joyce: Letters*. Ed. Stuart Gilbert. New York: Viking, 1925.
Kitchin, George. *A Survey of Burlesque and Parody in English*. Edinburgh: Oliver and Boyd, 1931.
Leavis, F.R. *New Bearings in English Poetry: A Study of the Contemporary Situation*. Ann Arbor: University of Michigan Press, 1932. Rpt. 1960.
Leick, Karen. *Gertrude Stein and the Making of an American Celebrity*. Studies in Major Literary Authors. New York: Routledge, 2009.
Lewis, Wyndham. *Time and Western Man*. London: Chatto and Windus, 1927.
Lovecraft, H.P. *The Ancient Track: The Complete Poetical Works of H. P. Lovecraft*. San Francisco: Night Shade Books, 2001.
Lyall, Mary Mills. *The Cubies' ABC*. New York: G.P. Putnam's Sons, 1913.
Marquis, Don. "The Gertrude Stein Club Grows." *New York Evening Sun*, 18 September 1914.
– *Hermione and Her Little Group of Serious Thinkers*. New York: D. Appleton and Co., 1916.
Mirrlees, Hope. *Paris. A Poem*. Richmond: Hogarth Press, 1919.
Molony, J. "Letters to the Editor. Marionette, and Play the Fife and Drum." *New Age* 15, no. 3 (1914): 311.
Monro, Harold. *Some Contemporary Poets*. London: Leonard Parsons, 1920.
O'Brien, Edward J. "Four O'clock: Men as Trees Walking." *Coterie*, no. 5 (1920): 23–4.
Palmer, Herbert. *Post-Victorian Poetry*. London: J.M. Dent and Sons, 1938.
Pattee, Fred Lewis. *The New American Literature, 1890–1930*. New York, London: The Century Co., 1930.
Pearson, John. *Façades: Edith, Osbert, and Sacheverell Sitwell*. London: Macmillan, 1978.
Pound, Ezra. "Poems." *Poetry* 3, no. 2 (Nov. 1913): 53–60.
– "Salutation." *Poetry* 2, no. 1 (April 1913): 6.
Richardson, Christina Leonora Annabel. *Parody*. English Association, pamphlet no. 92. London: English Association, 1935.
Samuel, Horace Barnett. *Modernities*. Ten Studies. London: Kegan Paul & Co, 1913.

Savage, Henry. *A Long Spoon and the Devil. Being Fish Quaint and Queer from the Spoon River, the Property of Edgar Lee Masters, Poached by H. Savage, Etc.* [*a Parody of the Spoon River Anthology*]. London: Cecil Palmer, 1922.

– *Songs and Satires.* London: Renaissance Press, 1946.

Selver, Paul. "Perpetuum Mobile: A Pantoum, More or Less." In *Wheels* (Sixth Cycle), ed. Edith Sitwell, 55–6. London: C.W. Daniel, 1921.

Shakespeare, William. *The Tragedy of Hamlet, Prince of Denmark.* In *The Norton Shakespeare.* 2nd ed. Ed. S. Greenblatt, W. Cohen, J.E. Howard, K.E. Maus, and A. Gurr. New York: W.W. Norton, 2008. 1696–1784.

Sherman, Stuart Pratt. *Points of View.* New York: Scribner's, 1924.

Shrdlu, Etaoin. "Bastille by the Bay." *San Quentin News*, 28 November 1957: 2.

Sitwell, Edith. "Aubade." In *Selected Poems*, 95–6. Harmondsworth: Penguin, 1952.

– *Poetry and Criticism.* New York: Henry Holt and Co., 1926.

Smith, Paul Jordan. *The Road I Came; Some Recollections and Reflections concerning Changes in American Life and Manners since 1890.* Caldwell, ID: Caxton Printers, 1960.

Squire, J.C. *Collected Parodies.* New York: George H. Doran, [1921].

– "Editorial Notes." *London Mercury*, February 1920: 385–90.

– "Editorial Notes." *London Mercury*, August 1928: 337–46.

– "The Man Who Wrote Free Verse." *London Mercury*, June 1924: 121–37.

– "Poetry." Rev. of *Out of the Flame*, by Osbert Sitwell. *London Mercury*, August 1923: 436–7.

– "Short Cuts to Helicon." In Squire, ed., *Life and Letters*, 26–31. London: Hodder & Stoughton, 1920.

Stone, Constatia. "Letters to the Editor. Imagisme." *New Age* 16, no. 16 (1915): 438–9.

Taylor, Bert Leston. "Contemporomania. From 'a Line-o'-Type or Two.'" *Chicago Daily Tribune*, 11 April 1913: 6.

– *A Penny Whistle; Together with the Babette Ballads.* New York: A.A. Knopf, 1921.

Tracy, Daniel. "Investing in 'Modernism': Smart Magazines, Parody, and Middlebrow Professional Judgment." *Journal of Modern Periodical Studies* 1, no. 1 (2010): 38–63.

Tzara, Tristan. "To Make a Dadaist Poem." In *Seven Dada Manifestos* and *Lampisteries.* Trans. Barbara Wright. London: John Calder, 1977. 39.

Untermeyer, Louis. "Disillusion vs. Dogma." *The Freeman* 6 (17 January 1923), 453. Rpt. in *T.S. Eliot: The Critical Heritage*, vol. 1, ed. Michael Grant. New York: Routledge and Kegan Paul, 1982. 151–3.

– *Heavens.* New York: Harcourt, 1922.

– "An Introduction." In *Modern American Poetry: An Introduction.* Ed. Louis Untermeyer. New York: Harcourt, Brace and Howe, 1919. vii–xi.

– "Irony De Luxe." *The Freeman*, 30 June 1920: 381–2. Rpt. in *T.S. Eliot: The Critical Heritage*, vol. 1, ed. Michael Grant. New York: Routledge and Kegan Paul, 1982. 126–30.

– *Modern American Poetry: A Critical Anthology*. Ed. Louis Untermeyer. New York: Harcourt, Brace and Company, 1925.

Ward, Christopher. "The Judge." *The Triumph of the Nut, and Other Parodies*. New York: Henry Holt and Company, 1923. 79–83.

Weber, Max. *Cubist Poems*. London: Elkin Mathews, 1914.

Wetherell, J.E. *Later English Poems 1901–1922*. Ed. J.E. Wetherell. Toronto: McClelland and Stewart, 1922.

Widdemer, Margaret. *A Tree with a Bird in It: A Symposium of Contemporary American Poets on Being Shown a Pear-Tree on Which Sat a Grackle*. New York: Harcourt, Brace and Co., 1922.

Woolf, Virginia. "Modern Fiction." In *The Common Reader*. London: Hogarth Press, 1925. 184–95.

Permissions Credit Lines

Richard Aldington
"Penultimate Poetry" © The Estate of Richard Aldington. 'Richard Aldington's poem "Penultimate Poetry" reproduced by kind permission of Richard Aldington's Estate c / o Rosica Colin Limited, London.

Max Beerbohm
Work by Max Beerbohm is reproduced with the permission of Berlin Associates.

Hart Crane
"America's Plutonic Ecstasies" and "OF AN EVENING PULLING OFF A LITTLE EXPERIENCE (with the english language)" 1923, from COMPLETE POEMS OF HART CRANE by Hart Crane, edited by Marc Simon. Copyright 1933, 1958, 1966 by Liveright Publishing Corporation. Copyright © 1986 by Marc Simon. Used by permission of Liveright Publishing Corporation.

Samuel Hoffenstein
"Birdie McReynolds", "The Moist Land--A Parody of Eliot's Poem", from YEAR IN, YOU'RE OUT by Samuel Hoffenstein. Copyright 1930 by Samuel Hoffenstein. Copyright renewed January 1958 by David Hoffenstein. Used by permission of Liveright Publishing Corporation.

Knox, Edmund George Valpy
Work by E.V. Knox is reproduced with the permission of Dr Maria Lake, granddaughter of E.V. Knox.

Rose MacAulay
"Weekend at the Hoppers" by Rose Macaulay reprinted by permission of Peters Fraser and Dunlop (www.pfd.co.uk) on behalf of the Estate.

Harold Massingham
"Recipe for an Imagist Poem" by Harold Massingham reprinted by permission of The Society of Authors as the Literary Representative of the Estate of H J Massingham.

Ezra Pound
"Salutation" by Ezra Pound, copyright 1928 by Ezra Pound. Used by permission of New Directions Publishing Corporation.

F.R. Scott
F.R. Scott's "Sweeney Graduates" is reprinted with permission of William Toye, literary executor for the estate of F.R. Scott.

Paul Jordan Smith
The work of Paul Jordan Smith is reproduced with the permission of Paul Jordan-Smith. The images are reproduced with the assistance of the Paul Jordan Smith Papers, Department of Special Collections, Charles E. Young Research Library, UCLA.

Sir John Collings Squire
The work of J.C. Squire is reprinted with the kind permission of Roger Squire.

James Thurber
"More Authors Cover the Snyder Trial" by James Thurber. Copyright © May 7, 1927 by Rosemary A. Thurber. Reprinted by arrangement with Rosemary A. Thurber and The Barbara Hogenson Agency. All rights reserved.

E.B. White
"Is a Train" by E.B. White courtesy of the White Literary LLC.

Index

www.ingramcontent.com/pod-product-compliance
Lightning Source LLC
LaVergne TN
LVHW090146080826
844660LV00013B/686/J

* 9 7 8 1 4 4 2 6 4 4 8 2 3 *